THE

GANJAM DISTRICT

MANUAL

THE
GANJAM DISTRICT
MANUAL.

BY

T. J. MALTBY,

EDITED BY

G. D. LEMAN

GYAN

Published by

Gyan Publishing House
5, Ansari Road
Daryaganj, New Delhi-110002
Phone: 011-47034999, 9811692060
E-mail: books@gyanbooks.com

Distribution Network
gyanbooks.com
India, USA, Canada, UK, Australia

ISBN: 978-93-6280-440-2 (PB)
First Published, 1880

2nd Impression 2024

Printed at: Gyan Press, Delhi.

THE GANJAM DISTRICT MANUAL
Author: T. J. MALTBY, Edited by G. D. LEMAN

THE

GANJAM DISTRICT

MANUAL.

BY

T. J. MALTBY,

LATE MADRAS CIVIL SERVICE

EDITED BY

G. D. LEMAN, M. C. S.,

AGENT TO THE GOVERNOR AND COLLECTOR OF THE DISTRICT.

MADRAS:

PRINTED BY W H MOORE, AT THE LAWRENCE ASYLUM PRESS.

1882.

CONTENTS.

CHAPTER I.

GENERAL DESCRIPTION OF THE DISTRICT.

CHAPTER II.

DESCRIPTION OF THE ZEMINDARIES AND PROPRIETARY ESTATES.

CHAPTER III.

PORTS PLACES OF INTEREST, &c.

CHAPTER IV.

THE MALIAHS.

CHAPTER V.

HISTORICAL ACCOUNT.

PAGES.

CHAPTER VII.

THE GANJAM DISTRICT.

CHAPTER VIII.

CLIMATE AND DISEASES.

CHAPTER IX.

POPULATION, CASTES, LANGUAGES AND RELIGION.

CHAPTER X.

REVENUE HISTORY.

CONTENTS.

PAGES.

CHAPTER XI.

AGRICULTURE AND MANUFACTURES.

CHAPTER XII.

SCARCITIES, FAMINE AND THEIR PREVENTION.

PAGES.

CHAPTER XVI.

THE MUNICIPALITIES AND THE LOCAL FUND.

CHAPTER XVII.

APPENDICES.

APPENDICES.

THE GANJAM DISTRICT.

CHAPTER I.

GENERAL DESCRIPTION OF THE DISTRICT.

CHIEF RIVERS — CLIMATE — RAIN-FALL — TAMPARAS — PEOPLE — THREE DIVISIONS IN THE PLAINS—THEIR OFFICERS — THE PRINCIPAL DIVISION, GOOMSUR TALUQ—THE PRINCIPAL ASSISTANT'S DIVISION, CHICACOLE TALUQ—THE SENIOR ASSISTANT'S DIVISION, BERHAMPORE TALUQ — THE MALIAH TRACT — ITS OFFICERS—ITS LARGER DIVISIONS.

Ganjam is the most northern District of the Division of the Madras Presidency called the Northern Circars.

It lies between 18° 12' 45" and 20° 25' 40" North latitude and East longitude 83° 33' 20" and 85° 15' and is bounded on the north by Cuttack and Puri of the Bengal Presidency, east by the Bay of Bengal, south and west by the Vizagapatam District.

Its area is 8,313 square miles or thereabouts. Population by the Census of 1871, 1,520,088.

It is of convenient shape, but the head quarters of the Collector and his Chief Assistant have not been selected in sufficiently centrical places.

The district is one of the most beautiful in the Presidency. The Eastern Ghauts running on its western side approach to within 15 miles of the sea at Baruva, behind which rises one of the highest peaks in the district—Mahendragiri. The hills are for the most part beautifully wooded and the country between them and the sea is undulating, interspersed with rocky hills and fine topes.

The district is divided into plains and maliahs. The plains are of course the country below Ghauts. The maliahs, the hilly country above Ghauts, are chiefly inhabited by Khonds and Savaras, aboriginal inhabitants of Hindustan.

The rivers as may be imagined with the hills so close to the sea, are not very large. The chief are the Rushikulya, the Vamsadhara, and the Langulya or Nágavali.

The Rushikulya's course is about 100 miles. It rises near Daringabadi in the Chinna Kimedi Hills, is joined by the Mahanadi at Aska and enters the sea at Ganjam. The Vamsadhara is 145 miles long. It rises in the Jeypore hills of the Vizagapatam District, enters the district at Battili and the sea at Calingapatam. The Langulya hardly belongs to the district. It is its southern boundary for a few miles and enters the sea at Mofazbandar.

Besides these there are the Godahodo, a tributary of the Rushikulya, the Bahuda which runs into the sea at Sonnapur, the Mahendratanaya which passes through Mandasa and runs into the sea at Baruva, and another of the same name in Parla Kimedi. All of them are utilized for irrigation purposes more or less.

None of the rivers are used for navigation though wood rafts are floated down both the Vamsadhara and the Rushikulya; the Vamsadhara is navigable as far as Battili; and the Rushikulya as far as Aska during the rains, but as the banks are high and steep, the current strong and the people without much enterprize, there is little boat traffic on them.

The hills being so near the coast the rivers are liable to sudden floods but they seldom do much damage.

The climate is as pleasant as any in the Presidency. In the rains, which last from June to November, it is oppressive and close by the sea, but the heat is tempered by the rains away from it.

The hot weather lasts only about the 3 months of March, April and May, while the cold is very pleasant indeed. Both

Europeans and Natives are liable to fever which is also a most frequent cause of death to the latter.

The average rain-fall is 43 inches.

The shallow depressions close to the coast and also further inland sometimes filled with good and sometimes with brackish water, are known as *Tamparas*. The Chilka lake is the largest and best instance. The scenery on it is beautiful, especially near Birkul in Cuttack District, where its borders are studded with green islands and hills.

The people of the district may be divided into Uriyas, Telugus, Khonds and Savaras. The Musulman population is very small.

The Khonds and Savaras inhabit the hills, and the line which divides the Uriyas and Telugus may be drawn from Kassibugga* to Parla Kimedi.

The people are for the most part Vishnuvites.

The roads are pretty good. They used to be famous, but from one cause or another, the money to spare for their upkeep has become less and less in the last ten years and now it is a very difficult matter to get them in order again. The larger rivers have been left unbridged, but there are a sufficiency of smaller bridges on the main roads. Road-making was only commenced in the district in 1854 and then complaints were made by the Engineers that the wheels had no iron tyres and were not round but hexagonal so doing great damage.

The District above Ghauts pays no revenue to Government, and its management devolves on the Collector as Agent of the Governor, assisted by a Special Assistant Agent and his other usual officers, who also have special official designations, the Sub-Collector being called Principal Assistant, and the Head Assistant, Senior Assistant Agent.

* *Note.*—Mr. Hunter, on Mr. Lyon's authority, says Ichapur but this is too far north.

In the plains for revenue purposes the District is divided into three Divisions, which are made up as under :—

1. The Collector's or Principal Division :

Goomsur taluq and the Zemindary estates of

Atagada,	Biridi,
Palur,	Kallikot and
Humma,	Bodogoda.

2. The Principal Assistant Collector's Division :

Chicacole taluq, within which are 28 small proprietary villages and the zemindaries of

Parla Kimedi,	Tarla.
Tekkali and	

3. The Senior Assistant Collector's Division :

Berhampore taluq, which includes 7 small estates and the Zemindaries of

Sergada,	Chikati,
Dharakot,	Jalantra,
Chinna Kimedi,	Mandasa.
Pedda Kimedi,	

Each of the Divisions contains a Government taluq, and to each of these, as a matter of course, there is a Tahsildar assisted by the following Deputy Tahsildars for the Revenue, and Sub-Magistrates for Magisterial work.

(1.) Goomsur Tahsildar.

Surada Deputy Tahsildar.

(2.) Chicacole, Tahsildar.

Tekkali and
Narasannapet. } Dy. Tahsildars.

(3.) Berhampore Tahsildar.

Ganjam,
Purushottapur,
Ichapur and
Sompet. } Deputy Tahsildars.

Besides these there are the Berhampore Town Magistrate, the Deputy Tahsildar and Sub-Magistrate of Aska Division and the Sub-Magistrate of Parla Kimedi. The charges of the above officers are given in the Appendix.

The Ramagiri Magistrate who is stationed at Udayagiri in the Pedda Kimedi Maliahs formerly exercised Magisterial jurisdiction in the Parla Kimedi Maliahs, but this charge has been more recently transferred to the Sub-Magistrate at Parla Kimedi below Ghauts, as that town is nearer and in every respect more conveniently situated for the bulk of the Maliah population attached to that zemindary.

The settlement of the district was undertaken in Fasli 1287, and finished in Fasli 1289. The rates for wet vary from Rs. 5-8-0 to Rs. 1-4-0, and for dry from Rs. 4 to annas 4 per Acre.

In describing the various divisions it will be best to take the Government taluq of each first. The Zemindaries and proprietary estates that lie within them will be found separately noticed where necessary in Chapter II.

Goomsur Taluq—This is a third class taluq and consists of the two ancient zemindaries of Goomsur and Surada which were confiscated by Government after the rebellion in 1836.

It is bounded on the north by the Daspalla and Nyagar Zemindaries of Cuttack; on the east by the Atagada Zemindari, on the south by the Bodogada and Dharakot Zemindaries and the Berhampore taluq, on the west by the Eastern Ghauts which lead up into the Agency tracts or Maliahs.

By scale it measures 1,246 square miles. Its villages are numbered at 1,116, many of them small hamlets. And its population 162,693.

The taluq is wild, with thick forests, especially on its east and north frontiers, in fact one-half of its area or 600 square miles is much of it fine sal wood forest; wild beasts and game abound, tiger, panther, bear, sambur and spotted deer. Towards the centre and south it is hilly with beautiful well-watered and fertile vallies running towards the sea. To the north and east the land is very good indeed. Its natural advantages are great for the rains are so plentiful (and they seldom fail) that it is only for sugar-cane cultivation that artificial irrigation is wanted as a rule.

The chief towns are Russellkonda, population 2,625, where the Tahsildar resides, and Surada, population 3,116, the residence of the Sub-Magistrate.

The only irrigation work of any importance is a fine tank, the Bori Sagaram, near Gangupur. It was constructed by Government in 1861 at a cost of 10,749 Rupees; has been kept in repair at an average yearly cost of 70 Rupees and waters 1,632 acres of land, the yearly profit by extra water-rate over and above what used to be paid being 1,845 Rupees, a notable instance of an inexpensive but productive Government work.

The taluq is divided as follows:—

Khandams or Divisions.	*Mutahs or Sub-Divisions.*	
Ballipadra ...	Páyelpada. Ballipadra. Vishnuchakrum. Bavanipuram. Bugudá. Koracholi.	These Mutahs are the best cultivated in Goomsur, and are situated in extensive plains not devoid of jungle.
Bodoborosinghi.	Potosinghi. Salingiá. Peruju. Bondhágotso Kidika.	These five Mutas were formerly included in the Maliah country, but were assessed in 1863.
	Buttapilli. Nuagodo. Rogodo. Gondribedo. Malo.	Half jungle and the other half open.

Vonnagiri ...	Jaksabádi. Vonnagiri.	Half jungle and the rest open.
	Dakshanagodotolo. Padiyá.	Very open land but contain some scrub jungle.
	Pántsogodotolo. Birakot.	Contain much jungle and but little open land.
	Durgaprasád. Darpangia. Gidipuhalli. Sárábadi.	Formerly included in the Maliah country, but assessed in 1861 and incorporated with Goomsur.
Kullada ...	Kukulubá. Gallari.	Contain much jungle.
	Jagannáthprasad. Uttorogodotolo. Púrbogodotolo.	About half is jungle and the rest open land.
	Chokapad. Posorá. Challi. Ghátigudá.	These four were assessed in 1863 and brought under Goomsur, but are above Ghauts and form, strictly speaking, a part of the Maliahs.

The *Goomsur and Surada Paik Inams* deserve notice. After the termination of the Goomsur campaign in 1837, it was not considered advisable to deprive the *Paiks*, or armed retainers of the Goomsur family, of their service lands, upon which most of them were dependent for their livelihood. This body of men were part of the feudal system which formerly prevailed in Ganjam, and were originally appointed to protect the plains against the inroads of the Khonds of the adjoining hill country. They also attended the Rajah's person and his family, and assisted in the collection of the revenue by watching over the crops and seeing that the Ryots did not make away with them before the Zemindar's share was secured. The Paiks have a good knowledge of the country, are plucky and reliable, and have a supreme contempt for a Khond. Mr. Russell remodelled the establishment in 1837, but instead of confining the Inams to one or two Mutas of the taluq only, he distributed them over the country. Some 10,000 acres of land were made over to the Paiks at a small quit-rent, and 6 Sirdars, 69 Naiks and 1,244 Peons were confirmed in their appointments. Their descendants still continue to hold their lands and are formally appointed by the chief Revenue officer in charge of the taluq. The Paiks* hold their lands during life, dependent upon their good conduct and the faithful discharge of their duty of doing armed service when called out. They receive daily batta when on service and were now to a considerable extent utilized as guards at the Salt Factories in the manufacturing season.

Surada, the Sub-Division of Goomsur, may be described in the same terms as Goomsur. It was a distinct Zemindari, but was sold for arrears of revenue about 1833, and was bought by the Goomsur Rajah. When his country was resumed, Surada was resumed with it. The Joro Nadi runs through it, but can hardly be said to water it, for unless it overflows, the ryots never use the water.

The Mutas of Surada proper already named in Goomsur are:—

(1.) Nuagodo.
(2.) Gondibeda.
(3.) Malo.
(4.) Rogodo.
(5.) Salingia.
(6.) Pochangi.
(7.) Peruju.
(8.) Bondagotso.
(9.) Kidika.

The chief food products of the Division are about—

Paddy............	37,099	Garce.
Ragi..............	3,555	„

Besides these, dholl, chamalu, green gram, cotton, oil seed of different sorts and sugar cane are grown.

* *Note.*—The G. O., No. 1,110; dated 13th July 1867, dealing with the matter whether the Paik's Inams of Goomsur and Parlakimedi should be enfranchised or not by the Inam Commissioner, decided that for the time they were to be left untouched and no subsequent order has issued. There are similar Paiks, 468 in number, with 52 Sirdars in Parlakimedi. These are the retainers of the Bissoyes or Hill Chiefs.

The people are for the most part cultivators and are fairly prosperous, but they are improvident, and like all natives want more enterprize and energy and more willingness to take advantage of the favorable circumstances in which they are.

The roads in the taluq are :—

		Miles.
(1.)	Portion of the road from Gopalpur to Kalingia	46
(2.)	Road from Aska to Pippalaponka	30
(3.)	Road from Aska to Korcholi	27
(4.)	Road from Ballipadra to Russellkonda ...	16½
(5.)	Road from Russellkonda to Kullada	4

Chicacole Taluq.—This is a second class taluq and consists of the Haveli lands of the old Chicacole Circar.

It is bounded on the north by the Parla-Kimedi and Tekkali estates, on the east by the Bay of Bengal, and on the south and west by the Vizagapatam District.

It measures 451 square miles, and its villages are 372 in number, of which 146 are Government, 78 Inam, and 148 Zemindari.

The country rises gradually from the sea towards the northern boundary of the taluq. There are a few hills here and there, and the Vamsadhara flows through it. In fertility it does not bear favorable comparison with Goomsur; it is far less wild, has been longer under cultivation, and has not the benefits of such a plentiful rainfall.

Its irrigation works are river channels from the Vamsadhara and Langulya, viz., the Wadada, Dusi and Gajuli channels of the Langulya, and the Bhyri, Nyra, Purushottapur, Nagarikatakam, Jalmur, Polaki, Mabagam, Lukulam and Garibula channels of the Vamsadhara.

The taluq is divided into five Khandams, as follows :—

(1.) Uttara (north) Khandam.
(2.) Polaki.
(3.) Paltalagam.
(4.) Paschama (west) Khandam.
(5.) Dakshana (south) Khandam.

} All well cultivated. [(2.)–(5.)]

Its chief towns are Chicacole, where the Tahsildar resides, population 15,587, and Narsannapet,* the residence of the Deputy Tahsildar.

The chief products of the division are :—

Paddy .... 30,000 Garce, and
Ragi .... 3,000 Garce ;

but oil seeds, sugar-cane, millet, and gram are also grown in more than sufficient quantities for the local demand, and there is considerable export from Calingapatam.

The people are for the most part cultivators, but a few of the old weavers are left. They are described as being "miserably poor," and certainly they do not seem to be as well-to-do as other natives ; at the same time they certainly are not in so bad a state as they have been described in the Settlement report as "barely existing."

The system of weekly markets which is common throughout the district, is found in this division.

The roads are fairly good save about Naupada, where the soil is sandy and roads being very expensive have not yet been made. The roads are :—

Trunk road from Chicacole to Kassibugga,	52	miles.
Road from Chicacole to Calingapatam,	16	,,
,, ,, ,, towards Palkonda,	12½	,,
,, ,, Alikam to Battili,	20½	,,
,, ,, Chintada to Gara,	12	,,
,, ,, Calingapatam to Parla-Kimedi viâ Narsannapet,	15	,,
,, ,, Jarjangi to Jagannadhapur towards Palkonda,	18	,,
,, ,, Naupada to Parla-Kimedi viâ Malapetta,	12	,,
,, ,, Tekkali Raghunadhapur to Hiramandalam viâ Tembur,	3	,,

* The population of Narsannapet cannot be ascertained as the town is made up of portions of several villages.

Road from Pundi to Varanasi viâ Parla-Kimedi, 10 miles.
„ „ Bommali to Raghunadhapur, 9½ „
Branch road to Srikurmam from the Chicacole to Calingapatam road, 2½ „
„ „ from 2nd mile of Calingapatam road to Mofuzbandar road viâ Arasavilli, 1 mile.
„ „ from Goppili *towards* Mandasa, ¾ „

Berhampore Taluq.—This is a first class taluq and consists of the old Mohiri Zemindary which was bought on behalf of Government at an auction for arrears of revenue in 1844, and of the old Pubbakondah and Ichapur Khandams.

It is bounded on the north by the Kallikot, Atagada, Biridi Humma and Palur Zemindaries and the Aska Estate; on the east by the Bay of Bengal; on the south by the Jalantra Zemindari; and on the west by Chikati, Chinna-Kimedi, Pedda-Kimedi, Sergada and Dharakot Zemindaries.

By scale it measures 521 square miles. Its villages are numbered 411, of which 346 are Government and 65 Agraharams.

The taluq is a fertile one; not such good land as Goomsur, but generally better than Chicacole. On the east the country is an open plain, but to the west there are some small ranges of hills.

The Kerandi or Mohiri hills which divide the Senior Assistant's division into two parts, traverse it in a north-westerly direction and occupy about 20 square miles of territory, separating the Government lands from the Zemindari tracts of Chinna-Kimedi, Pedda-Kimedi and Chikati. The range is about 2,500 feet high and contains about 30 hamlets inhabited by Khonds. These outlying Khonds are called Tinki Khonds. It is reputed to be very unhealthy, but is almost unexplored. The station of Sirkot in the Mohiri hills was occupied during the disturbances of 1818 by the Collector's

Sibbandi corps and for a long time previously had formed a refuge for a noted outlaw named Maharta and his adherents.

The chief towns of the taluq are Berhampore, which is the residence of the District Judge, Senior Assistant Collector, Tahsildar, &c., population 21,670; Ganjam, where the Deputy Tahsildar resides, population 4,163; and Chatrapur, the Head Quarters of the district. The population of this place is very small: it is composed of parts of 6 villages.

The Senior Assistant Collector's Division also includes Kallikot, Atagada, Chinna-Kimedi, Pedda-Kimedi, Chikati and Mandasa Zemindaries which will be found separately described.

The cultivation of the paddy chiefly depends on the rainfall; but there are a few irrigation works, viz., the Hiradhara channel from the Rushikulya which waters 9 villages in Purushottapur, and the Koratoli Tampara which irrigates 3,816 acres and is fed by the Jayamangalam channel of the Godahado.

To the south, near Ichapur, drainage works to carry off surplus waters are almost as much wanted as works to increase the supply.

The taluq is divided into three Khandams as follows:—

1. Ichapur. | 2. Mohiri. | 3. Pubbakondah.

The chief products are paddy, 37,930 garce and ragi, 10,637 garce; but oilseeds, sugar-cane and gram are also grown. The yield is more than the local demand and there is considerable export from Gopalpur.

The people are for the most part cultivators. Besides the ordinary weaving of common fabrics for native wear, there are at Berhampore weavers of fine cloths in silk, tusser silk and cotton.

There are weekly markets held at all the principal towns of the taluq as well as in some of the villages.

The roads in the taluq are :—

	Miles.
Road from Bengal frontier to Ganjam river...	25
Do. from Ganjam river to Berhampore ...	17
Do. from Berhampore to Chicacole frontier	44
Do. from Gopalpur to Ampuva bridge on the Trunk Road ...	6½
Do. from Berhampore to Aska ...	22
Do. from Damodarapalli on the Aska and Surada Road to Purushottapur on the Trunk Road ...	39
Do. from Aska to Humma on Trunk Road.	31½
Do. from Purushottapur to Trunk Road near Jagannadapur ...	13
Do. from Purushottapur on Trunk Road to Sonnapur ...	6
Do. from Trunk Road to Gopalpur ...	3
Do. from Trunk Road to Mandasa ...	9
Loop lines at Berhampore ...	5
Branch line from Trunk Road near Kanchili to the Port of Baruva viâ Sompet ...	5½
Road from Trunk Road near Korlam to Baruva	3½
Loop lines at Chatrapur ...	3
Branch lines at Ganjam ...	3
Branch roads at Aska ...	2

The Agency tracts at present under the jurisdiction of the Governor's Agent and Collector in Ganjam comprise the following Maliahs, or Hill Tracts :—Goomsur, Surada, Bodogoda Kattingia, and the Mutahs of Korada and Ronabha, Chinna-Kimedi, Pedda-Kimedi, Surangi, Jarada, Jalantra, Budarasingi, Mandasa, and Parla-Kimedi.

After the Goomsur war in 1836 it was considered necessary for the prevention of further disturbances that the administration of Criminal and Civil justice in the Hill Zemindaries should be removed from the ordinary Courts and placed under the Collector, and Act XXIV of 1839 was passed giving the Collector as Agent to the Governor, Fort Saint George, the necessary powers.

In 1845 the Government of India created a special Agency for the suppression of Meriah sacrifices and female infanticide throughout all the Hill Tracts of Orissa, and appointed Captain Macpherson, Agent under Act XI of 1845. All the Ganjam Maliahs, then under the Collector and Agent, were therefore transferred to him.

In May 1862 the Meriah Agency was done away with, and the Maliahs of Ganjam were retransferred to the Collector and Agent. In 1865 Goomsur proper with Surada were removed from the jurisdiction of the Agent, all Agency tracts below the Ghauts having been retransferred to the jurisdiction of the ordinary Courts. In 1869 the petty Chieftainships of Korada and Ronabha were restored to the Agent's jurisdiction, together with the Chokapád Mutáh of the Goomsur taluq.

In the Goomsur and Surada Maliahs the only collection made from the people is a small sum per acre of cultivation made in the Chokapad Mutáh.

The Chinna-Kimedi Maliahs were in 1872 taken from the management of the Chinna-Kimedi Zemindar. The Government collections made here are but a few rupees, paid by the Heads of Mutáhs at the yearly visit of the Agent.

The Pedda-Kimedi Maliahs are still under the Pedda-Kimedi Zemindar who collects from the Savara cultivators some 2,300 Rupees per annum and pays Rs. 500 a year for his Sanad.

The Parla-Kimedi Maliahs were in 1803, by the advice of the Circuit Committee, excluded from the Estate of the Parla-Kimedi Zemindar and Government, by proclamation, ordered that the Bissoyes and Paiks should pay their usual tributes direct to Government instead of as of old to the Zemindar. This order was never carried out in consequence of the difficulties of the country and the turbulence of the people, and in 1821, when the Estate which had been under management was about to be handed over to the Zemindar on his coming of age, it was recommended and sanctioned (by the Court of Wards as far as this District records shew), that the Bissoyes should in future pay their tributes to the Zemindar as of old and not to the Government direct. In 1834, Mr. Russell in his Report on Parla-Kimedi, para. 135, informed the Government that it was extremely desirable that the Bissoyes should still be considered tributary to the Zemindar rather than independent Chiefs paying direct to Government.

The Sanads under which these two Zemindars hold are special Sanads. The Revenue of the Hill tracts formed no part of the assets of the respective Zemindaries to which they happened to be attached, and the Zemindars are entitled only to receive the quit-rents that existed at the permanent settlement or which were then imposed on the Chiefs.

If there is a forfeiture for misconduct in their duties or an escheat from failure of heirs the reversion is in the Government not in the Zemindar, the latter always getting the quit-rent.*

The Civil jurisdiction is vested in the Governor's Agent who exercises the powers of a Civil and Sessions Judge throughout the Maliah tracts. Questions of disputed succession to landed Estates are decided by Government on the report of the Agent. The Maliah tracts are scheduled districts under Act XIV of 1874 and are excluded from the operation of the Local Fund Act.

The Special Assistant Agent has his head-quarters at Balliguda and he is required to reside in the hills for 7 months in the year. During the rainy season he lives at Russellkonda for the Hills are then very feverish.

There are three Sub-Magistrates in the Hill Tracts, viz., at Balliguda, Udayagiri in Goomsur and Udayagiri in the

* Special Commissioner's Proceedings, No. 104, dated 13th April 1881.

Pedda-Kimedi Maliahs. The Sub-Magistrate residing at Udayagiri of Pedda-Kimedi is called the Ramagiri Sub-Magistrate. Each Maliah Sub-Magistrate is invested with the powers of a Moonsiff for the trial of Civil disputes, but it is the express desire of Government that these powers should not be exercised where the parties can be induced to have recourse to a punchayet of their own people for the settlement of their disputes. Therefore these powers are ordinarily exercised in regulating and controlling the action of the Panchayats. Their procedure is guided by the Agency Rules drawn up by the Sudder Court under Act XXIV of 1839, under Government sanction.

Eighteen Hill Schools, fourteen under the Special Assistant Agent and two each under the Principal and Senior Assistant Agents, have been established and are attended by 735 boys and eleven girls. Of the boys, 117 are Khonds, 3 are Savaras and the rest Uriyas.—G. O., 8th October, 1878, No. 2032, J. D.

I give the following Sub-divisions and Mutáhs of the more important Maliah tracts.

Mutáhs of the Goomsur Maliahs, Population 49,750, *Khonds chiefly.*

1. Bara Mutáh
2. Othero „
3. Korada „
4. Hodogodo Mutáh
5. Tentuligodo Mutáh
6. Lanipoda
7. Chokapad.

Mutáhs of the Daringabadi Maliahs, Population 6,751, *Khonds chiefly.*

1. Daringabadi.
2. Kattingia.

Mutáhs of the Bodogoda Maliahs, Population 16,810, *Khonds chiefly.*

Mohono	Govindapur	Jorow
Lohagudi	Mirkot	Korchobadi
Kondho Odoba	Zhiliki	Gondogoto.
Budili	Odoba	

Mutáhs of the Chinna-Kimedi Maliahs, Population 46,264, *Khonds chiefly.*

Komonkolla	Kudutuli
Sarangada	Bargoma
Kurtumgar	Balliguda
Mondigar	Mirikia
Tumudibondho generally called	Pusangia
Tumariband	Gadapore
Kotgodo	Panigonda
Budaguda	Rumisi.
Mahasingi	

Mutáhs of the Pedda-Kimedi Maliahs, Population 29,512, *chiefly Savaras.*

Udayagiri	Nuagodo
Kojiripoda	Keradango Guma
Bodopoda	Ramagiri Guma
Zalarsingi Guma	Kotodesho Maliah.

Mutáhs of the Parla-Kimedi Maliahs, Population 19,201, *chiefly Savaras.*

Gumma	Kumulusingi
Gaiba	Konipuro
Serango	Gondahatti
Ojoyogodo (*i. e.* impregnable fort)	Lohkniyagodo, *i. e.* butter fort
	Naráyanapuro
Jirango	Námanogoro.
Raigodo	

The Surangi, Jarada, Jalantra, Bodarsinghi and Mandasa Maliyas are comparatively small and of little importance. Their inhabitants are chiefly Savaras.

CHAPTER II.

THE ZEMINDARIES AND PROPRIETARY ESTATES.

KALLIKOT AND ATAGADA—PALUR—BIRIDI—HUMMA — DHARAKOT — BODOGODA—KATTINGIA—SERGADA—CHINNA-KIMEDI —PEDDA-KIMEDI—CHIKATI —SURANGI —JARADA— JALANTRA—BUDARSINGI—MANDASA—TARLA—PARLA-KIMEDI—THE PROPRIETARY ESTATES OF ASKA, KURLA, DEVABHUMI, BARUVA, AND URLAM.

Origin of the Ganjam Zemindars.—The Zemindars of Ganjam, most of them, derived their power and estates from the Gajapati kings of Orissa, who granted them their lands on condition of feudal service and of keeping in check the wild aboriginal tribes of the hills—the Khonds and Savaras. Owing to the inaccessibility of their estates, the Zemindars gradually arrogated to themselves a rude kind of petty sovereignty and frequently waged war upon one another. Many of them appear to have been nominated to their estates by Purushottama Deo who ruled over Orissa in 1479-1504. The number of ancient Zemindaries is now eighteen.

Besides them, there were existing at the beginning of the century the Goomsur Zemindari which was the most ancient in the district, for when that Zemindari was declared by proclamation in 1836 to be forfeited for rebellion, the ruling family of the Bhondzo traced back their descent for a period of 875 years. The family is now extinct in the male line.* The country about Aska used to be a large Zemindari, but before the English established themselves in Ganjam, it was sub-divided between Goomsur, Bodogoda, and Atagada. The Kadamba "Vamsam" or family had been in possession of the Tekkali estate for a period of 375 years when the last Raja died in 1797 without legitimate issue. The ancient Mohiri Zemindari was sold for arrears of

* The last Zemindar died a State Prisoner in Vellore, having been deported there after the close of the war.

revenue in 1851, and in 1854 the Atagada estate became the property of the neighbouring Raja of Kallikot by purchase.

The present Zemindars of Parla-Kimedi, Pedda-Kimedi and Chinna-Kimedi claim descent from the ancient Gajapati kings of Orissa. The Zemindars all hold under a Sunnud-i-Mulkeut Istimrar granted at the settlement by the Government.

Owners of proprietary estates are registered, but have no Sanads. Their quit-rents were permanently assessed upon the estates held by them in 1804 and 1805.

At the present moment the Zemindaries of Parla-Kimedi, Chinna-Kimedi, Sergada, Jarada and the estate of Urlam are under the Court of Wards' management.

Kallikot.—The Kallikot Zemindari has a population of 41,311 distributed among some 235 villages. The approximate area is 231 square miles. It lies on the northern boundary of the Madras Presidency, adjoining the Banpur country in Orissa. The soil is generally very fertile, and is well supplied with water. Stretching as it does along the western shore of the Chilka lake, it possesses great natural advantages in the way of water-carriage. The yearly peishcush payable is Rs. 18,975-8-10.

The name of the present Zemindar is Sahib Mahurban Dostan Sri Narayana Mardaraja Deo. His fort or residence is about 15 miles from Rambha, beautifully situated in a basin surrounded and almost touched by the adjacent hills.

The Kallikot family is said to have been founded by one Rama Buya who exerted himself to clear the jungle and found villages. During the progress of Purushottama Gajapati Deo, King of Orissa, through the country A.D. 1374 he was an eye-witness of Rama Buya's ability and confirmed him as Zemindar of the taluq. At a later period the then Zemindar received credit for keeping the Mahrattas out of the district and obtained the title of Mardaraja Deo for his valor. The adjoining taluq of Atagada was bought by the Kallikot Zemindar in 1854 and now forms a part of his estate.

Atagada.—The Atagada (eight forts) estate is perhaps the finest in the district. The population is 76,301, and the area about 265 square miles. It contains 203 villages divided into three mutáhs or sub-divisions :—

1. Koladi Mutáh with 68 villages.
2. Bondakhandi Mutáh with 93 villages.
3. Bhitoro Mutáh with 102 villages.

The yearly peishcush payable is Rs. 59,929-1-9. On the north the estate is bounded by Bánpur and Nyagar in Cuttack, and on the south its limit is the River Rushikulya and the Government taluq of Berhampore. On the east it adjoins Kallikot, and on the west Goomsur. The country is mostly very rich and fertile, being watered by three small rivers. In the centre it is mountainous, and south-east of Koracholi in Goomsur there is an elevated tract of country known by the name of the Pandrapada Maliáhs chiefly covered with a dense forest and abounding in game. The Bissoi or Chief of this tract was formerly a feudal dependent of the ancient Zemindars of Atagada.

The Atagada estate was sold by auction for arrears of tribute on the 15th July 1854. The estate was at first declared to have been bought by Government on the ground that the Kallikot Zemindar who was actually the highest bidder, had not complied with the terms of the sale and paid in the prescribed deposit. Against this decision of Mr. Prendergast's, the then Collector, the Kallikot Rajah appealed to Government and the Government ordered that the amount of his bid should be accepted and the taluq made over to him. The old sanad was, as is usual, cancelled. The transfer of Atagada to the Kallikot Rajah, in spite of his being a nephew of the last Zemindar of Atagada, caused a great deal of dissatisfaction amongst the people and some disturbances took place. The causes are alleged to have been oppressive management. In 1873 the feeling of discontent which prevailed, culminated in the murder of Unnuva Rama Lingam Pantulu, the Zemindar's "patro" or manager. He was way-laid at night time by a band of armed malcontents, some 30 in number, and stabbed to death in the neighbourhood of Boirani, whilst on his way to Berhampore. Unfortunately the murderers were not convicted in spite of the exertions made both by the Police and the Magistracy to discover and bring to justice the perpetrators of this outrage.

The founder of the ancient family of Atagada is said to have been one Jagga Daso, a hermit, and the family was held in great esteem by the kings of Orissa.

Palur—Is a small Zemindari, having a population of 4,102 and being about 24 square miles in extent. It consists of 11 Jeroyeti and 4 Agraharam villages, and lies to the south of the Chilka lake. The soil is generally poor and the estate contains a number of salt swamps. The inhabitants have rendered themselves notorious by the illicit manufacture and smuggling of salt for which the country is in many respects very favourably situated. The name of the Zemindar is Sri Ramakrishna Gazendra Deo, and the yearly peishcush payable is 553 Rupees. The Zemindari is said to have been presented to Dasaradhi Soor, a Sirdar by Purushottama Gajapati Deo, King of Orissa, in A. D. 1489. From him the present Zemindar traces his descent.

Biridi—Is contiguous to the Kallikot Zemindari and, like Palur, also impinges upon the southern extremity of the Chilka lake. The village of Rambha which from time immemorial has been the principal port of the Chilka, is in the Zemindari. It has a population of 10,550. The approximate area is 47 square miles and the number of villages 62.

The peishcush is Rs. 4,456-13-0. The present Zemindar's name is Sri Vinayaka Sur Maharta Mardaraja Bramaravaraya. Like the other Zemindari tracts lying contiguous to the Chilka lake, the estate owes its origin to Purushottama Gajapati Deo, King of Orissa, who granted the taluq to Balaram Sur, one of his Sirdars, in the year 1489 A. D.

Humma—Lies near Ganjam and is the smallest Zemindari in the district. Its population is 2,766 and its approximate extent 9 square miles. The estate contains 13 villages, some of which are interspersed amongst the Government ones in the Tirustanam khandam of Berhampore taluq.

The name of the present Zemindar is Sri Purushottama Narayana Samantaraya Mahapatro Deo, and his peishcush is Rs. 1,163-0-4. Humma was formerly situated in the midst of a thick jungle which was the resort of thieves and plunderers. In order to protect travellers who passed along the high road adjoining it, Kapilendra Deo, King of Orissa, is said to have appointed one Madana Mohana Samunto to be Zemindar with the title of Samunta Raya Mahapatro A. D. 1228.

Dharakot.—The Dharakot Zemindari lies about 8 miles from Aska in a north-westerly direction, and adjoins Bodogoda on the north, and Goomsur on the east. It contains a population of 31,691 and 188 villages. Its approximate area is 125 square miles. It is traversed throughout its entire length by the Rushikulya river which meets its principal tributary, the Mahanadi, not far from Aska.

The Zemindari is divided into three Mutáhs or sub-divisions, viz., Jahada Mutáh, containing 85 villages; Konunagodo Mutáh containing 37 villages; and Sahasrango Mutáh, containing 66 villages.

The name of the present Zemindar is Sri Braja Sundara Singh.

The peishcush payable is Rs. 24,965-5-6. Dharakot formerly was a part of the ancient Khidsinghi Zemindari together with the neighbouring divisions of Surada, Bodogoda and Sergada. The name of the first Raja of Khidsingi was Sobab Chendra Singh, who is said to have received the countenance of the King of Orissa and ruled over the country for 39 years (A. D. 1168 to 1206). After seven generations had passed away Boliar Singh, a member of the ancient family, thought proper to divide the Khidsinghi country. To Damona

Singh, the son of his eldest son Gangadro Pattu Kumonaro, he gave the Bodogoda taluq. To his second son Haddu Singh, he gave Dharakot. To his third son Sunda Danoo Singh, he gave Surada, keeping Sergada for himself. This division took place in A. D. 1476.

Bodogoda, i.e. Great Fort.—This Zemindari adjoins the former Zemindari of Surada, now incorporated with the Goomsur Taluq. It is one of the wildest parts of the district and the inhabitants may be said to partake of the nature of the country. Attached to the Zemindari by name are the contiguous Bodogoda Maliahs which form a part of the charge of the Special Assistant Agent. The country is for the most part hilly and overrun with jungle, amongst which there is some fine forest land. The streams that water the country are the tributaries of larger rivers.

The population of the taluq is 12,400 and its approximate area is 141 square miles. There are 153 villages and three mutáhs or sub-divisions, viz., Kota, Jagari, and Korada Kona. The name of the present Zemindar is Sri Durga Mádhava Singh. His yearly peishcush, Rupees 4,230.

Kattingia.—On the west of Bodogoda we come to the small Mutáh of Kattingia which pays a quit-rent of 50 Rupees and is held by the Kattingia Muttádar, formerly a feudal dependant of the Bodogoda Rajas. In consequence however of a fight which took place in 1807 between the Kattingia Sirdar, assisted by the Chief of Surada, and the Godapore and Bodogoda Zemindars assisted by the Sergada people in which the Bodogoda Zemindar's son-in-law and two peons were slain whilst twelve other persons were wounded, a Sanad was granted to Kattingia with a view of preventing similar disturbances for the future.

Sergada.—The Zemindari is small but very fertile. The population is 9,422 and the approximate area is 24 square miles. The present minor is a second son of the Rajah of Chikati, having been adopted by the late Zemindar's widow.

The peishcush payable is Rs. 5,822-13-3 whilst the yearly income amounts to Rs. 18,314. The number of villages is 38. The Zemindari yields very fine crops of paddy besides other grains. It lies south-east of Dharakot and north-east of Chinna-Kimedi. The high road between Aska and Ichapur passes through it.

Pratápagiri or *Chinna-Kimedi.*—This formerly was a part of the adjacent Zemindari of Vijayanagar or Pedda-Kimedi, and along with that estate originally belonged to Parla-Kimedi. In 1607 the then Parla-Kimedi Rajah had two sons. To the younger son, Unanga Bheema Deo Kesari, he gave that portion of his estate called Unanga Bheema Deo Kimedi, and this estate was subsequently sub-divided into Vijayanagar or Pedda-Kimedi and Pratápagiri or Chinna-Kimedi. In 1768, when Mr. Cotsford took possession of the Ichapur province, he found the united estate in the hands of Bheema Deo, the most troublesome Zemindar in the district. At his death in 1776 one of his sons, Moni Deo, kept Vijayanagar or Pedda-Kimedi and the other, Jagannadha Deo, succeeded to Pratápagiri or Chinna-Kimedi, but since that date there were feuds and disturbances of a more or less serious character between the two families, till a recent decision (1876) of the Privy Council in appeal has decided that the estate is to be made over to the adopted son of the late Zemindar's widow who is a sister of the neighbouring Zemindar of Pedda-Kimedi. It is therefore to be hoped that the Estate will now enjoy the repose and peace of which it stands so greatly in need after the discord which has lasted for more than a century. (Vide Historical account of Ganjam.) The peishcush is Rs. 19,941-11-4 and the annual income of the Zemindari, Rs. 63,621.

The population of the Zemindari is 28,941 and its approximate area is 189 square miles. The number of villages is 159, and the Estate is sub-divided into five Mutáhs, viz.:—

1. Pratápagiri, containing 18 villages.
2. Sidhéshvaram „ 16 „
3. Gudari „ 10 „

4. Khari, containing 47 villages.
5. Othaisi „ 59 „

There are besides 19 Agraharams.

The Zemindar's 'godo' or fort is situated at Pudamari and there the Zemindars used to live.

The cultivation of Indigo has been attempted on this Estate with European Capital and the quality of the Indigo made was most excellent, but the enterprize was abandoned in consequence of the litigation and distracted state of the taluq that prevailed. The Godahado river flows through the Zemindari, and joins the Rushikulya river near Injili.

The extensive Chinna-Kimedi Maliahs (1,975 square miles which were formerly attached to this Zemindari), have been resumed by Government and their ancient feudal connection with Chinna-Kimedi, has therefore terminated.

Vijayanagar or Pedda-Kimedi.—The Raja claims descent from the ancient kings of Orissa, being a younger branch of the Parla-Kimedi family.

The Raja's 'godo' or fort was formerly at Vijayanagari. The present residence of the Zemindar is at Digupudi, a village containing 3,828 inhabitants.

The population of the Zemindari is 40,650, and its approximate area is 195 square miles, it contains 194 villages divided into 5 mutáhs: 1, Kara Mutáh; 2, Adupáda Mutáh; 3, Khari Mutáh; 4, Naupada Mutáh; 5, Gopalapuram Mutáh. At Naupada which is a large and important village, native cloths are manufactured. The Zemindar's name is Sri Lakshminaráyana Ananga Bheema Deo.

The yearly peishcush is Rs. 23,323-13-5. The Raja holds the Government Sanad for the Pedda-Kimedi Maliahs, which are attached to the Zemindari, and cover an area of 377 square miles.

Chikati.—This Estate lies to the south-east of Pedda-Kimedi and contains a population of 40,991, with an approximate area of 109 square miles. It is in general open and well cultivated. It is watered by the Báhudá river, which flows past Ichápur.

The number of villages is 129 and the country is divided into 6 mutáhs, viz. :—

1.	Krishnapuram	mutáh,	containing	15	villages.
2.	Bodopolonko	,,	,,	20	,,
3.	Jayantipuram	,,	,,	21	,,
4.	Kotilingi	,,	,,	11	,,
5.	Patrapuram	,,	,,	19	,,
6.	Talatampara	,,	,,	43	,,

The name of the present Zemindar is Sri Viswambhara Rajendra Deo.

The peishcush payable is Rs. 33,915-6-1. The Raja's residence is at Chikati, where he possesses a substantially-built house. A king of Cuttack is said to have granted this Zemindari to one Kasáno, a Sirdar, who conquered the country from the aboriginal wild tribes, and built a fort in A. D. 881.

Surangi.—This Zemindari lies south of Pedda-Kimedi and contains a population of 12,881, and an approximate area of about 75 square miles. The number of villages is 69. It adjoins that part of the Eastern Ghauts, known by the name of the Surangi Maliahs, which are attached to the Zemindari. The name of the present Zemindar is Sri Niládrichendra Harischendana Jagat Deo. His peishcush is 3,545 Rupees. Surangi is about 12 miles distant from Ichapur by a cross country road in a north-westerly direction. The Zemindar's "godo" or fort lies in a narrow gorge or recess at the head of a small valley. The wildness and loneliness of the country has, even in more recent time, made it a refuge for evil-doers. Quite recently one Bodro, a noted Savara murderer and malefactor, contrived for many years to elude the Ganjam Police in spite of all their attempts to capture him in these hills.

Jarada.—This is a small Zemindari adjoining Surangi and south-west of Chikati. It has a population of 5,927, and an approximate area of 38 square miles. The estate is hilly and jungly, but is tolerably well watered by a small stream that falls into the Báhudá river. It contains 29 villages. The name of the Zemindar is Sri Sáradhi Charana Sántara, and his peishcush Rs. 2,025.

Jarada is about 14 miles distant from Ichapur in a south-westerly direction.

Concerning the origin of this Zemindari it is related that one Visvambhara Singh Raya Turayi, formerly possessed a large tract of country in the Mahendra Maliahs. His second son, Veera Bhadra Singh, having subdued the hill people on a mountain named Jarasindu, the father bestowed it upon him and named it Jarada in A. D. 1440.

Jalantra.—Meaning "destitute of water" from *jala,* water, and *antaram,* without. This Zemindari lies about 11 miles south of Ichapur, Jalantra itself lying about 2 miles south-west of Kanchili, which is on the high road. The population is 18,175, and the approximate area 100 square miles. The estate contains 78 villages. The name of the Zemindar is Rama Krishna Chetroy Deo. His peishcush is Rs. 7,384-4-3. The Jalantra Zemindari is said to have been founded by Sri Purushottama Gajapati Deo, who halted in a jungle near the Mahendra mountain, when returning to Cuttack after his victory at Conjeeveram.—(Vide Historical Account). After subduing the neighbouring Savaras, he nominated his son, Govinda Chetroy Deo, to be Rajah, and called the place Jalantra, from the circumstance of its being a tract devoid of water. As an emblem of his having overcome and reduced the hill people to obedience, the King further ordered their net (Uriya Jâlo), with which they were accustomed to catch wild beasts, to be used as a sign by the Rajah.

Budârasingi—Is a small Zemindari extending along the foot of the Mahendra mountain between Jalantra to the north, and Mandasa to the south. The population is 3,244, and the approximate area is 22 square miles. The country is poor and considered unhealthy for strangers, and there is much bamboo jungle. The yearly peishcush is Rs. 525. The name of the present Zemindar is Sri Lakshmi Náráyana Nissunko Deo.

The family of the Budárasingi Zemindar traces back its descent to 1443. Its founder, one Damodra Nissunko, there is reason to believe, was a Savara Chieftain. The family has repeatedly intermarried with Mandasa, with whom it has also frequently been at feud.

Mandasa.—The population of the estate is 33,620, and the approximate area is 132 square miles. The number of villages is 166. The yearly peishcush payable is Rs. 14,035.

The Zemindari is generally open, and is separated from Parla-Kimedi by the Mahendra mountain. The paddy grown is said to be the best in Ganjam. The name of the Zemindar is Sri Rájamani Rája Deo, C.I.E.

The present Rája is one of the most enlightened in the district, and has done much to improve the town of Mandasa and his estate. Mandasa is about two miles distant from Haripuram which lies on the high road and contains a Zemindari school and a Post Office. It is not known when the Mandasa family first established itself here but the founder of the family, Pachendra Bammana Singh, is said to have been directed in a vision to settle in the Mahendra Máliah of the Kalinga Circar, and the tradition is that he came from Northern India, the Punjab.

Tarla.—Leaving Mandasa and proceeding southwards we enter the Tarla Zemindari in the sub-division of Ganjam. The estate is bounded on the south by Tekkali, and on the west by Parla-Kimedi. The population is 24,118, and contains an approximate area of 52 square miles. The number of villages is about 60. The country is tolerably level and well supplied with water.

The name of the present Zemindar is Sri Ráma Chendrasúrú Harischendana Deo. The peishcush is Rs. 4,000. The Tarla family originally came from Nagpore, and entered the services of the kings of Orissa. The first Zemindar's father is said to have been killed in battle at Kánchi (Conjeeveram), and upon the return of Purushottama Gajapati Deo from his expedition to the south, he made over the Tarla estate to his son, Sadásena Soor, in A..D. 1436.

Parla-Kimedi.—This estate is the largest and most important in Ganjam. It contains a population of 227,482 and an area, by actual survey, of 639 square miles. The yearly peishcush is Rs. 87,825-4-0 whilst the income derived from the estate is 4½ lakhs. Attached to the estate, but above Ghauts, are the Parla-Kimedi Máliahs inhabited by Savaras, which cover an area of about 354 square miles.

The chief town is Parla-Kimedi, with a population of 12,158. It is the head-quarters of a native Magistrate and of the Manager of the estate. There are also the following larger towns in the Zemindari:—

Battili,	population	...	...	2,311
Varanasi,	„	...	...	4,018
Hiramandalam,	„	...	...	3,167
Sarvakota,	„	...	...	1,490
Gurandi	„	...	...	2,293

Since 1830 the Zemindari has been administered by the Court of Wards, and its affairs are supervised by the Principal Assistant Collector, who lives at Chicacole. The present Zemindar, Sri Virapratáparudra Gajapati Narayana Deo, is a man of weak intellect and unfit to manage his own affairs, due probably to habits of debauchery, &c., for which the Oriya Zemindars used to be notorious. His children have not inherited their father's weakness, but are fine intelligent children. They are being educated by a private tutor under the orders of the Court of Wards, and it may be hoped that when they are old enough to do so they will set as brilliant an example of the advantages of good and careful education to the people of this district as the Vizianagram Zemindar's family—their neighbours—do in Vizagapatam district.

The Zemindari is full of hills, between which are numerous extensive and fertile valleys.

The highest mountain in the estate is Deodangar,* 4,054 feet above the sea-level, and there are some good sal wood forests near Serangi.

The whole country is singularly favored by nature and the Mango and Jack topes are the finest in the district. It is well supplied with rivers, channels, and tanks. "The rainfall "amounts to between †80 *and* 90 *inches yearly*, and owing to "the forest-covered hills which are scattered throughout the "estate, hardly a month passes without more or less rain falling." There are two teak plantations on the estate, one at Vallada and another at Kimedi. Since its administration by the Court of Wards the estate has been steadily increasing in value. Its public works are under the superintendence of the Estate Engineer who resides at Parla-Kimedi. Roads have been opened, and irrigation works improved and constructed. The lie of the country between the hills is particularly favourable to the construction of large reservoirs, and much may yet be done to improve the irrigation of the country. The Vamsadhara and Mahendratanaya rivers flow through the estate and Captain Rundall has suggested the construction of a navigable canal which would at the same time be available for irrigation purposes, between Battili and the great Salt Depôt at Naupada. Such a canal would be of incalculable benefit to the country as it would not only reduce the cost of carriage for salt and other articles, but would give additional stimulus to cultivation. If properly constructed it might also have the effect of preventing the disastrous floods which occur nearly every year

* Also called Ojjaigodo.

† These figures are out of Captain Rundall's report of 1854. They no longer apply. The rainfall is not, if it ever was, 90 inches, and the magnificent forest has become low scrub and impenetrable jungle under the untiring efforts of the hill people to extend their Kumeri cultivation. The Manager gives the rainfall to average 51·4 inches.

and which are productive of the greatest mischief. Captain Rundall remarks that the water required for the canal for six or eight months could probably be procured from the river Vamsadhara, and that the remainder might be obtained from reservoirs situated in the Kimedi hills, which, as before remarked, are particularly favourable for their construction.*

There are many fine tanks of large size in Parla-Kimedi, amongst which are the Rama Sagaram and Sita Sagaram near Kimedi, Brundavana Sagaram near Upalada, Krushna Sagaram near Gopilli and Chaitanya Sagaram, north-west of Parla-Kimedi. Other sources of irrigation are the Radha Sagaram, Sita Sagaram and Asarla Cheruvu.

The principal produce of the estate is paddy, but sugar-cane and dry grain are also grown. The yearly produce of paddy and ragi is estimated at paddy 16,112 garce, ragi 4,850 garce. The manufacture of indigo has also been recently attempted with more or less success. Other manufactures are cloth and muslin. At Parla-Kimedi baskets, mats and other articles of a fine texture are woven from the bark of a species of weed and are much esteemed in the district. The word Parla-Kimedi is said to be a corruption of the word "Pravála Khimundo," "the coral-headed and coral-eyed one," which was the name of the last of the aboriginal rulers of this tract. He was subdued by Callahumber, a son of Kapilendra Deo, of the Royal family of Orissa. This prince is said to have quitted Cuttack along with his brother's family in consequence of family dissensions and to have taken up his residence at Bissum Cuttack, then the chief town of Jeypore.

There are 503 villages in Parla-Kimedi, containing 64,062

* Captain Rundall's report, dated 6th November 1854, is to be found in ch. XII. A canal of the kind would only pay if the traffic on it paid. The increase to the cultivation would be very small and the natural supply of water is so good that no more could be got out of the Ryots for water than is now taken from them.

acres, assessed at Rupees 2,78,720. The country is divided into 24 Mutáhs, viz.:—

		Containing villages.			Containing villages.
1.	Soda	... 19	13.	Narayanapuram...	50
2.	Mahasingi	... 31	14.	Korsanda ...	4
3.	Labhara	... 17	15.	Gondahatti ...	9
4.	Gulenuru	... 20	16.	Goppili ...	20
5.	Irapadu	... 6	17.	Temburu ...	48
6.	Kurigam	... 18	18.	Sarvakota ...	35
7.	Kittalapadu	... 3	19.	Varanasi ...	20
8.	Neradi	... 9	20.	Liviri ...	3
9.	Khaspa	... 17	21.	Nivagam ...	20
10.	Jolla	... 10	22.	Bhaggu ...	24
11.	Gottipalli	... 11	23.	Nulakajodu ...	10
12.	Turpu	... 93	24.	Battili ...	6

There are 11 Bissois or feudal Chieftains in the Parla-Kimedi estate, of which 7 have their forts or "godos" in the Máliahs and four in the low country. They are as follows, and the four last in the low country: Gumma, Raigada, Jirangi, Serungo, Ojjagodo, Komalasinghi, Koipuram, Namanagaram, Gondahatti, Narayanapuram, and Lohuniagodo.

The roads in the Parla-Kimedi Estate are:—

		Length in miles.
1.	Gumma road from Varanasi road to Munisingi village	9
2.	Pálem and Tembore road	9
3.	Road from Chápara on the Pundi road to Kinchilingi viâ Gárabanda	12
4.	Nowtala road	7
5.	Gyba road	7
6.	Tekkalipatnam and Goppili road... ...	6
7.	Kimedi and Parápuram road	13
8.	Kimedi and Kinchilingi road	20

		Length in miles.
9.	Gárabanda and Goppili road	6
10.	Singapuram and Goppili road	5
11.	Gusadi road	5¼
12.	Road from Zemindar's Palace to Burgam ...	3¾
13.	Road from Kanduru to Basaba viâ Valuda ...	7
14.	Road from Gusadi road to Busagudi ...	2¼
15.	Road from Uppalada on Kimedi and Kinchilingi road to Gajapati Sagaram tank ...	3½

Besides the above roads which are paid out of estate funds there are the following roads maintained by the Chicacole Local Fund Board in the estate :—

	Whole length in miles.
28 miles of the road from Alikam to Battili ...	48¼
20¼ miles of the road from Calingapatam to Parla-Kimedi viâ Narsannapeta	35¼
13¼ miles of the road from Nowpada to Parla-Kimedi viâ Malapetta	25¼
17¾ miles of the road from Tekkali Raghunadhapur to Hiramandalam viâ Tembore... ...	20¾
29¼ miles of the road from Pundi to Varanasi viâ Parla-Kimedi	39¼
14 miles of the road from Addubhangi on the Varanasi road to Addubhangi on Palakonda boundary...	14
5 miles of the road from Mokhalingam to the Tekkali and Hiramandalam road ...	5
12 miles road from Chintáda to Gara	12

The permanent settlement of the estate was made in 1801 at the same time as that of the other estates, the management of the Court of Wards commenced in 1830. In 1861 a survey on what is called the block system was commenced and finished in 1867. In 1868 a rough classification of soils based on this block survey was made and the rates for the different soils were fixed. Complaints, however, were made that the classification and the consequent assessment on the various descriptions of soil were inaccurate, and a report by a skilled officer of the Settlement Department was ordered. This was made by Colonel C. J. Stuart in April 1880, and he reported that the boundary pillars of many villages had disappeared; that the configuration of the blocks on the ground was no longer traceable owing to extended cultivation while Porumbokes had in many instances become cultivated and dry lands were converted into wet. On this report the Court of Wards sanctioned a fresh survey to secure a field registry for the estate and this is now in progress.

The Court are now engaged in building the Zemindar a palace which will hardly cost less than 4½ lacs of Rupees before it is finished.

The population of Parla-Kimedi Máliah tract is returned at 19,201 and its approximate area is 350 square miles.

The management of the Court of Wards has been a very great success. They took the estate in charge in 1830 after the rebellion was put down. The peishcush, Rs. 87,825, which had never been paid except on compulsion was of course heavily in arrears and the people unsettled, and the lands left waste. Now it is one of the finest pieces of cultivated country in the district and the savings of 50 years amount to over twenty-four lacs of rupees.

Proprietary Estates.—The total number of proprietary estates in Ganjam is 47, most of them being in the sub-division.

These estates, originally thirty in number, were created by the sub-division of the Haveli or Government lands in 1803 and 1804, and were permanently assessed after the model of the permanent settlement, which was introduced into Bengal in 1799 by Lord Cornwallis. The Government lands of Chicacole were first sub-divided by Mr. Cherry, the then Collector, into twenty estates and were sold subject to a permanent quit-rent to the highest bidder in 1803. In the following year

(1804) the Haveli lands of Northern Ganjam were sold by public auction in a similar manner, having been sub-divided into ten proprietary estates with the exception of the Government lands rented to Captain Evans for the use of the Honorable Company's Stud. Most of the estates were, however, over-assessed and gradually reverted to Government. At the present day there are only five estates in the south remaining in the families of the original proprietors.

The four proprietary estates in the Northern Division are Aska, Kurla, Devabhumi and Baruva.

Aska, Kurla and Devabhumi.—These estates contain a total population of 16,704, and are now under one proprietor, the Aska Maluqdar. They are liable for a total quit-rent of Rs. 15,465-2-4.

The quit-rent is composed as follows :—

Rs. 8,449-2-3 for Aska.
„ 5,427-11-1 „ Kurla.
„ 5,188-5-0 „ Devabhumi.

The Aska estate originally formed a part of the Aska Zemindari which was dismembered about the beginning of the seventeenth century, during the Mogul Government of the Northern Circars (1560 to 1753) upon the death of Ram Rautu Rau, the last Zemindar, and was divided amongst the neighbouring Zemindars of Goomsur, Dharakot and Atagada.

The chief town is Aska with a population of 4,255. It lies on the River Rushikulya on the borders of Goomsur, and is the chief seat of the sugar trade in the Ganjam District.

Baruva—The Baruva estate lies on the sea coast about 30 miles south of Berhampore. It contains a population of 9,171, but has been recently sub-divided into Baruva and Petta.

The estate contains extensive plantations of cocoanut and palmyra trees and a good deal of cocoanut-oil is manufactured in the neighbourhood. The chief town is Baruva, one of the sea-ports of Ganjam, with a population of 6,739.

The yearly quit-rent payable is 7,800 Rupees. The estate lies in the jurisdiction of the Sompet Sub-Magistrate, which village is distant from Baruva about 4 miles by a metalled road.

Urlam.—This estate consists of 13 villages which were formerly under the possession of one Kannepalli Ramavadhanlu but which were put up to auction by Government for arrears of revenue about the year 1812. One Budhirazu Basavarazu, who was a Gumastah in the private service of Ramavadhanlu purchased it. He died in 1814 and his widow afterwards managed the estate. She had only three daughters, of whom one named Viyyamma married one Kaudukuri Perayalingam, and had a son Basavarazu Pantulu, the late proprietor; the other two daughters not having male issue. The estate therefore devolved on Basavarazu Pantulu in 1855. He was a very economical and business-like man and managed the estate with much care and diligence till his death in 1878. As his only son, Viswanadharao, was a minor, the estate came under the Court of Wards; the boy however died in 1880, from injuries received in the overturn of his carriage in Chicacole. His widow, Mahalakshnammah, is the present proprietrix without any issue. The estate still continues under the management of the Court of Wards.

The villages in the estate are:—

Jeroyeti Villages.

		Rent Roll.	
		In kind.	In money.
		Garce.	Rs.
1.	Urlam	253	902
2.	Devadi	80	491
3.	Gopalapenta	86	494
4.	Killam	103	481
5.	Mobagam	218	1,225
6.	Kobagam	104	381
7.	Chodavaram	100	238

Inam Villages.

		Rents. Rs.
8.	Venkatarayapuram	62
9.	Lukulam	1,200
10.	Pattanjavalasa	120
11.	Vanitamandalam	65
12.	Jennam	63
13.	Makivalasa	300
14.	Parvatalapeta subsequently acquired by purchase	228

Besides these there is a family property in the Godavery District consisting of a share in Kanchanapalli paying a yearly rent of Rupees 443.

The Inam villages pay money rents as well as the dry lands in the Jeroyeti villages, while for wet lands, half the gross produce is paid *in kind.* The proportion of dry lands to wet is estimated at about one to ten. The estate is devoid of hills or forests and no cultivable land is waste. Its demand for Fasli 1289 was Rs. 42,916 and the peishcush Rs. 13,580.

There are many other petty estates in the Sub-division too numerous and trifling to be treated in detail. They are shown in the Appendix.

CHAPTER III.

PORTS, PLACES OF INTEREST, &c.

GOPALPUR—GANJAM—SONNAPUR—BARUVA—PUNDI—BAVANAPADU—CALINGAPATAM—BERHAMPORE— CHATRAPUR— CHILKA LAKE—RAMBHA—ICHAPUR—SOMPET—MANDASA—MAHENDRAGIRI—ASKA—RUSSELLKONDA— PARLA-KIMEDI— CHICACOLE — MULAGAVALSA — PURUSHOTTAPUR—THE JOUGODO-TAPTA PANI—VARIOUS TEMPLES.

Gopalpur—(Formerly Mansurkota) is the chief port of the Ganjam District, and contains 2,416 inhabitants. It lies in latitude 19° 31′ north and longitude 85° 0′ east.

Gopalpur is a port of call for the steamers of the British India Steam Navigation Company. Its distance from Berhampore is 9 miles by road. The intense heat of May is tempered by the sea-breeze at Gopalpur considerably, and it is a pleasant place of residence for Europeans. The supply of fish is abundant. There are several bungalows at Gopalpur belonging to European merchants and others, and a public bungalow. Merchandise and other goods are landed on the beach close to Mr. F. J. V. Minchin's extensive godowns, not far from which is the Custom-house. North-east of Gopalpur there is a large back-water which separates it from the village of Mansurkota, which formerly gave its name to the port.

There is a Port Officer at Gopalpur who also has charge of the collection of Sea Customs. Within the limits of the port he exercises Magisterial powers and acts as a Justice of the Peace, in cases occurring on board ships in the roads. A light is exhibited at night time from the flagstaff of the Custom-house on the beach which is visible at a distance of 13 miles.* The port of Gopalpur is nothing more

* Arrangements are on foot for the construction of a light-house.

than an open roadstead similar to other ports on the eastern coast of the Madras Presidency. The depth of water in the anchorage varies from 8¼ to 9¼ fathoms at low water. The bottom at these depths is sand mixed with stiff mud, and is good holding ground. The rise and fall of the tide is about 6 feet. Under 7½ to 8 fathoms the bottom consists of sand and shells, through which an anchor easily drags. During the months of April, May and October more especially, the surf is frequently so high that communication between the shipping and the shore is interrupted for days together; but it is generally possible to communicate in the early part of the day. The prevailing wind is south to south-east, and during fully eight months of the year it blows at times very strongly. The surf rises very quickly, and being shorter and more chopping than the longer and more formidable-looking waves at Madras, is justly considered more dangerous to boats shipping cargo, &c., added to which the Masula boats are not so well manned, and the currents are stronger than at Madras. As a rule, the current runs with the wind. When the southerly winds commence to blow in February the current is found setting in strong to the north which it continues to do until towards the end of the south-west monsoon. The current then sets slightly to the southward and when the north-east monsoon sets in, it ultimately becomes a strong southerly current. The limit of the port on the north-east or Mansurkota side is at a distance of 1,160 yards from the Custom-house and on the south-west side at a distance of 600 yards from it. To seaward the boundaries of the port extend to where a depth of 12 fathoms is reached. No ballast may be discharged by ships within a depth of 12 fathoms.

The anchorage* for ships is with the Custom-house flagstaff on the beach north-west ½ west; centre of the large white godown on the beach from which the Aska sugars are shipped north, north-west ¼ west; Saddle-hill entirely detached from

* Finlay's Sailing Directory for the Indian Ocean, page 900, Second Edition, 1870.

the highland and appearing to the south over the beach sand hills west south-west and Mansurkota hill north by west about 1¼ mile from the shore.

Ganjam—Is about 13 miles north-eastward of Gopalpur. It contains 4,163 inhabitants and was formerly the chief town of the district. The handsome buildings that once adorned it have either fallen into ruins or been pulled down by the natives; and at the present day, with the exception of the picturesque looking fort, there is scarcely a vestige of its original splendour. The fort which was commenced in 1768 by Mr. Cotsford, the first resident in Ganjam, still forms an interesting ruin and recalls to mind the memories of former residents and chiefs in council who were engaged here partly in political and partly in commercial enterprizes for the good of the Honorable Company. The adjoining cemetery contains some interesting monuments which are gradually falling to decay. The severity of the fever which caused Ganjam to be given up as district head-quarters may be judged from the fact that the population of the town, estimated at 30,000 in 1815, had in 1818 diminished to 6,000. Many of the inhabitants abandoned the place, and the Civil and Military authorities removed to Berhampore, which lies 18 miles W. S. W. of it. Mr. Cherry first notices the prevalence of fever at Ganjam in 1802, but previous to that date it appears to have been as healthy as any other town in the Presidency.

The true causes of the epidemic of 1815 seem never to have been discovered, although a local committee was appointed to investigate them shortly after the outbreak. It seems clear that an utter want of all sanitary precaution had brought the town into a most unhealthy state at the time of the outbreak. Other reasons assigned were the brackishness and badness of the water-supply. Of late years the Local Fund Board has done much to improve the condition of the town by drainage.

Ganjam used to lie on the Rushikulya river, but in consequence of the river gradually shifting, the limits of the port have been changed from time to time. The river formerly emptied itself into the sea close to the fort, but its present mouth is nearly three-quarters of a mile farther north. During the rains the river is often in flood, and its overflow causes some damage to the surrounding country. The tide comes up the river, and at new and full moon, there is a considerable depth of water between its banks. During the floods a ferry plies across the river at the northern road, but it is fordable at most times.

The limits of the port of Ganjam, within which passengers and cargo may be embarked, were fixed from the godowns formerly belonging to Messrs. Shand and Co., on the south to Kappagantula Ramiah's godowns on the north. Ships usually anchor in the roads abreast of the fort in eight or nine fathoms, about two miles from shore. Ganjam is the head-quarters of a native Sub-Magistrate. The Conservator of the port at Ganjam is also Superintendent of Sea Customs. There are a Police Station and a Post Office here and a Salt factory described elsewhere.

Once this was the chief port of the district, now it is a rare thing for a ship to come there, and it is difficult to understand why it has been so thrown into the shade by Gopalpur, unless it be that the latter has had the advantage of British enterprize to bring it forward. Over Gopalpur, Ganjam has the advantages that boats can be loaded in quiet water at the Custom-house, and that they can be of greater capacity than boats that have to be dragged up out of the surf when loaded. It is said that the anchorage is not so good, and that there is generally more sea, but with larger boats one would suppose that the sea would not matter, and for anchorage Gopalpur itself is not very good.

Sonnapur (Sonnapuram)—Lies in lat. 19° 6′ north, and long. 84° 47′ east, and is now a port of no importance, although at one time (1768) the principal shipping place in the Ichapur province. The port is marked by a white obelisk and a white column, each 50 feet high. At 120 feet N. by E. from the column is the flag-staff, and between them is the Custom-house. The anchorage is with the flag-staff bearing W. N. W.

The Bâhudá river falls into the sea at Sonnapur, and forms with the sea, sandy bars which offer great obstruction to shipping. The trade that formerly went to Sonnapur is now gradually finding its way to Bâruva. The soil around Sonnapur was much injured by inundations from the sea in 1825, which have rendered it brackish and unfertile. Excellent edible oysters are found here which are much appreciated by the European residents of the District. During the hot weather Sonnapur is a pleasant place to camp at, as the sea-breeze renders the heat tolerable. It is two miles from the Surlá salt factory, and 14 from Berhampore, with which it is connected by a branch road leading into the high road between Ichapur and Berhampore.

Bâruva (Anglicé Barwah).—This port lies in lat. 18° 51' north, and long. 84° 35' east, and is 33 miles distant from Berhampore by road. South-west of Bâruva there are large topes of cocoanut trees. To the north there is a plain covered with sand drifts. The port is marked by two columns, black and white, 50 feet high, built on a site 15 feet above the sea, bearing north-west from the usual anchorage. The black one must be altered for it is invisible at sea at any distance. Bâruva forms part of the proprietary estate of that name. A new Custom-house and flag-staff have been recently constructed. A good deal of cocoanut oil is made in the neighbourhood and the trade of the port is increasing; native passengers from Burmah are frequently landed there.

Pundi (Anglicé Poondy).—This minor port is in latitude 18° 40' north, and longitude 84° 26' east, and is under the Sea Customs' Superintendent of Calingapatam in the Chicacole

---

Vide Findlay's Sailing Directory for the Indian Ocean, p. 900.

Division. It stands at the mouth of the Mahendratanaya river, having several rocks projecting a considerable distance seaward from north-east ¾ east. The port is marked by a white obelisk, 50 feet high on a hillock, 19 feet above the sea. At a few yards east of it is the flag-staff, 75 feet high, and north of it at the same distance is the Travellers' bungalow. As the obelisk, flag-staff and bungalow thus stand together on the hill, this port cannot well be mistaken by ships at sea. The anchorage is with the obelisk bearing north-west by west.

Bavanapádu—is a small port in latitude 18° 34′ north, and longitude 84° 20′ east, and 23 miles north-east of Calingapatam. At present it consists of nothing but thatched godowns and fishermen's huts. The ground is low and is a succession of sand-drifts. The port is marked by a column coloured black and white, 50 feet high, at 6 feet above the sea. The usual anchorage is with this beacon bearing north-west.

Calingapatam.—This port contains a population of 4,675, and stands on the south bank of the Vamsadhará river. The sandy point forming the south bank of the river is in latitude 18° 19′ north, and longitude 84° 7′ 30″ east. A light-house, 64 feet high, stands on the point, and the town is between the south bank of the river and this long low sandy point. A reef of rocks extends from the shore half a mile seaward. In passing vessels ought not to approach nearer than 8 fathoms. The best anchorage is in 6½ to 7 fathoms.*

Calingapatam is the only port which has any shelter, and which is not a perfectly open roadstead and unprotected between Coringa 150 miles south, and Dharma in Orissa 250 miles north. Communication between the shore and shipping is but

---

*Vide Findlay's Sailing Directory for the Indian Ocean, p. 900, 2nd Edition.

rarely interrupted, and the landing is much less uncertain than at Gopalpur. During the monsoons a large number of native vessels lie up in the river Vamsadhárá. The greatest depth of water over the bar is 14 ft. 6 in. and for 220 yards there is a depth of 12 feet. It is now (1882) a fortnightly port of call for the coasting steamers of the British India Steam Navigation Company.

Calingapatam is connected by means of a good metalled road with Chicacole, from which it is distant 16 miles. The country around is barren and dreary in the extreme. On the land side all is salt-swamp, and elsewhere nothing is to be seen but drifting sand without a blade of vegetation on it. It is the residence of a few European merchants, and is gradually regaining some of the importance which it formerly possessed. Its neighbourhood should prove of interest to antiquarians as it was formerly the site of the ancient city of Kalinga, and on a mound, that is clearly the site of an old city, are found after a shower small gold coins of very considerable antiquity. The little boys about make it their business to hunt for them, and they are from 4 to 2 annas in value. A late Salt Deputy Collector is said to have collected as many as 200 by making the boys bring to him for purchase all they found. At Dirghasi, on the opposite side of the river, is an old inscription that it is believed has never been deciphered.

Berhampore (*The city of Brahma*).—Berhampore is the chief town of the Ganjam District, and contains a population of 21,816 according to the Census of 1871. It is situated in latitude 19° 20′ north, and longitude 84° 50′ east. It is distant from Madras 664 miles, from Calcutta 325 miles, and from Nagpore in the Central Provinces 560 miles. The town stands on a rocky ledge 78 feet above the mean level of the sea, surrounded by an extensive cultivated plain, and in a direct line is seven miles distant from the sea. On the east and south this plain is open, and slopes towards the sea, but on the north and west it is bounded by the Mohiri or Kerandi hills, some 2,500 feet high, and distant about 8 miles from Berhampore.

There is no river near Berhampore, but there are numerous small tanks and irrigation channels which become swollen during the monsoon rains. The climate is generally healthy and bracing both to European and native constitutions. In November, December, January and February, the weather is very pleasant, the sky being clear, and the atmosphere cool, with heavy dews at night. The thermometer at this season ranges between 50° and 80° Fahr. The most trying months in the year are April, May and September, the two former on account of the excessive heat, and the latter by reason of the sultry oppressiveness of the air, which is frequently broken by copious falls of rain.

Berhampore is a Municipal town, and the residence of the Civil and Sessions Judge of Ganjam, and of the Senior Assistant Collector and Magistrate. The Head-quarters of a Native Regiment, the other wing being usually stationed at Sumbulpore in the Central Provinces, are also stationed here. The military lines are in Bápuram, where there is a Protestant and a Roman Catholic Chapel, a military hospital, and a parade ground for the sepoys, besides other military buildings. The situation of the military lines, which lie in a hollow, has been brought to the notice of Government, and V-shaped stone drains similar to those constructed by the Municipality in other parts of the town, have been laid down, but the place is not after all a very unhealthy cantonment.

Páta Barampuram is the exclusively native part of the town and adjoins the military lines. In the principal street, which has been widened and opened out, the chief native merchants and traders reside. The dispensary which is supported partly by Government and partly by the Municipality, lies on the outskirts of the town, and is under the charge of the Zillah Surgeon. It is a matter for regret that the remoteness of this institution should somewhat interfere with its usefulness. The other public buildings at Berhampore are the Civil and Session Court and the District Jail, which are situated on the high ground near the high road to Gopalpur and Chatrapur adjoining the village of Lanjipilli and west of the military lines. The District Surgeon acts as Superintendent of the District Jail, in which all prisoners sentenced to imprisonment for more than one month are confined, also all Civil prisoners. Prisoners sentenced to rigorous imprisonment are employed at work either in the large garden attached to the jail, or in making and repairing roads in its immediate vicinity.

Berhampore was formerly frequently ravaged by cholera, but since the establishment of the Municipality in 1867, the health of the town is steadily improving and much has been done to improve its sanitary condition. Unfortunately it is still subject to these attacks, which are in a great measure due to causes beyond the control of the Municipal authorities. The disease can be, as a rule, clearly traced to the return of pilgrims from Pûri or Jagannâth in the neighbouring district of Pûri. Feeble and sinking for want of nourishing food, and way-worn with the heat and fatigues of the journey, the poorer pilgrims are usually the first to fall victims to the fell disease, which they only too frequently bring with them in their train.

The chief industry in Berhampore is the weaving of tussur silk, which is manufactured into gold embroidered turbans, dresses and other articles of wearing apparel. These are usually of excellent quality. The common native cotton cloths are also woven. The ordinary artisans at Berhampore are, as a rule, a very indifferent set of workmen, and take but little pride in their work. The bazaars are well supplied with the ordinary necessaries of life. During the colder months of the year English vegetables such as peas, beans, cauliflower, asparagus and potatoes, can all be raised with success. English flowers also do well, and the quality of arrowroot grown here has been very favourably reported upon. Snipe, wild-fowl, and other game are plentiful during the season.

Chatrapur (*Sitarampalle*).—Chatrapur is only of importance as the head-quarters of the chief civil officer of the district. It lies on the high road between Berhampore and Cuttack, and is distant from Berhampore 12¾ miles and from the frontier of Bengal 28 miles. It is 112 miles from Chicacole. The public buildings at Chatrapur consist of a Subsidiary Jail, the Police Hospital and Police Lines, and the Collector's Cutcherry. The Máliah (Hill) Reserve Force of Constables is located at Chatrapur, which is also the head-quarters of the Superintendent of Police and a Medical Officer. The Onslow Institution was founded by A. P. Onslow, Esq., a former Collector, for the education of natives, and is supported by the rent of the Collector's house, and other property donated for that purpose. A weekly bazaar is held on Thursday evenings, and native cloths and other goods are brought from Berhampore and Ganjam for sale. Provisions for Europeans have usually to be brought from Berhampore, and even for natives the bazaar is but indifferently supplied.

The situation of Chatrapur is very beautiful. It stands overlooking the sea about 60 feet above sea-level, and in the Collector's compound are banian trees worth a long journey only to see. It is a healthy place, but relaxing. After the deadly outbreak of fever in Ganjam in 1815, from which Chatrapur is only five miles distant, the Collector's Cutcherry was located between 1816 and 1835 at Berhampore. In 1831, however, Mr. Eden, the then Collector, seems to have taken up his residence at Chatrapur, and in 1835 a sum of 5,000 Rupees was sanctioned by Government for the erection of a Cutcherry and public offices for the Collector. The sole reason assigned for abandoning Berhampore seems to have been that it was the property and residence of a Zemindar (Mohiri).

The Chilka Lake—Belongs rather to the Cuttack District, and for the purposes of this work is only a water-way by which produce can be brought to Rambha or to Ganjam at present by means of the Chilka canal and before long to Gopalpur, when the canal is extended.

The lake is 42 miles long and 10 broad. It is shallow, seldom exceeding 6 feet in depth. The water is brackish and there is a very slight tide at the southern end, the sea running into it at Manickpatam. The boats on it are the same curious things that are described as follows by Col. Cotton in a report dated 12th July 1856:—

"The trade of the Chilka is carried on in boats quite peculiar to "the lake, and in some respects well suited to it. They are made "of planks without ribs or keels, and perfectly flat-bottomed "with perpendicular sides. This form is necessary in the unim-"proved state of the landing places, as the lake is very shal-"low at the edges, except where a rocky knoll forms the "bank; and in such positions goods cannot be landed "with safety from the breaking of the waves. The bed of "the lake is all of the softest mud, and the slope from the "shore is so slight, that but for the rise and fall of the tide, "loaded boats could not approach the most favorable landing-"places within several hundred yards, and when the rise of "tide is slight, as it is at the south end of the Chilka at this "season, the boats can only be unloaded by the carts being "driven into the lake to meet them. These boats are poled against "the wind, and have mat sails when the wind is fair, set upon "two loose bamboos which come down upon the heads of the "crew, if the sail is by accident shaken in the wind. I never "saw boats so rude in their rig and consequently difficult to "manage, but even with these drawbacks and most lazy "working, the carriage on the lake is very moderate."

The lake swarms with wild fowl, especially on the Puri and sea side, and around the Island of Nálbunno. The scenery on it is very beautiful. Its port in the district is Rambha and the produce arriving there is at an average 67,078 maunds of rice and 584,136 maunds of paddy per annum.

At Rambha is the old house built by Mr. Snodgrass about 1792, as it is believed, from Famine funds. It stands in a beautiful situation overlooking the lake, and is now the property of Mr. Minchin, one of the partners in the Aska distillery and firm.

Ichapur—(City of delight) is a large village, or, more strictly speaking, agglomeration of villages, containing 12,493 inhabitants. It lies on the high road between Berhampore and Chicacole, 16 miles from Berhampore, and was formerly the residence of a Mussulman Naib during the Mussulman occupation of the Ichapur province, 1560-1753. Some small musjids or mosques are now the only architectural remains that serve to mark their rule, and even these are fast falling into ruin. Ichapur is now the station of the Deputy Tahsildar and native Sub-Magistrate. The public buildings consist of the Deputy Tahsildar's Cutcherry, the Munsif's Court, Subsidiary Jail and Police station, a Taluq school and a Post Office. The river Báhudá passes near Ichapur, and is spanned by a bridge on the high road. In the neighbourhood there are some fine betel gardens. The Surla Salt factory is about three miles distant, and is surrounded by extensive swamps.

Sompet—contains 2,716 inhabitants, and is the head-quarters of a Deputy Tahsildar and native Magistrate. The village is situated partly in the Talatampara mutâh of the Chikati estate, and partly in that of Jalantra. The public buildings consist of a Post Office, and an excellent Cutcherry built on Mr. Chisholm's plan. The village lies off the high road between Berhampore and Chicacole, but is connected with it by a road distant two miles from the public bungalow at Kanchili. The road to Sompêt is continued to the neighbouring port of Baruva, from which Sompêt is distant six miles. A large swamp near Sompêt affords good snipe, plover, and duck-shooting during the season.

Mandasa—The capital of the Zemindari of that name. It is a fine clean and well-kept town and is the residence of the present Zemindar who received the order of C.I.E. at the Empress Durbar held at Berhampore on the 1st January 1877.

The Zemindar's fort is prettily situated at the foot of the Mahendra mountain.

Mahendragiri—An outlying spur of the eastern ghauts, the Máliah country of the district. It was once proposed as a sanatarium for Calcutta. It is situate in latitude 18° 58' north and longitude 84° 24' east. The highest peak is 4,923 feet above sea-level and on a plateau facing the sea at a height of 4,578 feet there is a bungalow built by a former Collector and now kept up by the Rajah of Mandasa. There are three rooms in the bungalow and an out-house for servants. The temperature in the hot weather is quite 13 degrees lower than in the plains in the day time and by night the difference is much greater, but dense mists are very common. Good water is to be had, as a rule, not far from the bungalow itself, but in seasons of drought, water is not obtainable nearer than from the stream, that usually forms a half-way resting-place during the ascent of the mountain. The mountain is about 16 miles from the sea, and lies exposed to the sea-breeze, the nearest port being Bâruvâ, which can be seen from the bungalow. The slopes of the mountains are for the most part bare, and with the exception of hares, there is a comparative absence of animal life, although it is occasionally visited by bears, sambar and barking deer. Game is chiefly confined to the lower valleys, but the slopes of the hill are so steep that even the most ardent sportsman will not find himself much tempted to penetrate into their depths.

The flora of the plateau near the summit is quite distinct from that which clothes the steep sides of the hill. Violets and different kinds of ferns are common, amongst which is the common bracken fern (Pteris aquilina). The principal herbaceous plants on the plateau are :—

Crotalaria linfolia, L.
Anaphalis aduata
Jasminum grandiflorum
Tephrosia tinctoria
Cassia Macraei

Justicia procumbens, L.
Knoxia corymbosa
Conyza absentifolia
Sopubia delphinifolia
Colens barbatus.

The rarer ferns are :—

Hemionotis eodata, *Roxb.*
Pteropecis Wightianna
Acrophorus immersus, *Moore.*
Athyrium falcatum, *Knuze.*

Of edible fruit the wild raspberry, the wild mango, and a species of sloe-plum are common. The natives drive their cattle up for pasture at certain seasons of the year, and once a year large numbers of them make a pilgrimage from the low country to the temples on the top of Mahéndragiri, which offer some interest to archæologists.

The most conspicuous temple crowns the topmost peak of the hill, and is remarkable for the huge blocks of granitic gneiss, of which it is composed. The height of the temple is somewhat under 25 feet. There is a second temple, larger, on the same level as the bungalow, but lying some distance behind it. One other temple lies at the foot of the eminence on which the bungalow stands, but is hidden from view from above by a picturesque dell, encircled by a thick grove of trees. The natives assert that these temples were built by giants, evidently on account of the large size of the granite blocks employed. Besides the three principal temples, which are all of small size, there are a number of rudely constructed cairns or huts generally arranged in groups, and for the most part built of uncut stones. Their origin is unknown and there are no inscriptions visible to assist in determining their date. Presumably they were used as dwelling places by the old devotees.

The topmost temple has been struck by lightning and some of the stones misplaced and shattered in the most curious manner.

There are inscriptions inside the temple near the bungalow, and two curious iron rods have been put in apparently by the original builders, among the supporting stones of the entrance to the building The reason for placing them there is difficult to conjecture, for being only about the thickness of a man's wrist, their supporting power is very small as compared with the enormous granite masses that they lie beside. One rod is fixed in its place, apparently by molten metal poured in from above when it was put in position, and the other is not fixed but resounds loudly to the blow of a stick.

The temples, except that at the very top of the hill, are ornamented with small carvings, and are in the shape adopted by the worshippers of *Siva*, having the umbrella or chattram at the top.

There are three different ways leading to the top of Mahéndragiri. One is from Tumbâ in the Jalantra estate, where a Bissoyi or Hill Chief resides. This route is the nearest to Berhampore in a direct line, but is in reality the most inaccessible, as the road or track is a bad one. The second route from Berhampore is viâ Haripur on the Great Northern Trunk Road where there is a bungalow, and then on through Mandasa and Savarakota in the Mandasa estate, where there is another Bissoyi. Whilst the third route lies the farthest to the south in the Parlá-Kimedi estate, and, although the longest, is probably the easiest of the three. This route may be described as follows. From Kimedi to Gárabanda, 14 miles, the road is a good one. Six miles farther on, the ascent commences at Kinchilingi. From Kinchilingi to Koipúr there are 5 miles of easy walking. From Koipúr to the top of Mahéndra 6 miles—total 31 miles. This route is the most convenient for persons living in the subdivision of Ganjam, but for the benefit of those who may happen to be in the northern division, information concerning another road to the top viâ Haripur and Mandasa, may prove of use.

The best plan, in order to avoid the heat of the sun, is to start from the bungalow at Haripur, which is 2 miles from

Mandasa, at midnight. Riding through Mandasa by a torch light, if no moon is visible, some jungle is passed to Savarakota where there is a Bissoyi, who is a feudal dependent of the Mandasa Rajah's. The Mandasa Rajah, it should be stated, is most attentive and obliging in affording every assistance to the traveller. The actual ascent of the mountain begins at Savarakota, and either a horse or a pony may be ridden up as far as the half-way stream, which affords amongst the trees, a pleasant resting-place for breakfast. It is not advisable to take a horse beyond this spot, as the farther ascent is exceedingly steep and rugged. The rest of the journey therefore must either be accomplished on foot or in doolies, bearers being previously provided for those unable or unwilling to walk. The ascent of the mountain is a toilsome one, and it is with no small feelings of pleasure and exultation that the wayfarer finally finds himself in the verandah of the bungalow at the top.

Aska—The residence of a Sub-Magistrate, is prettily situate on the fork of the Mahanadi and Rushikulya rivers. It is a District Munsiff's station also, but is chiefly famous for the Aska Sugar Factory, now the property of a firm known as Messrs. Minchin Brothers and Co. The firm are distillers as well as sugar makers, and at present besides supplying Government with considerable quantities of Alcohol and Rum, are the Abkari renters of Ganjam.

Russellkonda (*Russell's Hill*).—This small town, situated in the midst of charming scenery, was named in 1837 at the termination of the second Goomsur campaign after Mr. Russell, the able Special Commissioner in Ganjam. The town lies at the foot of a small hill, and is in lat. 20° 56' north and long. 84° 37' east. The river Luharakhandi flows past the town, and is spanned by a good masonry bridge. The country is well supplied with good water. Mango topes are conspicuous, and the plain, which surrounds the town, is cultivated with paddy, cotton, sugar-cane, castor-oil and dry grains. The country is thickly studded with hills and jungle, and bears and other game abound. In the large garden attached to the jail, most excellent arrowroot is grown, besides all kinds of English and native vegetables. The climate is salubrious, but during March, April and May the heat is excessive, and the nights are very oppressive. During the rest of the year the weather is cool and pleasant, and from November to January the cold at night time is quite sharp. Russellkonda was occupied by troops for some little time after the Goomsur war to prevent further disturbances. It is no longer a military station, and the barracks for the sepoys are now used as the hill jail, in which natives of the Máliah tracts, sentenced to more than one month's imprisonment, are usually confined, the air of the sea coast having been found to be exceedingly fatal to them. The sea-air has a very decided effect in developing the germs of any latent fever, as district officers know to their cost.

The other public buildings besides the Hill Jail, are the Goomsur Tahsildar's Cutcherry, a Hospital in charge of a resident Apothecary and a Normal School for the instruction and training of the Uriya School Masters destined for employment in the district. In the rains when the hills are very feverish the Special Assistant Agent and the Assistant Superintendent of Police reside here. Russellkonda is the chief mart for the disposal of the produce of the hills, consisting chiefly of wheat, turmeric, wax, honey, hides and horns, which the Khonds exchange for salt-fish, iron, brass vessels, beads, &c. Large troops of Brinjaries and their pack-bullocks also pass through Russellkonda with salt on their way to the Boad Zemindari and the Central Provinces. The distance between Russellkonda and Balliguda is 56 miles. The population of Russellkonda is 2,625.

Severe thunderstorms are of yearly occurrence and the Jail and Taluq Cutcherry have both been struck at different times. Crows have also been picked up dead struck by lightning.

Parla-Kimedi—is the chief town of the large Zemindari of that name, and contains a population of 15,958. It is the head-quarters of the Assistant Superintendent of Police in the Chicacole Division, as well as of a native Magistrate. The Manager of the estate resides here. The Zemindar's palace will be a fine building, and is being constructed from the designs, and under the supervision of Mr. Chisholm, the Government Architect. The cost is estimated at about 4 lakhs. Parla-Kimedi is situate in an amphitheatre of hills and is in the midst of remarkably pretty scenery. The magnificent tanks or *Ságarams*, as they are termed locally, near Parla-Kimedi, are worthy of notice.

Chicacole (Srikakulam).—Chicacole is a Municipal town and contains 15,587 inhabitants and is the head-quarters of the Principal Assistant Collector and Magistrate who has charge of the Chicacole Division. It contains a noble mosque built in 1641 by Shir Mahomed Khan, the first Mussulman Faujdar, and has a large enclosed garden and burial ground. Chicacole enjoys a very salubrious climate. During the months of March, April and May the thermometer stands high, and generally ranges from 96° to 98° Fahr. owing to the strong south south-west winds which prevail at this season. Occasionally the thermometer will rise in May for a few hours as high as 102° or 104°, but these spells of great heat are almost always succeeded by a heavy thunder-storm, or a sea-breeze. On the whole, the heat is not very oppressive. From June till the end of October, the period of the south-west monsoon, more or less rain falls at intervals, and the prevailing wind is to the west, or a point or two to the northward of it. In November the wind changes to the north-east, when the cold season commences, lasting till about the end of February. At this season of the year heavy fogs with dew prevail in the morning and evening, and in the end of December and beginning of January the thermometer generally ranges from 54° to 58° or 60° in the mornings, sometimes falling as low as 52° Fahr.

The town lies on the north bank of the river Langulya, which was spanned by a fine bridge of 24 arches of 36 feet span each, till on the 9th October 1876 six arches of the bridge were washed away by a flood which also caused much damage to the town. As it only lies 48 feet above sea-level, it is exposed to considerable danger from floods. Chicacole was formerly celebrated on account of the very fine muslins made here, but the industry, like all other purely native industries, seems to have declined, as soon as it came in competition with machine-made goods. The quality of the muslins made is excellent. The great northern trunk road passes through the town, which is 567 miles distant from Madras. Chicacole was formerly a military cantonment, and is still an important recruiting station. It was also the head-quarters of the district Court until its transfer to Berhampore in 1864.

The public buildings consist of a public Cutcherry and other Offices, a Church, a Telegraph Office, a Lock-up, and a Post Office, besides minor buildings.

The Educational establishments consist of a Zillah school supported by Government, the Municipal and other private schools. The Civil Hospital and Dispensary is a useful institution, and is supported partly by Government and partly by the Municipality. Chicacole lies about 4 miles distant from Máfuzbandar, a former sea-port situate at the mouth of the river Langulya. The bazaars are well supplied, and turkeys and game-cocks abound, the latter being much affected by the Mussulman part of the population.

Mulagavalasa—In the Chicacole taluq, has a curious enclosure called the *Danta Vaktruni Kota*. It is said to be the old fort of Danta Vaktra, a giant who was killed by Krishna. Gold and silver coins are found there, and it would seem to be considerably like the Jougodo near Purushottapur.

Purushottapur—On the bank of the Rushikulya, residence of the Sub-Magistrate. The town is being gradually driven from the bank by the river encroachment; during the last 20 years, 4 streets have disappeared. This place is chiefly famous for the Jougodo or Lac Fort as it is called, which is in its vicinity, and towards the centre of which among some fine rocks is one huge granite mass which has an inscription of the Asoka edicts similar to those found elsewhere in India,—at Dhauli Girnar and Allahabad, &c. This particular inscription is addressed to the inhabitants of the Khephalinga hills, and two separate edicts which are found here and at Dhauli only are in this case addressed to the Ruler of Samapa. The inscription is fast disappearing in consequence of the scaling of the rock, and if Col. Cunningham is correct in giving the date of it at 250 B.C., there is little cause to wonder, but rather that it should have so long borne the sun and rain of the tropics, and yet retain any trace of the letters. Photographs and copies were taken of the inscription in 1871 and prior to that in 1858, and Mr. Minchin who took the photographs on both occasions has noted how the inscription has in the last few years become less and less distinct; now hardly one-half of the old inscription is left. The face of the rock was smoothed in some way to prepare it for the inscription which is graven into it, and the smoothed white surface is plainly visible some way off in contrast with the dark grey of the untouched granite rock. There are 3 smoothed places on the rock, each close to the other, about 20 feet by 16, and the letters are about 2 inches in length. There were four separate inscriptions, 3 in a row, and the last or fourth underneath the third one. This contains the two separate edicts addressed to the Ruler of Samapa.

The following extracts from Major-General Cunningham's C.S.I. *Corpus Inscriptionum Indicarum* are interesting, his preface recites that in his publication the Jougodo inscription appears for the first time.

" Asoka, the generally acknowledged author of these inscriptions, was the third Prince of the Maurya dynasty, and the grandson of Chandra Gupta who was happily identified by Sir William Jones with Sandrakoptos, the contemporary of Seleukos Nikator. Chandra Gupta reigned twenty-four years from B. C. 316 to 292. His son, Bindusâra, reigned twenty-eight years down to B. C. 264, when he was succeeded by

Asoka who reigned forty-one years and died in B. C. 223. I understand that Wilson to the last doubted the identity of Asoka Maurya with the Priyadarsi of these rock and pillar edicts. But as he firmly believed in the identity of Chandra Gupta and Sandrakoptos, his doubts as to the identity of Asoka and Priyadarsi were a manifest inconsistency. For as both Brahminical and Buddhist accounts agree in stating that Asoka Maurya, the grandson of Chandra Gupta Maurya, was king of Magadha for forty-one years as noted above, it is certain that he was a contemporary of all the five Greek Princes mentioned in the edicts of Priyadarsi. And as Priyadarsi also ruled over Magadha, we thus have two different kings of Magadha at the same time. The simple solution of this difficulty is the fact, mentioned in the Singhalese Dipawanso, that Asoka was also called Priyadarsi. The same fact is also stated in the Burmese life of Buddha, where Mahakasyapa is made to prophesy that 'in after times a young man named Piadatha (Piyadasi) shall ascend the throne and become a great and renowned monarch under the name of Asoka.' A strong argument in favor of the identity of Priyadarsi Devanampriya with Asoka, is the subsequent use of one of the titles by his grandson, Devanampriya Dasaratha, in the Nagarjuni cave inscriptions.

" As both the 10th and 12th years of Priyadarsi are mentioned in the rock edicts, the dates of their promulgation will be B. C. 251 and 249. Now as Alexander II of Epirus died in B. C. 254, the mention of his name in the edicts of Priyadarsi, which were promulgated just at that time, is the most satisfactory proof of the accuracy of the date which has been assigned to Asoka and most conclusively confirms Sir W. Jones's identification of Sandrakoptos with Chendra Gupta.

" That the Antiochus mentioned by Priyadarsi is not Antiochus the Great, as suggested by Wilson, is most fully proved by the omission of the name of Euthydemus of Bactria, the nearest Greek Prince on the frontier of India. It is equally disproved by the reference to the Governors (Samanta and

Samino) of Antiochus which shows that the revolt of the Eastern princes under Diodotus, Pantaleon and Antimachus had not then taken place. These edicts were therefore drawn up during the lifetime of Antiochus Theos, or certainly before B. C. 246.

" The following is James Prinsep's summary of the ' contents of the edicts' :—

' The first edict prohibits the sacrifice of animals both for food and in religious assemblies, and enjoins more attention to the practice of this first of Buddhistic virtues than seems to have been paid to it even by the Raja himself at least prior to the sixteenth year of his reign.

' The second edict provides a system of medical aid for men and animals throughout Piyadasi's dominions and orders trees to be planted and wells to be dug along the sides of the principal public roads.

' The third edict enjoins a quinquennial humiliation, or if we read the word, by the alteration of y to s, as anusasânam, the republication every five years of the great moral maxim inculcated in the Buddhist creed, viz., Honour to father, charity to kindred and neighbour and to the priesthood (whether Brahmanical or Buddhistical) ; humanity to animals ; to keep the body in temperance, and the tongue "from evil speaking" ! And these precepts are to be preached to the flock by their pastors with arguments and examples. This edict is dated after the twelfth year of Piyadasi's inauguration.

' The fourth edict draws a comparison between the former state of things, perhaps lawless and uncivilised, and the state of regeneration of the country under the ordinances of the beloved king. The publication of the glad tidings seems to have been made with unexampled pomp and circumstance and posterity is invoked to uphold the system. This edict is also dated in the twelfth year of Piyadasi.

' The fifth edict after an exordium not very intelligible, proceeds to record the appointments of ministers of religion, or more strictly Missionaries; and enumerates many of the countries to which they are to be deputed for the conversion of the young and the old, the rich and the poor, the native and the foreigner. Many highly curious points, especially as to geography, call for notice in this edict, wherein for the first time the name of the celebrated city of Pataliputra is made known to us in the ancient character.

'The sixth edict appoints in like manner pativedakas, informers, or perhaps more properly, custodesmorum, who are to take cognizance of the conduct of the people in their meals, their domestic life, their families, their conversation, their general deportment, and their decease. It also nominates Magistrates or officers for punishment, if the word antiyayika (S. antyayaka) may be so understood, so that in this edict we have a glimpse of the excellent system of moral administration for which the Greek and Persian historians give credit to our monarch, and we find it actually not very different from that followed twenty centuries later by ourselves, for we too have our Judges and our Magistrates, and further our missionaries are spread abroad among the people to drown them with the overflowing truths of our dharma, to release them from the fetters of sin and bring them into the salvation which 'passeth understanding!'

'The seventh edict expresses, not an order, but an earnest desire on the part of the king that all the diversities of religious opinion may be obliterated; that every distinction in rank and in tastes may be harmonised into one system of bhavasudhi, that peace of mind, or repose of conscience, which proceeds from knowledge, from faith and entire assent.

'The eighth edict contrasts the mere carnal amusements patronised by former Rajas with the more harmless and pious enjoyment prescribed by himself. The dhammayata or in Sanscrit dharmayatra, the festival of religion, is thus set in opposition to the Viharayatra, the festival of amusement, and it is stated to consist in the visits to holy people, in alms-giving in respect to elders, and similar praiseworthy sources of rational gratification. This edict is dated in (or rather after) the tenth year of Piyadasi's reign.

'The ninth edict continues the thread of the same discourse, by expatiating on the sources of true happiness, not such as the worlding seeks in marriage, in rearing children, in foreign travel and such things, but the dharma mangalam, the happiness of virtue, which displays itself in benevolence to dependants, reverence to one's pastors, in peace with all men, abundant charity, and so forth, through which alone can the blessings of Heaven be propitiated.

'The tenth paragraph comments upon yaso vá kìti và, the glory of renown, which attend merely the vain and transitory deeds of this world. The Raja is actuated by higher motives and he looks beyond for the reward for which he strives with heroism (parakramena) the most jealous, yet respectful.'

In his Chapter III, Major-General Cunningham describes the language as Indo Páli.

What the enclosure was it is not possible to say. It seems too large for a "fort;" it is a long square, the opposite faces being 858 yards by 814 yards respectively. The bank, an earthen one, even now in places is 18 feet high and 148½ feet across at the base, and it has two entrances on each side. Inside are found old tiles and debris of houses and coins after rain and in ploughing; but for the most part the coins are copper ones. I could hear of no gold coins being found recently, but the people say they used to find them. I am inclined to think it was an old walled town. Its name of "Lac" is from a tradition that it was made of "Lac," and was therefore impregnable, for no enemy could scale the walls they were too smooth and slippery, but its impregnability was destroyed by a spy who let the adversary into the secret that fire would melt the stuff.

There are also at Kesarapilli near the Malati Hill in Goomsur Taluk the remains of an old town and fort with a famous old well, and tradition has it that the king of this fort was he who

Note.—The eleventh, twelfth and fourteenth edicts are not at Jougodo.

destroyed the Jougodo. At the foot of the hill not long ago a herd boy tending cattle struck his foot against a plate of metal set on edge and the villagers' curiosity being aroused, they dug and found there an old temple in which there was a stone image of the size of a man. It was carried to Buguda where it was consecrated in a temple. The image is called "Virinchi Narayanaswami" or Suryanarayanamurti, the sun. The top of the temple is covered with copper sheathing.

Besides the places already mentioned there are none of archæological interest: there are no caves or Buddhist remains, no Cromlechs or old stone monuments.

Srikurmam—Is the only place of pilgrimage for Telugus in the district. The temple is sacred to Vishnu and is said to be a fine one decorated with the usual carving from which obscenity is not absent. There is also a temple of some fame at Vishnuchakram.

Tarini Amma Konda—Near Purushottapur, is a famous place of pilgrimage for Uriyas and there is a considerable yearly slaughter of sheep and kids in honor of the goddess.

At Kalláda, Buguda, and Arasavilly there are temples of some fame frequented by the worshippers of Jaggernath. And at Mukhalingam Siva is worshipped and the temple is a place of pilgrimage.

There is a hot sulphur spring called the Tapta Pani on the Ghaut road running up from Pudamari to the Pedda-Kimedi Máliahs, the water comes bubbling up in two places and is in temperature from 90° to 100° Fahrenheit. It is not frequented for medicinal purposes by the people; but one would think that it might be of use in that unpleasant disease which is believed to be common to the natives and the Scotch.

CHAPTER IV.

THE MALIAHS.

DESCRIPTION OF THE MALIAHS—THE THREE PLATEAUX—CHIEF PEAKS—FORESTS—PASSES—GHATS—ROADS—REST HOUSES—KHONDS—THEIR LANGUAGES—HEADMEN—MODE OF LIVING—WEAPONS—DRESS—MARRIAGE—BIRTH—DEATH—FOOD—FIGHTING—METAL VESSELS—CHASTITY OF THE WOMEN—PANOS—MERIAH SACRIFICE—THE REASON FOR IT—THEIR EARTH GODDESS—PRIESTS—THE TRACTS WHERE IT WAS PERFORMED—BUFFALO SACRIFICE—SUPERSTITION OF THE KHONDS—CULTIVATION—SAVARAS—BIRTH—DEATH—WEAPONS—DRESS—CULTIVATION—THEIR GODS—FIGHTING—EMPLOYMENT OF KHONDS AND SAVARAS IN GOVERNMENT SERVICE—ITINERATION OF DISTRICT OFFICERS—SUB-MAGISTRATES AND THE POLICE—TWO KINDS OF WILD DOGS—TREES.

The Máliahs or high lands are the irregular chain of the Eastern Ghats that lie to the north and west of the district.

There are three plateaux; one from the Boad frontier to a line drawn from Udiagiri in the Goomsur Máliahs and Sarangodo of Chinna-Kimedi; this is flat and uninteresting and differs but little in appearance and produce from the plains near the foot of the hills. The second is considerably higher with fine hills and valleys intersecting it in every direction and extends from this line to a line drawn from Nuagada in the Parla-Kimedi Máliahs to Mahendragiri. The third from this to the Vizagapatam frontier is again lower than the central one and less picturesque. The mean elevation of the central plateau is 2,000 feet, that of the other two is considerably less. Balliguda is 2,200 feet, Shubaranagiri 2,445 feet and Dusragam a little more above sea-level.

The chief peaks are Dodosoro, near Raikia 3,800 feet (in the Goomsur Máliahs), Singaraj 4,976 feet, and Mahendragiri 4,928 feet (in the Surangi Máliahs), and Deodangar or Ojjaigodo in Parla-Kimedi, which is 3,941 feet above sea-level.

The scenery of the central plateau is very beautiful and there are still in places remains of the old forest standing, but the continual clearing of the hill sides for the purposes of cultivation prevents the trees attaining any size except in places where cultivation is not possible. The forest is chiefly Sal, a very useful timber for building if well seasoned, but the only trees the hill people spare are fruit trees and trees from which they can procure liquor.

The best forests are on the slopes leading up into the hill country.

The chief passes into the Máliahs are to begin with the easiest, that from Russellkonda by Durgaprasad known as the Kalingia Ghat, there is a bandy road quite practicable for carts and continually used by them. At the top of the Ghat there is a road on to the Boad frontier which will be bridged throughout very soon. Working southward, the next Ghat is Pippalapanka by Gajellabadi to Daringabadi, a long and stony one: after that the Katingia Ghat from Surada viâ Mirkot to Katingia; the next the Hotspring or Taptapani Ghat from Digupudi to Lohagudi. South again comes the Puipani Ghat from Seringi viâ Nuagada to Cheligodo, and last the Munsingi Ghat in Parla-Kimedi from Kimedi to Gumma. These are all passable by loaded elephants and horses and men. There are other ways up and down used by the hill people, but they are better unattempted save by a good walker and climber.

From Kalingia, the top of the first Ghat named, besides the Boad road there is a road which will be completely bridged by next year to Balliguda, the head-quarters, and an alternative road to the same place viâ Sarangodo and Kurteli.

From Balliguda there are roads to Baracoma and Tumeribund; and that one which traverses the length of the Máliah country from Balliguda towards Gumma, known as the Grand

Military Road. Except those named as such none of them are bandy roads, and the Grand Military Trunk Road itself is but a track smooth and clear of jungle with a good ditch on either side, slopes into and out of difficult water-courses and rivers, and where possible wooden bridges.

There are mud bungalows at most of the usual halting places for the convenience of officers travelling, for the sparseness of the population, and the wildness of the people and their independence make it very difficult to get coolies in the cultivating season.

The hills are inhabited by Khonds, Gonds, Uriyas and Panos or Hill weavers from the Boad Frontier to Cheligodo in the Pedda-Kimedi Máliahs, and on the western sides bordering on Kalahandi, Jeypore and Vizagapatam are the Kutiya Khonds, the most warlike and troublesome of the hill people; between Cheligodo and Udiagiri we find Savaras mixed up with the Khonds and Gonds, while south of this, in the Parla-Kimedi Máliahs, there are only Savaras, Uriyas, and weavers who here take the name of Paidis.

It is not easy to trace the name "Khond." In Telugu they are "Kodu Vandlu," in Uriya "Kondho loko," and they call themselves "Kui" plural "Kuinga." I think that the English word is a feeble attempt at the Uriya. Lieut. Macpherson, who was Meriah Agent in 1846, thinks it may be from the Telugu, "Konda," a hill, or that "Kulinga" may have been the corruption of "Kuinga," and thence "Pulinda," a barbarian in Sanskrit and Tamil.* I do not know how or when the name first arose, but in 1767 the Collector of this district, then Mr. Cotsford, making a report on his district, speaks of the people called "Kodulu or Kodulu Vandlu," being well known to indulge in the performance of human sacrifice; but he does not call them Khonds.

Both the Khond and Savara languages are unwritten and have no character. Captain Frye, who was a very good linguist,

* Vizagapatam Manual, page 90.

took a great interest in the Khonds and wrote a grammar, and dialogues adopting for them the Uriya character, but this seems to have been a mistake. The language is Turanian or Nomadic,* and the Telugu character would have been more suitable.

There are many dialects in the language of the Khonds, and the Goomsur, Kuttiya, Chinna and Pedda-Kimedi people do not succeed in making themselves understood easily by one another. Bodogoda Khond is quite unintelligible to the other Khonds. The Goomsur Khonds, especially of Chokapad and about Udiagiri, speak Uriya generally, but pretend they do not.

The Khonds manage their affairs by means of headmen, variously called "Moliko," "Maji," and "Podoro." Each village has one, and he has under him a Pano to run messages, &c. Each mutáh has in the same way a headman, similarly called with the prefix of mutáh and Pát Maji in the Kuttiya country. These head people are of the tribe of the villagers—Khonds, Gonds or in the case of Uriya villages Uriyas. Each collection of mutáhs has for its Chief a Patro, in every case an Uriya.† This Patro the Khond people, unless he gives them offence, deem it their duty to, and do generally, submit to and obey. They are great sticklers for the right of descent in the case of their Patros, and are not easily satisfied if an heir is set aside without reason.

The Khonds will not generally live in the same village with Uriyas; and though they will allow Panos to live in the same village they make them occupy a separate street. A Khond village is generally only a few huts, built low on the ground by means of hewn slabs laid one after another. The roofs are always thatched. There is a pial in front and an enclosure for cattle behind.

The people are very shy and will generally run away if the village is invaded by a European stranger. If met on a jungle path they dive into its recesses, and it is very rare to see any

---

* The Vizagapatam Manual, page 85.

† Differently called in different mutáhs Bissoyi and Behra Dolloi.

women or girls about. They are improving and becoming less shy by degrees except the Kuttiyas who build their villages on the tops of the hills, and so are not in the way of being often visited.

The Uriya Patros have Uriya Paiks or armed peons living in the chief village or fort, and holding their lands on condition of service. They used to be of assistance if the Khonds were called out in defence of their Zemindar. Now they assist in putting down the Khonds if necessary.

In the Kuttiya country the Patros are chiefly Gonds, but the Goomsur men are proud of their descent from the Nalla Bongso caste or family.

The men all go about armed with a *Tangi*, a sort of battle-axe, the handle of which is covered in many parts with brass wire for protection and ornament. They use also bows and arrows when hunting or fighting, and are averse to the use of guns and gunpowder, saying the bow and arrows are the proper weapons of a Khond.

Major Macpherson gives the following description of them: "The Khonds are fitted by physical constitution to undergo "the severest exertions, and to endure every form of priva- "tion. Their height is about the average standard of Hindus "of the Peninsula. Their forms are characterized by strength "and symmetry. The muscles of the limbs and body are "clean and boldly developed. The skin is clean and glossy, "its colour ranging from a light bamboo to a deep copper "shade, the heel is in a line with the back of the leg, the foot "is somewhat larger than that of the Hindu, and the instep "not highly arched, although the Khond nevertheless has ex- "traordinary speed of foot. The forehead is full and expand- "ed. The cheek bones are high and rather prominent. The "nose is seldom though occasionally arched, and is generally "broad at the point. The lips are full, but not thick; the "mouth is rather large. The whole physiognomy is generally

" indicative of intelligence and determination, blended with " good humour."*

As regards the character of the Khonds they possess a great love of liberty They are faithful to their friends, brave, hospitable and laborious, and unlike the Hindus in the plains, they are too simple-minded to tell a lie, and prefer the truth. Death is preferred by them to transportation for life. Their worst vice is drunkenness which is almost universal amongst them. Occasionally they show their love for revenge, and even for brutal passion. Their favourite amusement is hunting which they pursue with an indefatigable ardour rarely abandoning the pursuit of a wounded animal, until they have run him down.

The toilet of the Khond is simple. It usually consists of a piece of coarse cloth worn round the loins, the ends of the cloth being red and hanging down like tails both in front and behind. The head-dress is more elaborate. The hair is worn very long, and drawn out in the fashion of a horn, inside which the Khond usually places his comb, pipe, and other little domestic requisites. Often the hair is bound with a piece of red cloth, and decorated with the bright feathers of the peacock or other bird. In the southern part they decorate the head with a white or colored fillet.

The women are seldom good-looking and are short in stature. Their dress consists of a skirt reaching a little below the knees. Nothing is worn over the bosom except ornaments. Like the men, the women invariably wear a small comb in the hair, and the younger females sometimes have five or six of them. Their ears are pierced at the edges in ten or twelve different places. The unmarried women wear pieces of broom in the ear-holes, whilst the married ones are distinguished by the small brass rings inserted in them. Sometimes instead of rings, they wear an ornament either of gold or brass made like a button. Covering the bosom the unmarried women wear a curious

* Lieut. Macpherson's Report upon the Khonds of the Districts of Ganjam and Cuttack—Madras, reprinted 1863.

ornament made by stringing together small pieces of a kind of grass, whilst strings of colored glass beads, made up like necklaces, reach almost down to the waist of the married ones. Nose-rings made of gold, silver or brass, with heavy brass bangles on the wrists, and hollow brass anklets are also worn. They tattoo the face and body.

The Khonds have no caste prejudices. Their ordinary food consists of rice, or dholl or other dry grain boiled into a kind of porridge. Wild game is eaten freely when procurable, but domestic animals are reserved for special occasions. Tobacco is regarded by them as one of the most necessary articles of existence, and they are universal smokers. Curiously enough they do not drink milk, although they possess numerous herds of both buffaloes and goats. Virtue and morality are at a very low ebb amongst them. Nearly all offences can be condoned by the payment of a penalty or "Poronja," and in cases of adultery the injured husband can, if he pleases, claim satisfaction of the adulterer. If he does so the woman remains with him as his wife.

Amongst the Khonds the parents arrange the marriages of their children. The bride is looked upon as a commercial speculation, and is bought and paid for in "gontis." A "gonti" is one of anything, such as a buffalo, a pig, or a brass pot, as for instance, a hundred "gontis" might consist of ten bullocks, ten buffaloes, ten sacks of corn, ten sets of brass, twenty sheep, ten pigs and thirty fowls. The usual price however paid by the bridegroom's father for the bride is twenty or thirty "gontis." A Khond finds his wife from among the women of any other mutáh than his own. On the day fixed for the bride being taken home to her husband's house, the pieces of broom in her ears are removed and are replaced by brass rings. The bride is covered over with a red blanket, and is carried astride on her uncle's back, towards the husband's village, accompanied by the young women of her own village. Music is played in front of the party, whilst in the rear are carried brass play-things such as horses, &c., for the bridegroom, and cloths and brass pins as presents for the bridegroom from the bride's father. On the road at the village boundary the procession is met by the bridegroom, and the young men of his village with their heads and bodies wrapped up in blankets and cloths. Each is armed with a bundle of long thin bamboo sticks. The young women of the bride's village at once attack the bridegroom's party with sticks, stones, and clods of earth, which the young men ward off with the bamboo bundles. A running fight is in this manner kept up until the village is reached when the stone-throwing invariably ceases and the bridegroom's uncle snatching up the bride carries her off to her husband's house. This fighting is by no means child's play and the men are sometimes seriously injured. The whole party is then entertained by the bridegroom as lavishly as his means will permit. On the day after the bride's arrival a buffalo and a pig are slaughtered and eaten, and upon the bride's attendants returning home on the evening of the second day, a male and female buffalo by the well-to-do or any less valuable present is presented to them to take away. On the third day all the Khonds of the village have a grand dance or corrobbery, and on the fourth day there is another grand assembly at the house of the bridegroom. The bride and bridegroom are then made to sit down on a cot, and the bridegroom's brother pointing upwards to the roof of the house, says "As long as this girl "stays with us, may her children be as men and tigers, but if "she goes astray, may her children be as snakes and monkeys, "and die and be destroyed!"

Marriages amongst the Khonds are usually celebrated during the hunting season, which opens about April, when they burn the grass and underwood of the jungle, and drive the wild beasts from their lairs to seek a refuge in the unburnt forest. This season is always one of drunkenness and revelry. The Khonds are very fond of dancing, and in every village there is a house called a "Dhangada" which is set apart for that purpose, and where the young men and maidens meet.

On the approaching birth of a child the men are all turned out of the house. The mother receives no assistance from the surrounding women, but herself divides the navel cord and bathes the child. Oil, usually castor-oil, is then smeared all over the infant's body, and it is then held before a hot fire and half roasted. When the string that has been tied round the umbilical cord falls off, the infant's head is shaved, and a month afterwards it is taken to its uncle's house, where a fowl is presented to the parents which they take home and eat. The mother is unclean for five days and no man may eat in the house till after that and until all old pots have been replaced by new ones.

Immediately after death, a cloth is wrapped round the corpse, but no cloths or valuables are removed. A portion of paddy and all the cooking utensils of the deceased are given to the village Sittra, and the body is then burnt. On the following day a little rice is cooked, put on a dish, and laid down on the spot where the corpse was burnt. An incantation is then pronounced, requesting the spirit of the deceased person to eat the rice and enjoy itself, and not to change itself into a devil or a tiger and come bothering the survivors in the village. Three days after death, the "Madda" or ceremony is performed. An effigy of the deceased is prepared of straw which is stuck up in front or on the roof of the house and the relations and friends assemble, lament and eat at the expense of the people of the deceased's house. Each person brings a present of some kind or other and on his departure the next day receives something else of slightly greater value.

If a man dies without male heirs his widow cannot inherit his lands or agricultural stock; both go to the Patro, a kind of escheat.

The death of a man in a village requires a purification which is made by the sacrifice of a buffalo on the 7th day after his death. If a man is killed by a tiger the purification is made by the sacrifice of a pig, the head of which, cut off with a *Tangi* by a Pano, is passed between the legs of the men in the village who stand in a line astraddle. It is a bad omen to him if the head touches any man's legs. If the Patro attends a funeral he gets the fee of a goat for firing his gun to drive away the dead man's ghost.

When a woman dies her pots and ornaments are thrown away.

The men are great drinkers (not the women) and they have ample means of indulging, for the "Solapa" or Sago palm which gives toddy or fermented juice for six months up to the rains, is very plentiful as also the Mohwa or Ippa tree from the flowers of which a strong spirit is distilled.

The food of a Khond is very varied; their usual meals are whatever grain they may happen to have made into a porridge (except rice which they boil as in the plains) with lumps of such flesh as may be at hand boiled and floating about in it. They eat the mango and use the pounded kernel as a sort of flour, numberless jungle roots, sweet potatoes and yams, and last not least the Mohwa flowers. Those they do not convert into spirit they store and eat dry (they are said to taste like raisins), while the stones are crushed by the Panos for the purpose of extracting oil.

The Khonds being very excitable and jealous of any encroachment on their village properties, used to be continually at war with one another, and even now their warlike propensities want watching.

Lieutenant Macpherson's account of a hill fight as detailed by an eye-witness is as follows :—

"At about 12 o'clock in the day, the people of Bora Des began to advance in a mass across the Salki river, the boundary between the districts, into the plain of Kurmingia, where a much smaller force was arrayed to oppose them. The combatants were protected from the neck to the loins by skins, and cloth was wound round their legs down to the heel, but the arms quite bare. Round the heads of many too cloth was wound, and, for distinction, the people of Bora Mootah wore peacock's feathers in their hair, while those of Bora Des had cock's tail plumes. They advanced with horns blowing and gongs beating when they passed a village. The women followed behind carrying pots of water and food for refreshments, and the old men who were past bearing arms were there giving advice and encouragement. As the adverse parties approached, showers of stones handed by the women, flew from slings from either side and when they came within range, arrows came in flights, and many fell back wounded. At length single combats sprang up betwixt individuals who advanced before the rest, and when the first man fell, all rushed to dip their axes in his blood, and hacked the body to pieces. The first man who himself unwounded slew his opponent, struck off his right arm and rushed with it to the priest in the rear, who bore it off as an offering to Loha Pennoo* in his grove. The right arms of the rest who fell were cut off in like manner and heaped in the rear, beside the women, and to them the wounded were carried for care and the fatigued men constantly retired for water. The conflict was at length general. All were engaged hand to hand and now fought fiercely, now paused by common consent for a moment's breathing. In the end the men of Bora Des although superior in numbers began to give way and before four o'clock they were driven across the Salki, leaving sixty men dead on the field, while the killed on the side of Bora Mootah did not exceed thirty. And from the entire ignorance of the Khonds of the simplest healing processes at least an equal number of the wounded died after the battle. The right hands of the slain were hung up by both parties on the trees of the villages and the dead were carried off to be burned.

"The people of Bora Des the next morning flung a piece of bloody cloth on the field of battle, a challenge to renew the conflict, which was quickly accepted, and so the contest was kept up for three days.

* The War God.

"The arms of the Khonds are a light, long-handed sword,* with a blade very curiously curved, the bow and arrow, and the sling—no shields are used. The axe is used with both hands, to strike, and guard, its handle being for the latter purpose partly defended by brass plates and wire.

"The Khond is peculiarly dexterous in a species of ricochet shot with the bow which it is difficult for a man to avoid: bending down, he makes his shaft fly, it is said, so as to strike the ground with its heel, at a short distance from its object, which it strikes in rising below the line of vision."

The Sittras are the metal-workers of the Khonds. They make their battle-axes, brass ornaments, &c. The brass they use comes from the low country, but the iron they make themselves, finding the iron stone chiefly in Boad and smelting and working it themselves.

Every Khond who has a position to keep up is the owner of one or more enormous brass vessels from two to three feet high, shaped like a chatty, which on grand occasions of feasts, &c., are filled with drink for the guests to help themselves.

Chastity is not known, or at least practised, by the Kutiya girls. They go naked till marriage and the unmarried men and girls sleep together in a house set aside for the purpose in some villages; in others, by invitation of the girl, any man she may fancy visits her at her parent's house. When a man proposes marriage to a girl he offers to buy her a cloth and after that she is expected to remain virtuous.

Infanticide of all females used to be practised by some Khonds, especially those of Daringabadi.

The Panos or Dombos are a degraded race, the Pariahs of the Máliahs, and the biggest thieves in the hill country. It is said that some tribes of them are of as ancient origin as the Khonds and that they are a separate race, but it is generally thought that they are the descendants of persons sprung from

* Not now used by the Khonds, and believed to be a misprint for the word "axe."

the admixture of the Khonds with persons from the low country. The Panos manage most of the commerce of the hills and act as interpreters between the Khonds and their neighbours. Their regular occupation is supposed to be the weaving of cloths which they barter with the Khonds for grain and other commodities. The Panos look up to the Khonds as their natural protectors and seek to identify themselves with them in every particular. As a rule they have no voice in the public councils unless they have acquired lands by purchase. As the full rights of citizenship in a tribe however are attached to property, the Khonds are, as a rule, opposed to the practice of selling their lands. When the meriah sacrifices were practised it was chiefly the Panos who supplied the Khonds with their victims. The Panos procured the meriahs for the sacrifices either by purchase, by barter, or by kidnapping them from the low country. On rarer occasions indeed the Panos did not even hesitate to sell their own children for the purpose.

As we know, the sacrifice of human beings was common to the ancient religion of India; in the present century the practice of "Satti" has counted its victims by thousands, and the principal article in the creed of the Thugs was the immolation or murder of human victims in honor of the goddess *Kali*. The Hebrew Scriptures frequently allude to the practice, which has not only existed amongst the most barbarous, but also amongst the most enlightened nations of antiquity.

The prevailing idea amongst the Khonds evidently was that the meriah sacrifice would avert the anger of the deity and was calculated to ensure for them good health and good crops, but more especially the latter. When however the Khonds found that the prevention of the meriah sacrifice did not interfere with the fertility of their fields, they willingly desisted from what was for them a very expensive ceremony.*

* Personal narrative of service amongst the wild tribes of Khondistan by Major-General Campbell.

In 1837 when Major Campbell first penetrated into the Khond country for the purpose of suppressing human sacrifice, five or six of the oldest and most influential Khond Chiefs made the following statement before him :—" We have always sacrificed " human beings. Our fathers handed down the custom to us. " They thought no wrong, nor did we. On the contrary we " felt we were doing what was right. We were then the " subjects of the Rája of Gumsur. Now we are the subjects " of the Great Government whose orders we must obey. If " the earth refuses its produce, or disease destroys us, it is " not our fault. We will abandon the sacrifice, and will, if " permitted like the inhabitants of the plains, sacrifice ani- " mals." With regard to the religious system of the Khonds, which has been so discursively written about by Major Macpherson, the following interesting account of their belief in connection with the meriah sacrifices appears to be more in harmony with facts, than the elaborate system, ascribed to them by that officer, whose sources of information are in this respect open to doubt.*

The Khonds believe that Tari Pennu, the Earth goddess, sends famines as a punishment for their sins in ceasing to worship her with human sacrifices. This monstrous belief will not surprise those who are acquainted with the reasons which were urged by them in its favour, and the objections they made to the abolition of the barbarous custom. To thoroughly understand this matter it will be necessary to notice, as briefly as possible, the religious doctrines of the Khonds. They believe in one Supreme Being, whom they sometimes call the God of Light, sometimes the Sun God. In the beginning he created for himself a consort, who became the source of all evil and the Earth goddess. Afterwards he created the earth; and walking upon it one day with Tari Pennu, he was so enraged with her, because she refused to scratch the back of his neck,

* The *Argosy*, November 1866.—" The name of the author of the article is, I regret to say, unknown to me.—T. J. M."

that he resolved to create out of the earth a new being, man, who should render to him the most devoted homage. He also resolved to create out of the earth all that was necessary for man's existence. Filled with jealousy, Tari Pennu attempted to prevent the fulfilment of these purposes, but only succeeded in altering the order of creation. Taking a handful of earth, Boora Pennu threw it behind him to create man, but it was caught by Tari, and cast on one side, whence arose trees, herbs, and all kinds of vegetable life. In like manner she intercepted, caught, and flung aside three other handsful of earth, which became respectively the fish of the sea, the beasts of the earth, and the birds of the air. Then, seeing what his rebellious consort had done, Boora Pennu put his hand on her head, to prevent any further interference with his will, placed a fifth handful of earth on the ground, and from it was the human race created The goddess then placed her hands over the earth, and said "let those beings you have made exist; you shall create no more;" whereupon the god caused an exudation of sweat to proceed from his body, collected it in his hand, and threw it around, saying—"to all that I have created:" whence originated love, and sex, and the continuance of species. At first the human race was sinless, went about unclothed, and enjoyed free communion with Boora. They lived without labour, and in perfect harmony. But all this was changed by Tari, who "sowed the seeds of sin into mankind as into a ploughed field." Then came the loss of innocence, which was followed by disease and death. The earth became a jungle, flowers became poisonous, and animals became savage. The god and goddess fiercely contended for superiority over the new creation; and the supposed result of this supposed conflict is the source of a division in the religious belief of the mountaineers. One sect—those who follow Boora Pennu—believe that he was victorious, in proof of which they allege the pains of child-birth which have been imposed upon the sex of Tari. The other sect—those who worship the goddess—believe that she was unconquered, and that although she is the source of all evils, she can confer every form of earthly benefit, indirectly, by not obstructing the good which flows from Boora, and directly, by her own act. They also believe that she appeared on the earth in a feminine form, called by them Umbally Bylee, and that while under this form she introduced order and the art of agriculture, as well as all other blessings, into the world. As Umbally Bylee, she was one day slicing vegetables, and accidentally cutting her finger, the blood drops fell on the soft barren mud, which instantly became dry and firm earth. "Behold the good change," exclaimed the goddess; "cut up my body to complete it." But regarding her as one of themselves, the people declined to do her bidding, and in order that it might be carried out they resolved instead to purchase victims from other peoples. This is the origin of what is variously termed the Meriah, Tokki, or Keddi sacrifice. At first its efficacy was confined to those who personally practised the rite, but afterwards Tari ordered that all mankind should be included in the benefits it was to confer. Hence the sect of Tari believe that the responsibility for the well-being of the whole world rests upon them. The practice of a rite so horrible on such purely benevolent principles is one of its most singular features. Thus it was no uncommon thing to hear the followers of Tari speak of the followers of Boora as poor uninstructed fools, who could not understand that, through the virtue of human sacrifices, all mankind, and they themselves, lived and prospered; while, on the other hand, the worshippers of the God of Light exclaimed "wretched men! they destroy life and devour human flesh without the apology of the tiger and the snake, and believe that they conciliate the gods." So contradictory is human nature, however, that those who uttered these lofty sentiments were themselves guilty of a crime no less atrocious than the one they so justly condemned—that of female infanticide.

The infanticidal tracts were confined to Pondrákholo, and other parts of the Surada Máliahs, where human sacrifices were unknown. And for this, they produced the authority of

Boora Pennu, who at the beginning of the world said to men, "Behold! from the making of one feminine being what have I and the whole world suffered. You are at liberty to bring up only as many women as you can manage." And yet these mountaineers have many noble virtues. They account as great sins the refusal of hospitality to a guest or his abandonment, the breaking of an oath, or promise, or pledge of friendship, or old law or custom, the denial of a gift, the contracting of debts, the payment of which was ruinous to a man's tribe, which is responsible for the engagements of all its members, skulking in time of war, and the betrayal of a public secret. Whoever was guilty of any of these sins, they believed would be born again, afflicted with disease, poverty and mental qualities which would render him infamous. The chief virtues were, of course, the opposites of the sins just enumerated, and in addition, the killing of a foe in public battle, death on the battle field, and (among the sacrificing tribes) being a victim to the Earth goddess. To be acceptable to Tari a victim had to be purchased, in which case the cost varied from fifteen to two hundred Rupees, or he must have been born a victim, that is to say, the child of a victim father, or he must have been dedicated to the Earth goddess while a child by his father or guardian. The victims, who were of both sexes, were lodged in the house of the village chief, in fetters, if grown up; at liberty, if children. They were looked upon as consecrated beings, and if at large, were eagerly welcomed at every door. They were in short, treated with a mixture of reverence and tenderness. But when the fancied necessity for a sacrifice arrived, that is, when any misfortune befell a family or a village in the shape of disease, loss of cattle, or want of rain, the Meriah was led out to die his horrible death. Ten or twelve days before the appointed time, the victim's hair, till then left unshorn, was cut off; and the people assembled to hear the Jáni, or priest address a preliminary prayer to Tari, in which he announced the intended celebration of the rite. Three days before the sacrifice all the people assembled together, and indulged in every form of wild riot and gross excess. The first day and night were passed in drunken feasting and frantic dancing. On the morning of the second day the victim, who had been kept fasting, was carefully washed, clothed with a new garment, and led forth from the village in solemn procession amid music and dancing. At a short distance from every village was the Meriah grove, composed of large forest trees casting a deep shade, and near to a rivulet called the Meriah stream. These groves were kept sacred from the axe, and were regarded by the Khonds as haunted ground. In the centre of the grove was fixed a post, at the foot of which, and bound to it, the victim was seated, and he was then anointed with oil, ghee, and turmeric. Finally, he was adorned with flowers, and in this posture was worshipped throughout the remainder of the day. At night the villagers resumed their licentious feasting, and on the morning of the third day the victim was given a little milk. The sacrificing priest then implored the goddess to shower down her blessings upon the people, by filling their homes with the voices of happy children, by increasing their cattle and poultry, and by adding to the fertility of their fields, so that by increase of wealth might come increase of worship. He next minutely recounted the origin of the rite, the principal features of which have already been described, and concluded by narrating the incidents which attended the first sacrifice of all :—" We obeyed the goddess, and assembled the people. Then the victim child wept, and reviled, and uttered curses. All the people rejoiced except those with whom the child had dwelt and the Jáni. They were overwhelmed with grief: their sorrows prevailed entirely over their expectations of benefit, and they did not give either their minds or their faith to the gods. 'The world,' said they, 'rejoices; we are filled with despair;' and they demanded of the deity, 'Why have you instituted this miserable heart-rending rite?' Then the Earth goddess came again and rested upon the Jáni, and said, 'Away with this grief! Your answer is this; when the victim shall weep, say to him—blame not us, blame your parents who sold you. What fault is ours? The Earth goddess demands a sacrifice; it is necessary to the world. The tiger begins to rage, the snake to poison; fevers, and every pain afflict the people—shall you alone be exempt from evil? When you shall have given repose to the world you shall become a god by the will of the gods.'" At this point in the proceedings it was usual for one of the villagers to personate the victim, and to endeavour to excite the compassion of the chief and the priest, when something to this effect was said:—"I knew nothing of your intention to kill me. I looked upon you all as my parents. When there was delicate food in the village, I was fed. When the child of any one suffered, he grieved; but if I suffered the whole village grieved. When did you conceive this fraud—this wickedness to destroy us You, O my father, and you, and you, O my fathers, do not destroy me. See! there are the palm trees I planted; there is the public building on which I laboured. Look behind you. The cows and the sheep which I tended look lovingly at me. All this time you gave me no hint of my intended fate. I toiled with you at every work with my whole mind. Had I known of this doom I had leapt from a precipice and died. Let the whole burden of my soul's grief, as I remember the past, lie upon you." This ceremony gone through, the victim was led from the sacred grove to the spot where the sacrifice was to take place. As it would have been contrary to the essential principle of the rite for him to have met his fate bound, or with any show of resistance, the bones of the arms and legs were sometimes broken, but more generally he was stupified with opium. This done, the Jáni wounded the Meriah with his axe, whereupon the crowd rushed at the victim, and stripped the flesh from his bones, leaving untouched the head and the intestines. These, and what remained of the unhappy victim, were carefully guarded till next day,

The Máliahs are but rarely visited with actual famine, although a scarcity of food may prevail.

when they were burnt, and the ashes scattered over the fields. Meantime, those who had secured a piece of flesh hastened home to bury it in their favourite fields. Such, then, was the mode in which the worship of the Earth goddess was conducted. But occasionally there was a deviation from this pattern. Thus, in one district, the victim was placed on a low stage, sloping on either side, like a roof, the limbs bound so as to confine, but not to prevent, his struggles, while hot brands were applied to his body, which caused him to roll upwards and downwards. As long as he was capable of moving or uttering cries was he thus tortured, under the belief that the fall of rain would be proportioned to the number of tears he shed. Next day he was cut to pieces. Every month in every year, till within a recent period, were these diabolical sacrifices carried on in the hill tracts of Orissa. Many British officers, but notably the late Major-General Campbell and Major Macpherson, were at various times engaged in the good work of suppressing them; and at last they succeeded in inducing the tribes to give up the practice, not because they were convinced of its wickedness, but because they saw that the British Government was very powerful. This led them to entertain a notion that the God of the English must be their own God of Light, who had not sanctioned the rite of human sacrifice; and hence they began to think that the battle waged between Boora Pennu and Tari Pennu had resulted in the total defeat of the latter. Favourable harvests helped to give strength to this half-formed conviction; but in relinquishing the practice they stipulated for permission, in the event of any misfortune befalling them, to denounce the Sirkar to the Earth goddess as its cause. In a word, they declined to take the responsibility of the change upon themselves.

Although by no means universal, there is no doubt that the sacrifice of human beings prevailed in the Khond Hill Tracts to an enormous extent previous to the establishment of the Meriah agency, and even subsequently. Lieutenant Hill, who was well acquainted with the Hill Tracts, estimated that at the

New Moon Feast on the 8th January 1841, as many as 240 Meriahs had been sacrificed. Between 1837 and 1854, Colonel Campbell was the means of rescuing 1,506 Meriah victims, of which 717 were males and 789 females. The practice of human sacrifices prevailed to the north of the Mahánadi, in Daspallá, Boad, and Sonpúr, and south of that river in the Goomsur and Chinna-Kimedi Máliahs and in Jeypore right away to Bastar, where the practice prevailed to an enormous extent. The victims were usually bought, and might be of any caste or sex or age, but grown males were the most esteemed as they were the most expensive. Children were purchased and reared for years with the family of the person who ultimately devoted them to sacrifice, when circumstances demanded a victim from him. The victims were usually treated with every kindness, and if too young to be conscious of their fate, they were under no constraint. Otherwise they were kept in fetters and guarded. Most of the victims rescued by the British authorities had been sold by their parents or nearest relatives, and the practice was apparently a common one. Persons of riper age were kidnapped, and there were* (chiefly Panos) individuals who followed a regular trade in human flesh, and supplied victims by forcibly seizing children. It was necessary that the victim should always be purchased, as the Khonds did not sacrifice criminals, or prisoners captured in war. The price of a Meriah victim was from 60 to 200 Rupees, and the payment was made in brass vessels, cattle or coin, or partly in each. The method of performing the "Meriah puja" differed however according to the tribe and place of performance.

Meriah is the name given to the human sacrifice by ourselves. The derivation of it is probably the Khond word which is "Mervi." This would soon be pronounced "merivi," and so "meriah." The Uriya Patros joined in the sacrifice with the Khonds and, in fact, it was their business to provide half the expense of a victim in the case of a public meriah, and in many

* Volume IV, "Madras Journal of Literature and Science," 1837. Report by Mr. Stevenson, Collector of Ganjam.

cases to kill the victim. The different ways of doing it seem to have been infinite, but it was more frequently a death of torture. In all the human sacrifice was accompanied by indulgence in the worst forms of sensual excess, and for a month prior to the day of sacrifice there was much feasting, intoxication and dancing round the victim, who was adorned with garlands, &c. On the day previous to the sacrifice he was intoxicated with "*solopo," toddy, and among some tribes made to sit at the bottom of a post on the top of which was an effigy of a peacock, and at the foot of which a brass effigy of the same bird was buried. The Khonds and others then danced round the post to the sound of music, and addressing the earth, exclaimed: "O God, we sacrifice to you, give us good crops and seasons and health." The victim was then addressed: "We have bought you with a price, not seized you, and we now sacrifice you according to custom. No sin rests on us." On the following day the victim was again intoxicated with toddy, and anointed with oil. Each individual present touched the anointed part, and wiped the oil on his own head. They then proceeded in procession around the village and its boundaries bearing the victim who was preceded by music and a long pole, at the top of which was attached tufts of peacock's feathers. On returning to the post, which was always placed near the village deity, (Jakari Pennu, represented by three stones they proceeded to dig a pit, and after having killed a hog in sacrifice the blood was allowed to flow into the pit. The victim who was usually in a state of senseless intoxication, was then seized by five or six persons, thrown into the pit, and his face kept pressed to the earth until suffocated in the bloody mire. All cries were in the meanwhile drowned by the noise of instruments. When the victim was supposed to be dead, the Jáni or priest cuts a bit of flesh from the body and buried it with ceremony near the brass effigy of the peacock and village idol, as an offering to the earth. The Khonds present then

* Sago Palm Juice fermented.

cut off pieces of flesh, and carried them to their own villages, burying the morsels with great solemnity in the boundaries of the villages or fields, or before the village idols. After the sacrifice of the human being, a calf was brought before the same post, and after its feet had been cut off, it was left there still living, until the following day, when the women dressed in male attire and armed as men, drank, danced and sang round the post. The calf was finally killed and eaten, and the Jáni dismissed with a present of rice, and a hog or calf.

*Captain MacViccar thus describes the mode of performing the sacrifice in Máji Desho, the country midway between Boad and Patna.

" On the day of sacrifice the Meriah is surrounded by the " Khonds, who beat him violently on the head with the heavy " metal bangles, which they purchase at the fair and wear on " these occasions. If this does not destroy life, an end is put " to his sufferings by strangulation by means of a slit bamboo. " Strips of flesh are then cut off the back, and each recipient " carries his portion to the stream, which waters his fields, and " there suspends it on a pole. The remains of the mangled " carcase are then buried, and funeral obsequies are performed, " and repeated a year afterwards. It was however more usual " for the fragments of flesh to be buried in the fields. When " a sacrifice took place, a deputation from all villages of Tari " Khonds within a certain radius attended it, and returned the " same day, or as rapidly as possible with the flesh, a little of " which was given to each head of a family. To secure its " arrival in time, it was sometimes sent by relays of men, and " conveyed with postal fleetness 50 or 60 miles."

The Kuttiyas had a curious arrangement of wood which they called the Hatti Mundo, elephant's head (from some slight resemblance), to which the victim was tied or before which he was sacrificed, and in the Pedda-Kimedi Máliahs they had a curious arrangement of upright poles, but generally

* Report dated 6th April 1851.

the sacrifice was performed in the sacred grove. And in some places, as it was thought necessary the victim should make no resistance, his legs and arms were broken before he was taken to the place.

In the Bálligudá taluk and down to Báminigám, the buffalo intended for sacrifice in place of the human being, is by pouring rice and water, declared sacred for a year previous, and is permitted to roam at will throughout the country, destroying the crops and eating the stored grain or anything else that it can get at. In the Kuttiyá country and south of Bámanigám, the buffalo is allowed none of these privileges, but has to work at the plough, like any other buffalo, until three days before the sacrifice. Before the eventful day arrives each night and generally throughout the day, the old men and women, the young men and girls all join together and dance and sing the praises of their god, hoping thus to propitiate the deity and obtain for themselves all the earthly blessings they have any idea of; sometimes a toy cock is made up and stuck on a pole, round which the people dance. On the day of the sacrifice the buffalo is paraded three times round the village, being severely beaten by every one whilst so led, after which it is taken to a place outside the village where a post has been firmly planted in the ground. A live cock is tied up, and *púja* having been made over some rice, it is placed in front of the bird. If the cock eats the rice there is a great rejoicing, for it is considered that the so doing is equivalent to the deity being actually present in the cock, and that it is the deity that eats the rice, and not the cock. The buffalo is then securely fastened to the post already alluded to, after which the chief Pújari (Jáni or priest) places his *tángi* or battle-axe seven times on the animal's neck, finally giving it one tremendous blow. This is the signal, upon which the Pújáris (worshippers) of every village engaged in the sacrifice, and who are all standing ready with knives in their hands rush in at the buffalo slicing off pieces of flesh from it, wherever they may get the chance.

Sometimes, but seldom, the heavy blow given by the chief Pújári kills the buffalo, but more frequently it lies groaning in a hideous manner for some five or six minutes. Each Pújari or worshipper takes the bit of flesh that he has managed to secure and some blood, and darts off to his village as fast as he can go. When he arrives there he at once buries it in the sacred grove and sprinkles the blood to the four quarters. The following day all return to the village where the sacrifice has taken place to eat the remainder of the flesh, and to get very drunk off toddy. The intention of the sacrifice is that all people may enjoy good health, that the hunting season may be a successful one, and that the crops may be good.

The village Pújáris have no precedence over other Khonds. They hold and cultivate land like the others, but at the place of sacrifice, the Pújári first eats the meat, and tastes the drink before the others commence.

Savaras.—The Savaras are divided into the following tribes:—

Sudda,	Lodoro,
Sannapania,	Jara, and
Méla,	Lombolanjia.

Of these the last are said to be the only remnant of the true aborigines. In dress, clothing and food, they resemble the Khonds; but the two races do not mix with one another, and the Khond looks down with more than a small amount of contempt on his Savara neighbour.

These people have a better idea of chastity than the Khonds, and it is said some of the women are old maids.

When a man has fixed upon a girl that he would marry, he plies her father with pots of liquor left in the house. If these pots of liquor are accepted and drunk it is a sign that the marriage is not distasteful to the girl's people, and the would-be bridegroom presents more liquor and two arrows to her father. If these are accepted there is nothing more to be done but to name a day when the girl is to be sent to the man's house which is done with tom-toming, drinking and feasting.

The system of Poronja, or compensation for damage done, exists among the Savaras also under the name of "Boroboria," and the penalty an adulterer may be called upon to pay is two he-buffaloes and a pig.

The birth of a child is not celebrated in any particular way but some impurity attaches to it and the family linen has to be washed and all the cooking pots broken and replaced by new ones.

The Savaras burn their dead and bury the ashes. A grand feast is given the day after the death, a month after the death, and on the anniversary. On the last occasion, they dance round the place where the body was burnt and set up a stone on end under some tree near the village in memory of the deceased.

Should a case of small-pox occur, the patient is left with food and drink in his house and the village is deserted by the villagers. If he recovers they return; if he dies, the corpse is thrown out into the jungle without burning or burial and the people will not return but build a new village elsewhere. While he is sick, none may visit the patient but those who have had small-pox.

The weapons of the Savaras are just like those of the Khonds, but their tangies or battle-axes have less ornamentation and are not so elaborate, and they do use a thing they call a sword.

They wear handsome neck-laces of brass beads, and the arrangement of their hair is sometimes very curious, the top-knot being drawn through a hollow bamboo from a half to one foot long and there tied in a knot and ornamented with bits of red cloth into which again are stuck peacock's feathers, a plume of white egret's feather or the like. One curious ornament is a piece of brass, half an inch wide and about a foot and half long, beaten out until it is quite thin and pliant.

This being polished up and shining and quivering with every movement of the man's head has a very curious effect.

The cultivation and the crops are much the same as those of the Khonds; but the paddy fields are for the most part built up and revetted with large masses of stones. The Savara villages are generally small like those of the Khonds. Their head-men are called Gomangos and these Gomangos are again under the Bissoiyis or Hill Chiefs whose duty it is to keep the country generally quiet.

They have the same propensities as the Khonds for hunting, but there is less game in their hills. When an animal is killed, one thigh is reserved for the Bissoi or the Patro as the case may be. A small piece out of the back is offered to the god of hunting and the rest is divided into shares among the hunters; of which shares the killer is entitled to two and the head.

Their gods, or rather goddesses are three in number: *Julva*, to whom they sacrifice goats; *Gangi*, who claims a pig, and *Jommo*, a fowl. At the time of worship they use the tom-tom and the worshipper dances before the goddess.

A sick person is supposed to be possessed by some goddess or other, and the priest is consulted (he bears the same name, *Jáni*, both here and in the Khond country) as to what goddess has possession of the unfortunate man; and when this is known, sacrifices are made to induce the goddess to abandon her victim.

The Savaras are not so pugnacious as the Khonds are. They get themselves up in a similar way with woollen clothes and leather protections; but the women, who may not be hurt by the combatants, mingle in the fight and endeavour to protect the men of their own side. One death was sufficient to put a stop to a battle and the disagreement was arranged by the women. In fact so much authority were the women supposed to have that in the Vizagapatam District it was, and perhaps is still, the custom to summon the women to Bhêt and inform them that they would be held responsible if they let their men quarrel or misbehave.

Bhêt is the name given to the meetings or assemblages to which the hill people are summoned by the Agent while making his annual progresses through the hills. They then make their offerings of a fowl, sheep, a few eggs or a basket of rice in token of their intention to behave themselves well in future.

On the whole, both the Khonds and Savaras are advancing in prosperity, and the country is being slowly but surely opened out. The hill schools are doing good work, although the attendance is as yet comparatively small. In some of the schools the sons or nephews of the headmen are employed as assistant teachers. Sufficient roads exist throughout the country, and the work performed by the Khonds is remarkable for its efficient and intelligent nature. The umbrella, as an emblem of civilization, has found its way into the country, and the Khond dressed in his national costume may be seen at fairs with an umbrella on one shoulder, and a battle-axe (*tángi*) on the other. The traffic of the country is much increased and the markets established in the Máliahs have attracted traders from all the neighbouring districts. They may be seen coming with silk and cotton from Sambulpore, others with brass bangles and chatties from Daspallá, besides the various dealers in the usual articles sold in low country bazaars. In 1878 for the first time bandy-loads of rice went across the Máliahs all the way from Sumbulpore in the Central Provinces to Russellkonda in Goomsur and returned, laden with salt, across the Máliah country of Ganjam and through Boad.

It must not however be supposed that the Khonds have entirely given up the desire to perform the meriah sacrifice or the belief in its efficacy. In the year 1880 an attempt was made and it was nearly successful to make a human sacrifice in the Kuttiya country of the neighbouring district of Vizagapatam.

They are very superstitious and believe in witches and devils who are supposed to roam about chiefly at night-time. They believe in a power possessed by certain of themselves of converting themselves into panthers or tigers and in that form compassing the death of their enemy (this is called becoming a "*Paltobhag*"), and a threat from one man to another that he will so convert himself has, in my own experience, caused a threatened man to murder the man who threatened him.

The cultivation of three kinds of paddy is practised by the Khonds, and the fields are prepared with great difficulty and great expenditure of manual labor. Being so hilly it is difficult to find any part of the country sufficiently level for a paddy-field and the sides of the hills where the water-courses come down have to be scooped out and levelled to make them. Their work however for this purpose is not so good as that of the Savaras. The dry crops are grown in the usual manner and are *dholl*, millet, *korralu*, *chamalu* and ragi. Besides these mustard, rape, and black and green gram are grown.

Turmeric is a special hill product. It is grown in the dry land and is some two years in the ground. It is necessary to cover the field over in the hot weather with a thick covering of leaves to prevent the plants being dried up and scorched by the sun.

Besides the ordinary cultivation of dry crops on level land both the Khonds and Savaras grow hill doll, and cholum, on the slopes of the hills which they clear for the purposes. This is a most wasteful method of cultivation, and is known in other parts of the country as *kumeri*. A piece of land cleared—the clearance is done with axe and fire—is kept under cultivation from two to three years. It is then abandoned and the forest trees grow over it again to be again felled after they are from eight to fifteen years old.

There are a few, both Savaras and Khonds, in the police force in the hills; but this is the only Government employment possible for them (save four Khonds as schoolmasters in the hills). As active and intelligent police officers they are perfectly useless, and they are no more to be trusted to abstain from bullying their own country people than are the ordinary low country constables; their enlistment is allowed because the number of applicants is few and they are very useful for communicating orders and the like to their fellow Khonds.*

In order that any ill-treatment of the hill people by their Chiefs, &c., may not pass undetected, the Government have ordered that the Agent shall make a tour through the hill tracts once in every year; that the Special Assistant Agent and the Assistant Superintendent of Police shall reside in the Máliahs for six or eight months in the year, and the Principal Assistant and the Senior Assistant shall make yearly visits to that portion of the hills which is under their jurisdiction. To enable these orders to be carried out (and it would be impossible without them) the Government have sanctioned a special equipage of elephants which are divided amongst the Agency officers.

The resident Sub-Magistrates have been stated in Chapter I to be three in number—one at Balliguda, one at Udayagiri (Goomsur), and one at Udigiri (Pedda-Kimedi Máliahs), who for distinction sake, is called the Ramagiri Sub-Magistrate. The police force is located as will be found in Appendix XXIII. The force may seem unnecessarily large, but the advantages of immediate action in a hill disturbance are supreme.

The natural history of the hills is included in the natural history of the whole district; but it is worth while to mention here the two kinds of wild dogs that are found in the hills. These are the *Bolia Kukuro* or "powerful dog" which hunt in pairs, and the *Khogo* which hunt in packs. They are very much feared by the deer and the appearance of them is sufficient to cause all deer within sight or hearing to get away from

* A recent order of Government directs that they be enlisted as Police as much as possible.

that part of the jungle. Even tigers are said to be afraid of them, but it is more likely that the tiger deserts the jungle in search of his food driven away by the dogs, but one instance is known where a tiger was really killed by them.

Of trees, the most beautiful are the Simili, or the silk cotton tree; the Bauhinia, with its geranium-colored flowers; and the Manna tree, which, with its magnificent yellow blossoms, reminds one of the English laburnum on a very gigantic scale. The Mango tree is a magnificent forest tree, and some in the hills are of a very large size. There are also two famous Banian trees, one at Sarangoda and the other at Chokapad.

CHAPTER V.

HISTORICAL ACCOUNT.

EARLY HISTORY—THE KALINGA KINGDOM—INVASION BY YAVANAS—INVASION BY THE GAJAPATI DYNASTY—EXTENT OF THEIR DOMINIONS—DECLINE OF THE GAJAPATI DYNASTY—THE MUSSULMAN INVASION—CHICACOLE AND ICHAPUR AS SEATS OF GOVERNMENT—CHICACOLE MOSQUE—MUSSULMAN RULERS—CHICACOLE CIRCAR ASSIGNED TO THE FRENCH—MONSIEUR DE BUSSY PROCEEDED TO GANJAM TO LEVY TRIBUTE—NORTHERN CIRCARS GIVEN AS INAM TO THE ENGLISH—FRENCH DID NOT ABANDON GANJAM—ATTEMPTS OF THE FRENCH TO TAKE POSSESSION OF VIZIANAGRUM WITH THE ASSISTANCE OF THE MOHIRI ZEMINDAR—MOHIRI ZEMINDAR ABANDONED THE FRENCH—FRENCH ABANDONED GANJAM SETTLEMENT—GANJAM SECURED BY THE ENGLISH AND MR. COTSFORD SENT AS ENGINEER AND RESIDENT—GANJAM IN DISTURBED STATE—PARLA-KIMEDI ZEMINDAR REFUSED TO SUBMIT TO AUTHORITY—MR. COTSFORD RETURNED TO MADRAS—MR. COTSFORD RESIDENT—HIS REPORT TO GOVERNMENT—ICHAPUR DISTRICT—CHICACOLE DISTRICT—RESIDENT'S PRECARIOUS POSITION OWING TO THE ARRIVAL OF MAHRATTAS IN CUTTACK—CERTAIN RAJAHS APPROPRIATED VILLAGES—RECOVERY OF KURLA—ATAGADA ZEMINDAR PROCEEDED AGAINST—ZEMINDARS STOPPED PAYING TRIBUTES OWING TO AN EXPECTED INVASION BY MAHRATTAS—ENGAGEMENT WITH GOOMSUR RAJAH WHO CAME TO TERMS—DISSENSIONS AMONG MAHRATTAS IN CUTTACK—GANJAM FORT—PARLA-KIMEDI ZEMINDAR PROCEEDED AGAINST FOR NOT PAYING TRIBUTE—ATAGADA ZEMINDAR PROCEEDED AGAINST FOR TRIBUTE AND AGREED TO PAY IT—CHIKATI AND BIRIDI ZEMINDARS PROCEEDED AGAINST FOR THE SAME PURPOSE—ENGAGE-

MENT WITH KALLIKOT RAJAH—FRESH TROUBLES IN KALLIKOT —PALEMPORES—PEDDA-KIMEDI ZEMINDAR IN ARREARS—ENGAGEMENT AT ALLADIGAM—PEDDA-KIMEDI ZEMINDAR CAME TO TERMS—DISPUTES BETWEEN HIS TWO SONS—MR. COTSFORD RETIRED.

The early history of Ganjam is involved in the natural obscurity that might be expected of a country covered with mountains and jungle, and only accessible with any degree of ease from the sea-coast.

Adrian and Ptolemy describe the coasts of Orissa as occupied by Kirradœ, a savage race, probably the ancestors of the aboriginal Khonds. The Sanskrit name of Orissa, of which Ganjam was once a part, is *Odráshtra* or land of the Ods or Uriyas and according to Lassen, ("Indische Alterthumskunde") was probably used to signify the northern portion of Kalinga, being derived from the Prakrit form of *Auttara*, northerly, from *uttara, oddara, odra.*

The district originally formed part of the ancient kingdom of Kalinga, which is supposed to have been founded in the ninth century before Christ. According to Elphinstone Kalinga extended from the Bengal frontiers of Orissa to the river Godávari, a distance of some 500 miles. The name still survives in the sea-port town of Calingapatam, not far from Chicacole, and in early times a place of importance. Kalinga was for many centuries the head-quarters of Buddhism in India, and on the authority of the Rájavali, Vijaya, a member of a royal family, who came from Kalinga, is said to have founded the Ceylon monarchy B. C. 833, and thus established another Buddhist kingdom. The relations of Kalinga with Ceylon seem to have been kept up for many centuries and in A. D. 275, it is stated, that the celebrated tooth of Buddha, a relic now at Kandy, was obtained by Mahasen, king of Ceylon, from the king of Kalinga.

The maritime invasion and conquest of the Orissan coast by the Yávanas under their leader Rokto Báhu has been so ably treated of by Dr. Hunter in the "Annals of Orissa," that it will not here be necessary to discuss whether the Yâvanas were of Ionian or Bactrian origin, nor whence they came. Cut off as Orissa then was from the rest of India, it is probable that the invaders arrived by sea and there are traditions existing to this effect.

The Yâvanas appear to have held the country for nearly a century and a half, when one Yáyáti Késari made his appearance, and about the year 473 A. D. founded the Lion Dynasty of Orissa. Up to this time the Buddhist religion had chiefly prevailed, but with the advent of the Késari line, it seems that Brahmanism came into vogue, and ousted the more ancient form of faith; and when Hiouen Thsang, the Chinese pilgrim, passed through the country in the seventh century, the Buddhist religion was dying out. The Késari kings are said to have ruled over Orissa for more than six hundred years and doubtless extended their sway over the neighbouring tract of Ganjam.

In the 12th century however an invasion from the south put an end to their dynasty, and the invader Chonanga Deo became the founder of the **Gánga Vamsam* or family, and assumed the surname of Gajapati, or Ruler of Elephants. With the arrival of the Gajapati line of kings the traditions of the district Rajas begin to assume a somewhat less mythical character, several of them tracing their descent to members of this family. The Gajapati princes gave to the country a long line of rulers, and their descendants even now occupy considerable territorial possessions in both Orissa and Ganjam. The Rajahs of Ganjam have morever always looked upon the kings of Orissa as their chief fountain of honour, and even at the present day they still acknowledge the Rajah of Jagannâth or Púri, a descendant of the ancient Orissan kings, as their Chief. The foundation of the town of Ganjam is usually attributed to a member of this family.

* The river Godávari is known by the name of Gánga.

Ananga Bhima Deo was probably the greatest of the Gajapati kings, and is said to have built the famous temple of Jagannâth at Púri, and to have reigned from 1175 to 1202 A. D. His grandson, Nursinga Deo, surnamed Langulâ, reigned from 1237 to 1282, and built another well-known temple, that of Kanárak on the sea to the north of Púri. He was a great warrior, and is said to have undertaken several expeditions to the south. It appears likely that his conquests extended as far as the Nellore district,* for a tradition exists of a monarch of that name having founded 185 Pagodas in the Udayagiri taluk which was for nearly 400 years under their control.

The dominions of the Orissan kings certainly extended beyond the river Kistna and their power was at its height in the thirteenth, fourteenth and fifteenth centuries. The wild nature of the country in Ganjam rendered their administration however merely nominal, and they were probably induced by these considerations to establish their own servants as Rajahs or Lords of the marshes to keep the wild aboriginal tribes of Khonds and Sávarás in check. As late as the fifteenth century we find the aboriginal inhabitants, more especially the Sávarás, still occupying portions of the plains according to local tradition, and it was probably not until the reign of Purushottama Deo that they were fairly driven back by the Hindus into the hilly fastnesses, where they still live.

Another well-known Orissan monarch was Purushottama Deo who reigned from 1479 to 1504. It is related in a native epic poem called Kánchi Kávéri that he went to war with the king of Conjeeveram, because the latter refused to marry his daughter to the sweeper of Jagannáth, an office filled by the kings of Orissa and regarded by them as sacred. The story goes that Purushottama Deo defeated the king of Conjeeveram, and took his daughter, Padmávati, prisoner. In-

* Vide Nellore Manual.

order to avenge the slight offered to him, the Orissan monarch declared that he would marry Padmávati, whose beauty was renowned, to an ordinary sweeper, but his prime minister took pity upon the princess, and presented her before the king, as he was sweeping the car of the God Jagannáth upon a feast day, and so induced his master to marry her. Purushottama Deo established many of the smaller Zemindars in Ganjam, whilst others were confirmed by him in their estates, upon their presenting themselves before him and tendering him their allegiance in the course of his progresses through the country.

Upon the death of Purushottama Deo's son Pratápa Rudra Deo in 1532, dissensions seem to have arisen amongst the different members of the Gajapati family and their power gradually declined during the sixteenth century. Taking advantage of the internal strife that prevailed, the Mussulmans invaded Orissa from the north under a General named Kalapahado. In the battle which took place between the contending armies, Telinga Mukunda Deo, the last of the independent kings of Orissa, was slain, and the Mussulmans overran the country about the year 1560, but it does not appear that they carried their arms beyond the Chilka lake.

It is here necessary to revert to the gradual progress made by the Mussulmans in the south by means of which they ultimately possessed themselves of the Ganjam province towards the latter end of the sixteenth century, although their possession of the country was but little more than nominal. Before however this took place one Hassan Gangu, a Mussulman adventurer of Afghan descent, had founded a kingdom in the Deckan in 1347, and as he took the surname of Báhmini, his dynasty was afterwards known by that name.

About the end of the fifteenth century the Báhmini kingdom split up into several smaller states such as Bijapúr A. D. 1489, Ahmednuggur in 1490, and Beder in 1498. In 1512 the kingdom of Golkonda or Hydrabad was founded by one

Sultan Kutb Shah, a native of Hamadan in Persia. The administration of this Mussulman adventurer was so successful that at the end of a long reign, he left a territory extending from the Godávari to beyond the river Kistna, and from the sea to a line drawn west of Hydrabad about the seventy-eighth degree of East Longitude.

In 1520 Sultan Kutb Shah, commanding the Mussulmans, defeated the forces of the united chiefs of Telingana at Kondapalli in the Kistna district, and there is reason to suppose that Pratápa Rudra Deo, the king of Orissa, was one of the chiefs who suffered discomfiture. It seems at any rate certain that the Orissan kingdom showed unequivocal signs of waning in the reign of this monarch. The Gajapati princes still however continued in power both in the provinces of Chicacole and Rajahmundry until sometime later.

About 1571, Ibrahim, the fourth monarch of the Kutb Sháhi line, took advantage of the uncertain rule in Orissa, and made himself master of the Godávari and other districts as far north as Chicacole. For about one hundred and eighty years the Ganjam district, which, including the Ichapur province, then known by the name of the "Chicacole Circar," was controlled either more or less directly by Mussulman authority from Hydrabad.

The principal seat of Government was at Chicacole, where the Fáujdar or Deputy of the Soubah resided, whilst a Sub-Governor or Naib resided at Ichapur. The revenues of the country were collected by these two Mussulman officials, as best they could, and remitted to the seat of Government at Hydrabad.

In the year 1641 Abdulla Kutb Shah sent Shir Mahomed Khán, who built the fine mosque or musjid at Chicacole, from Hydrabad to rule over the maritime dependencies north of the Kistna river. With the exception of a few mosques however, nothing now remains in the country to mark the time when the Mussulmans held their sway, and at the present day the Mussulman population is probably smaller than in any other district in the Madras Presidency. In 1687 the Kutb Sháhi kingdom came to an end with Abril Hussein, when the great Mogul Emperor, Aurangzebe Álamgir, asserted his authority in the Deckan, and established the government of the country on a firmer footing.

In 1707, upon the death of Aurangzebe, the Mogul empire may be said to have broken up and another period of anarchy followed, during which the Mahrattas rose rapidly into power. Finding no one in Central India to oppose them they soon overran the country from west to east, establishing themselves in the province of Orissa, north of Ganjam, about 1740. In the meanwhile the district of Ichapur in the Chicacole Circar continued to be administered by the Mussulman Fáujdars at Chicacole with the assistance of their Naibs at Ichapur.

In 1713 Asof Jah, who took the surname of Nizam-ul-mulk, was nominated Soubahdar of the Deckan by the Mogul Emperor at Delhi, and appointed one Anwar-ud-din Khan to be his Fáujdar at Chicacole in 1726. This man, subsequently better known as the Nawab of the Carnatic, ably administered the country for a period of fifteen years.

The following extract gives the names of the Mussulman rulers between 1726, the time of Asof Jah, Nizam-ul-mulk of the Deckan, and the cession of the Chicacole Circar to the French in 1753:—"Anaverdy Khan, father to the present Nawab, was "appointed a Naib by Nizam-ul-mulk and managed the Chicacole country from Fasli 1136 (A. D. 1726) to the (Fasli) year "1150, when he was succeeded by Jaffer Ali Khan who "continued as Naib to the (Fasli) year 1155, and then was supplanted by Ebadullah Khan. He continued in power till "1159, when Jaffer Ali having made interest at the Durbar, "Ebadullah was deposed by an order from Nazir Jung, and "Jaffer Ali again restored to his station. The Northern Circars being granted to the French in the (Fasli) year 1263

M. R., dated 8th June 1763.

"(1753) Jaffer Ali retired to Hydrabad, and Viziaram Raz "(Rajah of Vizianagrum) was appointed by Mr. Bussy to the "management of Chicacole. He continued in it for that year, "and in the latter end. of (Fasli) 1163 was succeeded by "Ibrahim Gaudy (Ibrahim Khan Gadidi).

"Ibrahim Gaudy being accused of ill-management and hav-"ing neglected to make remittances of the Circar rents in "(Fasli) 1166 Mr. Bussy marched with the troops he brought "with him from the Deckan in order to call him to an account "for the arrears due to the Company, who being unable to "satisfy the demands made by the French, and being alarmed "at the approach of their army fled to Cuttack and from "thence went to Hydrabad and joined the present Soubah "Nizam-ud-Doulah, who at that time began to have the pre-"eminence over his brother Salabat Jung. Anaverdy Ali "Khan was by Mr. Bussy nominated successor to Ibrahim "Gaudy, and remained one year in the station of Naib, when "the power and influence of the French in Indoston beginning "to decline, he and all their adherents were expelled from "the Circar by Gajapati Raz, nephew to Viziaram Raz, who "acted as Naib in the year 1163 (1753)."

In 1752 the struggle for pre-eminence between the French and the English in India was at its height. Mozuffer Jung, the Soubadar of the Deckan, had been slain in an affray whilst on his way to take possession of Golkonda, and with the assistance of the able and intrepid Comte de Bussy who commanded the Soubadar's French escort, Salabat Jung, third son of Asof Jah, was proclaimed his successor. Out of gratitude for the services that the French had rendered not only to himself but to his predecessor, Salabat Jung confirmed all the honours and privileges previously granted to Monsieur Dupleix, the distinguished Governor of Pondicherry. He also assigned to the French, with the other districts of the Northern Circars, the Chicacole Circar, for the pay and equipment of the French auxiliaries in the service. The French accordingly established themselves firmly in their capital at Masulipatam, at that time the strongest fortress and the most important place in the Northern Circars, and under DeBussy's instructions Monsieur Moracin lost no time in taking formal possession of the ceded territory.

The Chicacole Circar still continued however to be administered by a Mussulman Fáujdar subject to the authority of the French. In 1757 the collections from Chicacole became so slack and uncertain in consequence of the incapacity of Ibrahim Khan, the Fáujdar at Chicacole, that Monsieur DeBussy resolved to go thither in person, and settle the country, the independent chiefs of the province, with their family feuds and internal usurpations, having thrown every thing in disorder. Surajah Dowlah, the Nawáb of Bengal, had at the same time invited the French to co-operate with him against the English in Bengal where the latter were threatening the French Settlement of Chandernagore.* It became therefore part of DeBussy's designs to watch the course of events in Bengal, and be at hand if possible to assist the Nawáb against their common enemy.

* Vide Orme.

DeBussy accordingly proceeded northwards, and his forces were joined by Viziaram Raz, the Rajah of Vizianagaram, and other chiefs with an army of 10,000 men. He unfortunately permitted himself to be drawn into Viziaram Raz's quarrels with a neighbouring Rajah, and through his persuasion the French troops were allowed to assist in attacking the fort of Bobbili in the Vizagapatam district. The tragic termination of the assault is a well known subject in the Northern Circars. The Rajah and his adherents massacred their wives and children rather than allow them to fall into the hands of hateful enemies, and then fell themselves bravely fighting against their foes. Vengeance however pursued Viziaram Raz, the instigator of this murderous attack. An adherent of the Rajah of Bobbili killed him at the expense of his own life whilst he was sleeping in his tent. He was succeeded by his son Ananda Raz who afterwards became the worst enemy of the French in the Chicacole Circar.

Monsieur DeBussy deeply regretting the part that he had permitted his troops to take in the assault upon Bobbili, hastened to quit that part of the country. He first however placed a garrison at Vizagapatam and then proceeded into the Ganjam district along the line of hills to the north. The Zemindars of the district terrified by the fate of the Rajah of Bobbili, hastened to pay up their arrears of tribute, and it was not until the arrival of the French upon the borders of Goomsur that they met with any opposition. Here however the Rajah of Goomsur thinking himself secure in his fastnesses amidst the jungle refused to pay the tribute claimed by the French, and Orme thus describes the difficulties with which the collection was attended :

"This country (Goomsur) is much more extensive than that
1757. of any other of the ancient Polygars; it commences about 40 miles to the north-west of Ganjam extending about 50 miles in that direction and 20 in breadth. It is even more impenetrable than the country of *Bobbili, its forests consisting entirely of bamboos which grow closer, and resist the axe and fire better than any other vegetation, relying on which the inhabitants do not think it necessary to erect redoubts for the defence of their paths, but obstruct them with frequent and temporary barriers of bamboos wrought in a variety of entanglements." As DeBussy intended, for other reasons, to remain awhile in the northernmost parts of the Chicacole province, he resolved to employ his time in reducing the Goomsur country, of which the Rajah's arrears amounted according to Orme to 1,80,000 Rupees. "Day by day the troops were employed with excessive toil and fatigue in rooting up, cutting down, and

* The Bobbili Estates lie in the neighbouring District of Vizagapatam.

endeavouring to make their way through the forest. The whole district is estimated one of the hottest regions of Hindustan,* and is peculiarly subject to strokes of the sun, by which seven Europeans were in one day killed." Several barriers were forced or past, and the Zemindar beginning to think himself in danger made proposals which Mr. Bussy was equally willing to accept having lost 30 Europeans and a much greater number of sepoys in the little progress which the army had made. The arrangement was concluded in the middle of April.

1758.

DeBussy had in the meanwhile been expecting to hear from Surajah Dowlah, the Nawáb of Bengal, who had led him to expect substantial assistance in conducting his army to Bengal through the province of Orissa. In this expectation he resolved to remain near the frontiers of the Chicacole province, and accordingly marched his army from Goomsur to Ganjam, where Orme says the French had long had a trading establishment. Whilst they were encamped at Ganjam the French Commander received intelligence of the capture of Chandernagore by the English. DeBussy now convinced that no good could result from any further connexion with Surajah Dowlah, resolved to return to the Court of the Nizam at Aurangabad, and there to await an opportunity, if possible, of retaliating upon the English in the south. He accordingly left Ganjam in May 1758, and arrived shortly afterwards at Aurangabad with every prospect before him of establishing upon a secure footing the authority of the French in the Northern Circars.

Monsieur Lally, the Governor of Pondicherry, however required DeBussy's services at the siege of Madras, and recalled him in spite of his remonstrances, from his position in the north. DeBussy obeyed unwillingly, and in August 1758 made over the Government of Masulipatam and the Nothern Circars to the Marquis DeConflans.

* From March to June, away from the sea-coast.

In the meanwhile Ananda Raz, the Rajah of Vizianagram, dissatisfied with French rule, and offended with DeBussy, who had refused to rent the country to him, had been intriguing with the English in Bengal to drive the French out of their possessions in the Nothern Circars, promising them at the same time every assistance in his power. Lord Clive saw his opportunity, and in spite of considerable difficulties and much opposition, he managed to despatch a force of 500 Europeans under Colonel Forde to Vizagapatam. Colonel Forde's instructions were to effect a junction with the native troops of Ananda Raz and other native allies, and drive the French out of the provinces ceded to them.

The English force arrived at Vizagapatam in September 1758, and the first step that Colonel Forde took, after joining his troops to those of Ananda Raz, was to re-establish the factory of Vizagapatam, where the French had left a small garrison. He then marched straight against the French, and meeting DeConflans at Peddapore in the Godávari district, defeated him. Colonel Forde was so much encouraged by his success thus far, that he resolved to make no delay in attempting to carry Masulipatam by storm. Unintimidated either by the great odds against him or the vacillating conduct of his native allies, the English Commander carried the town, which was then the key of the French possessions in the north, after a short but severe struggle, in January 1759.

The Nizam who had been advancing to the assistance of his French allies, was now glad to conclude a treaty of alliance with the English. Impressed by Colonel Forde's successes, and his own capital and power being threatened by his brother Nizam Ali, Salabat Jung agreed to cede to the English all the Northern Circars, except Guntur, upon condition that the English should assist him with troops. Salabat Jung on his part bound himself to compel the French to quit the Dekkan, and not to suffer them to have a Settlement in the country. Salabat Jung's treaty with Colonel Forde in 1759 was confirmed by his brother Nizam Ali who murdered and succeeded him and was ultimately ratified by the Mogul Emperor's Farmán, dated the 12th August 1765. The Emperor by this Farmán gives the Nothern Circars as Inám or free gift to his good friends the English from April 1762.

It was not however until another treaty dated the 12th November 1766 had been concluded between the English and Nizam Ali, Soubah of the Dekkan, that the former determined to take actual possession of the grant. After the enumeration of other matters, the Soubah of the Dekkan agreed by this treaty "to write letters to all the Zemindars acquainting "them that they were in future to regard the English Com- "pany as their sovereign, and to pay their rents and obedience "to the said Company or their deputies without raising any "troubles or disturbances."

It was thus that the Northern Circars, including the Chicacole Circar of which the Ganjam district then formed a part, were finally secured to the English, and a road was opened to them which connected their Settlements in the south with those in the north. Upon the importance of this acquisition it is needless to expatiate.

The French in the meanwhile had not abandoned their Settlement at Ganjam. Owing to the unexpected capture of Masulipatam at the beginning of 1759, Monsieur Moracin who had been sent by Lally to assist DeConflans against the English found himself obliged to land his troops at Ganjam, which was the only port still open to them. Aware of the overtures made by Ananda Raz, the Rajah of Vizianagram, to the English in Bengal, Moracin thought his enforced stay at Ganjam a good opportunity of punishing him for his treachery. He accordingly entered into negotiations with Nárâyana Deo of Mohiri, "the principal Rajah in this part of the province. "The Fort and wood of his residence was called Mohirry, and "is situated 12 miles from the sea-shore and 20 miles W. S.
Vide Orme. "W. from Ganjam. Besides Mohirry he had "six or seven forts which lay more inland and further to the

"north. His constant force was 3,000 men, besides which he "occasionally hired from the other Polygars. The Rajah, "Viziaram Raz, during his administration under Monsieur "DeBussy in the province of Chicacole had, by some severities, "provoked the hatred of Náráyana Deo, which devolved after "the death of Viziaram Raz on his successor Ananda Raz."

Moracin accordingly proposed to Náráyana Deo that they should unite their forces and march first against the English Settlement of Vizagapatam, and afterwards against Vizianagrum, the principal residence of Ananda Raz. "If successful thus far they were to go on until joined by the French army of observation which was with Salabat Jung when Masulipatam was stormed; probably Salabat Jung would assist in retaking this place, and Náráyana Deo in reward was to be placed in all the advantages possessed by Ananda Raz. Náráyana Deo accepted the terms, but with no intention of prosecuting the expedition any further than the continuance of his own advantages. But the French troops having expected to land at Masulipatam were not provided with equipment for long marches, which it required much time to prepare at Ganjam. There were in the detachment 43 English soldiers who had been taken prisoners and had entered into the French service. Thirty of these men together made their escape soon after they landed, and after many hardships found their way to Cuttack in Orissa in the middle of May, where they were relieved by the English Resident, Mr. Grey, who sent them to Balasore from whence they were conveyed to Calcutta. Seven more arrived at Cuttack in June, and afterwards came in several other deserters of other nations." From these deserters the English derived information as to the proceedings of the French in Ganjam.

Orme 1759.

"It was in the beginning of July (1759) before Monsieur Moracin was ready to march, by which time he had expended all his ready money, and the subsistence of the detachment depended on the sale of some trumpery commodities and the precarious faith of Náráyana Deo, who however accompanied them with his troops. After three or four marches they were distressed to extremity for provisions which neither the army of Náráyana Deo nor the inhabitants of his towns would supply without money. At Berhampore, a town in the hills six miles before you arrive at Mohiri, the French soldiers entered the houses to get victuals; a fray ensued and blood was shed on both sides. Náráyana Deo with all the troops at once left them, and summoned the assistance of the neighbouring chiefs. The French detachment having no alternative marched back towards Ganjam. Náráyana Deo and his allies met them in the way and stood what they called a battle, but the European arms dispersed them as usual, and the detachment took post in Mansúrkota,* a town situated 8 miles from Ganjam in a country abounding in flocks and grain, where they collected provisions although surrounded by the enemy, with whom they commenced a negotiation of which Náráyana Deo seemed to be as desirous as themselves. To conclude it one of the French officers named Darvieu went to Náráyana Deo in his camp, but accompanied by 40 Europeans and the same number of sepoys. On their return they were attacked by the whole force they had visited, and all the Europeans, excepting three, were killed. The sepoys not being so much the object of this treachery suffered less."

"Mr. Moracin immediately returned to Ganjam, and encamped within and around the French Factory which is on the river-side, and threw up works sufficient to protect his detachment through the avenues of the town, which Náráyana Deo and his allies surrounded. Of the two ships which brought the detachment, the *Harleem* had been despatched to Arracan for provisions, and the *Bristol* had been driven ashore in a hard gale of wind before the troops marched to Berhampore. There

* Close to Gopalpur, but it is nearer 14 than 8 miles from Ganjam.

were on the stocks on the river-side a large snow, and in the river several smaller vessels belonging to the Factory, in which they intended to return to Pondicherry with the northern monsoon, after the English squadron should have quitted the coast. In the meantime they continued for many days skirmishing with the troops of Náráyana Deo who at length offered to retreat, which produced a cessation of hostilities, but no terms of reconciliation; for the demands of the French were in proportion to the injuries they had received; and Náráyana Deo only meant to save the expenses of the field, with security that the French troops would not make incursions into his country after his own should have returned to their quarters. This they promised and remained quiet."

In the meantime letters from Náráyana Deo to Colonel Clive arrived in Bengal requesting him to send a body of Europeans to take or destroy the whole of the French force with Moracin. "The Zemindar promised his assistance and the reports of the deserters confirmed the feasibility of their project. But the dubious state of the English affairs, and the decrease of their military force in Bengal scarcely permitted any further diminution of it. However, Colonel Clive, with his usual spirit of enterprise, determined to try the experiment. Sixty Europeans, half of them artillerymen, were embarked on the *Hardwicke* which had 100 Europeans as her crew. The ship sailed out of the river on the 30th September, and on the 7th of October anchored in the roads of Ganjam under Dutch colours. Two French officers immediately came on board to enquire news and were detained prisoners. Captain Samson then went ashore under a pass-port to Moracin, magnified the force he had brought, said more was coming, and proposed that he should surrender his whole detachment to avoid unnecessary bloodshed. But Moracin obtained juster intelligence. Samson then landed messengers who got to Náráyana Deo who, being by this time certified that the French detachment would soon go away of their own accord, had no further motive or inclination to renew hostilities against them, but nevertheless promised Samson that he would soon appear with his army, and again invest the town. A civil intercourse of messages continued between them until the 20th (October) when Samson being convinced that he intended to do nothing, sailed away for Bengal."

At the end of 1759 the French abandoned their Settlement at Ganjam, and no traces of their occupation remain at the present day.

No sooner had Nizam Ali, the Soubah of the Dekkan, voluntarily withdrawn all opposition to the cession of the Circars by the treaty dated the 12th November 1766, than the English Government at Madras at once took steps to secure Ganjam and the province of Ichapur by passing on the 2nd December 1766 the following resolution in Council. "As we have all "along intended that Ganjam should be "resettled as soon as our affairs with "Nizam Ali were concluded, not only on account of an investment to be made there and to promote the sale of our Europe "staples, but also to secure that barrier to the Circars to the "northward, and it being therefore necessary that the servant "sent should be one qualified for securing the Settlement, "Mr. Cotsford who may act both as Engineer and Resident, "is appointed to proceed thither: and as the northerly winds "will prevent our sending proper supplies of stores to Ganjam "till the month of March or April, it is agreed that Mr. "Cotsford do now proceed to the northward, make himself "acquainted with the investment at the different factories, and "if he has time that he do assist in finishing the fortification "at Vizagapatam; and if he finds the country sufficiently "settled to proceed to Ganjam, he is to survey the factory "and report to us its condition with that of the country about "it, and what stores it will be necessary to send thither, and "what prospect there may be of providing an investment and "disposing of any part of our European commodities."

Madras Records, 1766.

In obedience to these instructions, Mr. Cotsford proceeded first to Vizagapatam and afterwards to Ganjam early in 1767. He found the country to the north of Vizagapatam in a very disturbed state. Náráyana Deo, the Zemindar of Parla-Kimedi, the largest and most important Zemindari in Ganjam, had possessed himself of the country and refused to submit to the authority of the English, intercepting all communication between Bengal and Madras. In the interim between the departure of the French in 1759 and the arrival of the English in 1767, the country had been administered by Sitaram Raz of Vizianagrum, whose ambitious designs kept it in a constant state of disturbance. Mr. Cotsford wrote as follows about the misgovernment of the country at Ganjam. "Sitaram "Raz's general who protects the country, oppresses the Renter "of the Pergunnah, the Renter oppresses the Darogah or "Governor of the town, and the Governor the poor people "most severely." Mr. Cotsford however reported favourably upon the situation of Ganjam, and the chances of making an investment there, but as it was evident that nothing could be done in the district without the presence of troops, he shortly returned to Madras. In the following year 1768, Government determined to reduce Náráyana Deo, the refractory Zemindar of Parla-Kimedi; and Colonel Peach who was then in command of a Bengal battalion at Masulipatam, received orders to proceed against him. Mr. Cotsford was at the same time instructed to accompany Colonel Peach's force and to take up his appointment at Ganjam as Resident. The following resolution dated the 4th April 1768 was accordingly passed by the Madras Council. "Although "our intentions of settling a factory at Ganjam last year were "frustrated by the situation of affairs in the Chicacole Circar "and by the war with Nizam Ali, yet as we have constantly "kept that object in view, and our Reso- "lutions in the other department to reduce "Narrain Deo and the other rebellious Zemindars promise a "more favorable conjunoture, it is agreed that Mr. Cotsford

M. R. 1768.

"be again sent thither, and that the necessary instructions "for his conduct be accordingly prepared, and as it will be "necessary for a quantity of stores to be sent to Ganjam, "and a vessel will be wanting to transport the heavy stores "and baggage belonging to the Bengal detachment proceed-"ing against Narrain Deo: ordered that the Master Attend-"ant be directed to make enquiry for a well-found vessel "of about two hundred tons or upwards for those purposes "to be freighted by the Company so long as they may have "occasion to employ."

Mr. Cotsford arrived at Chicacole in April 1768, and caused the attested copy of the Nizam's firman to be read in open Cutcherry in the presence of Sitaram Raz, the Nizam's Fáujdar for the Chicacole Circar. The force under Colonel Peach soon afterwards defeated Náriyana Deo near Jalmur, in May 1768, and compelled him to take refuge in the Máliah country attached to his Zemindari. Upon the advice of Mr. Cotsford it was deemed prudent to put in the defeated Rajah's son as his successor in order to avoid complications and further disturbances. The actual management of the Parla-Kimedi country was however entrusted to Rama Jogi, the person nominated to be the new Zemindar's Patro (or Diwan) by the Company. Colonel Peach's battalion continued in the Parla-Kimedi Zemindari until the country to the south had been partially settled, and Mr. Cotsford meanwhile proceeded northwards to Ganjam and entered upon the duties of his appointment as Resident in July 1768.

1768.

The Chicacole Circar, as administered by the Mussalmans, had been divided and managed in three divisions, under the names of Ichapur, Chicacole and Kasimkota. Chicacole and Kasimkota being nearer to Vizagapatam were placed under the control of the Chief and Council at that place, but the Ichapur province lay too far to the north and rendered the presence of a Resident at Ganjam absolutely necessary to administer its affairs.

Mr. Cotsford gives the following description of the country that he was called upon to control: "The Ichapur district is the most northern province of the Chicacole Circar, "and was, before the cession of the Circars to the Company, "the boundary of the Soubahdary of the Deckan to the northward. The Chicacole province bounds it to the south-westward, the Bay of Bengal to the south-eastward, and "from N. E. to W. S. W. it is bounded in general by the "dominions of Jannoji, one of the principal Chiefs of the Mahrattas, but more "immediately by the Zemindaries tributary to the Soubah or Fáujdar at Cuttack "(Ganni Sambaji), who holds the government of the Cuttack countries by the "authority of Jannoji. It is divided into 19 Zemindaries "and 8 Pergunnahs." The town of Ganjam was at that time the principal sea-port of the district, but it had a formidable rival in Sonapore, which lay farther to the south.

Ganjam Records.—Letter from E. Cotsford to Charles Bourchier, Governor of Madras, dated 16th December 1769.

The Ichapur district itself extended as far as Kásibugga and included the small Zemindari tract of Tarla, the river at Poondy forming its boundary line. South of this line the Havéli lands of Chicacole and Kasimkota were under the management of Sitaram Raz, brother of the Vizianagrum Rajah, who acted as the Company's renter.

Upon Mr. Cotsford's first assuming possession of the country, his position was somewhat precarious, for to the north at Cuttack there was a large force of Mahrattas, whilst in the province itself there were nineteen Zemindars, all of a more or less turbulent character. His authority in the district was therefore liable to danger at the least appearance of any external troubles. The Zemindars, being semi-independent, entertained considerable bodies of feudal retainers, commonly called *paiks*, and in all could muster amongst them no less than 32,170 foot soldiers, whilst they held possession of 34 forts for the protection of their respective territories. It was therefore the Resident's chief care to provoke as little opposition as possible in his management of the country, and by gradually destroying the country forts he hoped to reduce the Zemindars to obedience. To assist the Resident in governing the country and collecting its revenues, an aggregate force of about 2,000 men, commanded by Captain Bandinell, the senior officer, were located in different parts of the country, but chiefly at Ganjam, Ichapur and Aska. To add to the difficulties of the Resident's position it was currently reported that the Mahrattas at Cuttack were about to invade the district. Mr. Cotsford's first care was to secure the revenue of the country, which, in the first year of our occupation, amounted to about 5 lakhs of Rupees. His second was to set about building a fort at Ganjam for the security of the Settlement and its stores. The renter of the 8 Havéli or *demesne* Government lands of the province was at that time one Dubbur Akkaji Pandit. Mr. Cotsford finding that this man possessed "ability and integrity accompanied with great activity," and that he moreover possessed "a perfect knowledge of the countries and the political interests of the Zemindars," resolved to renew the rents of the Havéli lands to him for 1769 in anticipation of the sanction of the Madras Council. In settling with the Zemindars however for their tribute, Mr. Cotsford experienced considerable difficulty and opposition. This was still further increased by a report from Masulipatam that the Nizam's son and Ibrahim Beg who had been renters of the province under DeBussy and the French, were preparing to invade the country.

Ganjam Records, 1769.

Of the nineteen Rajahs then in the province of Ichapur, Kissun Bhanj, the Rajah of Goomsur, was the most powerful. Besides four forts and two very strongly protected,* Palliems,

* Palliem is a tract of land under a petty Chieftain.

those of Vishnuchakram and Kotarikota, this Rajah had in his pay no less than 10,050 peons to which he was able to add, in times of emergency, another 1,000 men. The most troublesome Zemindar was, however, Bheema Deo, the Rajah of Vijayanagar and Pratápagiri, who had taken possession of the Havéli fort at Kurla and laid claims to that pergunnah. The Resident soon discovered that several other Ganjam Rajahs had taken advantage of the previous troubles to appropriate villages belonging to the Havéli (or Government lands). Two of the offenders in this respect had been the Rajahs of Goomsur and Atagada, but as their estates occupied the northernmost portion of the district bordering upon the Mahratta territory, the Resident was anxious to conciliate them as much as possible, "for with the force now here," he writes, "if the principal Zemindars are against us we cannot wage war but to "our own loss." The Resident was therefore content to recover thirteen Havéli villages from the Goomsur Zemindar out of the twenty-three that he had appropriated, and twenty-six others were recovered in a like manner from the Rajahs of Atagada and Mohiri.

Against the Zemindars of the Mahendramalei, whose estates lay in the south of the district, the Resident acted in a more vigorous manner and sent armed peons to take possession of the standing crops in the Zemindaries of Surangi, Jarada, Jalantra, Budarsingi, Mandasa, and Tarla upon their failing to settle satisfactorily for their tribute. "Without saucar security," the Resident writes, "it is the only way of dealing with them, for they cannot be trusted." Bheema Deo, the Rajah of *Vijayanagar and *Pratapagari, whose estates lay behind the Mohiri hills, meanwhile refused to give up the Company's fort at Kurla, and the Resident found himself obliged to send an armed force against him. As this Rajah kept up a total force of 4,900 paiks, and held ten forts and a palliem in different parts of his country, the Resident on the 19th October 1768 despatched against Kurla two companies of

* Pedda and Chinna-Kimedi respectively.

sepoys under Lieutenant Duncan, holding in reserve an auxiliary force of 1,000 peons supplied by Goomsur and 500 from Mohiri in case of resistance. Upon the arrival of this force at Kurla, Bhima Deo thought it prudent to give up the fort and agreed to settle for the payment of his tribute. Six other villages which he had appropriated were allowed to remain in his possession, as Mr. Cotsford did not consider it politic to press upon him at that juncture the Company's demands in full.

G. R. Letter to Madras Council, dated 25th Oct. 1768.

With regard to the tributes paid by the Zemindars of the district the Resident remarks that they were frequently out of all proportion to the size of their estates, and the ability of the Zemindars to pay. He hoped that, by gradually demolishing their forts and strongholds they might be reduced to a state of obedience that would give the Company an opportunity of apportioning their tributes to the size of their respective estates. Mr. Cotsford was however of opinion that, before this could be done, the Zemindars must be reduced by arms, for he says "they will not submit to it without compulsion. They will not even pay according to the agreements they now make without the assistance of an army in the field, which is the manner they have been accustomed to be treated in. The objections against depriving the Zemindars of their territories and placing others in their stead are, that there will be in general great difficulty in finding any one who will accept of such a place and can maintain himself in authority without the assistance of a considerable detachment from us, the Company running the risk of promoting a man equally unworthy as the one removed. The same may be said of them in the light of the Havéli lands, for our troops must support the renters in collecting the rents in which they will be much troubled by the adherents of the deprived Rajah, and have scope sufficient given them to defraud the Company if so disposed."

Mr. Cotsford's letter to the Madras Council, dated 26th December 1769.

Scarcely had matters been settled with the Rajah of Vijayanagar, when it became necessary to proceed against the Zemindar of Atagada for a similar refusal to come to a settlement for his tribute. This Rajah's estates lay on the northern bank of the Rushikuliyá river, and 4 companies of sepoys and the "Coffery" company with two 3-pounders marched from Aska, and took possession of the principal entrance or pass which leads to Atagada on the 5th October 1768. The pass lay near Boirani about 7 miles N. E. of Aska, and was formed by a hedge of bamboos, for the most part impenetrable with a good ditch before some parts of it. This hedge ran north and south for about 3 miles, and joined the hills at the two extremities. The entrance into the pass was protected by an earthen redoubt. After the hedge had been made practicable with hatchets, a company of sepoys entered and got behind the redoubt, whilst the rest proceeded to attack it in front. As soon as our men were perceived, however, the Atagada peons abandoned the redoubt. The Zemindar fearing to offer any further resistance agreed to settle for his tribute, and to restore ten villages of an annual value of Rs. 7,646 which he had annexed to his estate from the Government lands.

G. R. Letter to Madras Council, dated 21st Nov. 1768.

As the Bengal detachment under Colonel Peach was to leave the country in December 1768, and there were no other troops, Mr. Cotsford began to enlist a company of peons at a monthly cost of 290 Rupees. He also proceeded to store the fort at Ganjam with provisions, as news still kept coming from Madras that the Northern Circars were likely to be invaded by the Nizam and the Mahrattas. The Government forts at Aska, Kurla, and Ichapur were also garrisoned with a few sepoys, the better to secure the revenue and keep the Zemindars in check. The building of the fort at Ganjam had in the meanwhile been pushed on as much as possible, but in spite of every exertion, it was not at the end of 1768 in a position to stand a siege, in case the Mahrattas should invade the district. The Resident therefore thought it advisable to purchase a vessel and keep it in readiness at Ganjam, in case matters should come to the worst. Although all measures for the security of the country had been taken with as much caution as possible, the news of an expected invasion soon oozed out, and the Zemindars at once made a dead stop in their payments to the Company. As the Resident had received information of a secret road that led from the Mahratta country into Goomsur by way of Vishnuchakram, he resolved to get possession of that fort, which was reputed to be one of the strongest in the country, with the view of compelling the Goomsur Rajah to come to terms. Accordingly four companies of sepoys, a company of coffres and two 3-pounder guns marched on the 17th December 1778 from Aska in the evening and arrived at Vishnuchakram about sunrise the next morning, when it was perceived that some 600 or 700 Goomsur paiks were drawn up before the gate of the fort. The English detachment lost no time however in forcing their way, and taking possession of the gate, fearful lest the numbers of the enemy should increase. Upon the appearance of the English force the Goomsur Rajah retired to the hills, and thinking it more prudent not to offer any further resistance, he shortly afterwards gave immediate security for the payment of his tribute, and prevailed on the detachment to retire from the fort into camp.

M. R. Mily. Dept., 1768.

Colonel Peach's Bengal detachment quitted the Parla-Kimedi Zemindari about the 12th December 1768, and marched southwards to Vizagapatam, but they had hardly left, before disturbances commenced. Náráyana Deo, the rebel Zemindar, returned and compelled Ramajogi Pátro, whom he had put in as Diwán or Manager of the estate, to retire to Jalmur. He at the same time began intriguing with the Mahrattas in Cuttack, inviting them to attack us, and promising the co-operation of Sitarám Ráz, the Nizam's former Fáujdar, and of Bheema Deo of Vijayanagar. In the meanwhile dissensions had arisen amongst the Mahrattas, and, on the 24th January 1769, the Resident received a letter from Mr. Alleyn, the English Agent at Cuttack, informing him that Ganni Sambaji would be unable to make a raid into Ganjam, as Janoji had given positive orders to his generals and sirdars acting under the Fáujdar that they were by no means to molest the English, and were to obey no orders emanating from Ganni Sambaji. The Resident meanwhile suggested to the Madras Council the expediency of appointing a Resident or Chief at Chicacole, supported by five companies of sepoys for the management of the affairs of Kâsimkota and Chicacole "not only respecting the "rents of the Havéli lands, but of the different Zemindars dependent thereon, and to serve as a check "on Nârâyana Deo, who in all probability "would not long cease to break his promise of obedience, and "ravage the Havéli lands of Chicacole." Sitarám Ráz, the brother and Diwan of the Rajah of Vizianagram, still however continued to act as the renter of the Company's Havéli lands to the south, and it was not until 1787 that Mr. Cotsford's recommendation appears to have been acted upon.

G. R. 1769.

In the meanwhile the construction of the fort at Ganjam continued, and the Resident in April 1769 thus describes its condition: "The exterior wall is near eight feet thick, and "comprised of strong clay within, and sods laid horizontally "about 3½ feet thick on the outward side, well beat and "watered so as to make it very solid, which will not be so "liable, I imagine, to be cut by the heavy rains, as if composed of clay only.

"The Curvette which is within the ditch is principally made "for the getting clay for making the walls, though at the "same time it adds something to the strength of the place.

"The Magazine is sufficiently large to contain about "40,000lbs. of gunpowder, and from its construction, I "think it is bomb-proof. The walls of it are of large stones, "which were found in clearing the ground and making the "excavation round the fort. The Magazine is finished and "what powder we have lodged therein.

"The walls of the lodging are of clay though within are "timbers considerably large on which the beams supporting "the roof rest. The roofs are covered with tiles. I think "in about 20 days the whole of them will be habitable. They "will stand five or more years without needing any consider-"able repair. The sepoys' barracks have been begun upon, "only three days past.

"The artillery park is quite a temporary building and thatch-"ed: herein are now lodged all our guns and carriages, &c., "and all our stores in general are within the fort, one room "of the lodgings being repaired for the present for such of "the stores as require being kept with care. There are four "drains for the passage of the water out of the fort in the "rainy season. These are at present no further executed than "was absolutely necessary, that the raising the wall in the "parts might not be retarded, which is done by fixing therein "wooden spouts about ten feet in length, having apertures "about 9 inches square. They are made of 4-inch plank and "are fixed one foot above the level of the ditch or two below "the level of the country. The communication of these spouts "under the rampart will be by a passage in brick-work of 2 "feet wide and 3 in height, so that if by any means these "drains be stopped, the space will allow of persons going in "to make them clear.

"In laying down the covered way and glacis I have made "the places of arms before the gates more extensive than in "the other fronts, so as to allow of Ravelins being added if "you should approve of it.

"The fort with respect to the town appears to be extremely "well situated, as regards the connecting both together in "the case of a pettah wall being carried round the whole. "As I have in a former letter to the Chief Engineer written "concerning its situation with regard to strength I think it "unnecsssary to be more particular at present. I have "caused gabions about four feet high to be made, which in "the case of necessity may be placed on the wall at its present "height and fitted, which will serve as a kind of parapet, at "the same time increasing its height."

Bheema Deo, the Rajah of Vijayanagar, who had been suspected of intriguing with Sitarám Ráz and other Zemindars for the entry of the Mahrattas into the country, now again withheld his tribute. The Resident accordingly resolved to reduce him to obedience by taking the Rajah's principal fort at Pratápagiri. Three companies of sepoys accordingly marched at 9 o'clock at night of the 30th April 1769 under the command of Lieutenant Duncan from Aska, and arrived at Pratápagiri early the next morning. The nature of the fort is thus described. "It was about 120 yards square with towers "at the angles, and one in the middle of each curtain "except in the east front where there was a large gateway "projecting, as the gates in the country forts generally do: "the walls were not under, nor above 22 feet in height. A "ditch ran round three sides, which in many parts was deep "in water. On the western side only there was none, as the "soil which was rocky, would not admit of an excavation "being made without much trouble and expense. A ridge of "large hills ran close to it to the westward covered with a thick "wood, which extended to within 150 yards of the walls in "that front. On the other sides the country was entirely "open. The troops immediately upon arrival proceeded to "escalade the fort by means of ladders, which they had brought "with them for that purpose. Some confusion appeared to "take place amongst the peons stationed inside the pettah for "the protection of the fort, and Lieutenant Duncan at once "advanced one company to the gate. The other company was "drawn up between the fort and the pettah. The attention of "those within the fort being fixed entirely on the gate, two "of the ladders were applied to the walls, and a Havildar and "twelve sepoys ascended unperceived. When they perceived

" our sepoys to be within, and the greatest part of the garrison " cut off from the fort by those of ours stationed as above, " those in the fort retired with all precipitation through a " sally-port in the north front, but not fast enough to prevent " four men from being killed, and two wounded. Among the " former was the person commanding the fort; as these people " had stood on their defence they could not be saved. There " were found in the fort six small guns (country made), several " large Gingalls, a small quantity of powder and a small quantity " of rice." Hearing that his principal fort had been taken, Bhima Deo shortly furnished security for the payment of 20,000 Rupees. It was at first intended to occupy the fort permanently, but the detachment left to guard it under Ensign More, suffered so much from sickness, that with doubtful discretion it was restored to the Rajah on the 26th July 1769.

The next Rajah who had to be brought to terms was the Atagada Zemindar. On the 6th May the small English force again marched from Aska, and arrived before day-break at Bonapilli, a place about 4 miles from Boiráni. At this place there was one of the entrances that led into the wood serving as a natural obstacle to the approach of the fort at Atagada. The other entrance at Boiráni had been blocked up with strong timbers in four different places, and as the woods near Bonapilli were not so thick and the road better, it was determined to make the attack from that quarter. On the 8th May at day-break our force was drawn up in front of the gate, and two companies of sepoys were detached to get into the woods and come up behind it. Hatchets were also got ready to cut down the door in front. The fire from the detached sepoys soon gave notice that they had got into the wood. Upon the day breaking our people were discovered drawn up before the gate, and the enemy began to annoy them from the loop-holes in the gate-way with Gingalls. The sepoys who had forced their way through the woods on the other side now advanced and after 8 or 10 discharges from our field-

G. R. 1769.

pieces, the defenders of the gate thought fit to retire. In the afternoon our force moved forward with provisions for six days, and found that the enemy had not yet had time to impede our advance either to Atagada or Sangaram by felling trees and barricading the road. Sangaram was about 6 miles from Bonapilli, and the greater part of the road lay through dense woods. Three discharges of grapeshot however were found sufficient to clear it before the troops arrived at Sangaram. The Atagada Rajah's residence was secured from any sudden attack by its situation between two hills. It is described as being "almost, if not entirely, inaccessible, "for from one hill to the other a wall of stone twenty feet "high, was carried to a length of about 150 yards, and in a "direction, north and south. The wall itself was pierced by "a large gate-way with a square tower on each side of it." In the skirmish which took place eighteen of the Atagada people were killed, and about thirty more wounded. Our loss consisted of one lascar killed, with 1 coffre serjeant and three sepoys wounded. The Zemindar having been worsted, agreed to settle for his tribute for 1768, and pay up the arrear of tribute due for 1767.

In the meanwhile, neither the Kallikót Zemindar whose country adjoined the Chilka Lake, nor the Chikati Rajah had settled for their respective tributes. The Chikati man fled upon the troops moving against him, but after destroying his palliem at Chikati and another smaller fort, he agreed to arrange for the payment of nearly 50,000 Rupees then due. The operations against Kallikót lasted longer and were of a more difficult character owing to the nature of the country. The Biridi Zemindar, whose small estate lies not far from Ganjam, had also neglected to pay his tribute, and after reducing him to submission on the 26th October 1769 the troops under Captain Casemore marched to Rambha on the Chilka Lake on the 29th idem. On the same date Captain Auchmuty marched to Birabatti with three companies of the Bengal detachment.

While Captain Casemore's detachment proceeded towards Kallikót by land, another party consisting of the coffres and the 1st Company of grenadier sepoys under Lieutenant Rowles, and accompanied by the Resident went by water,* and disembarked on an island opposite the mainland at a village called Somala; soon after landing, some 300 peons were seen on the opposite shore. As they made a show of attacking the English force our party crossed over to them in the shallow water, and soon dispersed them killing two paiks and wounding three others without loss to themselves. A party of sepoys under Lieutenant More had, in the meanwhile, marched by land from Rambha towards Kanaka, where there was a pass formed by a hedge of bamboos and a parapet wall about three or four hundred yards in length running from the foot of the hills down to the Chilka Lake, but as Lieutenant Rowles' troops came up at the same time behind the wall from Somala, the enemy offered no resistance, and the detachment effected a junction at Somala. On the 2nd November the troops proceeded to Murda Ságaram, and the first obstruction they met with was at a pass, where there was a deep ditch, scarcely fordable, cut in the rock. The ditch was defended by two small forts on the declivity of the hill above it, and the march of our troops was retarded for nearly three hours. Fortunately flanking parties were sent up the hill to stop the fire of the peons, and these discovered and took possession of the forts which could not be observed from below. The detachment was therefore able to proceed without serious loss, but for the last three miles it was greatly pestered by parties firing on it the whole way under cover of the thick woods and jungle; and notwithstanding every precaution the enemy cut off a small portion of the baggage and also succeeded in gaining possession of the greatest part of the musket ammunition. The latter loss was however speedily recovered by a company that was immediately

G. R. 1769.

G. R. 1769.

* The Chilka Lake.

detached for that purpose. Our loss on this march consisted of a corporal of coffres killed and three sepoys wounded, together with about 16 camp-followers killed and wounded. On the 4th November a party consisting of the coffre company and two companies of sepoys marched under the command of Lieutenant Rowles to open the communication between themselves and the detachment under Captain Auchmuty, which had proceeded to Birabatti. A letter addressed to Captain Auchmuty by Mr. Cotsford on the 1st November from Somala did not unfortunately reach him till the 7th. He was thus prevented from attacking at the same as Lieutenant Rowles. In the meanwhile the party under Lieutenant Rowles marched about three miles from Murda Ságaram in the direction of Birabatti, but found the original road entirely blocked up by felled trees. Whilst opening a passage for themselves as best they could, the troops were attacked by the enemy in the rear. Our party however pushed forward and gained a redoubt between Murda Ságaram and Birabatti, but not without loss, as the troops had found themselves placed between two fires. The enemy twice attempted to dislodge the attachment from the redoubt after they had gained it, but without success. After sustaining considerable loss, the Rajah sent a principal person to Lieutenant Rowles with his sword, and proposed a cessation of hostilities provided the English would return to Murda Ságaram. As there was no probability of an attack being made by Captain Auchmuty from Birabatti, Lieutenant Rowles accepted the proposal and returned to camp about dusk. This affair cost us 24 in killed and about 28 in wounded. Amongst the killed were Ensign Main, 4 of the coffre company and 20 of the battalion, whilst Lieutenant Rowles was wounded. The loss on the Rajah's side consisted of about 30 killed, amongst whom was the Rajah's own brother, and 3 of his principal officers, and upwards of 50 wounded. Captain Auchmuty had, in the meanwhile, left a battalion under Captain Kerr at Birabatti and had marched with two of his battalions by the way of the Chilka Lake to Murda Ságaram where he arrived on the 10th November. On the next day a battalion and two field-pieces cleared the road and took possession of the middle redoubt without meeting with any resistance from the enemy. On the 9th Captain Kerr made himself master of the redoubt at Birabatti without loss, and by the 11th November at night the communication was open. There was another redoubt however, which led to the town of Kallikót about a mile from Murda Ságaram. As the English were unacquainted with its strength, it was judged advisable to get behind it by cutting a road through the woods, rather than deliver an attack from the front. On the 13th November this was successfully accomplished, and as the enemy retired without opposition the English were able to take possession of Kallikót on the morning of the 14th November. The Zemindar soon afterwards paid down 5,000 Rupees, and offered security for 21,000 Rupees more within a month. The Resident thought fit to accede to this, lest the collections from the other Zemindars should fall into arrears, owing to our attention being too exclusively taken up with Kallikót.

G. R. 1769 L., dated 22nd December 1769 to Madras Council.

The Bengal detachment soon afterwards commenced their march towards Bengal, although it was with difficulty that the Resident obtained the consent of Ganni Sambaji, the Mahratta Fáujdar at Cuttack, to permit the English troops to pass through their territory.

No operations of any importance appear to have taken place in 1770, although nearly all the Zemindars still continued to be in arrears with their tributes. One of them, Náráyana Deo, Zemindar of Mohiri, died on the 10th February 1770 and was succeeded by his son bearing the same name.

G. R. 1771.

In 1771, fresh troubles occurred in Kallikót. The Zemindar reported to the Resident that he was unable to pay his tribute in consequence of his brother Maun Sing having wrested all authority from him: and even threatened his life. At the request of the Zemindar the English troops were again sent into his country, and stationed there at his expense. As the road into the Cuttack countries lay through the Kallikót Zemindari, Mr. Cotsford considered it "alike advantageously situated for offensive or defensive war with the Mahrattas." The English force soon drove Maun Sing from the neighbourhood of Kallikót, and compelled him to take refuge in a distant and inaccessible valley called Puncally (Ponkhalo), where the inhabitants were well affected towards him. The troops traversed the country in all directions. The villages of the insurgents were burnt, and some of Maun Sing's peons were killed. Whereupon he left the country and took refuge in the hills between Atagada, Goomsur, and Puri, where he continued to lurk for some time. In August 1772, however, he gave himself up to the Resident and was kept in confinement at Ichapur and Aska, and the Resident refused to release him until he had paid for the expenses of the detachments sent against him. After remaining in confinement for three years, Maun Sing escaped from his prison at Aska and was shot through the body in an affray that he had with a party of his brother's peons in the Kallikót Zemindari in October 1775.

G. R. 1771

About the end of 1771 Mr. Cotsford writes: "Bheema "Deo (of Vijianagar) having agreed to pay in one month "28,000 Rupees of which I have already received 10,000, and "being moreover very old and infirm, no danger is to be "apprehended from his measures. The Zemindars of Chikati "and Mohiri being under age nothing is to be apprehended "from them. By the death of Rajender Deo of Chikati (who "was of a very refractory disposition) the spirit of opposition "is entirely broke in that part of the district. Our footing "in the Kallikót country gives us some advantage against "the Rajah of Atagada and the force we have is, I think, "sufficient to reduce him entirely after the first impression "has been made on his country, and our troops in possession "of Atagada, his place of residence." Many of the Zemindars of the district were, however, two years' tribute in arrears, and at the end of 1771 there were only the four Zemindaries of Bodogada, Sergada, Hummá, and Biridi against whom there were no balances. This was of course not a matter for surprise as the Ganjam Zemindars but rarely paid their tributes, except when they were obliged to.

The Resident's hands had hitherto been so fully occupied in coercing the refractory Zemindars of the district, that the Company's commercial operations were almost forgotten. Mr. Cotsford writes however in 1771: "I have, for some time "past, considered whether or not an investment may be now "attempted in this district, but on maturely considering it, I "think the Company will run some risk in "making contracts, as for the most part "the merchants live under the Govern-"ment of the Zemindars, particularly at "Berhampore which is under Mohiri, and where much cloth "is made, but they are *very insolent* and *not to be depended on* "preferring having dealings with private merchants in mus-"lins, &c., than making contracts with the Company for "Palempores. There is a considerable traffic between Sonna-"pur and Berhampore. At the former place broad-cloth, cop-"per and other foreign articles are imported, for which they "get grain, flowered-muslins and other cloth, stick-lac, &c. "This trade, I understand, was at the time Mr. Bussy came "into this country, carried on between Ganjam and Berhampore, "as formerly an investment might, with much greater success, "be undertaken than in the present situation. I have used "my endeavours to bring the merchants who import goods at "Sonnapur to move to Ganjam, and have given them cowles "setting forth that they should, in no shape whatever, meet "with any interruption in their trade, but on the contrary, be "aided and supported in what was just, and not contrary to "the public good.

G. R. L., dated 3rd Jan. 1771, to Madras Council.

"As the establishing the trade here would be the means "of our having great influence over the merchants at Berham-

" pore, it were to be wished that the means were fallen upon to " accomplish it. Besides this great advantage it would, in a mea- " sure, prevent the importation of arms and military stores."

The first shipment of Palempores from Ganjam to Europe appears to have been in 1771, and later on in 1779 the Court of Directors wrote: " As those (Palempores) from Ganjam are much approved you " must endeavour to send a larger proportion of that sort."

L., dated 22nd March 1771, G. R.

Subsequently in June 1779, a Mr. Fannin appears to have contracted to supply Palempores to the Company at Ganjam. Mr. Fannin proposed to carry on the business of investment in a systematic manner by establishing weaving villages and dividing the country into six divisions for the purpose of superintending the weavers " who are remiss and idle," and supplying them at proper times with cotton and thread for the cloths to be provided. Mr. Fannin urged with great reason that the weavers would make the greatest efforts of industry when living in perfect security from oppression, and that the Company's advances of money would be more safely recovered. Mr. Morgan Williams, the then Resident, appears however to have been less sanguine about the success of the scheme, and writes: " It cannot be doubted but if a sufficient number of weavers could be *assembled* in a few villages, the Company's investment might be carried on with certain ease and success, but the experience of the years proves the aversion of the people to remove from their old habitations, and that it is even with difficulty they can be prevailed upon to weave Palempores, they finding it more to their advantage to make muslins and different sorts of cloths for which they find a ready sale."*

Five villages were, however, assigned to Mr. Fannin as an experiment, but upon Balakrishna Naidu, the renter of the Havéli lands, objecting to the assignment as being contrary to his cowle,

* Mr. W. W. Hunter, in his "Annals of Orissa," is therefore mistaken when he says that the Resident advocated the *confinement* of the weavers in a pettah.

the villages were ordered to be resumed and the scheme came to an end.

In February 1772 news was received from the Chief at Vizagapatam that Gajapati Deo, the Zemindar of Parla-Kimedi, had fled from his estate in consequence of the enmity of and intrigues of Sitarám Ráz, the Company's Renter for the Chicacole Havéli lands. Mr. Cotsford discovered that he had retired to Rámagiri in the Máliah country, where he had placed himself under the protection of his uncle Bhima Deo, the Rajah of Vijayanagar. As this Zemindar would probably only advise him to place himself in antagonism to the Company, the Resident was anxious to persuade him to return to his own Zemindari, and for this purpose he sought an interview with him. Gajapati Deo came to the place of meeting about 7 miles distant from Vijayanagar, accompanied by Bhima Deo, who was attended by a force of about 3,000 peons. The Resident does not appear to have been successful in his endeavours to induce him to return to his Zemindari, as he, for a long time afterwards, continued to molest it after the Company had put in his brother, Jagannath Deo, to succeed him. Bhima Deo himself had been withholding his tribute for so long, and had fallen so greatly into arrears, that it became absolutely necessary to take steps for the better management of his Zemindari. The Resident was desirous of placing Bhima Deo's son, Moni Deo, in charge to manage the Zemindari, but his father had quarrelled with him six years previously, and Moni Deo sought our protection and accompanied the troops on their march.

Mr. Cotsford's Letter, dated 29th April 1772, G. R.

The troops of Ichapur received orders to proceed against Vijayanagar, the Rajah's chief residence, and as he made no signs of submission, the fort at Vijayanagar was occupied without difficulty. On the 12th April the detachment under Captain Bandinell arrived at Pratápagiri. A battery was raised against the fort, and a fire from an eighteen-pounder gun was directed against one of the bastions, but although 90 shots were fired in two days but little impression was made upon the wall of the fort which was exceedingly tough. Upon the arrival of fresh powder and shot from Kurlá it was discovered that the eighteen-pounder, which was a brass one, was cracked in many places, and gave evident signs of being near to bursting. As it would have involved too much delay to have awaited the arrival of another cannon from Ganjam, a general assault upon the fort with ladders was made on the 17th April at day-light. Four companies of sepoys and the coffres made the attack in different places, and upon our men getting on one of the bastions, the enemy gave way and fled so precipitately by that side of the fort, which was not attacked, that several fell and broke their limbs. The fort was occupied by about 250 men, and the enemy lost about 15 in killed and one wounded, whilst the loss on our side consisted of two killed and about 20 wounded. Amongst the latter was Lieutenant Trent.

L., dated 20th May 1772, G. R.

After leaving a company for the protection of Pratápagiri the detachment marched from thence and arrived at Alladigám on the 19th April. The fort was a small one, and on the 22nd at day-light, an attack was made on it by six companies of sepoys and the coffre company, who marched cheerfully and without confusion to their several stations. The walls of this fort were about twenty feet in height, ten of which formed the parapet with loop-holes therein to fire through, forming two lines. The rampart in the curtains was very narrow, many of our sepoys got to the top of the wall, but from the great height of the parapet could not descend into the fort. Others of our force with shorter ladders took possession of the loop-holes of the lower tier, and greatly annoyed the enemy. Many of the longer ladders broke down by the sepoys crowding too thick upon them, and this causing much confusion re-inspirited the enemy, and all attempts to gain the fort afterwards proved ineffectual. The attack lasted for nearly five hours, and was conducted with great spirit by Captain Bandinell. The garrison of the fore consisted of 200 men, but fearing another attack, they quitted the fort about 9 o'clock on the following night. Our loss had been considerable, for we had 27 killed and 202 wounded of all ranks. Amongst the former was Lieutenant Pennington, and amongst the latter were Captain Bandinell and Lieutenants Brulé, Hughes and Woodward. The loss of the enemy was only 8 killed and 25 wounded.

The check that Captain Bandinell had experienced at Alladigám served to enjoin upon him greater caution before proceeding against the next fort at Siddheswaram. The force accordingly marched from Alladigám (on the 4th May) and arrived before Siddheswaram. On the 8th at night a battery of two 18-pounders which had in the meanwhile been brought from Ganjam, was raised against the south face of the fort at a distance of about 200 yards from the walls. On the 9th May at day-light the battery opened fire, and by 11 o'clock the wall of the fort was greatly shattered, and large fragments began to fall from it, so that a breach therein appeared to be forming very fast. This so alarmed the garrison that they came to the resolution of quitting the fort, as they feared the resentment of our sepoys for the loss sustained at Alladigám, and were afraid to make an offer of surrender. Finding that the battery had ceased to fire on account of the excessive heat of the sun in the middle of the day, and observing the general slackness in the out-guards, the garrison poured out of the fort as fast as the narrowness of the gate would admit them. They were however, soon observed from the battery and the company stationed there for the protection of the guns immediately rushed up to the gate, and entered the fort. About 59 men who still remained in it now crowded together to one of the bastions, and having quitted their arms they sued for mercy. Fortunately there was an officer with our sepoys, who prevented them from exercising any acts of cruelty upon the prisoners. The garrison consisted of 120 men, and the outguard pursued those who had quitted the fort and killed and wounded 8 of them.

L., dated 6th June 1772, G. R.

Upon hearing that Siddheswaram was in our hands the garrison of the fort at Kotinada, consisting of 100 peons, quitted it, as the fort was not in so good a state of defence as the other forts. As all the forts dependent upon the Pratápagiri country were now in our hands, Bhima Deo sent his principal vakeel to the Resident with a letter expressing his great sorrow for his contumacy, and requesting a cessation of hostilities in order that his credit might be saved. The Resident accordingly sent Bhima Deo a cowle of personal safety, and on the 13th May he arranged a meeting with the old Zemindar. After Mr. Cotsford had effected a reconciliation between the father and son, arrangements were made for the better management of the Zemindari.

Bhima Deo consented to sign two deeds, by one of which he empowered his son, Moni Deo, to manage the two countries of Vijayanagar and Pratápagiri on his behalf, and by the other he gave to Moni Deo the Pratápagiri country on his death. The Vijayanagar country which had been formerly separated from Pratápagiri was to descend to Bheema Deo's favourite son, Jagannáth Deo. Moni Deo contrived, however, to retain possession of both countries upon Bheema Deo's death in 1776, and when Jagannáth Deo laid claim to Vijayanagar, because his father had willed it to him, the Company declined to support his pretensions. Jagannáth Deo subsequently became Rajah of Pratápagiri, but the adverse claims of the two brothers produced an irreconcileable hatred between them, which was productive of the worst consequences for the peace of the country during many long years.

At the end of 1773 Mr. E. Cotsford resigned his appointment as Resident on the plea of his failing health, and the Government of Fort St. George upon his departure expressed their appreciation of his able and vigorous administration of the country.

CHAPTER VI.

CHANGE IN GOVERNMENT—APPOINTMENT OF CHIEFS WITH A COUNCIL—APPOINTMENT OF MR. CHARLES SMITH AS CHIEF—EMPLOYMENT OF TROOPS IN CHIKATI, SURADA AND BODOGADA—MURDER OF THE SURADA RAJAH—QUARREL OF THE COMMANDING OFFICER WITH THE COUNCIL—MESSRS. MAUNSELL AND MORGAN WILLIAMS, PROVINCIAL CHIEFS—ABOLITION OF CHIEFS AND APPOINTMENT OF RESIDENTS—BALAKRISHNA NAIDU THE RENTER—DEATH OF KISSUN BHANJ, ZEMINDAR OF GOOMSUR—VIKRAMA BHANJ—HIS SUCCESSOR—HIS NON-PAYMENT OF TRIBUTE—SUBDUED BY THE ENGLISH TROOPS—VISHNUCHAKRAM AGAIN FELL INTO THE HANDS OF VIKRAMA BHANJ—ATTACK ON KALLÁDA AND THE RAJAH'S ESCAPE—VIKRAMA BHANJ'S RESTORATION TO THE ZEMINDARI—DISPUTE BETWEEN LACHMANA BHANJ AND VIKRAMA BHANJ—SUCCESSION OF SRIKARA BHANJ—MR. JOHN TURING, RESIDENT—APPROACH OF MAHRATTA ARMY UNDER CHINNAJI BABU—DESCRIPTION OF PASSES INTO THE MAHRATTA COUNTRY—MAHRATTA COMMANDER'S FRIENDLY NOTE TO RESIDENT—DISTURBANCES IN MADRAS—MUTINY AT VIZAGAPATAM—ARRIVAL OF FRENCH PRIVATEERS INTO GANJAM ROADS—COLONEL PEARSE WITH THREE THOUSAND MEN FROM BENGAL PASSED TO MADRAS—MAHRATTA COMMANDER ARRIVED WITH A NOTE FROM GOVERNOR-GENERAL—NARAYANA DEO, ZEMINDAR OF MOHIRI, MURDERED HIS PATRO—PROCEEDED AGAINST FOR ARREARS, AND GAVE OVER BERHAMPORE AND A GREATER PART OF HIS ZEMINDARI—ABOLITION OF RESIDENT AND APPOINTMENT OF A CHIEF WITH COUNCIL—QUARRELS AT COUNCIL BOARD—CESSATION OF HOSTILITIES BETWEEN THE ENGLISH, FRENCH, AND DUTCH—MR. MAUNSELL APPOINTED RESIDENT—REVENUE OF THE DISTRICT—TRADE DECLINED—COUNCIL ABOLISHED—MR. CRAWFORD, RESIDENT—ZEMINDARS OF PEDDA AND CHINNA-KIMEDI QUARRELLED AND

WERE BOTH CONFINED IN THE GANJAM FORT—DISTURBANCES BETWEEN ZEMINDARS—FAMINE AND ITS EFFECTS—MR. SNODGRASS, RESIDENT—RESIDENT ABOLISHED AND MR. BALFOUR APPOINTED COLLECTOR—MR. SNODGRASS RETURNED AS COLLECTOR—CONDUCT OF HIS DUBASH—MR. SNODGRASS REMOVED FROM OFFICE FOR DEFALCATIONS—MR. BROWN SUCCEEDED—EXTENT OF DEFALCATIONS—THE DUBASH IMPRISONED—GOOMSUR RAJAH'S REBELLION—FLIGHT TO THE HILLS—HIS SON PLACED ON THE THRONE IN HIS STEAD—CAPTURE OF REBEL JAGANNADHA DEO OF PRATAPAGIRI—HISTORY OF CHICACOLE DIVISION—SEETARAM RAZ'S LEASE—EMBEZZLEMENT BY MR. KEATING—PARLA-KIMEDI ZEMINDARI DECLARED FORFEITED AND PLACED UNDER COLLECTOR'S MANAGEMENT—TEKKALI ZEMINDAR DIED AND ESTATE MANAGED BY THE COMPANY—ENGAGEMENTS WITH INSURGENTS OF PARLA-KIMEDI—REVENUES OF THE CHICACOLE DIVISION.

Upon the retirement of Mr. E. Cotsford it was determined to alter the form of management of the Ganjam district, and Mr. Charles Smith was appointed Chief at Ganjam with a Council to assist him in the administration of affairs. Mr. Smith took charge on the 22nd February 1774, and the following appointments were made:—

Mr. Holland, Warehouse-keeper, Paymaster and Accountant.

Mr. Dynely, Store-keeper, and

Mr. Hudleston, Secretary,

whilst Mr. Maunsell, from whom Mr. Smith took charge, became second in Council.

There had been no military operations in Ganjam since 1772, but in 1774, 1775 and 1776 disturbances broke out once more. The Zemindars of Chikati, Surada and Bodogoda had all been remiss in their payments of tribute, and the troops were employed in the usual manner to demand payment at their gates. Murders and disturbances, together with the usual attendant consequences of military expeditions and assignments of villages to the Company, appear to have been constant throughout the period of Mr. Smith's tenure of office as Chief.

In June 1775 the Rajah of Surada was murdered by his brothers at the instigation of Vikrama Bhanj, the Rajah of Goomsur, and English troops were sent from Aska to occupy the fort at Surada and secure the revenue of the country. In Mohiri the Rajah's mother murdered the Patro in 1776, and in the same year Jagannath Deo, upon the death of his father Bhima Deo, made his first attempt to gain his share of his patrimony.

These incidents were varied by quarrels between the Council at Ganjam and the Commanding Officer, Captain Lysaght, at Aska, and the latter was at last removed from the command for beating the Company's renter, Cursojee Lallah.

Owing to the non-payment of tribute, there were assignments of villages in Chikati, Dhárákót, Kallikót, Pratápagiri and Bodogoda, and wherever there was an assignment it was usual to send thither a Tahsildar to collect the revenue on behalf of the Company. The Company's troops were constantly employed either in demanding the tributes of the Zemindars, who but rarely paid without either compulsion or threats, or in quelling disturbances and calling the murderers of the Company's Tahsildars to account. When a Zemindar was refractory the troops were quartered upon him, and he was made to pay for their keep.

In September 1777 Mr. Smith was recalled, and Mr. Maunsell became provisional Chief and continued in office as such until 1778. In May 1778 Mr. Morgan Williams was appointed Chief in Council, and in 1779 the Council at Ganjam was abolished, and Mr. Morgan Williams was appointed to be Resident with the well known Mr. Snodgrass as his Assistant.

On the 25th September 1779 the Ichapur district was rented to Balakrishna Naidu, formerly the Company's dubash, for a period of 10 years, and the Zemindars instead of paying their tributes as heretofore to the Resident or Chief in Council, were ordered to pay their tributes through the renter into the Company's treasury. The Council at Ganjam respectfully protested against a change in the system of renting the country, that virtually withdrew all the power from their hands, but apparently without effect.

Balakrishna soon found himself quite unable to cope with the difficulties of his position although assisted by the Company's troops, and upon falling irretrievably in arrears with all his payments, and giving great dissatisfaction to all the district Zemindars, his own cowle was finally revoked in October 1781 by an order from the Court of Directors at home.

Kissun Bhanj of Goomsur had died in 1773, and his son, Vikrama Bhanj, who succeeded him, never paid a rupee of tribute between the date of his death and 1778. During Mr. Cotsford's time the tribute of the Zemindari was only 30,000 Rupees, but previous to the confirmation of his second son, Vikrama Bhanj, this amount had been raised by the Company to 50,000 Rupees. A provision of nine jaghire villages was at the same time stipulated for on behalf of Lachmana Bhanj, the elder son; but Vikrama Bhanj obstinately refused to grant to his brother a Sanad for this jaghire, and the jaghire villages became a source of constant dispute for several years. Vikrama Bhanj's contumacy with regard to his brother's subsistence, and his obstinate withholding of the tributes due, at length compelled the Company, after several years of patient forbearance, to send troops into Goomsur for the final reduction of the country.

Accordingly in 1778 the troops stationed at Aska overran the whole of the Goomsur country, which was the only one that had not been effectually reduced by Mr. Cotsford. Vishnuchakram and other strongholds were occupied by the troops, and the Zemindar was compelled to take refuge in Mahratta territory. During the whole of 1778 and 1779 the troops from Aska remained posted in the Goomsur Zemindari, when Mr. Oakes appears to have had charge of the administration. Vikrama

Bhanj however still continued at large, and was able to foment disturbances by means of his adherents. The crops were destroyed by the paiks, and the Rajah's menaces and cruelties frightened away the country people. The Company's troops meanwhile suffered greatly from sickness and Vikrama Bhanj taking advantage of their reduced numbers, began cutting off small detached bodies and murdering the sepoys. The post at Vishnuchakram fell into the enemy's hands, and Vikrama Bhanj cruelly tied up and murdered 23 of the Company's sepoys, after they had surrendered themselves.

These daring atrocities naturally led to renewed expeditions and reprisals against the enemy. In a secret attack made by the Company's troops upon Kalláda, Vikrama Bhanj only escaped capture by a singular incident. As the Hircarrah who was leading the way for the Company's troops to follow, had just passed the Gumá or fort, he was suddenly seized by a tiger, and the Company's sepoys firing to make the brute quit his hold, gave the alarm, and put an end to all hopes of a successful surprise. A considerable number of paiks perished however on this occasion from the fire of the sepoys. A second attempt to surprise the Rajá was somewhat more successful, but the Rajá although wounded in the thigh and elsewhere by musket shots still managed to make his escape.

Being hard pressed, however, Vikrama Bhanj shortly afterwards took refuge with Sitarám Ráz of Vizianagram, and borrowing money from him, he proceeded to Madras in 1779. By means of the most scandalous falsehoods and misrepresentations, he succeeded in persuading the Madras Council to reinstate him in the Zemindari, and Lachmana Bhanj who had meanwhile been put in as a Zemindar, was once more turned adrift by Government to make room for Vikrama Bhanj, who in attempting to return to the district, was seized by Sitarám Ráz and detained at Tekkali for debt. At the request of the Resident, however, he was released and returned to Goomsur to dispossess his brother. The disturbances however still continued, and when Mr. Stone became Chief in 1782, it became the duty of the Council to decide, which of the two brothers should be finally put in as Zemindar of Goomsur. Lachmana Bhanj was the one upon whom their choice unanimously fell, as they had no confidence in his brother. The Zemindari was in an impoverished state from constant disturbances and Lachmana Bhanj agreed to pay a lakh of Rupees yearly to the Company, as one of the conditions on which he was to hold the country. The inhabitants had however fled to other parts where their property was more secure, and Lachmana Bhanj was unable to meet his engagements, and seems to have died in 1788. He was succeeded by his son Srίkara Bhanj, who afterwards gave the Company a great deal of trouble.

On the 21st March 1780 Mr. John Turing succeeded Mr. Morgan Williams as Resident, and the latter was recalled. In June the unwelcome news reached the Ganjam Settlement, that the Mahratta army had arrived at Cuttack from Nagpore, and that they were concentrating their forces, amounting to 25,000 men, at Cuttack, whilst the fort at Ganjam was still in an incomplete state in spite of occasional repairs.

There was only one battalion in the district, besides the Sibbandy corps raised by Mr. Cotsford, which was employed under the renter, Balakrishna Naidu. The Mahratta army at Cuttack was commanded by Chinnaji Babu *alias* Jannoji Babu, the second son of the Mahratta Chief at Nagpore, and as an English army under Captain Goddard was acting at that time against the Mahratta Peishwah at Poonah, the Resident lost no time in communicating his fears of an invasion to the Madras Council, and set about putting the fort at Ganjam into a better state of defence.

Captain Bruce, who commanded the troops at Aska, was at the same time directed to reconnoitre all the passes leading from Ganjam into the Mahratta country, with as much privacy as possible, and to report his opinion as to the best way in which the country might be defended in case of an invasion. Accordingly in his letter, dated the 29th June 1780, Captain Bruce describes fully all the different passes leading into the Ichapur country, and says that, if the Mahrattas attempt to enter the country, they will do so either "by the way of "Champnegar, or Manickapatam, or very likely by both." He proceeds to state: "a small force, not able to face them in the "field, has no other hopes of protecting the country, than by "seizing the pass of Champnegar and establishing a strong "pass at Maloude," which pass Captain Bruce describes as follows:—

"The pass of Champnegar leads from the Bowanapur "(Bánopur Zemindári) country into the upper part of the "Kallikót Zemindary. It is about one koss through; the "road pretty good for carriages, the jungle not excessively close. "It is fortified with a Tatt and Goomah* at the village of "Champnegar. The Bowanapur (Bánopur) country being "quite open up to this pass, as is the Kallikót on this one side "of it, and the Mahrattas in possession of it, makes this pass "the most favourable for them, should they attempt to disturb "the tranquility of this district."

The apprehended invasion however never took place and in July 1780, one Sheikh Mahomed Kamul, the Commander of the fort at Manickapatam, not far from the frontier of Ganjam, was sent by Jannoji, the Mahratta Chieftain at Cuttack, with a message assuring the Resident that it was not the intention of Rajah Modoji Bonslu of Nagpore "to break the friendship "that had subsisted so many years between the English and "the Nagpore Government, that it was their interest to keep "on friendly terms with the English, but being in a certain "degree subject to the Peishwah at Poonah, they had been in "some measure obliged to send out this army from Nagpore, "and that we might judge of their disposition by their having

* A kind of native fort.

"been *seven months* on a march that they might have performed "in six weeks." About the same time Warren Hastings, the Governor-General of India, wrote to Mr. Turing and informed him that, although the designs of the Mahrattas appeared uncertain, yet it would be better to meet them as friends, and so conciliate them to our Government.

The Resident meanwhile had, in a letter to the Madras Council, expressed a sincere wish that "the "gentlemen in Bengal might be able to ac-"commodate matters with the Nagpore "Rajah, and so remove any apprehension of an invasion from "the army at Cuttack."

L., dated 5th Oct. 1780, G. R.

Whilst the aspect of affairs was thus dark in Ganjam in 1780 it was still more so elsewhere in India, for Háidar Ali, the usurper of the Mysore throne, was threatening to invade the Carnatic and lay siege to Madras. The English were at the same time at war with the French and the Dutch, and there was a general combination against them throughout India to drive them out of the country. It was evident therefore that the Resident in Ganjam would not get much assistance from elsewhere. He was advised by the Council at Madras to draw together his troops as much as possible, and as these were but few in number, he experienced no difficulty in obeying these instructions. At the same time he put the fort at Ganjam into a better state of defence than it had ever been before. The parapet was raised, the ditch, that had partly silted up, re-excavated, and the fortifications were generally strengthened. All superfluous stores were removed from Aska, and two six-pounder guns were despatched thence in boats and arrived safely at Ganjam by the river Rushikulyá. The troops stationed at Aska were also ordered to be ready to move at a moment's notice. The Resident writes: "By training the coffres and las-"cars they are capable of working the guns; "but we want a few non-commissioned officers and gunners

L., dated 21st Aug. 1780, G. R.

"whom I hope your honor will think proper to send to "our assistance." This request, however, does not appear to have been complied with as the Presidency was itself in want of both troops and money, and soon afterwards advertised a loan for 6 lakhs at 8 per cent. interest.

Early in October 1780, the Settlement at Ganjam was startled by the news that the 1st Circar battalion at Vizagapatam had revolted, and fired upon their officers as they were issuing forth from the Chief's house after dinner. The ostensible reason for this conduct appears to have been that they were under orders to sail from Vizagapatam for Madras, where their services were much needed, but there is reason to suppose that Gajapati Deo, the Ex-Zemindar of Parlá-Kimedi, had a good deal to do with the matter. The mutineers after killing five or six of the officers took some of the others prisoners, and at the same time took possession of the fort. Mr. Casamajor, the Chief, also fell into their hands, but afterwards managed to escape on board a vessel in the port at Vizagapatam.

The Resident at Ganjam upon receiving information of this outbreak, at once directed Captain Bruce at Aska to march to Chicacole, take the command of the troops there, and proceed against the mutineers, who had placed themselves under Captain Brulé, a prisoner for treasonable correspondence, whom they had released. News was received, however, that the mutineers had quitted Vizagapatam for Parla-Kimedi, and that the Chief had been able to resume charge of the Settlement. Captain Bruce was accordingly directed to return to Aska. The mutineers subsequently dispersed of their own accord and Gajapati Deo, who had ostensibly exerted himself to protect the English prisoners from violence, was reinstated in the Parla-Kimedi Zemindari by the Madras Government, as a reward for his somewhat doubtful services on the occasion.

The fears of an immediate Mahratta invasion had scarcely been allayed before a fresh enemy appeared on the Ganjam coast in the shape of French privateers. This effectually prevented the Resident from sending supplies to Madras, although the calls for assistance from the Presidency were both frequent and urgent. The oxen, grain and other provisions, which the Resident had been anxiously waiting for an opportunity to send to Madras could not therefore be despatched.

The first French privateer seen off the coast was the *St. Ann*, carrying 18 carriage six-pounder guns and swivel, and manned by 60 Europeans and 40 coffres. Her Commander, Monsieur Champden, (sic) sailed into the Ganjam roads under English colors, and landed two English prisoners of whom he wrote: "Their honesty makes me regret being obliged to dispossess "them of what the fortune of war puts in my possession." He at the same time expressed a hope that the Resident would "render them that assistance which it is not in my power to "give them." The two prisoners were Captain Orphin and Mr. Collier respectively the Master and Chief Officer of an English ship that had become the French privateer's prize. The Resident hearing that the *St. Ann* was not alone, at once took steps to secure the safety of the native vessels lying at Sonnapur and Baruva, and despatched thither small bodies of troops for the protection of those ports. The *St. Ann* did not leave the Ganjam roads in peace, for she shortly afterwards seized a sloop coming from Bengal, and belonging to the port of Sonnapur. The Tindal making a show of resistance was cut down and killed, and the owners of the goods were so frightened that they jumped overboard, and were drowned. The sloop was plundered of 10 chests of opium, a quantity of pepper and rice and a sum of one thousand rupees. She was then allowed to sail to port. At the beginning of 1781 another French privateer, the *Solomon* of 40 guns, commanded by Captain de Rignon, stole into the Ganjam roads late one evening, and rifled and carried away two snows that were lying at anchor. French privateers continued to intercept English vessels during the whole of 1781, and in December of that year the Chief of the Godavery district warned the Resident at Ganjam that there were no less than 48 French vessels cruising for prizes in the Bay of Bengal.

In the meanwhile Haidar Ali Khan after devastating the Carnatic, was laying waste the Tanjore country, and Sir Eyre Coote was watching his movements at Cuddalore. Troops were despatched from Bengal to co-operate with Sir Eyre Coote in the south and ten battalions of sepoys, under the command of Colonel Pearse, arrived at Ganjam on the 17th March 1781. Together with camp-followers their numbers amounted to about 30,000 people. Soon after their arrival in the district sickness broke out amongst them and raged, as Colonel Pearse said, "with alarming fury." Until the outbreak, which was probably cholera, had somewhat abated, the troops were placed under cover at Ichapur, where the inhabitants, much to their praise, readily gave up their habitations for the use of the sick troops. After a long and harrassing march, in which Col. Pearse lost large numbers of his men both by sickness and desertion, he seems to have effected a junction with the main army near Madras in the month of August 1781.

In June 1781 a body of Mahratta cavalry (300 strong) arrived at Ganjam soon after Colonel Pearse's troops had quitted the district and the Commander, Abba Purushottama Pandit, brought a letter from Warren Hastings, the Governor-General, and gave out that a still larger body of cavalry was to follow and join Colonel Pearse's detachment on their march southwards. As they were greatly in want of money, the Resident was induced to advance them 5,000 Rupees, but upon refusing to pay over any more sums without the special sanction of Government, the Mahratta cavalry returned to Cuttack, and the proffered assistance of the Mahratta Chieftain came to nothing after all. On the 1st July 1781 Sir Eyre Coote defeated Haidar Ali at Porto Novo.

The Bengal detachment had scarcely left the district before the Resident received information that Royguru, the Patro of the Mohiri Zemindar, had been murdered at Berhampore on the

6th April 1781. G. R. 1781. The murder appears to have been instigated by Moja Deo, the Rajah's brother, and connived at by Náráyana Deo himself, who upon hearing of his Patro's death at once seized all his effects, and placed his family in confinement. Upon the Rajah of Mohiri refusing to deliver up the murderers and even making the chief of them, one Gopi Maharta, his Patro, Mr. Turing directed Captain Bruce to proceed with his detachment and take possession of the fort at Mohiri, which was about 6 miles from Berhampore. The fort at Mohiri was accordingly occupied, but as sickness of a severe type broke out amongst the troops they were withdrawn, and the walls of the fort demolished. As the arrears of the Zemindari amounted to over 65,000 Rupees, Mr. Turing sent peons to seize the crops, and the Zemindar who had fled at the first alarm, thought fit to dismiss Gopi Maharta, and agreed to assign and make over to the Company's management the greater part of his Zemindari, including the town of Berhampore, in satisfaction of the arrears due by him.

Gopi Maharta, the murderer, however, still continued at large with his adherents, but he was eventually captured and condemned by the Resident to work in chains for life on the fortifications at Ganjam. One Cursojee Lallah became renter of Mohiri, for which he agreed to pay yearly to the Company a sum of 60,000 Rupees. On the 10th December 1782, Náráyana Deo, the Zemindar of Mohiri, was himself murdered in his house at Berhampore by about 20 peons, and his two illegitimate brothers, Moja Deo and Sano Deo, were generally supposed to have instigated the deed. They contrived, however, to keep out of the way, and appear even to have succeeded in securing a monthly pension for their support, upon condition that they should live in a quiet manner and refrain from disturbing the peace of the country. This, however, they both of them failed to do, and the Mohiri Zemindari became the seat of almost continuous disturbances for a period of nearly 40 years.

On the 19th May 1782 the office of Resident was abolished and Mr. Turing was succeeded by Mr. John Maxwell Stone, who was assisted by a Council composed of Messrs. Robert Munro and Vincentio Corbett with Mr. Daniel Russel as Secretary. The Council was afterwards increased to five members. On Wednesday the 29th May 1782, it was agreed at the Council meeting that the following appointments take place:

Mr. Munro, Store-keeper and Accountant; Mr. Russel, Pay-Master and Secretary; Mr. Mierop, Assistant under the Accountant; Mr. Hare, Assistant under the Secretary and Reader of Divine Service; Messrs. Stone and Trice, Assistants under the Secretaries.

In 1783 quarrels took place in the Settlement at Ganjam which continued almost without intermission until 1786. They appear to have originated at the Council Board out of jealousy of the Chief, Mr. John Maxwell Stone, on account of his retaining the immediate management of Havéli lands in his own hands, and the other Members of the Council complained that the whole power of the Settlement was absorbed by Chengulroy, the Chief's dubash or manager.

The quarrels of the Council Board at Ganjam at length became so notorious as to call for the interference of Government. Mr. Henry Crawford was accordingly deputed to Ganjam in 1784 to investigate the complaints and counter-complaints made by the different Members, and upon receiving his report upon the subject, Government came to the conclusion 'that the disputes originated from private pique to the Chief.' They reduced the number of Members of Council from five to three, but continued in office Messrs. Munro and Russel, two of the former Members. Mr. Munro especially had been one of the Chief's principal opponents, and the change made by Government does not therefore appear to have been productive of much good, for disagreements still continued to prevail in the Ganjam Council until 1785 in which year Mr. Stone died.

Mr. Thomas Cooper, formerly of the Council, seems to have got into trouble in 1784, but whether this was due to the active part which he took in the quarrels of the Settlement does not appear from the records. He complains to Government in August 1786 that he has been for two years under suspension without any specific charge being made against him, and bewails his hard fate, stating that after 19 years' service, he only receives 8½ Pagodas a month for his subsistence. Upon being called upon to pay a debt that he owed to the Company, he tendered to the Council 6 candies of lead at 10 Rupees per candy, an offer which the Chief and Council did not consider themselves at liberty to accept without a reference to the Presidency.

On the 21st July 1783 (?) the welcome news was received at Ganjam that a preliminary peace had been signed at Versailles on the 20th June 1783, which produced a cessation of hostilities between the French, Dutch, Spaniards and Americans, and the English. The proclamation notifying the fact was publicly read out to the Garrison in the fort of Ganjam.

On the 6th June 1785 Mr. Robert Maunsell, who had taken Mr. Stone's place at his death, delivered over charge of the settlement to Mr. Morgan Williams who now succeeded as Chief in Council. About the same time the Board of Revenue and a Board of Trade appear to have been established in Madras.

In 1787 the Circuit Committee, composed of Messrs. Saunders and Hugh Maxwell, arrived and commenced to investigate the revenue resources of the district. Their report, dated 25th April 1788, forms the chief data upon which the permanent settlement was afterwards effected in the Ganjam district by Mr. Peter Cherry in 1804.

G. R. 1787.

Mr. Morgan Williams, in a report dated 31st December 1787, describes the revenues of the Ichapur district as on the increase, and estimates its population at 465,755 souls. The total revenue of the country, excluding the whole of the Chicacole Sub-division, is given as 6,35,252 Rupees, but the item of salt, which in 1787 produced but very little revenue, was not included in this estimate.

The trade of the district is described, however, as being on the decline, partly in consequence of a recent order prohibiting the importation of Ganjam salt into Bengal, and partly in consequence of Tanjore then commencing to supply the Madras markets with the grain that they formerly drew from Ganjam. The greatest restraint on trade, however, was the heavy duty levied on piece-goods and grain at the inland Chowks of the district, which amounted to 11 and 10 per cent. respectively. The inland duties added to the export ones were therefore so heavy as to be a practical prohibition of exportation, and instead of 200 vessels being found in the ports of the district, not even 20 could be found calling for freight in 1787.

On the 19th May 1790 Mr. Morgan Williams was appointed Member of the Council at Madras and left for the Presidency. He was temporarily succeeded as Chief in Council by Mr. Munro, but the days of the Council in Ganjam were numbered.

On the 17th November 1790 Mr. H. Crawford, who had been previously Collector of the Chicacole Division, was appointed Resident, and the Council abolished "owing to the great want "of energy in the proceedings of administration there, and "various inconveniences which have arisen from the present "constitution of authority in that district." Messrs. Thomas Snodgrass and Edward Hare were appointed to be Assistants to the Resident.

Troubles were meanwhile rife in the district, and a famine unparalleled in the history of the country was about to add its horrors to existing disturbances. So great did these appear to be that in May 1790, Mr. Munro declared that human foresight could set no limit to them.

The first disturbances broke out in Mohiri. The lease of the Mohiri estate which had been granted to Cursojee Lallah in 1781 expired in 1786, and on the 7th April 1786, the wife of the deceased Zemindar, Kruspru Periya Máhádévi by name, was formally appointed the Ráni of Mohiri. Cursojee Lallah, however, still continued to manage Mohiri for her until 1789 in which year he was barbarously murdered in the fort at Ganjam. It was generally supposed throughout the country that the murder had been committed by the instigation and connivance of Sáno Deo, one of the two illegitimate brothers of the late Zemindar.

Encouraged by the disturbed state of affairs, Sáno Deo made his escape from Aska in 1789, and joining his brother, Moja Deo, they betook themselves to a course of outlawry, having for their fastness the Mohiri Hills, not far from Berhampore. In 1790 Mr. Nathaniel Webb, the Havéli Collector, complained that Sáno Deo had plundered several Government villages near Ichapur. The troops were but few, and the Resident seems to have been almost powerless to protect the country from the troubles that desolated it.

About the same time Moni Deo, the Raja of Vijayanagar, and Jagannáth Deo of Pratápagiri, the two sons of old Bhima Deo, were waging open war with each other, refusing to submit their quarrels to the Company's arbitration and impoverishing each other's estates. In 1790 Moni Deo, assisted by Sáno Deo, made an irruption into the Zemindari of Pratápagiri, burning 12 villages and plundering 12 others. From 1790 to 1793 Moni Deo appears to have resisted all the Company's efforts to reduce him to submission, and in 1792 he even inflicted a check upon the troops sent against him under Captain Little. He was finally reduced in 1793 with the assistance of his brother Jagannáth Deo. Both Moni Deo and Jagannath Deo, however, continued their quarrels, and in 1800 they were both in confinement in the fort at Ganjam for troubling the peace of the country.

Farther to the south Sáno Padsha, the brother of the Jalantra Zemindar, recently deceased, assisted by the Tarla Zemindar, had taken possession of the Zemindari to the exclusion of his brother's child who was the rightful heir. Assisted by Sáno Deo, Sáno Padsha carried off the minor and his mother from the fort at Jalantra to the Bodogoda hills, and kept them in confinement for no less than five years. In the meanwhile Sáno Padsha enjoyed the Estate, and the Company found themselves forced to acquiesce for want of means to constrain him. It was not until 1797 that the usurper was finally driven out of the Jalantra country by an armed force sent against him by Mr. Snodgrass, the Resident, under Captains Fletcher and Spencer. Sáno Padsha then took refuge in the Jeypore country, and afterwards in Parla-Kimedi.

Still further south, the Budarsingi Zemindar in revenge for some affront had invaded the Mandasa country and burnt 16 villages in May 1790. The Rajah of Mandasa had retaliated in August by collecting an armed force of 300 or 400 men and sending it to surprize the Budarsingi Zemindar by dawn of day in his fort. An engagement ensued in which several lives were lost on both sides. The Budarsingi Zemindar received a wound in his arm and another in his breast, but made his escape to the neighbouring Máliahs. He appears to have abandoned the cultivation of his Zemindari lands, and for three years continued to resort to predatory excursions for subsistence.

About the same time the Surangi Zemindar was imprisoned in the fort at Ganjam for assisting Sáno Deo and neglecting to pay up his arrears, whilst the efforts of Sáno Deo himself to plunder and disturb the country were either alternately assisted or connived at by nearly every Zemindar in the district.

It was therefore no wonder that, with all the troubles of famine and rebellion prevailing from one end of the district to the other, Mr. Henry Crawford, the Resident, announced to Government that he was unable to reduce the refractory

Zemindars until "the situation of affairs in the Carnatic will "admit of an addition to our military strength."

For three years a terrible famine desolated the land. The crops had been very scanty in 1789, and on the 7th November Mr. Crawford issued a proclamation suspending all import and transport duties on grain and other edibles in the Company's Havéli lands. The Famine does not seem to have extended much to the north of Ganjam, and at Púri the people lived in the midst of plenty. In the Ichapur and Chicacole countries, however, the people died in thousands. The exportation of grain was forbidden from the sea-ports, and a guard of sepoys was stationed at Kanchili to prevent exportations to the south. Government seem to have done their best to mitigate the horrors of famine, but were powerless to control the evil in an efficient manner. In the Chicacole division, Mr. Keating, the Collector, calculated that an average of 3,000 poor people had daily subsisted on the Company's bounty for a period of two years. The importation of paddy for the relief of the people was ordered by the Board of Revenue, and we find from the Chicacole records that in June 1792, 10,519 bags of rice were dispatched from Calingapatam to Mr. Snodgrass, the Resident at Ganjam. Large quantities of rice also appear to have been imported from Cuttack viâ the Chilka lake, of which the utility has always been conspicuous in times of famine.

The country was plunged in a state of misery and desolation truly deplorable. Whole tracts were depopulated, and people were not forthcoming to cultivate the lands. The paddy ordered by Government preserved the lives of many, but we have no accounts to tell us of the thousands that died nor of the amount of loss inflicted upon the district by the falling off in its revenues. Mr. Warricker, Assistant Collector, writes on the 15th January 1792 to Mr. Keating, the Collector at Chicacole "I was an eye-witness of the melancholy effects "of famine. About six persons were gathered round a fire "and were feeding upon the carcase of a dog killed on suspicion "of its being mad." Mr. Warricker mentions that the village of Kodur, which had been populous and paid 3,000 Rupees yearly to Government, did not in 1791 contain more than 20 souls, and those feeble and emaciated from famine. The cattle died for want of sufficient pasturage, and in 1792 even the tanks had long since dried up. The duration of the famine was increased by the failure of the dry crop in 1792, and the floods that happened in that year did further damage. The famine seems to have been at its worst about Chicacole, and the Zemindaris of Jalantra, Mandasa, &c., around the foot of Mahendragiri, seem especially to have suffered. Jalantra is described as depopulated, but doubtless the disturbances caused by Sáno Padsha had aggravated the sufferings of the people, besides driving a great many of them away.

Chicacole Records, August 1791.

In 1791 Mr. Thomas Snodgrass who had been connected with the district as early as 1780 as Paymaster, became Resident and continued in office until 1793, Mr. Webb managing the Havéli lands. During Mr. Snodgrass' tenure of office as Resident, he seems to have exerted himself with considerable energy and zeal, not only in reducing the refractory Zemindars but in battling with the horrors of famine. His name is still familiar in the district as the builder of the grand-looking old house at Rambha on the borders of the Chilka lake, which, there is reason to suppose, was constructed as a famine work about 1792. No records exist, however, for Mr. Snodgrass' tenure of office, and there is consequently no information forthcoming as to the manner in which he employed the labour of the people upon the famine works which he promoted upon so large a scale. Government appear to have found fault with him for the lavish way in which he spent the public money in relieving the distresses of the people, for in spite of his talents, Mr. Snodgrass did not exercise very much control over expenditure.

During Mr. Snodgrass' absence at the Presidency in 1793 to take the Revenue oath prescribed by Act of Parliament, the Renter of the Kallikót Zemindari and the sureties of some of the Zemindars stated that they had paid various sums into the hands of Gopaul Kishnamma, the Resident's dubash, for which no receipts or credit had been given. The Acting Resident, Mr. Gordon, and the Havéli Collector, Mr. Webb, were accordingly directed to enquire into these charges, and pending the result of the investigation, Mr. Snodgrass was told to remain at the Presidency. The result of the enquiry was unfavourable, and Government considered Mr. Snodgrass' conduct very reprehensible in suffering Gopaul Kishnamma to exercise an improper degree of power in the Ganjam district, where he appears to have acted in the double capacity of Public Interpreter and Private Dubash to the Resident. Gopaul Kishnamma was found guilty of embezzling public money, and was ordered to refund 17,150 Rupees. As he failed to make full payment of this sum as ordered, he was confined at Ganjam, but finally disgorged the whole amount and was released.

In 1794 the office of Resident and Chief at all the settlements along the coast was abolished, the office of Collector was established, and Mr. Walter Balfour was appointed Collector at Ganjam. Unfortunately the general Reports of the Board of Revenue (printed) do not supply the details of administration between 1793 and 1800, and the District records of these eight years are said to have been destroyed by Mr. Brown who relieved Mr. Snodgrass in 1800.* The disturbances caused by Sáno Padsha, the usurper of Jalantra, and by the quarrels

* According to a statement signed by Mr. Spottiswoode, the Collector, Mr. Brown burnt some of the records and the white-ants destroyed others. What Mr. Brown's object was in burning the records is unknown. His conduct in this respect is all the more extraordinary, when it is remembered that he was sent up to Ganjam by Government to investigate the charges made against Mr. Snodgrass, whom he succeeded in the district as Collector. There is a story current in Ganjam that Mr. Snodgrass not only dropped his accounts into the Chilka lake in order that they might not be a testimony against him, but that he threatened Mr. Brown's life if he ventured to come to Rambha where Mr. Snodgrass usually resided. I can find nothing in the Records, however, to substantiate either of these stories.

of the district Zemindars, still continued to distract the country and impoverish the revenues, whilst bodies of banditti headed by Sáno Deo and Moja Deo, burnt and plundered the villages both in the Havéli and in the Zemindari lands.

In 1797 Mr. Snodgrass returned to the district as Collector, and made his administration notorious by the wholesale corruption which he allowed to prevail in every department of Government. He appears to have abandoned all control over the affairs of the district, and to have given up his extensive powers to his dubash, Jagannatha Ráo, whilst he himself resided at Rambha, ten miles away from his Cutcherry.

Defalcations of the revenue, coupled with fraud and wholesale oppression, were the speedy results of such an administration. The Zemindars of the district were disgusted with the treatment that they experienced at the hands of the dubash, and the country was brought to the brink of ruin by the wholesale corruption that prevailed. Jagannatha Ráo the dubash, kept up a small Court of his own at his dwelling at Ganjam, where Zemindars and their Patros as well as Renters and Peshkars appealed and sought for audience.

Mr. Wm. Brown's Report, dated 15th March 1802, G. R.

To quote Mr. Brown's own words: "He had in his train "sepoys, peons, and a multiplicity of attendants, and as an in-"dispensible addition to the character, he supported the capti-"vating allurements of a despotic dancing woman to encourage "and promote intrigue, dissipation, and extravagance." The public departments of the district from top to bottom speedily became all equally corrupt, and every species of extortion and oppression was practised for the purpose of extorting money. Mr. Snodgrass himself neglected all means of obtaining authentic information, and left the entire conduct of affairs to the native servants of his Cutcherry with the natural consequence of a widespread dishonesty. This state of affairs apppears to have lasted from the 3rd March 1797, until August 1800, but the falling off of Revenue in Ganjam had, in the meanwhile, become so great that Mr. Snodgrass was removed from office, and an investigation ordered by Government.

Mr. Snodgrass gave the following reasons for the very great deficiency of the public Revenue : the failure of the rains and consequent loss and reduction of crops, the low price of grain, the scarcity of specie, the disaffection of the Zemindars, the disturbances raised by the Khonds, and the want of sufficient military force in the district. Whereupon the Board of Revenue after criticising Mr. Snodgrass' different reports, observe that, "a more extraordinary statement in extenuation of a gross defalcation of Revenue (has) we believe never before been submitted by a Collector."

Mr. William Brown was appointed to succeed Mr. Snodgrass, but upon arriving in the District in August 1800, it was some time before Mr. Snodgrass could be prevailed upon to deliver over charge to him. At length on the 31st August Mr. Snodgrass gave over charge of the district to Mr. Brown, who found an Augean stable to clean out at the Cutcherry, and the Zemindars of the district upon the eve of revolt.

The whole administration of the province required revision; and Mr. Brown in one of his sesquipedalian and very ungrammatical and unintelligible periods, states that he found the province "once a most flourishing and delightful tract of country" reduced to "nearly the last ebb of a depopulated and frightful waste capable of recovering, however, from the brink of utter dilapidation and ruin, and likely by a wise and honorable system of Government to rise superior to its apparent destiny and yield in importance and splendour to no province." Pending further investigation, Mr. Brown detained Jaganatha Ráo in prison, and Government appear to have intended at first to prosecute both Mr. Snodgrass and his dubash in the Courts of Adawlut, but as no Courts had yet been established in Ganjam, the intention was apparently abandoned. The extent of Jaganatha Ráo's embezzlements was therefore never exactly ascertained. Some idea of them may, however, be gathered from Mr. Brown's subsequent reports and from the fact that, in Mohiri alone the amount unaccounted for was upwards of 68,000 Rupees, whilst in the Khandams of Aska, Pubbakonda, Mantreddi, Tirustanam, Mansurkota, and Baruva they were probably not far short of 1,00,000 Rupees (vide Mr. Brown's reports on the above Purgannahs for the year 1801). The disturbed state of the country and the rebellion of the Goomsur Rajah occupied too much of Mr. Brown's time, during his comparatively short stay in the country, to allow of his bringing a public prosecution to a successful issue.

Mr. Brown meanwhile set to work with energy to re-assure the minds of the inhabitants, and to take the best steps he could to preserve the peace of the country and secure its Revenues. In his report, dated the 15th March 1802, he details at considerable length all the occurrences that had taken place since his arrival in the district in August 1800. Mr. Brown's investigations do not, however, appear to have given entire satisfaction, as the Board writes to his successor in May 1803, "No information has been derived from the "examination of Mr. Brown's report which could reward the "labour imposed on Government or the Board by its prolixity." It must be admitted that the reproof is not unmerited. The Board of Revenue stated with reference to the charges made against Mr. Snodgrass that "adverting to the general "character of Mr. Snodgrass' talents and to the proofs of "ability which his writings contained," they do not consider themselves at liberty to attribute "the heavy defalcation of "Revenue in Ganjam to the ignorance or to the imbecility of "the Collector." They thought it their duty therefore to record that there was convincing proof that "that failure was derived "from the deepest source of corruption." Mr. Snodgrass was dismissed from the service, but the charges of corruption brought against him were never verified, although there is not the slightest doubt that his neglect of his duties was grossly culpable. The enquiry against Jagannatha Ráo dragged on for many years. Mr. Brown upon quitting Ganjam left with his successor a sealed packet which was said to contain the most material documents relating to the conduct of Jagannatha Ráo, but when opened by the Collector the very documents, which were most likely to afford satisfactory proof of Jagannatha Ráo's guilt, were deficient. After undergoing an imprisonment of nearly seven years, Jagannatha Ráo was at last released by an order of the Foujdári Adawlut.

A general revolt of the Zemindars was one of the consequences of Mr. Snodgrass' mal-administration of Ganjam. Strikara Bhanj, the Zemindar of Goomsur, was the first to take up arms against the Company. As early as May 1799 he had been joined by Sáno Pádsha, the Pretender to Jalantra, and by Parla-Kimedi Jagannath Deo, both of whom had been endeavouring to incite him to rebellion. Strikara Bhanj had succeeded his father Lachmana Bhanj in 1788, but disgusted at the situation in which he found himself with his country in the hands of the money-lenders who had made themselves securities for the Revenue, he resigned his Zemindari and went on a pilgrimage. His son, Dhanunjaya Bhanj, meanwhile held the Zemindari until 1795 when his father returned and expelled him from the country. From 1797 to 1800, little or nothing had been paid into the Treasury, and the Zemindari continued like the rest of the district in a state of the utmost disorder and confusion. Strikara Bhanj himself absconded and declared that the course he had taken was forced upon him by the ill treatment and frauds of the Agents employed by the Collector, Mr. Snodgrass. Mr. Brown, after his arrival in the district, at first entertained hopes of reclaiming Strikara Bhanj to obedience, but these expectations proved fallacious.

Mr. Russell's Report, dated 12th August 1836.

Taking advantage of the confusion of affairs that prevailed after Mr. Brown's arrival in the district, Jagannath Deo of Pratápagiri and Moni Deo of Vijayanagar, both escaped from custody at Ganjam, and were soon at the head of their respective followers.

Encouraged by the attitude of the Goomsur Rajah, a combination of the District Zemindars was the result. Aska and Berhampore were threatened on the one side by the force of Moni Deo, and on the other by nearly the whole body of Goomsur Paiks. To prevent the junction of these two bodies, the troops under Lieutenant-Colonel Smith made a rapid march at night time, and appeared most opportunely before Sergada at day-break. Moni Deo's men had been joined by the Zemindar of Sergada and his adherents, and were in full march for Goomsur, when a lucky shot from a six-pounder cut off the Zemindar of Sergada's head, and the enemy, startled by the occurrence, at once took to flight. This stroke of luck so terrified the Dhárákót and other rebel Zemindars that they made no further attempts to join the Goomsur Rajah in his rebellion. Jagannath Deo, the Ex-Zemindar of Parla-Kimedi, had meanwhile fled from the south, and joined Strikara Bhanj, whom it therefore became necessary to reduce by force.

Colonel Marly, a Bengal Officer, was appointed to command the troops in the district, and reached Ganjam on the 2nd May 1801 with two battalions of the 6th Regiment B. N. I. At Ganjam this force was joined by the 1st battalion, 10th Regiment M. N. I., from Chicacole, and a detachment of artillery. The troops at once marched into Goomsur and arrived at Gogu on the morning of the 9th May, when proclamations were issued declaring Strikara Bhanj a rebel, and offering a reward of 10,000 Rupees for his apprehension. The Zemindar's adherents collected in force at Kallida, and on the 14th May 1801, the troops under Colonel Marly's command* attacked a very strong stockade there. The rebels were driven off in every direction, and the stockade taken by the troops, six of whom were wounded. On the road to Durgaprasád the troops were assailed by the enemy with

1801. Mr. Russell's Report, dated 12th August 1836.

their fire at every point favourable to an attack, and as the march lay through jungles, the enemy could always make good their retreat. Three men were killed and five wounded on this march which lasted for two days. On the 23rd May the barriers and stockade at Durgaprasád were carried after some resistance, and the enemy fled to the hills which surrounded the place, from whence they kept up an annoying fire. Their better knowledge of the country enabled them at the same time to elude pursuit. Having established posts at such places as appeared best calculated for the protection of the country, Lieutenant-Colonel Marly returned to Aska in June 1801 with the rest of his force, and published the proclamation of Government formally deposing Strikara Bhanj, and appointing his son, Dhanunjaya Bhanj, Zemindar, in his stead. The country was however not yet reduced. Other minor engagements with the troops followed, and in the course of these, the fort at Kalláda was twice retaken by the rebel party before being finally occupied by the Company's force. The main body of the forces eventually returned to Ganjam, and Strikara Bhanj meanwhile continued at large in spite of the reward offered for his apprehension. In December 1801, Colonel Marly returned with his detachment to Bengal. Mr. Brown made a vain attempt to seize Strikara Bhanj, and at length induced him to acquiesce in the accession of his son by allotting for his support certain Mutáhs in the Zemindari. His presence, however, served to keep the country unsettled and disturbed, and both Strikara Bhanj and his son Dhanunjaya Bhanj were destined to give a great deal more trouble to the Company before it had done with them.

Although the troops employed had only partly reduced Goomsur, their presence in the field was an opportunity not to be lost for overrunning the Zemindaris of Pratápagiri and Vijayanagar, thereby producing an impression upon a part of the country which had been, for the past ten years or more, in a most distracted condition.

Moni Deo was deposed and his son, Balabhadra Deo, appointed Zemindar of Vijayanagar in his stead, whilst the Pratápagiri country was made over to Chandra Moni Deo, the son of Jagannath Deo. The latter had been charged with murdering his Pátro, and was not considered fit to retain his Zemindari, and Moni Deo's contumacious spirit was only too well known. Both Moni Deo and Jagannath Deo became declared outlaws, but favoured by their respective sons and the wild nature of the country, they contrived for a long time to elude recapture. The ancient feud however between the two families was not suffered to die out, and the sons naturally favored their father's pretensions.

In 1804 Moni Deo quietly returned to his Zemindari upon the death of his son, Balabhadra Deo, and Chandramoni Deo came to terms with Moni Deo to make common cause against the Company. An expedition was sent against them under Colonel Durand, but appears to have been withdrawn, and proved a failure chiefly owing to the imbecility of the then Collector. In 1805 Government offered a reward of Rs. 5,000 each for Moni Deo of Vijayanagar, and Jagannath Deo of Pratápagiri. The latter was finally captured in August of the same year, and the following extract explains how his capture was effected :—"On the "12th instant, Sirdar Lachminarasu (of whose good conduct "I have before had occasion to speak in several instances "with two Jamadars and 200 peons made a forced march "of 12 coss through a most dreadful jungle and came upon "the rebel (Jagannath Deo of Pratápagiri) at day-break at the "village of Becroocotah on the borders of the Bodogoda "Zemindari. The rebel, independent of the peons he had "with him, had stationed a small party on the entrance "of the village with direction to fire immediately on seeing "the Police Peons. By this signal the rebel was apprized "of the approach of the Sirdar's party which, however, had "been divided into three divisions to enter the village at

G. R., 1805.

"three different points. At once the rebel being prepared by "the signal, had got his people collected, and they received "our peons with a heavy fire of matchlocks which, I am sorry "to say, killed one or two men and wounded the Sirdar and "five or six more. Our peons were not backward in return-"ing the fire, and although the peons of the rebel separated "after their own discharge to aid his *return, yet they did not "effect it so securely." The Sirdar was again wounded, but the rebel was captured and a sword presented to the Sirdar for his meritorious conduct.

In 1803 the Sibbundy corps which consisted of 5 companies, each 175 strong, was ordered to be disbanded in consequence of mutinous conduct at Baruva where they were then stationed. To preserve the peace of the country, the Collector raised a corps of 500 peons which took the place of the Sibbundy corps.

In 1804 the Courts of Circuit were abolished and stationary Courts introduced in their stead, Mr. Cherry exchanging the office of Collector for that of Magistrate and Judge. He was succeeded as Collector by Mr. F. A. Robson who held office until September 1806. Owing to the introduction of the salt monopoly in 1805, an alarming scarcity of salt prevailed at Ganjam and throughout the district. Mr. Cherry, however, exerted himself in his usually energetic manner, and salt was largely imported from Cuttack to meet the more pressing wants of the people.

It is now necessary to turn to the history of the Chicacole division between 1767 and 1802, in which year it was incorporated in the Ganjam District. Previous to this date, it had formed the 3rd division of the Vizagapatam District, and included Kasimkota, now attached to Vizagapatam. The limits of the 3rd division extended from Chinna Pantulu Daba, 20 miles south of Chicacole, to Kásibugga, 50 miles north of it. Upon the acquisition of the Northern Circars, the district was rented out to Sitarám Ráz, the brother of Viziarám Ráz, Rajah

* (?) Escape.

of Vizianagram, for a period of 10 years until 1777. In 1777 the rent of the country to Sitarám Ráz appears to have been renewed for a further period of ten years, which expired in 1787. Sitarám Ráz's management of the country was most oppressive, and seems to have been highly detrimental to the Company's interests. The country was rack-rented in a wholesale manner, and the renters took what share of the produce they pleased, leaving the remainder to the ryot. Sitarám Ráz dispossessed the Brahmins of their charity lands or Agraharams, and, in recompense, bestowed upon them Havéli villages. The manufacturers and artizans of the country emigrated in large numbers and went to other places where they were less oppressed. At the expiration of Sitarám Ráz's lease, Mr. Henry Crawford was appointed in 1787 the first Collector of the Chicacole Division subject to the authority of the Chief and Council at Vizagapatam. Mr. Crawford estimated the probable revenue of the country at four lakhs, including the two large Zemindaris of Parla-Kimedi and Tekkali. The alienations made by Sitarám Ráz had been considerable, so that all lands not uninterruptedly enjoyed for twenty years were ordered to be resumed. As in Ganjam, so in Chicacole, the land Customs were numerous and burdensome, preventing the produce of the country being sent from those parts where it was plentiful to others where it was scarce.

Chicacole Records, 1787.

Upon Mr. Crawford proceeding to Ganjam as Resident in 1790, Mr. Michael Keating succeeded him. The Havéli lands of Chicacole were rented out to one Ramavadhanulu in 1791, but the Renter fell in arrears, and the Company seized his ships and other property at Calingapatam in satisfaction of their demands. In 1794 the Chief and Council at Vizagapatam were abolished, and Mr. Keating was directed to correspond direct with the Board of Revenue. Mulberry, cocoanut and opuntia plantations, and cochineal seem to have engaged the Company's commercial attention, but the success of these ventures does not appear to have been great. In 1797 Mr. Keating got into trouble, and was charged with embezzling a sum of 1,19,380 Rupees out of 1,73,414 Rupees allotted for the repairs of the 898 tanks which had been breached or damaged by the monsoon of 1795. Captain (Lieutenant) Pitman was, at the same time, charged with collusion, and Mr. Keating was removed, and made way for Mr. Andrew Scott in 1797. The country during the administration of Messrs. Crawford, Keating, and Scott continued in a more or less disturbed state. Gajapati Deo, the Zemindar of Parla-Kimedi, whom the English had put in as Zemindar upon the defeat of his father Náráyana Deo in 1768, was declared to have forfeited his Zemindari in 1797 for repeated breaches of his engagements, and for disobeying the orders of the Collector at Chicacole. The management of this extensive Zemindari was accordingly placed under the Collector, and Durgá Ráz, a relation of the Kimedi family, was appointed Manager in 1799.

In 1797 the Zemindar of Tekkali died, the last of a long and noble race, the Kadamba 'Vamsam' or family, and his estate which had been for 375 years in the possession of the same family, was converted into Havéli or Government land and managed by the Company.

Vide C. R. for January 1798.

During the years 1799 and 1800, disturbances in Kimedi took place concurrently with those in Goomsur, in consequence of which both the Chicacole and Tekkali Havélies suffered material injury. The Zemindar, Gajapati Deo, and his son had been sent to Masulipatam, but this step did not have the effect of quieting the insurgents who, besides laying waste the country, attacked the detachments posted at Varanasi and Kimedi. The former was compelled by the peons of the Doratanams to retreat out of the Zemindari, and the latter to capitulate on condition of being allowed to retire with their arms. After these successes the insurgents proceeded to take possession of the Tekkali Havéli, and to burn and plunder the villages at will. Jagannath Deo, the brother of Gajapati Deo, for whom he had been removed from the Zemindari in 1780, had, in the meanwhile, joined the insurgents who numbered a body 5,000 strong. 8 companies of Native Infantry, a detachment of Cavalry, and a brigade of six-pounders were sent against the insurgents. After some delay the rebels were finally reduced by Colonel Vigors with the assistance and advice of Durgá Ráz. During the course of the operations, Lieutenant Youngson, a British officer, was taken prisoner and carried off into the Máliahs. His release was finally effected.

As a reward for the services rendered by him, Durgá Ráz was appointed Manager, and for 13 years his administration of the country was most successful. In 1802 Gajapati Deo died, and his son, Purushottama Náráyana Deo, succeeded him. Upon the death of the latter in 1805, the Parla-Kimedi estate was managed by Durgá Ráz, subject to the Court of Wards, as Purushottama Nárayana Deo's son was only 12 months old when his father died. Jagannath Deo who had joined the Goomsur Rajah in his rebellion, and for whose capture Government offered a reward of Rs. 10,000, was seized and delivered up by the Zemindar of Surada in 1804, and sent as a prisoner to Masulipatam.

Mr. Cherry was the last Collector to succeed to the management of the Chicacole country in 1800, and in 1802 when Chicacole was incorporated with Ganjam, Mr. Cherry became the first Collector of the united Province.

With regard to the revenues of the Chicacole Division they never seem to have exceeded by much Mr. Crawford's first estimate of 4 lakhs. The jama or rent paid by Gajapati Náráyana Deo for Parla-Kimedi was 86,000 Rupees, whilst for Tekkali, the last Zemindar, Ram Kistna Jagga Deo, had paid 24,472 Rupees yearly. The average gross collections of the Chicacole Havéli lands from Fasli 1202 to 1206 (1792-1796) were 2,94,760 Rupees, making a grand total of 4,05,232 Rupees.

CHAPTER VII.

THE GANJAM DISTRICT.

MR. CHERRY, COLLECTOR—IMPORTANT CHANGES IN MANAGEMENT—PERMANENT SETTLEMENT—PETTY DISPUTES BETWEEN ZEMINDARS—MOHIRI ZEMINDARI ATTACHED FOR ARREARS—PART OF GOOMSUR ATTACHED—MOHIRI SOLD—PARLA-KIMEDI PLACED UNDER COURT OF WARDS—DISTURBANCES IN PARLA-KIMEDI—DURGA RAZ HANGED—FEVER AT GANJAM AND ITS FATAL EFFECTS—REMOVAL OF TROOPS TO BERHAMPORE—IRRUPTION OF PINDARIES—MR. CAZALET APPOINTED COLLECTOR AND MAGISTRATE—GOOMSUR DECLARED FORFEITED AND DHANUNJAYA BHANJ MADE STATE PRISONER FOR MURDERING HIS MOTHER AND FOR SIMILAR CRUEL ACTS AND TORTURES—STRIKARA BHANJ REINSTATED—DISTURBANCES IN MOHIRI—SARSUNGI MAHARTA, INSURGENT, CAPTURED AND SENT TO GOOTY—MOHIRI ZEMINDARI MADE OVER TO KRISHNA CHANDRA DEO—TWO FACTIONS IN PARLA-KIMEDI—DISTURBANCES IN PARLA-KIMEDI—SIR T. MUNRO—PARLA-KIMEDI ZEMINDARI MADE OVER TO YOUNG RAJAH, BUT TAKEN AGAIN UNDER COURT OF WARDS—INSURRECTION—GOPINADHA PATNAIK AND GODIYAPADHI KRISHNAMA DORA—MR. RUSSELL APPOINTED SPECIAL COMMISSIONER TO REPORT ON CAUSE OF CONTINUAL OUTBREAKS—ARRIVAL OF TROOPS IN KIMEDI — CAMPAIGN—CERTAIN BISSOYIS HANGED — PARLA-KIMEDI IN PEACE—STRIKARA BHANJ GAVE UP GOOMSUR TO HIS SON DHANUNJAYA BHANJ—DHANUNJAYA BHANJ FLED TO MALIAHS AND DIED—MR. RUSSELL AGAIN AS SPECIAL COMMISSIONER—GOOMSUR OVERRUN AND CERTAIN FORTS OCCUPIED BY THE ENGLISH—INSURGENTS FLED INTO THE HILLS—TROOPS PURSUED THEM—KHONDS RESISTED BUT SUBDUED—PEACE—GRANTS TO SIRDARS, PAIKS AND NAIKS CONTINUED—ATAGADA ZEMINDAR REWARDED FOR ASSISTANCE—GOOD EFFECTS OF MR. RUSSELL'S

ARRANGEMENTS—SURADA TRIBUTE REDUCED—SURADA FELL INTO ARREARS AND PURCHASED BY GOOMSUR—DISTURBANCES IN SURADA—GANJAM DISTRICT IN PEACE—PUBLIC WORKS AND OTHER IMPROVEMENTS IN GOOMSUR—SIBBUNDI CORPS FORMED TO CHECK KHONDS—FAMINE—NOMINATION OF GOVERNOR'S AGENT —MERIAH SACRIFICE, ITS SUPPRESSION—MOHIRI ZEMINDARI ATTACHED FOR ARREARS AND BOUGHT IN BY GOVERNMENT—INROADS OF SAVARAS,—FRAUDS IN SALT—ATAGADA ZEMINDARI SOLD FOR ARREARS AND BOUGHT BY KALLIKOT—DISTURBANCES IN ATAGADA SUPPRESSED BY MR. DAVIDSON—KUTTIYA DISTURBANCE AT ORLADONI—CHOKRO BISSOYI, RINGLEADER—SAVARA DISTURBANCE UNDER RADHAKRISHNA DANDASANA—FAMINE IN GANJAM, CUTTACK, PURI AND BALASORE—RELIEF HOUSES—FAMINE ORPHANS—LOSS TO GOVERNMENT BY FAMINE —DEFICIENCY OF IRRIGATION WORKS—RISING OF THE KUTTIYA KHONDS AGAIN—URIYAS MURDERED—POLICE SUPERINTENDENT AND ASSISTANT SUPERINTENDENT SUPPRESSED THE DISTURBANCES.

Mr. Peter Cherry, who succeeded Mr. Brown in 1802, was the first Collector of Ganjam as now constituted. In 1803 the Ganjam District comprised all the territory north of the Langulyá river near Chicacole, and extended from Mofazbandar on the sea coast in the south to Priagi on the Chilka lake in the north. It included four distinct Havélis, and 21 Zemindaris, including the large and important one of Parla-Kimedi, recently added. The disorganized state of the Ganjam district generally may be imagined, however, from the fact that the uncollected balances of Revenue amounted in 1804 to 18,25,651 Rupees, and extended over a period of 10 years, viz., from 1795 to 1804 inclusive.

Mr. Cherry's management of the country was vigorous and praiseworthy. His administration was marked by four important changes. 1*stly.*—The incorporation of the country north of the Langulyá river at Chicacole with the present Ganjam district in 1803. 2*ndly.*—The introduction of the Permanent Settlement. 3*rdly.*—The establishment of Courts of Judicature, and *4thly*.—The sale of the Havéli or Government lands in Ganjam and their formation into Proprietary Estates.

A general spirit of insubordination prevailed amongst the Zemindars of the district. Strikara Bhanj, the rebel Zemindar of Goomsur, had fortified himself in a part of the country, whence it was impracticable to dislodge him, whilst the Zemindars of Pratápagiri and Vijayanagar continued openly disaffected. In spite of these adverse circumstances, the Collector managed by perseverance, and his conciliatory and judicious conduct, to collect a larger Revenue by 1,52,374 Rupees than in the previous Fasli.

Under great disadvantages Mr. Cherry gathered the necessary information for the Permanent Settlement, and successfully effected its introduction into the district. Mr. Cherry wrote in December 1803: "I consider the introduction of the Permanent Settlement as offering the only prospect of permanent peace to this district." It required, however, something more than even a Permanent Settlement to produce peace in Ganjam. The progressive decline of the Revenues had been brought about almost as much by the evil consequences of *temporary expedients* as by petty warfare and famine. It was evident that a fluctuating management and a rack-renting system would not restore the prosperity of the country.

A special Commissioner was appointed to investigate the extent and resources of the district, with the view of arriving at a correct opinion of the tributes that might, at all times, be levied in perpetuity from each Zemindari with safety and a fair prospect of realization. The report to Government on the subject is dated 19th May 1804.

In 1806 disturbances broke out between the Bodogoda Zemindari and the small estate of Katingia which bordered it on the west and served as a barrier against the predatory excursions of the Khonds. The Bodogoda man was in the habit of paying the Sirdar an annual contribution to purchase his forbearance, but alleged that the Sirdar was his servant, an assertion indignantly denied by the latter. On the 11th March 1807, an engagement took place between the Sirdar of Katingia, assisted by the Zemindars of Surada and Gadapore on the one side, and the Zemindar of Bodogoda, assisted by the people of Sergada, on the other. The Zemindar of Bodogoda's son-in-law was killed together with 2 peons whilst 12 others were wounded. To prevent similar disturbances in future, a Sanad was granted to the Sirdar of Katingia by Government.*

In September 1806 Mr. Robert Alexander became Collector and Mr. Samuel Skinner filled the office of Magistrate. In 1807, the Mohiri Zemindari which had been restored to Krushna Periya Máhádevi in 1804 fell into arrears and was placed under attachment. The Goomsur Zemindari still remained in a disturbed state owing to the intrigues of the old Zemindar, Strikara Bhanj, to whom Mr. Brown had made over for his subsistence the Máliah districts of Kukulubá, Galéri, Jaksabádi, Pántso Godo, and Uttoro Godotolo of Goomsur. In 1807-08 Strikara Bhanj got into trouble with the Khonds, and in 1808 Danunjaya Bhanj, his son, had acquired sufficient influence to oblige him to quit the country, to which he did not return until 1815. For many years he wandered about in the garb of a religious mendicant or Bairági, visiting most of the cities and places of pilgrimage in the western provinces of Bengal, and travelling thence to Nagpore and Madras, where he finally procured from the Governor a passport permitting him to return to Goomsur.

In November 1808 Mr. G. F. Travers became Collector, but was shortly afterwards succeeded by Mr. Hugh Spottiswoode in 1809. There was a scarcity of salt for a second time in 1809 owing to continued rain, and to the fact that the quantity of salt manufactured was limited to the probable consumption. The Collector therefore suggested the importation of 300 garces of salt for two successive years, which certainly seem

* General Report of the Revenue Board, dated 10th October 1807.

absurd, if we consider the present unbounded capacity of Ganjam for the production of salt.

The Zemindari estates of Dhárakót, Kalikót, Chikati, and Atagada were in arrears, and part of the Goomsur Zemindari was attached for the same reason.

In 1810 the Mohiri Zemindari was attached for a balance of Rs. 33,169-2-6 and sold by public auction. The last Rajah of Mohiri, Náráyana Deo, had married the sister of the Chikati Zemindar. The Rajah was murdered in 1786 by his own brothers, Sano Deo and Moja Deo, and as he left no heir and the perpetrators of the murder were excluded from the succession, the Zemindari escheated to the Sirkar. At the recommendation however of the Chief and Council at Ganjam, founded on the policy of conciliating the inhabitants of the country, Government re-called the Ráni in the year 1786 from Chikati, where she had sought an asylum after her husband's death, and confirmed her in the possession of the Zemindari by a Sanad in the usual form. The Ráni of Mohiri however became involved in difficulties with her brother-in-law, Moja Deo, the former rebel, who laid claims to Mohiri, and although illegitimate had sued the Ráni in the Civil Court. In 1809 an order was passed by the Court confirming a Rájinámá or agreement, alleged to have been made between Moja Deo and the Ráni, and ordering that the Ráni should hold the Zemindari during her life and that it should afterwards revert to Moja Deo. The Ráni shortly afterwards fell in arrears, and Mohiri was attached and sold.

For a period of about eight years, the district had been comparatively quiet, and since the sale of the Mohiri Zemindari in 1810, the regularity with which the Revenue had been collected was unexampled. In 1814, however, the district again began to assume a tumultuous and threatening appearance, more especially in the south.

The Parla-Kimedi Zemindari still continued under the Court of Wards during the minority of Rája Jagannáth Gajapati

Náráyana Deo. The latter's grandfather, Gajapati Deo, had been dispossessed of the Zemindari by Government for repeated acts of hostility and rebellion, and the estate had been placed under the Collector's management in 1805, on the death of the minor's father, Purushottama Náráyana Deo. Previous to this, at the time of the permanent settlement, the proprietary right to Parla-Kimedi had been declared vested in Gajapati Deo and his heirs, by the usual Sanad-i-Milkeut Istimrár.

The management of Padmanábha Deo, who had succeeded his father, Durga Ráz, as Manager in 1813, became so unpopular with the Bissoyis and Doras of the country as to lead to serious complications. The insurgents, instigated probably by the Gajapati Patta Máhádevi, the widow of the late Zemindar, and by Durga Ráz, the son of Jagannáth Deo, a former Zemindar, began to create disturbances by burning and plundering the villages. Government accordingly made preparations to put down the disturbances by force, and Colonel Fletcher was appointed to command the troops in Ganjam. The Magistrate, Mr. Woodcock, and the Collector, Mr. Spottiswoode, were at the same time directed to proceed to Kimedi to enquire into the complaints made by the Bissoyis against the Manager, Padmanábha Deo.

In an interview that the Collector and Magistrate had with the insurgents, the latter appear to have had some thoughts of seizing their persons, for the Jeringi Bissoyi is said to have suggested that course to the Bissoyi of Gumá, saying, "Are not the golden sparrows flown into our cage, why should we part with our prize till the object we have in view is obtained? Let us then, with one accord, catch them by the feet, and let them be watched with care until this promised answer from the Government arrives." In spite of this suggestive speech however, the interview passed off without disturbance. Pending the negotiations that ensued, the insurgents had committed no further acts of aggression, and the Magistrate was unwilling that the troops should act until he had made a further reference to Government. The apparent tranquillity that ensued, led to the troops not being employed at all. Padmanábha Deo was removed from his post of Manager, and one Kanukurti Narasingarao was appointed in his stead. The lull was, however, only momentary, and disturbances soon broke out again and continued with but little intermission until 1817. The lenity of Government on this occasion was therefore clearly misplaced.

Padmanábha Deo had in the meanwhile retired to his estate at Tekkali, but in October 1816 his intrigues seem to have once more made the Zemindari the scene of rebellion. At the beginning of 1817 one Gudipati Lachanna commenced the disturbances by burning Nagarikatakam and five other villages in the Karakavalasa estate. Mr. Spottiswoode promptly entered the Zemindari with four companies of sepoys from Vizianagrum, and found the passes stockaded, but the presence of the troops appears to have temporarily prevented further outrages. No military operations were, however, attempted, and the troops were subsequently withdrawn, but not before Durga Ráz, the grandson of a former Zemindar, who was directly concerned in the disturbances, had been caught and hanged. A solitary instance of well-timed severity was not, however, in itself sufficient to quell the rebellious spirit of the Bissoyis, Doras, and Paiks of Parla-Kimedi.

Fever at Ganjam.

In August 1815, a most dreadful epidemic fever broke out in Ganjam, which had hitherto been the chief town of the district. The public buildings of the station, as well as the houses and gardens of the Civilians are described as having been upon a scale of grandeur surpassing almost every other station in the Madras Presidency.* Under the influence of the malignant disease which attacked the inhabitants, Ganjam was reduced in a very short time from a populous town of 30,000 souls to one of

* Statements such as these are difficult to realize at the present day, when there scarcely remains a single habitable house in the station.

less than 6,000. From 20 to 30 deaths occurred daily, and a panic seized upon the inhabitants who fled from the fever-stricken place in large numbers. All the principal merchants in the place died, and many Europeans. The deaths in the Collector's and Magistrate's Cutcherries were so numerous that public business was at a stand-still.

In November 1815 the troops were removed to Berhampore, whilst the Collector transferred his treasury first to Mansúrkota, and afterwards to Berhampore as being more central. With the exception of Chicacole, which was entirely free from it, the fever seems to have overrun the whole district. About Sonnapur the people are described as being so weak from its effects, as scarcely to be able to reap the standing crops in their fields. The causes of the outbreak do not appear to have been clearly traced in spite of the enquiries made. Mr. Woodcock, the Magistrate, was of opinion that the fever was due to the low situation of Ganjam, and to the prevalence of standing water in the fields around. The filthy state of the town seems to have had a good deal to do with it, as Ganjam had previously been as healthy as any town in India. The prevalence of fever was, however, noticed by Mr. Cherry as far back as 1803. Upon the present occasion the fever proved fatal to between 20,000 and 30,000 people and continued throughout the district for more than three years.

The Pindaries were an off-shoot of the Mahratta armies, who had taken to robbing and plundering the country, when their Chiefs could no longer afford to pay them. Consequent upon the disturbances in Parla-Kimedi, and, there is reason to suppose, instigated by Padmanábha Deo, the ex-Manager, the Pindaries made an irruption into the Ganjam District in December 1816. Their strength seems to have been between 4,000 and 5,000 men, and they were well mounted, although but ill armed. They entered the district through the Jeypore country, and proceeded northwards burning and plundering as they went. The Ichapur and Mansurkota Parganás seem especially to have suffered from their ravages, and as they spread over the country in small detached bodies, it was difficult to account for their movements. The troops at Berhampore prevented their molesting that town, and near Boirani a body of Pindaries, 1,000 strong, were surprised by Lieutenant Borthwick and a small force, and completely routed. Before leaving the district, however, for the northwards, they succeeded in looting Ganjam under the very nose of the Commercial Resident. The destination of the Pindaries was supposed to be the rich temple of Púri, but before reaching that place, they appear to have turned off to the west and disappeared, no more to return.

In 1816, the Collector was invested with Magisterial powers, and the separate office of Magistrate was abolished. In 1817, Mr. Spottiswoode left the district upon Sick Certificate, having been for nearly 2½ years in tents, constantly moving about.

Mr. Spottiswoode was succeeded by Mr. Peter Reade Cazalet on the 25th July 1817. The country was now in a most distracted state. There were disturbances prevailing in Goomsur and Mohiri, and fresh troubles were momentarily expected to occur in Parla-Kimedi. The loss of Revenue that resulted from this state of things was so serious, that Government resolved on the 20th October 1818 to depute Mr. Thackeray as a Special Commissioner to investigate the causes of the disturbances existing in Ganjam. After furnishing three interesting reports upon the state of the country, respectively dated the 8th February, 15th February, and 30th March 1819, Mr. Thackeray returned to his permanent appointment of Collector of Bellary.

Goomsur, 1814.

In 1814, Dhanunjaya Bhanj, Rája of Goomsur, was openly accused of murdering his own mother by his father Strikara Bhanj. Other atrocities being also alleged against him, summonses were issued to the witnesses by the Magistrate Mr. Woodcock, but the Rája refused to allow them to be served. As he still continued to resist the processes of the Criminal Court, his Zemindari was declared to be forfeited to Government by a proclamation dated the 21st May 1815. The Zemindar showing no signs of yielding obedience, the troops, under Colonel Fletcher, were marched from Aska into Goomsur, and took possession of the fort at Kallâda without opposition on the 20th May. In an attempt that the troops made to capture the Zemindar, they accomplished a forced march of 19 hours, and only failed through the extreme fatigue which they had endured. Dhanunjaya Bhanj, however, shortly afterwards gave himself up to the Collector, and the troops returned into Cantonment in June 1815, after having had the satisfaction of liberating upwards of a hundred miserable prisoners, a great many of them in irons, who had been illegally kept in confinement by the Zemindar at his own sweet pleasure.

After a long and exhaustive enquiry,* Dhanunjaya Bhanj was committed to take his trial before the Court of Circuit by Mr. Travers, the Magistrate. The evidence was, however, deemed insufficient on the ground that the witnesses against him were "either persons who had been maltreated by him, or the relations of such persons." He was therefore acquitted, and sent to Chingleput as a State prisoner. There can be but little doubt, however, that Dhanunjaya Bhanj was guilty of the most atrocious and inhuman crimes in spite of his acquittal by the Court of Circuit for the extraordinary reason given above. Amongst other outrages he was charged with murdering his mother and his own son, besides three out of four of his wives. Blue-beard himself could scarcely have held a candle to him. His father, Strikara Bhanj, was one of his chief accusers.† Colonel Fletcher, who commanded the troops

* Letter dated 18th August 1815, from Magistrate to Chief Secretary to Government, with Enclosures.

† Colonel Fletcher, the Commanding Officer, was subsequently tried by Court Martial for plundering the Zemindar's property, the Government remarking that under any circumstances the property of the Zemindar could not have been claimed as prize, but should have been preserved inviolably by the captors with a view to its regular confiscation, or as the case might be.

against him, calls him "that tyrannous monster, the bare recital of whose fiendish acts makes humanity shudder." In the gloomy fort at Kalláda he appears to have been in the habit of immuring prisoners who had excited his vengeance, and unfortunate women, the victims of his lust, and starving them to death by slow degrees. Some he confined in stocks, whilst he bent the hands of others with heavy stones, or tied them to stakes, in the sun, and left them to a lingering death.

In one well alone no less than 18 skulls were found upon its being searched by the Magistrate, Mr. Travers. The troops, upon occupying the fortress, also found ample evidence of the tortures that had been practised, and their suspicions were afterwards confirmed by the testimony of the numerous prisoners whom they subsequently released, when they so nearly captured the Zemindar in his flight. And yet this monster in human form was not only acquitted, but was actually afterwards reinstated as Rája of Goomsur in 1832.

In 1818, Strikara Bhanj, ex-Zemindar of Goomsur, who had been confined under a Military guard ever since 1815, escaped from Berhampore and returned to Goomsur, where he was soon at the head of a party, and virtually recovered possession of his Zemindari. Two persons named Dora Bissoyi and Báhu Bolendro, both of them afterwards noted rebels, obtained possession of the country, and for two years they succeeded in passing off a female child upon the authorities, (if there were any) as Balabhadra Deo, the son of Dhanunjaya Bhanj, who was generally believed to have been murdered by his own father. Strikara Bhanj upon escaping from confinement, however, got possession of the child, and sent it in to the Collector, and for 14 years after this he seems to have managed the country fairly, and paid his tribute of 75,000 Rupees a year with regularity. Upon Mr. Thackeray visiting the Ganjam district in the following year (1819) Strikara Bhanj was formally reinstated in the Zemindari upon the 3rd May 1819.

Thus after having been declared a rebel in 1801, having

wandered as a Bairagi since 1808, and having been a prisoner since 1815, Strikara Bhanj found himself once more in possession of the country of his ancestors. A pension of 8,000 Rupees was at the same time granted to Dhanunjaya Bhanj out of the Revenues of the Zemindari, which he continued to draw at Chingleput.

Mohiri, 1880.

The management of the Mohiri estate which had been secured in 1810 by Bandam Chalamaya, the Cutcherry Shroff,* was in the meanwhile most unsatisfactory. With the permission of Government, Mr. Spottiswoode had undertaken the management of the taluq on the 14th November 1816 at the request of the Bandam family. The Collector received a commission of 1½ per cent. for managing the taluq, and thus appears to have become the servant of his own shroff. Moja Deo was still alive, living at Chicacole, and the taluq peons had a grievance upon being dispossessed of their Inam lands. A body of peons, headed by one Sarsungi Maharta, formed a retreat at Sirhoot in the Mohiri hills not far from Berhampore, and betook themselves to a course of outrageous plunder. On the 8th March 1817, Maharta entered the town of Berhampore by night with his adherents, and burnt and plundered nearly the whole of it, threatening to return on the following night to complete the work of destruction. Efforts were made to capture him, but in vain. The Bandam family was unpopular, and Maharta professed the cause of the ancient Zemindari.

Disturbances continued in Mohiri throughout the whole of 1818. Troops were stationed at Ichapur and Berhampore to protect the country and peons and rangers were employed to guard the villages from Maharta's ravages. The whole province appears, however, to have aided and abetted the insurgents to the full extent of their power. The Police of the district consisted of 3 regular corps of Infantry, a corps of Hill Rangers under Captain Jobson, whilst grants of

* Nominally bought by Bhagavan Mahanti, a merchant of Mantreddi, for 38,000 Rupees.

money were allowed for secret service, and yet with all this not a native could sleep in his bed in safety. Maharta still continued at large in spite of a reward of 10,000 Rupees offered for his capture, and people were mutilated, murdered and robbed, or carried up into the hills, where they were kept until they paid ransom. In 1818 an attempt seems to have been made to seize or drive Maharta from the Mohiri hills, but the expedition ended disastrously. Three hundred men and seven officers including Captain Jobson and Mr. Mason, the Assistant Collector, died either from fever or exposure on service. Maharta was eventually captured, but instead of being hanged as a rebel, he was sent to Gooty as a State prisoner. Sirhoot, the post on the Mohiri hills that he had so long made his stronghold, appears to have been occupied by Sibbandi peons under the orders of the Collector. In 1830, however, Lakshmana Bissoyi, Maharta's nephew, surprised the post in company with 400 insurgents, intending to procure Maharta's release. He appears to have come from Goomsur together with the insurgents who accompanied him, and was subsequently given up in 1835 by Dhanunjaya Bhanj, and transported for life. Like his uncle, however, he burnt and plundered Government villages in the interim, although not to the same extent.

The Mohiri Zemindari was finally repurchased from the Bandam family by Government on the 18th October 1820 for 35,000 Rupees, and made over to Krushna Chandra Deo, the reputed son of Moja Deo, on the 17th July 1821. Pending the majority of the young Zemindar, the estate was managed by Mr. Cazalet under the Court of Wards. The former Ráni of Mohiri, Krushna Periya Máhádevi, received a pension for herself and her relations varying in amount between 9,000 and 12,000 Rupees yearly, and as late as 1833 appears to have made a final appeal to Government to be reinstated in the Zemindari.

Besides enquiring into the affairs of Mohiri and Goomsur in the north, Mr. Thackeray's attention was directed to those

23

of Parla-Kimedi. The Raja was still a minor. There were eleven Hill Bissoyis, each with a small fort, who were supposed to act as the police of the country, and prevent the Savaras or Hill people from breaking into the country and plundering it. To aid these Bissoyis and attached to them, there were a number of peons, and both Bissoyis and peons were paid by grants of land. There were besides some hundreds of turbulent town peons. The Swaji Máhádevi or young Rája's grandmother, and the Gajapati Máhádevi, the widow of the rebel Zemindar Gajapati Deo, were rivals for power in the country. Each Ráni had a party amongst the Bissoyis and peons. The country itself was under the Collector's management, but Subba Rao, the Government Manager, had in 1818 imprudently mixed himself up with the party of the Swaji Máhádevi against the Patta Máhádevi, and the Guma Bissoyi who supported her. The Gajapati Máhádevi, who was possessed of considerable influence in the *Zemindari*, disgusted at the slights to which she was exposed from the Manager's party, quitted the Zemindari in 1818, and proceeded to Chicacole. One disturbance now commenced to follow another.

The Bissoyis of the country were in some measure considered as holding their lands or Mokhasas at the will of the Rája. In the course of the quarrels and intrigues that had taken place between the two opposite factions, the Bissoyi of Roigodo had been turned out in October 1817, and one Dandaséna, the brother of the Guma Bissoyi, put in his place. Dandaséna again was turned out of Roigodo by the Manager and the Swaji Máhádevi's influence, whereupon in September 1818 Dandaséna and his people began to burn and plunder villages, as was the custom, and to demand the return of the Gajapati Máhádevi. These quarrels were always a good pretext for robbing and plundering, the unfortunate ryots being the sufferers, and the Bissoyis and peons, originally the police of the country, the gainers. Consequent upon Mr. Thackeray's report, however, Mr. Sub-Collector Bird was appointed to have especial charge of the Hill Zemindaris in Ganjam, and his head-quarters were located at Parla-Kimedi, but in other respects no more effectual means were taken to preserve the peace of the country. Upon his death he was succeeded by Mr. Bayard, an officer well acquainted with the Uriya language, and long resident in the country. As long, however, as the two factions resided in Parla-Kimedi, the Zemindari could have no peace, and reconciliation between them was not to be thought of.

In 1822 Sir Thomas Munro, Governor of Madras, paid a visit to the Ganjam District. In 1820 and 1821 the disturbances amongst the Bissoyis and town peons of Parla-Kimedi still continued in spite of the exertions of Mr. Sub-Collector Bayard to prevent them. In order to secure the peace of the Zemindari it was determined to deliver the country over at once to the Minor Rája, Jagannath Gajapati Náráyana Deo, without waiting for his coming of age. The young Rája was incapable and sensual, and Gopinátha Patnáyak, the new Manager, gave offence to the more powerful party under the Guma Bissoyi. The town peons, who were the bullies of Parla-Kimedi, moved away their families, and commenced burning and plundering. The Zemindari continued in a disturbed state between 1822 and 1830, and the country was alternately managed by Gopinátha Patnáyak, Padmanábha Deo, and the Gajapati Máhádevi. Constant fights took place between the rival factions, who met and fought out their quarrels in the streets of Kimedi. The Revenues of the country naturally suffered, and in 1829 the Zemindari was attached for arrears. The work of plunder and destruction however still continued, and the Rája was gradually lapsing into a state of imbecility, the result of self-indulgence. The Zemindari was at length once more resumed by Government in 1830, and its affairs placed under the Court of Wards.

Padmanábha Deo, who had previously been so ready to foster existing disturbances, and had repeatedly been denounced by the then Collector, was now foolishly re-appointed to the management. The policy followed was a temporising one, and the Government of the country was weak. Padmanábha Deo proved to be as obnoxious as ever, and a conspiracy was formed against him amongst the Bissoyis and the town peons, which in 1831 again culminated in an insurrection. The secret instigator of the disturbances was Gopinátha Patnáyak, who had been the Rája's Manager in 1822, but there were many others in the country who did not care to conceal their professions. The chief of these was Godiyapádhi Krushnama Dora.

In January 1832 Mr. Ogilvie assumed charge of the Ganjam Collectorate. The Government had been hitherto under the impression that the disturbances could be put down, without the presence of troops, by means of peons. The Bissoyis, Doras, and peons of the Zemindari were elated by former successes and encouraged by the comparative impunity, with which they had been so long allowed to carry on their excesses. In the course of these disturbances, the ryots had been murdered by the Savaras, and depredations were committed upon their property and cattle by the insurgents. Frequently they had been outraged in their own persons, or through the dishonour of their wives and daughters, and the country was gradually being abandoned by its cultivators. Last but not least, the Collector of the district was powerless, as Government had disapproved of his repeated proposals to call in military aid, and declare martial law. In October 1832 Padmanábha Deo died, and a temporary lull in the disturbances was the result.

The attention of Government had, however, at last been drawn to the serious results likely to accrue if the disturbances in Parla-Kimedi were suffered to continue. Whilst the Bissoyis, Doras and peons continued to possess themselves gradually of additional villages, land and money at the Rája's expense. The lawlessness of these men originally began at the end of 1813 and had continued to prevail in a more or less open manner for a period of 19 years.

On the 11th December 1832, Mr. George Russell, the 1st Member of the Board of Revenue, was appointed Special Commissioner to ascertain the causes which had led to these continual outbreaks, to devise and carry out measures for their suppression, and to recommend what future course he thought best suited to prevent their recurrence. He was invested with extraordinary powers including that of proclaiming martial law, if necessary in the Zemindari.* Brigadier General Taylor was Commanding the Division in the Northern Circars, and Major Baxter was appointed to command the troops in Parla-Kimedi.

Parla-Kimedi, 1832.

Mr. Russell's first enquiry was to ascertain who were the real instigators of the disturbances. Having obtained positive proof against Gopinátha Patnáyak, the ex-Manager, and Rákana Chandrudu, who was the Sirdar or Chief of the town peons in Parla-Kimedi, he proceeded to take them into custody. In May 1833 the fort at Gumá was occupied by the troops upon the Gumá Bissoyi failing to give up Godiyápádhi Krushnama Dora, a noted rebel of 1831, but no real opposition was offered to the troops. The Zemindari had remained in a state of comparative peace since Mr. Russell's arrival, and no further outrages were reported, except by the Savaras. The Special Commission sitting at Chicacole had, in the meanwhile, sentenced the prisoners sent for trial by Mr. Russell to transportation for life, that being the highest penalty in their power to inflict. The inhabitants had expected the public execution of their oppressors, and they learned with dismay that their lives had been spared. Hitherto there had been no direct act of rebellion, except in Guma.

In August 1833 Mr. Russell saw however fit to issue the proclamation of martial law, by which act treason and rebellion became capital crimes. Negotiations were commenced with the Bissoyi of Jeringi to deliver up the rebel Godiyápádhi.

During Mr. Russell's temporary absence at Masulipatam, Major Baxter, anxious to secure Godiyápádhi, sought for an

* Mr. Russell's report, dated 1st November 1834.

interview with the Jeringi Bissoyi at his own fort in order the better to secure the object he had in view. This was a fatal mistake. With a misplaced confidence in the people whose suspicions were easily aroused, Major Baxter, accompanied by a small body of troops, proceeded on the road to Jeringi. His movements were known to the Bissoyis, and he was fired upon by an unseen enemy, receiving a ball in his only remaining arm. The wound subsequently proved mortal The first shot had been fired, and the signal for a general revolt of the Bissoyis, the Doras, and the peons attached to them, had been given. Of the 1,100 town peons of Kimedi some 600 now threw off the mask, and joined the insurgents. It would serve no purpose to atttempt to describe in detail the different operations of the campaign.

The country was woody and hilly, the paths unknown, and the people disaffected. Caution was therefore necessary. Jeringi and other forts in the Eastern Division were gradually reduced with but trifling loss, and the Bissoyis of Roigodo and Lawanyakota were captured and hanged. The insurgents met with defeat at every point. Their principal leaders either died or were captured, and by April 1834, the campaign in Parla-Kimedi was at an end, and the troops were gradually withdrawn. The most efficient means of repression were found to be the destruction of the insurgents' villages and grain.

The anarchy which had existed for so many years had hitherto united all the turbulent classes of the country in one interest. It was Mr. Russell's object to separate the Bissoyis in the hills from the Doras in the plains and to crush out the insolence of the peons of the
1834. four streets in Kimedi town. The connection that had so long subsisted between the Bissoyis themselves was also effectually broken. The two Bissoyis of Roigodo were hanged along with 13 other insurgents, whilst 103 of the town peons were sent to Vellore as State prisoners. Some 25 other insurgents had been previously sentenced to transportation for life by the Special Commission sitting at Chicacole. As regards

the town peons of Kimedi, their numbers were considerably reduced. Only 200 were retained in employ in Kimedi, whilst waste land was allotted to others who had rendered services, sufficient to afford them a comfortable subsistence, subject to a light quit-rent after 4 or 5 years' tenure. This latter arrangement proved highly advantageous in many ways.

The moral effect of the troops' operations was great, as it taught the inhabitants to respect the power of Government by enforcing obedience. Kimedi had been in a state of open rebellion for years, the authority of Government had been despised, whilst the rebellious spirit of the peons and their leaders had been allowed to continue for long almost unpunished. The measures taken to suppress the prevailing anarchy were not more severe than necessary, and the country has ever since reaped the benefits of the measures so judiciously taken by Mr. Russell to ensure its future peace.

We must now turn to the affairs of Goomsur. Strikara Bhanj had continued to pay the tribute of 75,000 Rupees fixed upon his Zemindari with regularity from 1819 until 1830-1831, when he fell into arrears to the amount of 77,623 Rs. Being unable to make any satisfactory arrangements for its liquidation, he intimated his wish to the Collector to retire from public business, and give up his Zemindari to his son Dhanunjaya Bhanj.

Dhanunjaya Bhanj was accordingly recalled from Chingleput where he had been in confinement ever since 1815, but before he arrived, the old man had changed his mind and refused to surrender the country to him. Strikara Bhanj was, however, compelled to submit, and finally retired to Jagannath in 1832 on a pension of 8,000 Rupees per annum.

The Zemindari was then formally made over to Dhanunjaya Bhanj for the second time, subject to the condition that he was to discharge the balance due by his father for former years. On the 9th December 1833 Dhanunjaya Bhanj bought the Surada Zemindari for 8,000 Rupees, the Zemindar having died without issue in 1830, but *wilfully* continued to neglect his engagements with Government.

In 1835 the Collector, Mr. Stephenson, announced to the Zemindar that, if the arrears were not discharged within one month from the date on which the announcement was made to him, the Zemindari would be resumed agreeably to the terms of the Sanad granted to him in 1832. This the Zemindar failed to do, and retired to his stronghold at Kalláda. The troops moved forward from Aska, where they had assembled pending the negotiations of the Collector with the Zemindar to induce him to submit quietly, and occupied Goomsur on the 3rd November 1835. Kalláda was taken possession of on the 9th, but upon the arrival of the troops at Galéri, the Zemindar's adherents opened fire upon the camp, and thenceforward did all in their power to oppose their progress. Dhanunjaya Bhanj himself had fled into the Máliahs at the commencement of the operations and died there at the end of 1835. The treasure which he had taken with him was plundered by the people around him, and as it amounted to upwards of 70,000 Rupees, it served to enable his adherents to continue the disturbances. Mr. Stephenson, the Collector, had meanwhile represented to Government that the country must be completely reduced, if peace were wanted, and that some persons vested with greater powers than himself should be appointed to take the conduct of affairs in Goomsur.

Mr. Russell was accordingly once more selected to undertake the office of Special Commissioner, and joined General Taylor's camp in Goomsur at the commencement of 1836. The force in the field consisted of the 49th and 8th Regiments, 2 Companies of the 21st, and detachments of the 3rd and 10th Regiments together with 4 howitzers. The active advisers and supporters of Dhanunjaya Bhanj's rebellion were his illegitimate brother Brundávana Bhanj, Jagannath Bhanj, a member of the family, and Dora Bissoyi, a Boniá Khond. Besides these men there were other leaders, whom it became necessary to capture and bring to justice as open rebels. It will be sufficient here to point out

Goomsur, 1836.

Note.—Vice S. 34 of Mr. Russell's report, dated 11th May 1837.

the principal events of the two campaigns in Goomsur. The strongholds at Kolláda, Galéri, and at Durgaprasád below the ghauts were occupied, and the country over-run in every direction. The troops occupied the positions they had gained, and by constant enterprises in which the rebel party were frequently surprised and suffered severely, compelled them to seek shelter in the distant mountains bordering on Daspallá and Nuágodo (Nyágarh.)

On the 14th February 1836 the troops under Captain Butler ascended the ghauts for the first time, and entered the Máliah country of Goomsur in pursuit of Brundávana Bhanj and the family of the late Zemindar who were supposed to be at Udayagiri. Their object was not only to capture the members of the Rája's family, but to recover at the same time the treasure that he was known to have left behind him when he died. The troops met with some opposition from the Khonds when ascending the ghaut, but subsequently established friendly relations with the inhabitants. The Khond Chieftains, however, mindful of the rights of hospitality, still refused to deliver up the refugees.

Whilst negotiations were still pending, some men of the detachment misconducted themselves, by forcibly seizing fowls in the villages of the Khonds, and this produced a quarrel with the inhabitants, which led to the sepoys losing their lives. Instigated by Dora Bissoyi, the Máliah Chief appointed by the Zemindar, the Khonds of Goomsur first began by cutting off all small escorts, and at last ventured to attack stronger detachments under European officers.

One detachment of 35 men was attacked by the Khonds in the Kurmingia pass whilst escorting prisoners between Udayagiri and Durgaprasád, and 13 of them were killed, besides the two European officers, Lieutenant Bromley and Ensign Gibbon. This disaster would probably never have occurred, had not the two English officers been deserted by the Native officer of the detachment and most of the sepoys.

Reprisals were the result, and the Khonds were soon made sensible of their inability to cope with our troops.

The insurgents had soon no place that they could rely upon as a safe retreat, and the neighbouring Zemindars of Daspallá and Nuágodo (Nyágarh) were reluctantly compelled to deliver up the rebels who had sought refuge in their territories. The approach of the rainy season, however, made it necessary to desist from further active operations. The troops were accordingly withdrawn from the Máliahs, and those not absolutely necessary to command the low country in Goomsur, were marched back into cantonments in June 1836.

Further hostilities in Goomsur were suspended during the monsoon of 1836, but one of the chief insurgents, Dora Bissoyi, was still at large in the Máliahs, and although closely pursued upon several occasions, he had hitherto managed to escape capture. Mr. Russell determined meanwhile to detain in the low country the Bissoyis and other Chiefs who had given shelter to Dora Bissoyi, with the object of inducing them by kind treatment to serve us faithfully when hostilities were resumed. It was necessary, however, to pursue the advantages that the troops had gained, and a system of compromises, already too long pursued, was no longer to be thought of.

In November 1836 the troops commanded by General Taylor once more simultaneously ascended into the Máliah country by different passes, and entered upon the second Goomsur campaign. The operations were everywhere successful, and the losses on the part of the troops but trifling, consisting chiefly of camp followers murdered by the Khonds. A large number of rebel Chiefs took refuge in the territory of the Bôd Rája who sent information of their retreat. Troops from both the Madras and Bengal sides accordingly moved simultaneously into the Bôd Zemindari, and the rebels were at length put into our possession.

The insurrection was now practically at an end. Considerable numbers of the rebels had been either hanged or transported. Dora Bissoyi had escaped to the Patna Zemindari, but having obtained the promise of his life from the Commissioner of Cuttack, he came in and eventually surrendered himself. The Khonds sought for peace by putting us in possession of all the ringleaders of their tribe. None of the Chiefs, except Dora Bissoyi, remained at large, and all his relations of any note together with his Sirdars and most of the peons had either been killed or taken. Dora Bissoyi himself was a wanderer, and his influence in the Máliahs had been completely broken. In the low country he had never possessed any. New Molikos (Chiefs) were installed in the place of Dora Bissoyi's late adherents, and his own office was conferred upon Sam Bissoyi of Hozágodo, who had rendered us considerable assistance in the course of the two campaigns.

Collector to Board of Revenue, dated 4th October 1836.

With regard to the paiks or military dependents of the Goomsur family, it was not considered advisable to put down the system found to prevail, as they were a numerous body of men, who were mostly dependent upon their service lands for a livelihood. The establishment was therefore remodelled, and grants of land were made for life to the Sirdars, Naiks, and Paiks of Goomsur, dependent upon their good conduct, and the faithful discharge of the duties of their office. Instead, however, of being confined to one or two Mutahs only, the paiks were distributed over the country. Six Sirdars were appointed, 69 Naiks, and 1,244 Paiks and over 50,000 Bharnams of land (*i.e.*, about 10,000 acres) were made over to them at a small quit-rent.

The only Zemindar in the district who had rendered any assistance was the Rája of Atagada whose estates adjoined Goomsur. As a reward his tribute was reduced from 55,000 to 52,000 Rupees.

The arrangements made by Mr. Russell gave great satisfaction. The Government had previously resolved to confirm the former forfeiture of the Zemindari, and the announcement was received throughout Goomsur with complacency by the people. The members of the Bhanj family, nearly all of them illegitimate, were removed from the country, and small pensions allotted to them, whilst other persons who had done good service to Government during the two campaigns were suitably rewarded. Sundara Sing, for instance, a member of the Surada Zemindar's family, was granted the village of Lanjapalle near Berhampore, upon Mokhasa tenure. The exertions of the troops throughout the campaign had been most praiseworthy in spite of their suffering considerably from fever, and the 8th Regiment had been so much weakened by it after the first campaign, that it was not considered prudent to allow the regiment to enter upon the second.

The conspicuous services rendered by Mr. Russell were publicly acknowledged by Government, and the ability, energy, and firmness with which he had carried out all the measures adopted by him were justly commended. The system of warfare had been for the rebels to burn the villages, and force the inhabitants to desert the open country. In this way more than three-fourths of the villages in Goomsur were destroyed, and the country at the end of the war was almost depopulated.

The impression produced by Mr. Russell in the Ganjam District has been a lasting one, and his tours through the country "hanging some and transporting others," as a native letter naively puts it, were indirectly productive of the greatest advantages. The rebellions and disturbances that had been prevailing in the country, ever since we had taken possession of it in 1768, were at last effectually stamped out, and the district restored to a state of peace and security. It was only right, therefore, that the man who had done so much for the good of the country should have his name commemorated in a lasting manner. Government saw fit to locate a regiment in Goomsur, and the name given to the new cantonment was that of Russellkonda or "Russell's hill." At the present day Russellkonda is the chief town of the Goomsur Taluq, and one of the prettiest spots in India.

It has already been stated that Surada became annexed to Goomsur by purchase in 1833. Adjoining Goomsur, the Zemindars of Surada were always considered to be more or less subject to their more powerful neighbour. At the time of the Permanent Settlement Koonja Sing, the reigning Chief, distinguished himself by the active aid he afforded to the public authorities in the suppression of disturbances then prevailing. The Zemindari had previously paid a yearly tribute of 5,000 Rupees, but as an acknowledgment of the Zemindar's services in 1805, Government had reduced the assessment to 2,500 Rupees. Upon the death of Koonja Sing, his widow took possession of the country. Her right was, however, disputed by other members of the family, and the Zemindari became the subject of litigation in the Civil Courts. It was finally made over by the Civil Court to Lakshmi Náráyana Sing, the nephew of the last incumbent, in 1829. This individual was, however, much disliked by the inhabitants and hill people, and disturbances were at once commenced by the widow of the last Zemindar aided by the persons of most influence in the country. The chief leaders in these disturbances were Sundara Sing, Conjan Sing, Mohana Sing and Gopi Sing. In consequence of these disturbances the Zemindari had, in the meanwhile, fallen in arrears. It was therefore determined to sell the estate by auction for the arrears due, in the hopes that Dhanunjaya Bhanj, the neighbouring Zemindar of Goomsur, would buy it, as he was supposed to be the only person likely to be able to manage it to advantage.

Surada, vide Mr. Russell's report, dated 11th May 1837.

Surada was accordingly sold at public auction to Dhanunjaya Bhanj for 8,000 Rupees on the 9th December 1833, but their new master proved even more obnoxious to the inhabitants than their old one. The disturbances continued, and to such an extent was the country laid waste by the rioters that, out of 69 villages which Surada had previously contained, only 9 remained in 1835, all the rest having been either burnt or abandoned. At the commencement of the first campaign in Goomsur, the Goomsur insurgents under their leader, Hattiram, had made Rogada, a small tract, subject to Surada, their head-quarters, but the measures taken by the troops were so well considered that they were entirely dispersed, and were never again able to make any stand.

Surada had been repeatedly transferred to new claimants by the Civil Courts, and latterly to Dhanunjaya Bhanj by sale. In the confusion that ensued, all had taken up arms in their turn to support their pretensions, and the country had been rendered utterly desolate. The first object in view was therefore to restore confidence in order to bring back the cultivators, who in 1837 had so long deserted their fields that the traces of where they had been were scarcely visible. The Zemindari was therefore rented out at a nominal rent upon a quadrennial lease to influential persons, and upon its expiry, upon a triennial one. In six years' time (1836-1842) the revenue of the country had increased from Rs. 2,060-13-8 to Rs. 12,127-9-0.

The ancient Surada Zemindari now forms a part of the Goomsur Taluq, and is administered by a Tahsildar who resides at Russellkonda.

Since the termination of the second Goomsur campaign the Ganjam District has enjoyed for 40 years the blessings of almost unbroken peace, if not prosperity.

Owing to the failure of the crops in Goomsur in 1836, combined with the desolate state of the country from the previous disturbances, a partial famine prevailed throughout the Goomsur Taluq. Public works were authorised in 1837 for the relief of the distressed, and private charities were organised by the officers of the 17th and 43rd Regiments at Nattinga, Vishnuchakram, and Russellkonda.

Captain Campbell, an officer of experience and well acquainted with the Goomsur and Máliah country, was entrusted in 1836 with Revenue powers as the Collector's Assistant, and commissioned to raise a small Sibbandi corps of armed peons, who were disciplined and commanded by him. These were intended to check the Khonds, with whom we had for the first time been brought into contact in 1836, should they attempt to renew their former predatory incursions into the low country.

There had been bad years in 1837 and 1838, but in 1839 the season was so disastrous that the inhabitants were put to the greatest distress, and many of them emigrated, whilst cholera and other diseases carried off multitudes of those who remained. The distress was greatest in the northern taluqs of the district, but it affected all the estates in the district more or less. The south-west monsoon had been tolerably copious, but the drought that prevailed in the district after September was so severe that more than 10 per cent. of the cocoanut trees in the Tirastanam withered and died from its effects.

Famine, 1839.

In the same year certain tracts in Ganjam and Vizagapatam were removed from the jurisdiction of the ordinary Civil Courts, and the Collector of Ganjam was nominated Agent to the Governor of Fort St. George, and charged with the special administration of all the ancient Zemindaries attached to the Collectorate.

Upon the troops penetrating into the Máliah country in 1836, the practice that prevailed amongst the Khonds of sacrificing human beings was prominently made known to Government by Mr. Russell. Instructions were issued for the suppression of these barbarous rites, and in 1845 Captain Macpherson was appointed the first Agent for the suppression of the Meriah sacrifices under Act XXI of 1845. Large numbers of Meriah victims were rescued by the different officers of the Meriah Agency, who traversed the tracts of country inhabited by the Khonds, between the

Meriah Agency.

Mahánadi and Godavari rivers, in every direction, and the Agency was finally abolished on the 18th December 1861. The following are the names of the various officers, who contributed to the suppression of the Meriah sacrifices, throughout the Hill Tracts of Ganjam and Orissa, between 1845 and 1861, viz.: Captain Macpherson, Dr. Cadenhead, Dr. Pinkney, Captain Frye, Colonel Campbell, Captain MacViccar, Captain McNeill, and Lieutenant Crawford.* The success of the Meriah Agency in effecting their object has been more especially noticed in connection with the manners and customs of the Khonds, and the Máliah country of Ganjam.

The reinstated Zemindar of Mohiri who was of unsound mind and without issue, had fallen in arrears, and about the end of 1844 the estate was taken under the Collector's management. The arrears in 1850 amounted to Rs. 1,64,280-1, and Mohiri was therefore put up to auction, and bought in by Government for 100 Rupees. Pensions were at the same time allotted to the Zemindar and to the rest of his family. It is to be observed however, that the last Zemindar of Mohiri would never have been Zemindar at all, had it not been that the Government saw fit to buy back the Mohiri estate from the Bandam family for 35,000 Rupees, and put in Krushna Chandra Narendra Deo as the legitimate son, which he was not, of Moja Deo, the illegitimate brother of a former Zemindar.

In 1852 there were some disturbances in Chinna-Kimedi or Pratápagiri in consequence of the Zemindar claiming the right of levying taxes from his tenants. The matter caused an enquiry, and the District Zemindars were expressly forbidden to levy the taxes known as *Dwárábhodá* or House Tax, *Thiyábhodá* or Standing Tax, *Porodzá Mágunì* or direct payment of the ryots to the Zemindar, besides all other extra cesses which they are precluded from levying by the terms of their Sanad-i-Milkeut-Istimrár.

* The records of the Meriah Agency appear to have been destroyed as I have been unable to discover their existence either at the India Office in London, or in India.

Sáurá disturbances.

In March and November 1853 inroads were made upon different parts of Parla-Kimedi by the Savaras, but they were quickly put down by the troops, who burnt the crops and drove off the cattle as the most efficient means of punishing them for the outrages. The Savaras were supposed to have been instigated by the Patta Máhádevi and disaffected Bissoyis of Parla-Kimedi.

In July 1854 Mr. Prendergast took charge of the district from Mr. Knox, and was engaged for a considerable time in enquiring into extensive frauds principally in the Salt Department, which there was every reason to suppose had been going on for the past nine years. As the frauds in the Salt Department had been connived at by Government servants in the Sheristadar's department, Mr. Prendergast suspended the Huzoor Sheristadar.

For a long time past the Atagada Zemindar had been constantly in arrears with the payment of his peishkush, in spite of the Government having deducted 3,000 Rupees a year, as a mark of their approbation for his good conduct during the Goomsur disturbances in 1835-1837. In 1841 the Zemindari had been sold by public auction on account of arrears amounting to Rs. 40,097-8, and bought in on account of Government for Rs. 61,C00. The sale was not, however, confirmed by Government, and Atagada was restored to the Zemindar. In spite of this warning, the Zemindar again fell in arrears, and in July 1851 the estate was once more sold, and bought in by the Collector for 1,00,200 Rupees. Upon the arrears being paid, with the exception of Rs. 2,466-7-10, the estate was once more restored to the Rája. When Mr. Prendergast took charge in 1854, the Zemindar was in arrears to the extent of Rs. 39,150-15-0, and as he neglected to pay the tribute it was sold by auction on the 15th July 1854. Mr. Prendergast knocked down the estate on behalf of Government though their's was not the highest bid, on the ground that the highest bidder, the Zemindar of Kallikót, had failed to pay up the prescribed deposit there and then. The Kallikót Zemindar was, however, a nephew of the Atagada Rája, and upon a reference being made by him to Government they gave orders that the Atagada Zemindari should be made over to him and the amount of his bid accepted. The transfer of Atagada to the Kallikót Zemindar created a great deal of dissatisfaction throughout the country, and in November 1855 the ryots of the taluq entered into a combination amongst themselves to withhold their kists or rents from Kallikót. Upon this the Zemindar naturally appealed to the Collector of the district to interpose his authority. As Mr. Knox, the Collector, was engaged at the time in the Jamabandi of Mohiri, he deputed his Assistant, Mr. Davidson, to proceed to Boirani where the ryots were assembled, and use his influence with them to induce them to pay their kists to the Kallikót Zemindar. The ryots, some 700 or 800 in number, expressed their willingness to pay their kists to Government, but persisted in their refusal to pay their kists to another Rája than their own. After the necessary formalities Mr. Davidson placed six of the most prominent leaders under arrest, and confined them in his tent. This act so aroused the feelings of the assembled mob that there was every appearance of a serious riot ensuing, but owing to the coolness and discretion of Mr. Davidson, the people were at length prevailed upon to disperse. The ringleaders were subsequently punished for their contumacy, and the Atagada Rája was warned that he would be removed from his fort at Atagada, if any more disturbances took place in the country.

A rising of the Kuttiyá Khonds and several of the hill Mutahs took place in 1857, and the Khonds attacked the Agent's camp at Oorladoni, but the attack was speedily repulsed, and five Khonds were killed, whilst a Deloyat of the Agent and two camp-followers were wounded. The Agent was accompanied by between 200 or 300 Sibbandies and one company of native infantry. Two or three days later the Agent's camp was again surrounded by the reinforced Khonds who were chiefly Borikia Khonds of Kalahandi, and Khonds of the Kuttiyá country. The reason for the rising was as follows: In 1855 a Meriah victim had been secretly sacrificed in the village of Kidili in the Borikia Mutáh of the Kalahandi Zemindari, which adjoins the Ganjam Máliah country. For this offence, Rendo Maji, the Head of the Mutah, was arrested with his son Palaso Maji, and confined for two years at Russellkonda. In 1857 the Agent took his two prisoners in irons through the hills on his annual tour in the direction of their Mutah in hopes that it might afford a deterrent example. On reaching that part of the country it became evident that ill feeling existed, and the Khonds of Korikiya and other Mutahs refused to come in for the customary visit *(Bheto)* to the Agent. The attack upon the camp followed soon afterwards as already mentioned, but through the agency of the friends of the imprisoned Majis, the insurgent Khonds were induced to come in to visit the Agent. Rendo Maji and his son were released in due course, but no punishment was apparently inflicted on the rioters.

Between 1855 and 1856 there had been some slight disturbances in Goomsur where Chokra Bissoyi was the leader of gangs of robbers. He endeavoured to gain over the sacrificing Khonds to his side by promising them a renewal of the Meriah rite, which the officers of the Meriah Agency had practically put a stop to by their operations in the Máliah country.

In 1859 the Zemindar of Sergada died and was succeeded by his nephew the Rája of Bodogoda. His succession to the estate was, however, disputed by the widow of the Sergada Zemindar on the ground that her deceased husband had given her authority to adopt a son. The estate remained under the Zemindar of Bodogoda until 1872 when it was ultimately made over to the adopted son by Decree of the Civil Court.

In 1856 and 1857 there were some rather serious disturbances amongst the Savaras in the Parla-Kimedi Zemindari, headed by Radha Krishna Dandaséna of Gaibá. Some 50 villages were burnt or plundered by the Savaras, but upon the troops under Captain Wilson penetrating into the Savara country, the disturbances were quickly suppressed. The villages and crops were burnt down, and Dandaséna was caught and hanged as a rebel in 1857. The reprisals of the troops upon this occasion, and their penetrating into the heart of the Savara country had an excellent effect in preventing disturbances for the future. Most of the Bissoyis and Doras in Parla-Kimedi gave most efficient assistance to the troops acting independently against the rioters, and the Bobbili, Goomsur, and Vizianagrum paiks were usefully employed upon the occasion.

Sávará disturbances, 1856.

Between 1865 and 1866 a famine of the most unparalleled severity desolated the country, and slew between 10,000 and 15,000 people by actual starvation. The number of deaths *reported* was 10,898, but there is no doubt that the total loss of life by starvation was greatly in excess of this return, as many hundreds must have perished, of whom no account was kept. The northern part of the district suffered chiefly.

Famine, 1865.

In November 1865, another rising of the Khonds took place in the Máliahs of Ganjam. In June 1865, the Subarnagiri Patro had contracted with Captain Stuart, the District Superintendent of Police, in common with other Patros in the Hills, to clear and open an ordinary village road through the Mahásingi District, which skirts the Kuttiyá country on the west. The Subarnagiri Patro received an advance of money for this purpose, and proceeded to construct the road with the aid of his subordinate Patros and the villagers of the neighbouring Uriya and Khond villages. In the absence of the Subarnagiri Patro from the spot the work was delayed, and the Khonds seem to

Khond rising 1865. (Vide the report of W. Robinson, Esquire, C.S., Inspector-General of Madras Police, dated Russellkonda, the 24th January 1866.)

have been dissatisfied, especially the Kuttiyá Khonds, either at the allotment of work made to them by their Uriya Patros, or at the way in which they were treated. They accordingly quitted their work, and upon being recalled, they murdered the two Digalos or village watchers sent after them on the 13th November 1865 at Bollampallam, a Kuttiyá village not far from Gumagur.

The murder of these two unfortunate men was the signal for a general rising of the Kuttiyá Khonds, and as soon as the Subarnagiri Patro's authority had been openly resisted, the Khonds resolutely attempted to expel the Uriyas from their country. The rising was, however, chiefly confined to the Kuttiyá country of the Chinná-Kimedi Máliahs and was restricted to the Mutahs of Subarnagiri, Mahásingi, and Kalihandi, the latter not being attached to the district. They burnt the Uriya villages, and murdered all Uriya or Páno inhabitants, both men, women, and children who fell into their hands, besides carrying off their property. They also attacked Tumariband where they were repulsed by the Sub-Magistrate with Paiks and a few Constables. Reprisals on the part of the Uriyas soon however took place. The reinforcements of Police arrived from the plains, and Pákala Suriyá Náráyana Patro, the Sub-Magistrate of Udayagiri of Goomsur, at once took decisive steps to protect the inhabitants. Upon the arrival of Captain Stuart, the Superintendent of Police, and Mr. Goodrich, the Assistant Magistrate, the disturbances may be said to have terminated with the night attack on Kuripuji, when the Khonds received a lesson which taught them the wisdom of submission. By the end of 1865 the rising was over.

Fortunately the disturbances in the Hills had been confined to a somewhat isolated portion, or the consequences might have been more serious. It had, however, one beneficial effect for the Khonds, which was to draw the attention of Government to the necessity that existed for stationing European Officers in the heart of the Hill tracts, and thus securing the rude inhabitants from the oppression of their alien neighbours, the Uriya Paiks, and the Sundis or liquor sellers who live in their midst.

Since the famine of 1865 and the concurrent disturbances in the Hill tracts, chiefly amongst the Kuttiyá Khonds, the Ganjam District has, on the whole, been remarkably free from events of an untoward nature. It is sufficient to add that the district is gradually increasing in prosperity, and that it only needs a well-considered scheme of irrigation, and the utilization of the Rushikulyá, Vamshadhárá and Langulyá rivers to secure it permanently against famine and floods, so as to render it in every respect one of the finest provinces in the Madras Presidency.

CHAPTER VIII.

CLIMATE AND DISEASES.

CLIMATE—MONSOONS—DISEASES—CHOLERA—FEVER—SMALL-POX—BERIBERI—DYSENTERY—DIARRHŒA—RHEUMATISM.

The climate of Ganjam is usually pleasant and salubrious, and offers a favourable contrast to other parts of the Madras Presidency. Although the extremes of heat and cold are greater than in more southerly districts, yet both are very sensibly modified by the sea-breezes that blow along a line of sea-coast that extends for 135 miles. April and May are the two hottest months in the year, and December and January the two coldest. In May 1872 the heat registered at Aska, 30 miles inland, was 119½° Fahr., but along the line of sea-coast the thermometer but rarely rises to more than 90° Fahr. The heat in the interior is however very intense and trying to the European constitution, during the hot season, as apart from the direct heat of the sun the presence of numerous rocky mountains serves to retain and absorb an immense amount of heat. Large fires on the mountains are also common in April and May, as the hill-people are in the habit of burning down the jungle in order to promote the growth of the young grass for the cattle grazing, as well as to clear the hill sides for cultivation. This practice is very destructive to the forests. In the Máliah country the heat is as great or greater than in the plains, but in December hoar-frost is not uncommon, the thermometer not unfrequently falling as low as 30° Fahr., even in the low country the cold at this season is very sharp and piercing, more especially about Russellkonda.

A very strong southerly wind blows throughout April and early May, and the stronger it is the better the chance of a good monsoon.

The south-west monsoon may be usually expected to burst in Ganjam about the 15th June, and with occasional breaks it lasts, until October, when the north-east monsoon, less pronounced in its character, may be said to take its place.

September is usually an oppressive, close, and disagreeable month happening midway between the south-west and north-east monsoons.

Gales and storms are not uncommon in September and October, and the rain sometimes continues for days and nights together, but cyclones have never been known to pass into Ganjam. Hail-storms occur occasionally and the hail-stones are of an unusually large size and very destructive. The hail-stones for instance that fell on the 6th May 1866, are described as being as large as pigeons' eggs, whilst others again are said to have been the size of mangoes. Floods in the district occur almost yearly, and are destructive to the crops, but generally to nothing else. Owing to the comparative proximity of the mountains in Ganjam to the sea, the rivers rise with great rapidity, and their beds are then not sufficiently broad to carry off into the sea the torrents of water poured into them from the mountains. Both canals and reservoirs are required in Ganjam to regulate the distribution of water, as the rivers are dry in the hot season and the country parched up with heat, whilst at other times nearly all the water runs to waste.

**Diseases.*—The diseases peculiar to the district are chiefly malarious fevers and beriberi. Rheumatism, diarrhœa, dysentery, dyspepsia and diseases of the skin also prevail. Cholera is not endemic, but exists as an imported disease from Puri, whence the crowd of pilgrims who visit the shrine of Jagannath spread the disease throughout the whole of India. Indeed Mr. Hunter, B. C. S., states that it is propagated thence to Vienna and other parts of Europe.

The fever is sometimes preceded by a cold fit or ague lasting from half an hour to two hours, when it is followed by the hot

* From Notes kindly supplied to me by Honorary Surgeon J. Hargreaves.

stage with great restlessness. Gastric irritability, and sometimes delirium take place. The hot stage lasts from two to three hours, and is followed by free perspiration, which leaves the patient considerably weakened and prostrated. A peculiarity of these Máliah or jungle fevers, is that after the patients have been apparently free from any attacks for months, they again suffer from it on approaching the sea-coast. Ten to twenty grain-doses of quinidine preceded by aperient medicine, wholesome food, and avoiding exposure to the night air soon relieve the patient, but permanent benefit is only to be obtained by change of air, and a removal from the locality.

Fever, as everywhere else in India in the Plains, is the most fatal of the District ailments and its fatality is due to the habits of the people who go scantily clothed in the cold weather, sleep on the ground and eat for their early meal that most abominable of nasty food the cold and sour remains of the previous day's evening meal.

A further reason for the prevalence of fever is to be found in the Sanitary Commissioner's remarks on Godaveri fever as quoted at page 83, Gódaveri Manual.

" My conviction is that the periodical accessions of fever in the Godaveri District are due to the geographical position of that district in respect to malarious lands to the north and west, and that fever is due to the northerly winds of the north-east monsoon sweeping over the malarious jungles of the hill tracts of the Northern Circars before they reach the Godaveri District. In respect to individual taluqs and estates, Mr. Wright has shewn the correctness of this observation, and that the taluqs which are the most open to influences from the sea have the least fever, while these parts of the district, which are exposed most to the winds which have blown across unhealthy jungles have had the highest ratios of fever prevalence and mortality. The results of five years' registration demonstrate in a very clear manner that the intensity of fever in any taluq has no relation to the extent of irrigation of the lands, but is solely due to its geographical position and its exposure to malarious winds during the north-east monsoon."

The situation is identical except that the malarious northerly wind blows on to the plains directly from the hills. Cholera generally and with reason put down to the people passing through the district on pilgrimage to Puri, sometimes falls with fatal effect on the district. Of late years there has not been a serious epidemic due probably to the fact that the recent famine has reduced the number of pilgrims.

The deaths from small-pox are generally considerable in number for the people have till lately been persistent in their rejection of vaccination, but matters are improving a little. The Uriyas used all to prefer inoculation but the practice is certainly not as common as it used to be. A few years ago the profession of "Uriya Tekal" or inoculation was followed by some of the Uriya Brahmins who found themselves able to make a living by it.

Beriberi.—This disease is not peculiar to the Ganjam District, but is endemic throughout the whole of the Northern Circars from Masulipatam to the borders of the Chilka lake, a distance of about 400 miles. The symptoms are numbness of the legs with a peculiar tottering gait, accompanied by loss of sensation, and sometimes attended with fever. The natives have much faith in the use of a black oil called *malkankini*, and a diet consisting of wheaten cakes, and some dried mutton with warm water for drink.

The disease sets in after the south-west monsoon, and is supposed to have a malarious origin.

Dysentery.—This disease prevails after the hot season and setting in of the rains, but not to a very great extent. The symptoms are not severe, and are easily cured.

Diarrhœa—Is not a prevalent disease, though it shows itself occasionally, especially when the tanks and wells are low, and the water strongly impregnated with saline matter. It is easy to cure.

Rheumatism—From venereal disease, is very common and very obstinate to treat.

Itch and other skin diseases are very common, particularly amongst the Uriya population, whose dirty habits are sufficiently indicated by the fact that they wash their foul cloths in the same water used for bathing and drinking purposes.

CHAPTER IX.

POPULATION, CASTES, LANGUAGE AND RELIGION.

THE ARYAN AND ABORIGINAL RACES—LANGUAGES—CONDITION OF THE PEOPLE—THEIR COTTAGES—FURNITURE—FOOD—THE URIYAS—THEIR MODE OF CLOTHING—EDUCATION—RELIGION—MARRIAGES—COOKERY—FAMILY POLLUTION ON BIRTHS AND DEATHS—DIVISIONS OF CASTE.

There are in Ganjam two Aryan and two Aboriginal races forming the bulk of the population of the Collectorate. The two Aryan races are the Uriyas and Telugus, and the two Aboriginal, the Khonds and the Savaras who are confined to the mountainous tracts of the district. As the Khonds and Savaras have been separately dealt with, the following remarks apply only to the people inhabiting the plain country. In the northern division the bulk of the people are Uriyas who abound in the ancient Zemindaries and the more mountainous parts of the district where their colonies are frequently found scattered amongst the ruder aboriginal tribes. The Uriya language resembles Hindustani, and in a still greater degree Bengalee, of which it appears to be the parent. The written character is akin to Sanskrit and there is a considerable literature dating back to the eleventh century. One of the best known and most celebrated authors in the language was Upendro Bhondzo, one of the Rajahs of Goomsur. The Uriya language extends inland westwards towards Raipur of the Central Provinces and northwards as far as Midnapur in Bengal. It is spoken by nearly eight millions of people. The Uriya population of Ganjam may be estimated at two-thirds the total population of the entire district, although some have put it down as one-half.

There is no clearly defined line between the Uriya and Telugu country, but the limit may be fixed at Kasibugga as south of that line Telugu chiefly prevails.

Telugu, the second language of the district, is a soft harmonious tongue and has not inaptly been termed the Italian of the east. The Telugus are more enterprizing and pushing than the Uriyas, and their colonies are found along the sea-coast as far north as Puri. Most of the Government clerks are Telugus.

Ganjam forms a kind of debateable ground between the northern and southern portion of India, and owing to the prevalence of different races the number of castes in the district is very large, no fewer than 283 having been counted up.

Nearly half of the working population is engaged in agriculture, but the ryots are usually poor and in debt in spite of the low rates of assessment prevailing.

Thrift and economy are but little practised, and what Mr. John Stuart Mill calls "the effective desire of accumulation" is chiefly conspicuous by its absence. The bulk of the population have not even the means of clothing themselves properly, and although the climate is in their favour for the greater part of the year, yet during the colder months, they suffer a great deal from the weather.

The cottages of the ryots are usually mud huts with a thatched roof, the walls of which are formed of wooden lattice work plastered over with wet clay or mud which becomes hard after exposure to the sun and air. Sometimes they are built of brick and tiled. The ordinary mud cottages stand the rains, but indifferently, and when a flood occurs, the mud walls are apt to get undermined by the water and the whole building then comes down by the run. Fires are common during the dry season owing to the usually inflammable nature of the roof. The accommodation consists of two or three rooms at the back, small and badly ventilated, whilst the entrance or front part is reserved as a stall for cattle. The pial or verandah outside is used as a place for gossiping from and in the warm weather forms a convenient sleeping place with the simple addition of a rush mat.

The furniture of the cottage consists of a sleeping cot or "charpoy" which is a light wooden frame work, with cocoanut coir rope, or thread made of hemp or flax stretched or woven across it and standing on four legs (Uriya Khoto, and in Telugu Mantsamu), some rush or reed mats for lying on (Uryia Potti, and in Telugu Tsapa), some bell metal cups and vessels for drinking and eating (Kongsa and Tattiya), one or two brass pots for water and a large bamboo cradle for securing the household rice or paddy (Uriya Luduro, and in Telugu Ponaka). Earthen pots either red or black (Handi in Uriya, and Kundalu in Telugu) are also indispensable.

The ordinary ryot has usually three meals a day, but if very poor, he has to satisfy himself with two. The hours for meals are at 6 A.M., at noon, and in the evening about 7 P.M. A porridge or soup made of ragi called "Ambali" is the food of the masses, but this is varied with curry and rice and dholl mixed with pepper water.

Fish is eaten by certain classes when procurable and there is a considerable trade in the Hills with the Khonds who are very fond of salt fish.

Uriya Brahmins are not forbidden fish and the only two things that are forbidden to all Uriyas except the Bavuri people are beef and fowls.

The Uriyas are unintelligent, lazy and unenterprizing men as compared with the other inhabitants of the Madras Presidency. The men wear the usual cloths that Madras Natives adopt, but the women wear scantier and in texture thinner garments than I have seen anywhere. Among all classes there is a strong affection for Haldi or Turmeric, and with it they smear their clothes and themselves to such an extent that one or two in a room or even a few of them collected in the open air are most unpleasantly offensive and hardly bearable to a European.

The women cover the bosom, but do not wear the bodices common further south. The poorer class women wear a great amount of coarse brass-bangles on each arm. They were found in one instance, the woman wearing about the usual amount, to be ten lbs. in weight. Their wrists and hands are generally marked with a horny substance like a great corn induced by the friction of these bracelets.

They arenot an education loving people. The better class, out of, as they say, intense love for their children, let them please themselves at the very time they should be at school, and a well-educated Uriya is a rarity.

They are Hindus and follow the Hindu religious books, Vedas, Sastras and Puranas, and have their three sects of Dwytam, Adwytam, and Visishtadwytam. They are very much given to sacrifices and to making vows of a sacrifice to be made hereafter in return for a benefit desired and in Vysákham or April the time of the great feast on a Hill near Purushottpur it is said that from 10,000 to 12,000 goats and kids are slaughtered. These are not however wasted, for the carcasses are carried down and eaten at the bottom.

Their marriages are arranged much as other Hindu marriages are. They do not use the Tali. The Sudras and castes other than Brahmins instead of it use a gold bead which is put on the neck of the bride. The Brahmins use no symbol but at the ceremony tie the fingers of the bride and bridegroom together.

The Brahmin and Vaisya girls must be married before puberty, not so with the Kshatriyas and Curnams. Sudra girls if a real marriage has not been arranged in time, can be married to the sun and if this ceremony is performed, they are eligible for marriage with man, notwithstanding that they have arrived at womanhood. Widows and divorced wives of the Sudra caste can marry again.

The Uriya Brahmins are not forbidden to eat flesh. They also eat off bell metal plate, and are not restricted to the use of leaf platters, but report has it that the cookery of the Uriya generally is bad, and that they have no knowledge of the culinary art. All classes of them have a great dislike to moving from their native place and an Uriya living among persons not of his own race is utterly miserable. The Uriya Brahmin when he eats meat, must kill the animal as a sacrifice, therefore they do not purchase mutton, &c. The Uriya month ends with the full moon.

An Uriya Brahmin family observes the pollution of birth for 10 days, then bathes on the 11th day, but the mother of the child is unclean for 21 days, during which time she is left alone and may not interfere with cooking, distributing food and the like. A name is given to the child on the 11th day.

In other castes the pollution of a birth is not strictly observed.

On the death of a relative, Brahmins and others mourn for ten days and bathe on the 11th day. The well-to-do Brahmins perform daily rites for 10 days commencing from the day on which the dead body is burnt, others from the 7th to the 9th day only. On the 11th the funeral rites are performed by the offering of rice-balls. On the 3rd, the kinsmen and other connexions eat the powdered leaves of the Margosa (Vépa Chettu) which is called "Pittakhai." On the 11th day, beaten or parched rice, tyre, sugar-water and other things which are not cooked are supplied to Brahmins. This is called "Nisunkudi." The rich also get cakes to be prepared for them; monthly and yearly ceremonies are performed. Kshatriyas likewise observe these ceremonies, but they do not perform them personally. A Brahmin who is called "Po Brahmin" is deputed for the purpose.

Sudras do not perform daily ceremonies, but on the 11th day they bathe, replace their earthenware pots by new ones, and feed their relations andBrahmins according to their ability. "Pittakhai" is observed by all classes.

The customs and manners of the Telugu people of the district are exactly similar to those of the neighbouring district of Vizagapatam, and therefore it seems unnecessary that I should re-write the information that will be found in the Manual of that District.

Population, Castes, &c.—The following comprise the principal divisions of caste, as they exist in Ganjam :—

The Brahmins, who form the highest, the most polished, and the most intelligent class amongst the Uriyas, are chiefly employed in Government and priestly offices, and consist of:—

Dánua,	*Sau,*	*Holua, or*
Padia,	*Sárua,*	*Tosso.*
Bhodri,	*Guhária,*	

The *Holua,* or cultivating Brahmins, are a peculiarity of Orissa.

The Kshatriyas form the second highest or warrior class, and are comparatively numerous in Ganjam, the Zemindars and their relatives belonging chiefly to this caste. They consists of :—

Tsandulo,	*Bogolo,*	*Tsuáno,*	*Khondáito.*

The illegitimate children of Zemindars are usually distinguished by the surname of *Sánto* or *Bháipuo.*

Traders and shopkeepers.—In the Chicacole division the *Kalinga Komatis* principally prevail. Amongst the Uriyas they are termed *Boniyá* and comprise :—

Boniya,	*Ogrogatiboniya and*	*Boniyakorono.*

Writers and Accountants are called :—

Korono,	*Mahanti,*	*Patnaik,*	*Karnam.*

The agriculturists who form in Ganjam the great bulk of the population, comprise the following Uriya castes :—

Kálinji,	*Kampo,*	*Uriya,*
Dolua,	*Kudumo,*	*Bosontiya,*

and amongst the Telugus the *Telaga, Velama* and *Reddiki* castes.

The shepherds are also a numerous tribe, and go by the name of *Goudo, Bátogoudo* and *Solokhondiyagoudo* amongst the Uriya. The Telugus call them *Golla.*

The weavers are chiefly known amongst the Uriyas as *Derá, Tonti* and *Rongoni*; and amongst the Telugus as *Devángulu, Salelu* and *Pattusalelu.*

The fishermen are comprised in the following Uriya castes: *Keuto, Tiáro Kondrá* and *Nándiya.* The Telugu castes are *Jalaru, Palle* and *Mila.*

The distillers and toddy-drawers are known in Uriya by the name of *Sundi,* and in Telugu as *Yátavállu* and *Segidi.*

The barbers are called in Telugu *Mangali,* and in Uriya *Bondhári.*

The oil-mongers are called respectively *Teli* and *Teluhulavallu.*

The artizans comprise chiefly the following Uriya castes: *Sunari,* goldsmiths; *Kummáro* and *Luháro,* black-smiths; *Khodra* and *Konsári,* workers in bell-metal, &c.; *Korti,* sawyers; *Bodhái,* carpenters; and *Chitrokaro,* painters.

The agricultural labourers belong chiefly to the *Bauri* caste amongst the Uriyas, and the *Bói* caste amongst the Telugus.

Religious mendicants are drawn chiefly from the lower classes of Sudras and Pariahs of the Vaishnava faith, and are called *Boishnobo* and *Satani.*

Potters are called in Uriya *Kumbharo,* and in Telugu *Kummari.*

The washermen are respectively *Dhobi* and *Tsakali.*

The workers in leather amongst the Uriyas are included in the *Jagali,* and amongst the Telugus in the *Madiga* castes.

Tank-diggers are called *Mathiya* by the Uriyas, and *Uppari-vallu* by the Telugus.

The Pariah castes occupy the lowest rank in Hindu society, and are obliged to reside apart.

They comprise amongst the Uriyas *Samuntiya* or firewood-sellers, *Hadi* or scavengers, and the *Kodalo* and *Dandasi*.

The Pariahs amongst the Telugus are called *Mala* and *Tsat-sidi*.

The village watchmen in Northern Ganjam are usually *Dandasis*, and many of them are great thieves.

In the southern part of the district the watchmen are called *Bariki*, and it is their duty to guide the traveller on the march from place to place, changing at the different stages.

In the Hill country the *Panos*, who are by profession weavers, and the *Dombo* caste, who are tom-tom players, take the place of Pariahs in the plains.

Other wandering and predatory tribes are in Ganjam, chiefly confined to the following castes: *Sampua*, or snake-catchers; *Tsodaimora*, or bird-catchers; *Pothoriya*, professional stone-cutters, but addicted to snaring antelope by means of tame bucks which they keep for the purpose of decoying the wild ones; and *Khela*, jugglers. These are Uriya castes. The Telugu castes are the *Yerukalavallu*, who practise palmistry and fortune-telling; *Gangireddivallu*, who lead about performing oxen; *Garadivallu*, jugglers; and *Domaravallu*, who are gymnasts by profession.

CHAPTER X.

REVENUE HISTORY.

CHICACOLE AND KASIMKOTA HAVELI LANDS—TAX ON MANUFACTURES AND SALT—SEA CUSTOMS—ACCOUNTS FOR YEAR ENDING MAY 1788—ICHAPUR HAVELI LANDS—SALT REVENUE—HORSE BREEDING BY CAPTAIN EVANS—CHICACOLE AND TEKKALI HAVELI LANDS—DEMAND AND COLLECTION FROM 1811-12 TO 1873-74—DIVISION OF PRODUCE—CHICACOLE SETTLEMENT—BERHAMPUR SETTLEMENT—BENEFITS RESULTING THEREFROM—GOOMSUR SETTLEMENT AND RESULTS—ABSTRACT OF FINANCIAL RESULTS FROM THE SETTLEMENT.

When the English began to use the power that devolved on them by the firman of the Delhi Emperor in 1766 of taking the management of the Government of the Northern Circars, they found the lands that were under cultivation divided into the Havéli lands, and lands under the management and control of the Zemindars. The Havéli* lands of this District consisted of those of Chicacole with which those of Kasimkota, now part of the Vizagapatam District, were mixed up and those of the Ichapur District. In 1767 a ten years' lease of the former lands was granted to Sitaramraz, the brother of Viziaramraz, the-then Zemindar of Vizianagram. After the expiry of this lease it was renewed for ten years and after that it would seem because his management was found to be oppressive, the

* The Havéli lands consisted of the old demesne or household lands of the Sovereign, and tracts near to towns resumed by the Mahomedans and appropriated for the peculiar support of their numerous garrisons and establishments. These lands the local Foujdars and Nawabs always retained under their immediate management parcelling out the rest of the country into Zemindaries. The Revenue Agents of the ancient Hindu Rajahs were known as Deshmukhs or Desapandyas ; each functionary administered the affairs of a small circle of villages "Hunda" making the settlement of each village either with or through its headmen, and received for compensation certain lands rent-free. The Vizagapatam Manual, pages 114 and 115.

Havéli lands were divided amongst numerous renters. This was in 1787 and the results in rents are shewn below :—

	RS.	A.	P.
Bommali, &c., purganahs and villages...	1,39,034	14	0
Kuppili and dependencies	7,420	0	0
Siripuram, &c.	25,370	0	0
Wungarada, &c.	4,850	0	0
Kottakota, &c.	2,838	6	0
Ravolavalsa...	1,050	0	0
Totada	424	7	0
Goruntla..	672	0	0
Gokarlapalli and Tadivalasa	2,300	0	0
Kammetta	1,045	0	0
Koyam	6,304	0	0
Kasimvalasa	1,183	3	0
Nyra, &c...	4,614	0	0
Puttivalasa...	1,100	0	0
Makivalasa...	1,155	0	0
Kintali	4,000	0	0
Arasavilli...	6,792	8	0
Polatta	737	10	0
Vedullavalasa...	1,000	0	0
Modanlavalsa	500	0	0
Honjongy	498	14	0
Seermahomedpuram.	1,500	0	0
Acharala...	850	0	0
Boodumur	2,662	6	0
Mantanah...	1,417	8	0
Padapandu	1,300	0	0
Nagarikatacum purganah	11,560	0	0
Gontey	1,075	0	0
Jurjeam	258	8	0
Land Customs, &c....	13,420	0	0
Salt pans of Naupada and Womaravilli.	18,273	0	0
Total...	2,65,206	4	0

Tho Karakavalasa purganah and ten villages were rented to one Datla Venkataraz for Rs. 40,000, as shown below.

		Collections for 1786.		
1.	Karakavalsa purganah	14,200	0	0
2.	Purushottapuram and dependencies...	5,975	0	0
3.	Ponnam	1,241	8	0
4.	Singipuram	4,706	0	0
5.	Ampolu	3,341	0	0
6.	Buravilli	2,692	12	0
7.	Ambalavalasa	1,157	0	0
8.	Salihundam	2,601	0	0
9.	Kottur Sowdam...	1,051	10	0
10.	Byri	2,932	8	0
11.	Kopagum	315	0	0
	Total...	40,120	6	0

Eighteen villages which would not rent were kept under Amani or management. They produced a net Revenue of Rs. 27,676.

In Fasli 1197-98 we first find the division made between the Kasimkota and Chicacole lands to the effect that Rs. 3,09,000 were collected in Chicacole against Rs. 62,000 in Kasimkota, but this will not give the exact amount because the shrotriems and similar villages are not divided. The kists were then payable in four instalments in August, October, December and February ; one-fifth of the rent on the two first occasions, three-tenths on the last two. Besides the rent of the lands, the State used to collect land customs, salt revenue and a duty on cloths.

The Schedule of moturpha, a tax levied upon different manufactures, &c., and on looms in Chicacole and its dependencies is given below for the year 1787.

	Per Annum.		
Fisherman at 1½ per mensem	237	0	0
Gajulu people or manufacturers of bangles at Rs. 14 per mensem	140	0	0

	Per Annum.		
Goldsmiths, from 1 Rupee to Rs. 6 each house per annum	54	0	0
Potmakers, from 2 Annas to 1 Rupee per house.	116	0	0
Oil people, from 8 Annas to Rs. 5	43	0	0
Milk people, from Rupees 1 to 3	102	8	0
Washers, from ¼ to Rs. 30	73	0	0
Pachili people or green sellers, from 1¼ to 3...	34	0	0
Segidi from 1 Rupee per each house. ...	240	0	0
Shoemakers, 4 Annas	27	0	0
Boat rice sellers, Rs. 2 each	25	0	0
Jalari people, 4 Annas	11	0	0
Cowkeepers, 3 Rs.	10	0	0
Rangareez people or painters, at 1½ ...	10	0	0
Jalagadugula people, 1 Rupee each ...	5	0	0
Bamboo people, 1 Rupee	3	0	0
3 small hamlets in the vicinity of Chicacole ...	53	0	0
Looms, at 8 Annas	449	8	0
Total...	1,633	0	0

The Cotanparcha or duty levied for affixing a Government Stamp on cloths from the loom was as follows :—

1. On all cloths or muslins valued Rs. 2 or under, per piece ... ... 5¼ dubs
2. Do. from 2 to 15 Rs. do. ... ... 9¼ do.

   Exclusive of the above, a duty of nearly 2½ Rs. per cent. was levied on muslins and other fine cloths of the foregoing valuations.
3. On all cloths and muslins value Rs. 15 to 100, per piece ... ... 7½ per cent.
4. Handkerchiefs ... ... 1 dub each.

The price of salt sold at Naupada was Rs. 40 the garce. It was a policy of the Mahomedan Government to confine the making of salt to their own Havélies prohibiting the manufacture in any of the Zemindaries.

Sea Customs.—The grain exported to Madras from December 1788 to October 1789, was as follows:—

	Garces.
Paddy	8,426
Rice	1,004
Natchney	263
Wheat	37
Horse gram	93
Gingelly and Lamp oil seeds	16
Red gram	17
Green gram	0
Black gram	4
Cholum	0
Other kinds	11

The duty levied on the above was one Rupee per Calingapatam garce of paddy and natchney* and two Rupees on rice and other grains.

In Appendix 36 will be found an interesting letter under date 1787, on the management of the Chicacole Havéli lands.

The following is an abstract of the Account Current appended to Mr. Crawford's letter, dated 27th September 1788, to the address of the Chief, &c., Council at Vizagapatam.

Receipts from June 1787 *to May* 1788.

	RS.	A.	P.
Rented villages	2,90,478	0	0
Customs	8,952	12	0
Stamp duty	2,684	14	9
Shrotriem	8,386	14	6
Amani villages	27,676	7	0
From the village of Tamada resumed by authority	1,700	0	0
Repayment of advances to the Amani villages	386	4	0
Salt	2,317	14	0
From Karakavalasa purganah & 10 villages..	40,120	6	0
Fees on cowle to the renter of the Karakavalasa purganah villages ...	200	0	0
Villages of Doopulavalasa resumed by authority	20	0	0
	3,82,923	8	3

* Ragi.

Charges—	Rs.	A.	P.
Advance to the farmers of 18 villages under Amani towards the cultivation ...	6,153	0	0
Charges for collections	25,686	11	7
Pensions and charitable allowances ...	365	0	0
Remitted to Vizag. Treasury	3,35,000	0	0
	3,67,204	11	7
Balance on hand on 31st May 1788 ...	15,718	12	8
	3,82,923	8	3

In regard to the Ichapur Havéli lands the information is not quite so good. The first account of the rent we have is Rs. 1,30,000 about 1767, but in 1779-80 the Company's Dubash, Balakristnama, rented the Havéli lands and Zemindaries for 4½ lakhs. In 1781 this lease was resumed because Balakristnama fell in arrears and the Zemindars complained of having to pay their rents to him. In 1781-82 we find the following statement of the payments due by Zemindars and the collections made from various purganahs.

		Rs.
1.	Tarla	3,000
2.	Budarsingi	700
3.	Humma	2,000
4.	Palur	2,000
5.	Biridi	4,000
6.	Beeraghur	4,000
7.	Surangi	4,000
8.	Jarada	2,000
9.	Jalantra	5,000
10.	Mandasa	15,000
11.	Sowrerah	3,000
12.	Sergada	6,000
13.	Atagada	37,000
14.	Pratapagiri	22,000
15.	Chikati	35,000
16.	Dharakot	25,000
17.	Kallikot	34,000
18.	Vizianagram	25,000
19.	Goomsur	15,000
20.	Mohirri	30,000
	Total Rs...	3,08,700

			Rs.
1.	Poobakonda	... ...	68,516
2.	Ichapur	... ...	48,502
3.	Baruva	... ...	7,000
4.	Kurla	... ...	6,000
5.	Mantridi	... ...	14,471
6.	Tirastanam	... ...	29,280
7.	Mansurkota	... ...	4,000
8.	Aska	... ...	10,000
9.	Restored villages	...	25,198
		Total Rs...	2,12,967
		Grand Total...	5,21,667

In 1783 the Circuit Committee were appointed and after 4 years they made their report in 1787. Appended is an interesting statement of the Collections of the Ichapur District compiled by the Committee.

Years.	Collections from Government lands. Rs.	A.	Collections from Zemindars. Rs.	Sea-Customs. Rs.	Total. Rs.
1768-69 ...	1,04,447	0	1,52,268	......	2,56,715
1769-70 ...	1,30,146	9	2,82,711	......	4,12,863
1770-71 ...	1,27,531	0	2,06,125	25,239	3,58,895
1771-72 ...	1,34,000	0	2,29,626	17,157	3,80,783
1772-73 ...	1,59,000	0	3,00,792	31,856	4,91,648
1773-74 ...	1,52,787	0	1,87,816	10,104	3,50,707
1774-75 ...	1,50,917	0	3,92,187	15,483	5,48,587
1775-76 ...	1,42,933	0	3,30,103	5,115	4,78,151
1776-77 ...	92,600	0	2,65,941	9,246	3,70,786
1777-78 ...	1,29,157	0	2,29,502	10,358	3,69,017
1778-79 ...	1,64,260	0	3,10,398	11,100	4,85,758
1779-80 ...	......		3,00,000	2,292	3,02,292
1780-81 ...	......		3,76,000	.....	3,76,000
1781-82 ...	1,41,312	0	2,37,605	3,192	3,82,109
1782-83 ...	2,02,055	0	2,91,495	9,270	5,02,820
1783-84 ...	2,08,508	0	3,99,123	4,000	6,11,631
1784-85 ...	2,08,483	0	4,30,746	15,592	6,54,820
1785-86 ..	2,02,406	0	4,32,277	10,568	6,45,251

The above statement shows an increase of Revenue Collections from Rs. 2,56,715 to Rs. 6,45,251 in eighteen years of English rule.

Salt was only manufactured at Ichapur and Mansurkota in the Ichapur District. The collections amounted to only Rs. 10,000 during the year 1788, but the profits and mismanagement were great, for the Circuit Committee say "In consequence of several of the "Zemindars and Havéli purganahs being prohibited from "supplying themselves with any other salt than what is made "at Ichapur and Mansurkota, it is in the power of the renters "of the salt farms to exact what price they please; and we "accordingly find this necessary of life selling on the very spot "where it is made two and three hundred per cent. dearer "than in places 40 miles inland which are not subject to this "restriction; this hardship falls heavily upon the poorer sort "of people."

Letter to Board, 25th April 1788.

In 1798 an attempt was made at horse-breeding by Captain Evans with some mares, some of his own and some that had been used in the Mysore war. That turned out a failure, but Captain Evans by his energy did a great deal for the cultivation of the lands about. He also planted a very great number of cocoanut trees along the sandy tract that runs from Mansurkota to the Rushikulya river When the horse-breeding was pronounced a failure by Government, Captain Evans applied for permission to carry it on himself and obtained a ten years' lease of a large tract of country near Chatrapur for Rs. 93,941. His management of this was very successful. He improved the irrigation works, especially the Koratoli Tampara, and is said to have introduced the cultivation and manufacture of Indigo. He died in 1810, having just obtained a renewal of his lease for 20 years; and in 1814 an arrangement was made with his heirs that till the expiry of the lease they should receive Rs. 15,000 a year and half the produce of the cocoanut trees.

The several Estates or Hundas (twenty in number) forming the Chicacole and Tekkali Havélies were sold outright subject to the payment of a perpetual rent on the 30th June 1803. Eight of these estates, comprising 109 villages, however reverted to Government between 1809 and 1811, the purchasers having become insolvent and unable to manage them, and by 1845 some other estates had lapsed. Of the twenty estates, six now appertain to the Vizagapatam District, five and a part of the sixth remain in the possession of the proprietors and eight and a part of the last referred to have lapsed to Government; these make up the present 146 villages of the Taluk.

The gradual growth and variation of assessment, and the collections of land revenue may be gathered from the following statement.

Year and Fasli.		Demand.	Collection.	Year and Fasli.		Demand.	Collection.
		Rs.	Rs.			Rs.	Rs.
1811-12	1221	1,59,371	1,58,763	1843-44	1253	1,47,143	1,27,577
1812-13	1222	1,34,064	1,30,253	1844-45	1254	1,35,379	1,32,250
1813-14	1223	1,03,810	1,00,198	1845-46	1255	1,32,290	1,31,756
1814-15	1224	1,19,057	1,18,609	1846-47	1256	1,44,167	1,42,198
1815-16	1225	1,28,421	1,11,044	1847-48	1257	1,45,617	1,43,525
1816-17	1226	1,35,311	1,17,684	1848-49	1258	1,44,080	1,42,833
1817-18	1227	1,34,572	1,14,223	1849-50	1259	1,45,119	1,42,040
1818-19	1228	1,37,762	1,14,684	1850-51	1260	1,40,865	1,35,938
1819-20	1229	1,02,351	1,01,649	1851-52	1261	1,41,346	1,34,643
1820-21	1230	1,06,428	1,02,943	1852-53	1262	1,69,827	1,68,359
1821-22	1231	1,12,575	1,09,563	1853-54	1263	1,72,762	1,62,973
1822-23	1232	1,07,347	1,07,347	1854-55	1264	1,57,175	1,53,414
1823-24	1233	99,229	98,823	1855-56	1265	1,61,100	1,60,944
1824-25	1234	1,09,107	1,09,087	1856-57	1266	1,63,659	1,63,580
1825-26	1235	1,13,337	1,13,337	1857-58	1267	1,66,666	1,66,354
1826-27	1236	1,13,624	1,13,624	1858-59	1268	1,73,876	1.73,375
1827-28	1237	1,14,883	1,14,883	1859-60	1269	1,76,876	1,73,739
1828-29	1238	1,17,072	1,17,065	1860-61	1270	1,78,231	1,74,997
1829-30	1239	1,16,558	1,16,533	1861-62	1271	1,81,193	1,80,831
1830-31	1240	1,16,951	1,16,951	1862-63	1272	1,86,513	1,86,443
1831-32	1241	1,20,650	1,20,577	1863-64	1273	1,90,279	1,90,124
1832-33	1242	1,20,500	1,19,681	1864-65	1274	1,92,655	1,92,631
1833-34	1243	1,27,217	1,27,063	1865-66	1275	1,89,053	1,88,000
1834-35	1244	1,33,959	1,32,294	1866-67	1276	1,95,943	1,91,955
1835-36	1245	1,46,288	1,44,320	1867-68	1277	1,97,273	1,92,000
1836-37	1246	1,46,419	1,39,471	1868-69	1278	1,95,830	1,89,790
1837-38	1247	1,45,792	1,35,671	1869-70	1279	1,97,678	1,86,919
1838-39	1248	1,45,187	1,41,409	1870-71	1280	1,97,710	1,87,607
1839-40	1249	1,46,490	1,39,041	1871-72	1281	1,97,815	1,79,355
1840-41	1250	1,49,711	1,39,897	1872-73	1282	1,98,812	1,82,872
1841-42	1251	1,50,741	1,38,583	1873-74	1283	1,99,377	1,71,793
1842-43	1252	1,49,069	1,32,371				

The following Extract from Sir T. Munro's Minute, dated 7th January 1823, shows how the produce of land used to be divided between the landlord and the tenant :—

" Under the old Hindu Government they (the people) paid " half of the produce in kind, but after the Mahomedan con- " quest the Zemindars employed in the management of the " country imposed a shist or fixed assessment on the land, to " which extra assessments were afterwards added, by which " the share of the ryots was reduced nominally to one-third, " but actually to one-fifth of the gross produce in rice-lands, " which formed the chief cultivation of the country : in dry " grain the shares of the ryot and Government were equal. " These were the shares which prevailed in the Chicacole " Circar." This division of the produce seems to have continued till the introduction in 1817 of the ryotwari settlement.

This settlement was at first commenced in Patrunivulsa, a village close to Chicacole, under the immediate direction of the Collector: the fields including arable and waste lands were measured, classified, and assessed. The assessment was based upon a valuation of the average of the total produce of the wet and dry lands from Fasli 1220 to 1226.

The proposals for the last settlement were made in 1874 by Mr. Goodrich, the Deputy Director for the Chicacole Taluq. He proposed the grouping of irrigated wet under three classes with reference to the certainty of the sources of supply, (1), all irrigation from river channels or tanks similarly fed in the first group, (2), ordinary tanks with a fair capacity for receiving and storing drainage in the second group and (3), the smaller tanks. For the first group the failure of water was presumed to be improbable and it was therefore treated as superior while the irrigation under the other two groups was held to be more or less precarious.

Rice and ragi were selected the staple crops, the area under the former during a selected year (Fasli 1284) being

68 per cent. of the total area under cultivation, and the proportion on which ragi was raised being about one-quarter of the whole. In fixing the commutation rate therefore these grains were adopted as the standards for irrigated and unirrigated lands. It was intended that the rate should be regulated by the prices prevailing during the 20 years ending 1864, but the adoption of this series of years would have resulted in an abnormally low average in consequence of the growth in the Export trade in rice, the improvement of communications and the attention paid to irrigation works which in this taluq afford a perennial supply of water. The rise in prices seemed likely to be permanent, Mr. Goodrich therefore based his calculations on the prices which ruled during the 20 years ending 1874 exclusive of the famine year 1865-66. The rates arrived at were Rs. 93-5-4 per garce for paddy and Rs. 105 for ragi, Mr Rundall considered the rate for paddy too high and recommended the commutation rate Rs. 80. The rates proposed for wet lands ranged from Rs. 7 to Rs. 1-8-0 an acre and for dry Rs. 5-8-0 to Annas 8. These rates would have caused an increase of Rs. 33,326 or 20 per cent. on the then existing demand for wet, viz., Rs. 1,63,909. For dry there was a decrease of Rs. 391.

The Board of Revenue, however, considered that an increase of 20 per cent. on the wet demand was excessive, and as the ryot in the Chicacole Taluq was described by Mr. Goodrich as "only having just the quantity needed to main-" tain life of the coarsest food," the Board were not convinced that the enhancement was justified. They remarked "they "cannot therefore submit these proposals to Government with "their support. There are several unsatisfactory features "in the scheme, the commutation rate classification and grain "values appearing to require revision, which preclude the "acceptance of money rates based on data, the accuracy of "which is open to question and the Board therefore resolve to "remit the scheme to the Director for reconsideration."

The revised proposals which were submitted with the Director's report, dated 21st January 1879, resulted in an increase of 10,159 acres in area and Rs. 20,433 in assessment over the Revenue Demand of Fasli 1287. The Government approved of these proposals in their Order, No. 739, dated 27th March 1879, Revenue Department, which embodies the brief and concise reports of the Deputy Director of Revenue Settlement and the Director.

The settlement in 1878, of the Berhampore Taluq resulted in an increase of 15,901 acres in area and Rs. 27,506 in assessment.

The number of villages excluding those in the Mohiri Hills amounted to 339. The wet lands were classified in three groups numbered 2 to 4. Those irrigated by the Bahuda and Godahaddo rivers, by *tamparas* or lakes and by the better tanks and hill streams of reliable quality under No. 2, those by the ordinary tanks under No. 3 and by rain-fed tanks under No. 4. 20,849 acres of land were specially treated as "Manawari" or rain-fed at an assessment of Rs. 32,208, the rate per acre varying from Rs. 2-8 to Annas 12. The area of the garden lands, 678 acres, was assessed at Rs. 2,385 the rates being two, viz., Rs. 4 and Rs. 2-8. The area in which are the Government cocoanut* plantations, has not been treated by the Settlement Department. The Revenue accounts for Fasli 1287, show that there were 448 acres of this plantation paying a revenue of Rs. 1,365; the rate is Rs. 3-8 an acre. 5,526 acres have been registered as lands irrigated by baling assessed at Rs. 10,541 exclusive of the abatement of one Rupee per acre for lift. The allowance will be continued as long as the area is irrigated by baling. The fields watered from Itifak wells are not liable to any 2nd charge. There being very little 2nd crop grown the Ryots in the Taluq did not agree to compound the charge for second crop though the consequent advantages were fully explained to them.

* Planted by Captain Evans, see page 219.

All occupied lands (525 acres) in the waterspread of tanks have been registered as wet and the unoccupied as Poramboke.

The financial results of the settlement are briefly given below and are compared with the Revenue Demand for Fasli 1287.

	As per Revenue Demand of Fasli 1287.		As per Settlement.	
	Area. Acres.	Assessment. Rs.	Area. Acres.	Assessment. Rs.
Irrigated 2nd group...	31,919	93,906	34,149	1,18,216
3rd group...	31,991	82,403	35,529	87,472
4th group...	3,324	7,559	3,948	6,712
Total...	67,234	1,83,868	73,626	2,12,400
Unirrigated 1st group.	63,974	98,443	73,483	97,417
Grand Total....	1,13,208	2,82,311	1,47,109	3,09,817

On the whole there was an increase in area of 15,901 acres or 12 per cent. and in assessment of Rs. 27,506 or 10 per cent. on the figures in the Revenue accounts for Fasli 1287. The percentage of increase in wet and dry over the Revenue figures is 10 and 15 respectively in area, that in assessment for wet is 16 while for dry there is a decrease of 1 per cent.

In irrigation Berhampore is not equal to Chicacole and has not therefore the first group irrigation. The increase is most marked in the assessment of wet lands, the rates are moderate and vary from Rs. 1-4 to Rs. 4-8. The dry rates vary from Annas 8 to Rs. 4.

Mr. Spedding briefly summarizes the benefits resulting from the new settlement.

" All anomalous revenue rates have been got rid of and " equitable ones substituted for the locality and irrigation " capability. Lands irrigated by Government sources and " hitherto registered as dry have been transferred to wet and " those not irrigable by such sources, have been placed in the " respective heads of dry and rain-fed paddy lands according "to circumstances. Pattahs have been transferred to actual "holders of lands and joint pattahs subdivided where the "parties concerned agreed thereto in writing. Lands were "allotted for public purposes such as extension of village sites, "grants of lands for threshing floor and assignments for "jungle or hill porambokes and for pasturage. The grievances "of all kinds represented by each individual pattahdar were "heard and relief granted where necessary according to "circumstances."

There are 908 villages in the Taluq of Goomsur of which 140 are agraharams, but the Survey Department did only survey 558 villages, 74 of these being agraharams. The Settlement Department confined their operations only to the 248 villages which are situate in the open country between Aska and Russellkonda. Of the remaining villages some are occupied by the Khonds or are in the Máliahs while some are so feverish and unhealthy that it was not thought advisable to incur the risk of visiting them. Mr. Clerk, the Deputy Director, says the part settled is the garden of the District, the lands being on the whole very good and those situated in the valleys along the brinks of the rivers exceedingly rich. A large area is under sugar-cane cultivation which is in this part of the District in great demand for the Aska Sugar works. The ryots are in a prosperous condition.

There is no first group irrigation in the Taluq. The rivers Loharakandi, Mahanadi, Buda, Baguva and twelve good tanks have been placed in the 2nd group, hill streams and ordinary tanks in the third and the inferior tanks in the fourth. 232 villages fall under these groups there being no wet at all in the remaining 16. Considerable difficulty was experienced in ascertaining the fields in ryots' occupancy as it had been usual to charge on the total holding without entering any particulars in the Pattas granted to the people. The fields were, however at length determined and the Revenue system is now the same as in other parts of the District.

There is no second crop in the Taluq. 15,517 acres of land have been registered as Manavari* and classed under Dry. The assessment is Rs. 27,237 the rates varying from Annas 12 to Rs. 2-8 per acre. The extent of garden lands is 121 acres and the assessment Rs. 450, the rates being Rs. 4-0-0 and Rs. 2-8-0 per acre.

The lands were in the first instance classified fieldwar but were subsequently converted into blocks. They have been for the most part classed in the third taram (black clay), fourth taram (black loam) and fifth taram (black sand)—596 acres of land have been treated as irrigated by baling, the revenue derived being Rs. 1,532. For baling a reduction at 1 Rupee an acre is made. The occupied area within the waterspread of tanks is 29 acres, the unoccupied area has been registered as Poramboke.

The rate on wet lands varies from Rs. 4-8 to Rs. 1-4 and on Dry from Rs. 4 to Annas 4. The occupied area under wet and dry is shown below with the assessment fixed as compared with the figures in the Revenue accounts.

	As per Revenue Accounts.		As per Settlement.	
	Area. Acres.	Assessment. Rs.	Area. Acres.	Assessment. Rs.
Wet ...	23,781	74,756	27,409	83,013
Dry ...	28,670	47,831	37,883	57,474
Total...	52,454	1,22,587	65,292	1,34,487

The unoccupied area is—

	Acres.	Assessment.
Wet... ...	22	60
Dry	9,029	9,072
Total...	9,051	9,132

The result of the settlement is an increase of Rs. 11,900 or 10 per cent. on the Revenue demand of Fasli 1287: the increase in area being 24 per cent.; the average rates are somewhat lower than formerly though there has been an enhancement of Revenue.

* Watered by Rainfall only.

The following is an abstract statement showing the Financial Results of the Settlement of the three Taluqs in the District.

		As per Revenue Accounts.		As per Settlement.	
		Extent.	Assessment.	Extent.	Assessment.
		Acres.	Rs.	Acres.	Rs.
Chicacole ...	Dry	22.968	34,783	28,262	34,028
	Wet	43,782	1,65,591	48,647	1,86,779
	Total...	66,750	2,00,374	76,909	2,20,807
Berhampore...	Dry	63.974	98,443	73,483	97,417
	Wet	67,234	1,83,868	73,626	2,12,400
	Total...	1,31,208	2,82,311	1,47,109	3,09,817
Goomsur ...	Dry	28,670	47,831	37,883	51,474
	Wet	23,784	74,756	27,409	83,013
	Total...	52,454	1,22,587	65,292	1,34,487
Total ...	Dry	1,15,612	1,81,057	1,39,628	1,82,919
	Wet	1,34,800	4,24,215	1,49,682	4,82,192
	Grand Total ..	2,50,412	6,05,272	2,89,310	6,65,111

It will be seen that the total result shows an increase of Rs. 59,839 or 10 per cent. in assessment and 16 per cent. in area.

The following is an abstract showing the area both occupied and unoccupied land falling under each money rate in the District.

Rates.			Occupied.		Unoccupied.	
			Acres.	Rs.	Acres.	Rs.
Wet ... Rs.	5	8	7,553	41,426	34	189
	4	8	33,043	1,47,309	237	1,068
	3	8	41,865	1,14,939	590	2,064
	2	8	39,895	98,244	981	2,430
	2	0	22,272	43,165	1,746	3,506
	1	8	3,553	5,227	665	1,003
	1	4	1,501	1,882	64	80
Total...			1,49,682	4,82,192	4,317	10,340

Rates.	Occupied. Acres.	Occupied. Rs.	Unoccupied. Acres.	Unoccupied. Rs.
Dry ... Rs. 4 0	821	33,293	89	357
2 8	5,547	13,930	378	947
2 0	16,034	32,383	1,165	2,335
1 8	18,591	28,129	169	271
1 4	47,428	59,615	7,990	9,965
1 0	34,023	34,367	10,919	10,912
0 12	6,940	5,304	6,669	5,138
0 8	8,110	4,086	11,598	5,800
0 4	1,686	446	425	107
Govt. cocoanut plantation at Rs. 3-8	448	1,366	...	...
Total...	1,39,628	1,82,919	39,402	35,832
Grand Total...	2,89,310	6,65,111	43,719	46,172

It is said that the District has been lowly assessed, the highest rate being only Rs. 5-8 against Rs. 12, Rs. 10-8, Rs. 9 and Rs. 7-8 an acre elsewhere, but this is the first time the District has been settled, and the old Ryotwari assessment was fixed in a very haphazard way as a lump assessment liable to increase for new cultivation, was fixed on each village.

CHAPTER XI.

AGRICULTURE AND MANUFACTURES.

THE DIVISION OF THE TELUGU YEAR—CLASSIFICATION OF THE SOIL—IRRIGATION CHANNELS—WET CROPS—SECOND WET CROP—IMPORTATION OF ORISSA RICE—MODES OF CULTIVATION OF RICE—COST—THE SEVERAL KINDS OF PADDY GROWN—THE TELUGU AND URIYA EQUIVALENTS FOR PADDY IN ITS DIFFERENT STAGES OF GROWTH—SUGAR-CANE—METHOD OF CULTIVATION—DESCRIPTION OF THE NATIVE SUGAR MILL—THE COST OF SUGAR-CANE CULTIVATION—DALWA PADDY—RAGI CULTIVATION—CUMBU OR GANTELU—KORRALU AND CHAMULU—PULSES—WELL CULTIVATION—THE FRUIT OF THE DISTRICT—THE WARUM OR DIVISION OF THE CROP—WAGES OF LABOURERS—PRICES OF GRAIN AND PULSE—THE LAND TENURES—WEIGHTS AND MEASURES—MANUFACTURES—HANDICRAFTSMEN—BERHAMPORE TUSSER AND SILK CLOTHS—CHICACOLE MUSLINS—ASKA SUGAR AND RUM FACTORY.

AGRICULTURE.

The division of the Telugu year has been described in the Vizagapatam Manual. For agricultural purposes we need only consider the 3rd to the 17th of the twenty-seven divisions or Kartés of from thirteen to fourteen days each into which it is resolved. They are given with the English monthly equivalents and the usual agricultural operations that are carried on in each.

Divisions of the Luni-Solar year according to the Telugu Calendar.

Number.	Kartés or Asterisms of the Lunar Zodiac.	Duration in days.	Approximate date of commencement of each Karté or Sun's entrance.	Agricultural operation.
3	Kruttika ...	14	9th May ...	Ploughing.
4	Rohini ...	14	23rd May ...	If there is rain, cotton, gingelly, korralu sown.
5	Mrugésira ...	14	6th June ...	General sowing if rain falls.
6	Arudra ...	14	20th June ...	Useless for any agricultural purposes.
7	Punarvasu ...	14	4th July ...	Sowing if there has not been rain before; if there has been, transplantation of ragi, sugar-cane supported, Pulses sown.
8	Pushyami ...	14	18th July ...	
9	Ashésha ...	14	1st August ...	Paddy transplanted. Gathering of crops put down in Rohini.
10	Makha ...	14	15th August ...	As above, also ragi harvest begins.
11	Pubba ...	14	29th August ...	
12	Uttara ...	13	11th September	Last paddy transplanted. Pyra or 2nd crop in dry land put in.
13	Hasta ...	14	25th September	Garden crops put down.
14	Chitta ...	13	9th October ...	Weeding, &c., so many insects about that anything sown now is not expected to live.
15	Swati ...	15	22nd October ...	
16	Visakha ...	14	4th November.	Paddy harvest.
17	Anuradha ...	13	19th November.	Paddy harvest and rains are over.

The classification of soil as made by the recent Settlement Department shows that regar land predominates in the Government taluks (but little survey has been made in the larger Zemindary tract); next in quantity we have red soil then sandy and, last of all, alluvial, of which there is very little indeed.

The regar or black soil is most suitable for wet or paddy cultivation. The sandy for the ragi cultivation.

Where the rain is sufficiently frequent in the vicinity of the hills rain-fed paddy is grown, *i.e.* that for which none or but very small tanks are used (Manavári).

The following is the list of river channels irrigating the lands in the three Government taluks.

GOVERNMENT TALUKS.

Goomsur Taluk.

1. Bodonadi,
2. Lukharakhandi,
4. Bhagura,
3. Soronadi.

Chicacole Taluk.

1.	Vadada Desa Gedda.	From the Langulia River.
2.	Dusi Gedda.	
3.	Gajuli Gedda.	
4.	Bairi Desa Gedda.	From the Vamsadhara River.
5.	Naira Gedda.	
6.	Purushothapuram Desa Gedda.	
7.	Nagarikatakam Gedda.	
8.	Jalmuru Desa Gedda.	
9.	Polaki Desa Gedda.	
10.	Mobagam Gedda.	
11.	Lukulam Gedda.	
12.	Gareebula Gedda.	

Berhumpore Taluk.

1.	Bellupada River channel	From the Bahuda River.
2.	Lothaputti do.	
3.	Rattakanna do.	
4.	Haripuram do.	
5.	Kolingani Dhumku Nalla.	
6.	Kasapuram River channel.	

7. Jayamangalla nalla, a branch of the Godahado River.
8. Heeradharabutte, a branch of the Rushikulia River.

Besides the above, the larger irrigation works of note are the Boiri Reservoir, south-west of Gangupur in the Goomsur taluq, and the Koratoli tampara in the Berhampore taluq fed by a branch of the Godahado River.

The Parla Kimedi tanks are named in Chapter II.

As elsewhere, the crops grown are divided into wet (Telugu Pallam, Tamil Nanjah) and dry (Telugu Mettu, Tamil Punjah). What used to be called Totaccal or garden crops, are now properly classed as dry.

Paddy and sugar-cane are the chief wet crops of Ganjam. The former is the staple crop of the district, is of a very fine quality and largely exported.

The earlier the season, the better, as a rule, is the harvest; but except in Uddanam, a tract of country near Ichapur, "there is no custom" to raise a second crop in this district.

Large quantities of the coarser rice grown in Orissa are imported across the Chilka lake for food while the native good rice is exported.

The paddy is sown both broadcast and in beds for transplantation. The system followed does not differ from that adopted all over India; if broadcasted, the field is manured more or less according to the Ryot's ability; if transplanted, the nursery bed alone is manured. Buffaloes are used for ploughing the wet land by those who can afford them, and the district breed of these ungainly beasts is not bad, but the cattle are very undersized and poor.

Transplantation is most practised in the southern part of the district. For it, nursery beds are prepared by about seven ploughings and heavy manuring with cattle stall and other refuse till the ground is quite pulverized. As soon as a supply of water is secure or anticipated, the seed sown thickly is twice ploughed in, and the young plants which spring up very quickly are carefully tended and watered. The larger fields to which a month later the young plants are taken, are prepared by three ploughings, but generally without manure. When they are put out finally the young plants are generally planted about a distance of two inches or so from each other. From 15 days after transplantation the fields require a constant and ample supply of water. I am not aware that the amount per acre is determined, but the more the plants grow the greater is the quantity of water required.

After the crop is cut it is deposited in heaps and left for several days to dry; it is then brought to the threshing floor where the grain is threshed, either by the hand, striking the bundles against a cart so that the grain falls underneath, or by treading it out with cattle.

Where the broadcast system is resorted to, no nursery beds are required; the fields are manured about May and thrice ploughed till about June when the seeds are sown broadcast and spring up after a shower of rain. After one month's growth of the plants, the land requires to be continually watered and the crop is kept clear of weeds by ploughing in the furrows.

The charges incurred in raising a paddy crop by each of the two systems on an acre of wet land which pays a Jeroyiti assessment of Rs. 4-8 a year, may be thus estimated:—

The Broadcast System.

	RS.	A.	P.
Ploughing and sowing ...	2	0	0
Manure	0	8	0
Seed	1	8	0
Weeding	1	0	0
Reaping	0	8	0
Threshing	0	4	0
Repairing bunds, letting water, &c...	0	8	0
Government Kist... ...	4	8	0
Total Rs...	10	12	0

The Transplantation System.

	RS.	A.	P.
Ploughing the seed bed ...	0	8	0
Manure	0	4	0
Seed	1	8	0
Taking the young plants out of the seed bed and carrying them to the transplantation ground ...	0	12	0
Ploughing for transplantation ...	1	8	0
Transplanting	1	0	0
Repairing bunds	0	2	0
Reaping	0	8	0
Threshing	0	4	0
Government assessment ...	4	8	0
Total Rs....	10	14	0

In each of the systems the land yields a produce of two-thirds of a garce of paddy, the average value of which is Rupees 25.

The following is a list of the different descriptions of paddy cultivated in the principal Division :—

1.	Pascha Bhogo	... Very fine.	Grown to a small extent.
2.	Sunnakhilo	... do.	
3.	Dasaradhi	.. do.	
4.	Ratnachudil	... do.	
5.	Nodiyaroso	... do.	
6.	Jagannadhavallabho	... do.	
7.	Kolajhari	... do.	
8.	Parujatako	... do.	
9.	Chikatisoru	... do.	
10.	Jillipayaga	... do.	
11.	Munda Bonuli	... do.	

No.	Name		Quality	Remarks
12.	Bhojana	...	Very fine.	Largely grown.
13.	Maharaja Ponyagu	...	Fine.	
14.	Narayandas Pryagi	...	do.	
15.	Kottaragodi	...	do.	
16.	Kristnakojelo	...	do.	
17.	Boyahunda	...	do.	
18.	Moyipala	...	Coarse.	
19.	Chinnamali	...	do.	
20.	Bankayi	...	do.	
21.	Kolakonuyayi	...	do.	
22.	Kartika Kotta	...	do.	
23.	Bhindiyarayi	...	do.	
24.	Nimmayi	...	do.	
25.	Bamsomuli	...	do.	
26.	Oriyasalli	...	do.	
27.	Bangara Madhavy	...	do.	
28.	Duddho Bankayi	...	do.	
29.	Loghuvasa	...	do.	
30.	Kajalo Mongo	...	do.	
31.	Mantara	...	Very coarse.	Grown to a small extent.
32.	Duddhomoni	...	do.	
33.	Kokharuva Moyipalo	...	do.	
34.	Kola Biliagy	...	do.	
35.	Kusuma	...	do.	
36.	Piya	...	do.	
37.	Panichi	...	do.	
38.	Boraponko	...	Very fine.	
39.	Jhariphullo	...	do.	
40.	Sonna Bankoyi	...	Fine.	Largely grown.
41.	Pinpuru Mundiya	...	do.	
42.	Sogododhuli	...	Coarse.	
43.	Baromunya	...	do.—Largely grown.	
44.	Kosichompa	...	Fine.	
45.	Santanipatto	...	Coarse.	

46.	Gunta	...	Coarse.
47.	Tulasivaso	...	Fine.
48.	Koliya	...	Coarse.
49.	Gongavalli	...	Fine.
50.	Kondua	...	Coarse.
51.	Moyipalo	...	do.
52.	Kolasora	..	do.
53.	Panisondho	...	do.
54.	Ojanosoli	...	do.
55.	Œtnasitolo	...	do.
56.	Belindi	...	do.
57.	Machokonta	...	do.
58.	Noyikonda	...	do.
59.	Osinisutta	...	do.
60.	Sunnaphullo	...	do.
61.	Parijatoko	...	do.
62.	Holidigundi	...	do.
63.	Jiri	...	do.
64.	Magurakotta	...	do.
65.	Sómachinnomali	...	do.
66.	Kosichompa	...	do.
67.	Bonokjulo	...	do.
68.	Mukutakera	...	do.
69.	Dalipohara	...	do.
70.	Sojini	...	do.
71.	Kolakoranda	...	do.
72.	Kali	...	do.

The women engaged in the operation of transplantation have a practice of indulging from time to time in a peculiar cry somewhat resembling the Tyrolese "Yodel."

The young paddy plants raised in seed beds are called in Uriya "Toli" and in Telugu "Akulu." The growing rice stalks after transplantation are called in Uriya "Dhanno Gotcho" and in Telugu "Chénu." Rice in the husk is termed

"Dhanno" in Uriya and "Dhányamu" in Telugu. Raw rice deprived of the husk is called in Uriya "Uváchávulo" and in Telugu "Pachchi Biyyam."

The lower classes are in the habit of eating what is called boiled rice, that is rice first boiled (or steamed) in the husk, the husk being afterwards removed by beating in the usual way, but the machine used is a long lever working in a hole in the floor, the lever is raised by the women with their feet and allowed to fall on the rice; it is termed "Usunachávulo" in Uriya and "Uppudu Biyyam" in Telugu. Cooked rice is called in Uriya "Bhato" and in Telugu "Annamu," the common term for ordinary food. Another preparation of rice is "Chuda" in Uriya and "Atukulu" in Telugu, which is rice boiled in the husk, then husked and afterwards beaten flat; in such state it is fit for immediate use. "Kanji" is the thick liquid water in which rice has been boiled.

The most profitable crop in Ganjam is sugar-cane, and the quality of the cane is most excellent. As a rule, however, only the more wealthy ryots can afford to grow it, as it takes ten months reaching maturity and requires one-third more water than rice. It also demands more care and attention than any other crop, and it so takes it out of the land that it should lie fallow in the next season. It is chiefly cultivated about Aska in Goomsur, Surada, Dharakot, and Atagada in the north, and in the south in the Parla Kimedi Estate.

Bears are very fond of the sweet cane and play great havoc in the sugar-cane fields at night-time in spite of fences and watchers.

The ground is first manured well by enfolding sheep and cattle, and by spreading over it stored manure and gingelly oil cake, which last is considered essential. It is ploughed up thoroughly some fifteen times and flooded when the operation of planting commences. For its propagation a supply of the canes of the last year is reserved, which are cut into pieces of about 8 inches in length and are planted out at a distance of one and half feet or so from each other. In the absence of rain the field is, at this stage, flooded every four days. The shoots generally appear fifteen days after planting. The earth is loosened round the stems with a hand hoe and the weeds, if there be any, are removed. The field now requires to be watered every ten or fifteen days according to circumstances, unless there is rain. About August, when the canes are from 3 to 4 feet in height, a stake is stuck into the ground by the side of each plant which is tied to it by its long leaves for the purpose of supporting it. Each cutting produces some 5 or 6 canes, and some ten months after planting they are fit to be cut. The canes are generally an inch or so in diameter and from four to six feet in length. The native sugar-mill consists of two vertical cylinders wrought on a perpetual screw between which the canes are passed as they revolve upon each other. The juice expressed is conveyed to an iron pan, and as soon as this pan receives a sufficient quantity of juice it is removed and placed upon a fire and the juice slowly boiled with a little chunam (lime). It is then passed out into pots that can hold 15 seers in the principal Division (5 in the Sub-Division.) The resulting jaggery is then ready for the market. The cost of the cultivation of an acre of cane in 1856 was estimated to be Rs. 150, the return Rs. 200 ; now, Rs. 174 and 230 respectively. The greater quantity of the cane grown is converted into sugar, &c., at the Aska Factory.

If the means of irrigation exist, a second crop of paddy called Dalwa paddy or of green gram(*a*) is sometimes raised on paddy land.

Dalwa paddy is also raised in low lands from which the water is not off in time for the planting of the larger crop. This paddy takes a lesser time to ripen than the big paddy.

The wet lands are also used for oil seeds between April and May.

(*a*) Phascolus Mungo.

Of dry crops, that most valued and on which the agricultural population depend for their food, is the ragi(*b*) or in Telugu "Chollu," in Uriya "Mandia."

It is raised on sandy, easily drained land, and once started will support a drought that would ruin the paddy crop; but at the same time the rain that is liked by the natives for the paddy is too much for it.

This crop also is transplanted; the roots of the young plants being placed in each furrow, are covered up by the earth moved by the plough in its next course.

Cumbu(*c*) "Gantelu" is not much grown here, but more in the north than the south, and the same may be said of Cholam(*d*) or "Jonnalu," but this latter is more used in the Hills.

Korralu(*e*) and Chamalu(*f*) are neither a very favorite crop, but Chamalu is the principal dry crop of the Hill country.

The pulses grown are in their order here given. Horse gram(*g*), black gram(*h*) and red gram(*i*). Of the latter, a kind called Hill doll or red gram is very much grown in the Hill clearances in the Máliahs.

Of special crops, the chief are oil seeds(*j*), cotton(*k*) and tobacco(*l*).

The beauty of the topes in the district has been noticed.

The cultivation of turmeric as a special Hill product has also been noticed and an account of all crops grown will be found in the Appendix. Well cultivation is not much favored in Ganjam. On the banks of nearly all the rivers, and especially near towns and large villages, Picotas are used to raise water for cane and garden crops, but well cultivation is hardly practised at all.

(*b*) Eleusine Coracana. (*c*) Penicellaria Spicata. (*d*) Sorghum vulgare.
(*e*) Panicum Italicum. (*f*) Oplismenus Frumentaceum.
(*g*) Dolichos Uniflorus. (*h*) Phaseolus Roxburgii. (*i*) Cajanus Indicus.
(*j*) Sesamum Indicum and Ricinus Communis.
(*k*) Gossypium Indicum. (*l*) Nicotiana.

The district can hardly be said to be famous for its fruit. There are no good mangoes(*a*) to speak of, and the plaintains are of the ordinary coarse kind, seen everywhere. The jack(*b*), abominable to the nose of a European, flourishes and smells in Kimedi and the Tamarind(*c*) is found everywhere about the district. A large loose-skinned orange(*d*) found in the Hills of Pedda Kimedi is the only fruit worthy of note save those grown in a few native and European gardens. European flowers and vegetables do very well in the cold weather.

Barwa is famous for its cocoanut trees, and there is considerable amount of oil and coir manufactured from them.

Payment for agricultural labour is made either in kind, that is in grain, or in money. When paid in kind, the average monthly payment of a labourer is 40 Madras measures or seers with a cloth in the cold weather and perquisites at harvest time. When paid in money and hired all the year round, the labourer's wages are about two and half rupees a month, but perquisites are thrown in.

As compared with other parts of India, the daily wages of coolies are low, and the cost of living in Ganjam is less than elsewhere. The different daily rates of hire for the years 1850, 1851, and 1871 and 1876 were as follows :—

	1850.	1851.	1871.	1876.
Coolies ...	9 pice to 1 a.	1 a.	1 a. 8 p.	2 as.
Women do. ...	9 pice	6 to 8 pice	1 a.	1 a. 4 p.
Bricklayers ...	2 as. 8 p.	2 as. to 3 as.	4 as.	6 as.
Carpenters ..	2 as. 8 p.	2 as. to 3 as.	4 as.	6 as.
Blacksmiths ...	2 as. 8 p.	3 as.	4 as.	6 as.

The following table exhibits the different prices of food-grains, &c., for the years 1850, 1860, 1870 and 1876, per Madras garce of 9,874 lb.

(*a*.) Mangifera Indica. (*b*.) Artocarpus Integrifolia.
(*c*.) Tamarindus Indicus. (*d*.) Citrus Aurantium.

	1850.	1860.	1870.	1876.
Best rice ...	Rs. 104	Rs. 223	Rs. 278	Rs. 320
Common rice ...	96	267	257	267
Best paddy ...	41	68	117	125
Common paddy...	39	18	104	105
Wheat ...	169	309	578	290
Salt ...	155	185	319	336
Ragi ...	52	...	124	133

The land tenures of the district may be briefly classed under three heads :—

1. *Ryotwári* or individual holdings.

2. *Kosht Gutá*, i. e., Villagewár system of joint rent and responsibility.

3. *Mustajári*, or the Renting-out system.

The two first systems are chiefly confined to the Government Taluks, whilst the Mustájari system prevails in the Zemindari tracts. The Kosht Gutá or Villagewár system is a relic of the past, and is rapidly giving way to the Ryotwár system, which is common throughout the Madras Presidency. Government ryots are allowed a right of occupancy in their lands as long as they pay their kists, or periodical instalments of rent. The document that sets forth the extent and boundary of each ryot's holding together with the amount of rent that he has to pay and the dates of payment is termed a patta. The number of pattas held in Ganjam in various years will be found in the Appendix. The rent is paid in money. In the *Kosht Gutá* system an entire village is rented out to the whole body of ryots who make themselves jointly and severally responsible for the payment of the Village Revenue, irrespective of the amount of land which they may choose to cultivate. Immemorial waste (*anádi banjar*) in Gumsúr is sometimes rented out on the Cowle system upon favourable rates of assessment for periods of three or eight years gradually increasing to the full assessment of lands of similar quality in the neighbourhood.

The Mustájari system is resorted to when money is scarce or when the landlord wants ready money or wishes to save himself the trouble of dealing with the ryots individually. The privilege of collecting the rents of the village or villages is put up to auction and sold to the highest bidder. This leads to a system of rack-renting. The Mustájar or renter makes an advance of money to the Zemindar and collects what he can in kind from the ryots who suffer accordingly. The usual rate for wet lands is a half share, but it is said that even more than that is sometimes paid by the ryots. For dry lands it is usual to take a money rate, but any arrangement the Mustájar likes he can make. Very little use is made of Act VIII of 1865, either by the landlord or tenant; but there is no doubt that the Zemindari ryots pay a good deal more for their lands than their fellows who cultivate Government lands. They are not, however, compelled to pay at fixed times and fixed amounts, but have much more license to pay when and how it is convenient to them, and it is for this reason that they are contented with their position.

Weights and Measures.

Weights and measures in Ganjam vary very much, and reform in this respect is much needed. The túm (toom) which is the most common measure of capacity in the district, varies so much that it is scarcely found to be the same at any two places 15 miles apart. Of nine different kinds of túm in use in the district the average has been found equal to 254·8 tolas or a little over 6 lbs. It must be further noted that there are two kinds of measures prevalent, viz., the Bikká and the Sikká, of which the Bikká is $\frac{5}{8}$ of the Sikká.

I.—*Weights.*

15 tolás	...	...	make	1 solá.
4 solás	...	...	„	1 addá.
4 addás	...	...	„	1 túm (toom), 1 túm = 3 seers of 80 tolas each.
4 túms	...	...	„	1 náuti = 12 seers.

II.—*Measures.*

4 giddas	make	1 solá.
2 solás	„	1 tavvá.
2 tavvás	„	1 addá.
4 addás	„	1 túm or kuncham.
4 túms	„	1 náuti.
20 náuties	„	1 bharnam.
120 náuties	„	1 Itchapúr garce.
150 náuties	„	1 country or Calingapatam garce.
240 náuties	„	1 sea-port garce.
400 náuties	„	1 Madras garce.
1 Madras garce	„	4,800 seers.
In Chicacole 3 seers (each 80 tolás)	„	1 kuncham or túm.
20 kunchams	„	1 putti.
30 putties	„	1 garce.

III.—*Land Measures.*

8 cubits or godzo make 1 rod or Nolo = 13 feet Engl :
1 rod square = 1 kuntá or 169 sq. ft.
50 kuntás = 1 bharnam of irrigated land = 8,450 sq. ft.

In Ganjam 5 bharnams are reckoned as equal to 1 acre.

The bharnam (in the Northern Division) is really a measure of capacity, viz. :—

4 túms	=	1 náuti, and
20 náuties	=	1 bharnam.

In Chicacole the garce being a measure of capacity is in the same manner made use of as a land measure, viz., for that extent of land which may be ordinarily expected to yield a garce of paddy.

The measure of *distance* in Ganjam is the Kós, which is any distance between 2 miles and 2½ miles according to circumstances.

MANUFACTURES.

The manufactures of the district are those necessary for the people and little more. The village weaver makes the ordinary cloths, which are always used by those who can afford them in preference to English manufacture and the village potter, blacksmith, and carpenter satisfy, in a rough but sufficient way, their other wants.

In Berhampore there is a manufacture of Tusser as well as fine silk cloths, but the last is in the hands of a few people who can afford to advance money for the material that the weavers cannot afford. The demand is very small and does not extend beyond the next district, Vizagapatam.

In Chicacole there is a very considerable manufacture still of muslin cloths, many of them very handsomely finished with gold thread. The common Chicacole muslin is also still made and is hawked about the country as far south as Masulipatam, but the manufacture is nothing to what it used to be. Beyond these two industries and the Sugar and Rum Factory at Aska, there is none of note in this district.

The Factory at Aska is managed by a firm composed of European and Native partners. The original value of the plant and machinery is estimated at 60,000£, and the Factory is furnished with machinery of the best construction driven by steam-power, for the generation of which there is a large consumption of fuel.

*The process employed for the manufacture of sugar is that termed in German the "Diffusions-process." It consists, shortly speaking, in chopping up the sugar-cane into small shavings by means of rapidly revolving knives, and the juice of the cane is then extracted by a thorough saturation in water. The saturated extract is afterwards boiled down into sugar, after undergoing various processes of cleansing and refining. It is calculated that by the "Diffusions-process,"

*These particulars have been kindly favoured by F. J.V. Minchin, Esq.. of Aska.

some 80 per cent. of sugar is extracted out of a possible 90 per cent. in the cane. By the native method of manufacture, which is of the rudest description, a large percentage of the sugar-cane juice remains unextracted, and is thus wasted. The refuse of the sugar-cane is used for fuel and burnt. The process employed is a continuous one, and fine white sugar can be bagged from the cane within 48 hours without the use of animal charcoal. When charcoal is used the time required is 72 hours.

The yearly out-turn of sugar from diffusion is now (1880) about 8,000 bags of 1½ cwt. each of first product, valued at 1,60,000 Rupees. The Factory turns out from cane 14 tons of sugar in 24 hours. 100,000 gallons of syrup are also manufactured yearly valued at 25,000 Rupees. Centrifugaled "Chini," or jaggery deprived of its syrups by the centrifugal process, is also at times largely manufactured, when there is a demand for home shipment. This phase of the sugar industry is however threatened with extinction on account of the unremunerative prices obtained in the raw sugar market at home, owing to the failure of sugar-refining as a trade, caused by the bounty on the export of refined sugar from France. The refining power of the Aska Factory is equal to 2,000 tons of refined sugar of a value of Rs. 6,00,000. Since the demand for the jaggery of the Ganjam District for export, sugar-refining has been almost abandoned in favor of diffusion. The season of manufacture for sugar is that of the cane season, from January to the end of March. The jurors of the Paris Exhibition of 1878, granted a silver medal to Messrs. Minchin and Co. for their exhibits of sugar.

The distillation of rum and other liquors is carried on in the most approved fashion, and the liquors manufactured are much superior to those formerly distilled by the Odiya "Sundies," in whose hands the liquor traffic formerly lay. The rum is chiefly manufactured out of the surplus syrup, which it is not found profitable to convert into sugar. For making country spirits, rice and mowa flowers (*Bassia latifolia*) are principally used. Besides rum and rice spirit, cognac and milk punch are manufactured. The Factory also possesses one of Barnett's patent Soda-water machines. The out-turn per year of rum is 150,000 gallons proof spirit. The distillery possesses two column stills, each capable of delivering from 1,000 to 1,200 gallons of proof spirit in the 24 hours. The spirit reservoir lined with Portland cement which is attached to the distillery has a capacity of 16,000 gallons.

The Factory contains, besides the machinery and buildings connected with the manufacture of sugar and rum, a cooperage for making casks and a complete establishment for casting in iron and brass. In the busy season of the year it affords employment to 1,000 men and women, of whom 300 are mechanics, brick-layers, coopers, stokers, engine-men and men engaged in the foundry. During the idler months of the year from 300 to 400 persons are employed, chiefly mechanics.

The establishment of the Aska Factory on so large and important a scale in the midst of a district, at one time one of the wildest in India, has given not only a considerable stimulus to the cultivation of sugar-cane, but at the same time has been the means of imparting to many of its inhabitants a skill as mechanics which they would have had no opportunities of acquiring elsewhere. It has thus indirectly borne no inconsiderable share in the development of the district and its welfare.

CHAPTER XII.

SCARCITIES, FAMINE AND THEIR PREVENTION.

FAMINES BETWEEN 1789 AND 1866—THE FAMINE OF 1865-66—COLLECTOR'S APPLICATION FOR RELIEF REFUSED BY GOVERNMENT—RELIEF HOUSES—STRUGGLE BETWEEN THE POOR AND STARVATION—DEATHS BY PRIVATION—GOVERNMENT SANCTIONED RS. 10,000 WITH EXCELLENT RESULT—RS. 20,000 MORE RECEIVED—CHILKA CANAL WORK STARTED—SEED PADDY DISTRIBUTED——DISTRESS AMONG WEAVERS HOW TREATED—ORPHAN CHILDREN PLACED UNDER MISSIONARIES—COST OF FAMINE TO GOVERNMENT—OBJECTION OF BETTER CLASSES OF PEOPLE TO TAKE COOKED FOOD—APPREHENSION OF A FAMINE IN 1878—SLIGHT RELIEF GRANTED—HIGH PRICES OF GRAIN CAUSED DISTRESS—WANT OF WORK IN THE FIELDS—MR. RUNDALL'S SCHEMES OF IRRIGATION—COLONEL COTTON'S APPROVAL—CAPTAIN BECKLEY'S SCHEME—THE FAMINE COMMISSIONER'S PROPOSAL TO STORE GRAIN AGAINST FAMINE, NOTED—THE SCHEME OF CONNECTING THE CHILKA LAKE WITH CALINGAPATAM—THE CHILKA CANAL SHOULD BE EXTENDED AT LEAST TO GOPALPUR.

The famine and scarcities that have fallen upon the district are four, viz., between 1789 and 1792, between 1799 and 1801, between 1836 and 1839 and between 1865 and 1866.

There have been besides times of scarcity but not of such extent as to require special notice.

The two first are of the last century and for the purpose of this work may be passed over, it is not unlikely that the disturbed state of the country had much to do with them. We have no record of them.

The third a period of scarcity rather than of famine also occurred when the country was disturbed by the Goomsur war. Prices rose exceedingly; rice that had been selling at 70 seers a rupee rose to 25 seers a rupee, and ragi from 100 to 40. The next four years' prices continued very high.

The last was the famine of Orissa.* The rainfall of 1863, 1864 and 1865 had been scanty in the whole district, but especially so in the principal division where it was recorded to be 29·39, 20·44 and 18·05 inches, and by September 1865 when the usual import of rice by road from the north was found to be failing, prices had risen so that the quietness of the district was imperilled by threatened grain riots.

By January matters were so strained that the Collector applied for special relief for the people to the Government, but his application met with a curt refusal.

In February he called upon the Zemindars to feed their people and proposed a subscription in the district, both of which met with a ready compliance. Relief houses were opened by the various Zemindars and in the Government Taluks.

In March it was clear that famine was in the land, but the Government while sanctioning a few small works would not approve of the Chilka Canal, a large work proposed. Things went on from bad to worse and in May the Government having called for a special report the Collector recorded that an universal struggle between the poor and starvation was going on, that 200 deaths from starvation were reported, but that of 1,543 deaths reported from small-pox and cholera many had been due to want and hunger, and that the ryots preferred death to taking cooked food which in consequence of the limited means at his command, was the only form of relief, he the Collector, could offer.

---

* Extracted from a Report by a District Officer compiled after the famine of 1866.

In May the subscriptions, local and from Madras, were Rs. 8,700 per mensem, Government help, except the sanction for roads already named, being nothing, and by this time the relief houses were so beset by starving people clamorous for food that the distribution of such food as could be afforded was made with much difficulty and only with police to keep order. On the last day but one of the month came a Government telegram of a grant of 10,000 Rupees.

Being now awake to the urgency of the case the Government did all that could be done to assist the people and the officials of the district and as rapidly as possible, arrangements for the relief of all who were in need of it were made. By the end of June matters had vastly improved and a further supply of Rs. 20,000 was sent from the North-West Famine Fund.

In July the excavation of the Chilka canal was started.

In August the Board of Revenue sent up seed paddy at the Collector's request, and with this and the improved state of affairs it became possible to afford relief to all cases that could be reached.

In October a further grant of rice was made by Government to the Relief Fund, and by the end of the month the prices began to fall and the numbers at the relief houses which were 8,000 in July fell to 6,000.

In November the early paddy was cut, and this and the imports from Cuttack and the feeding of the poorer classes caused an absolute glut of food grain in the markets.

In the meantime the state of the weavers had attracted attention and advances for cloth to be made had been given them.

The number of parentless children that were saved from death was 537, and they were distributed among the Missionaries to educate.

The cost of the famine to Government may be tabulated as follows :—

			Rs.
1.	Remissions and refunds to ryots	...	1,25,405
2.	Cost of seed grain given	...	29,000
*3.	Cost of rice given to ryots for food	...	85,000
4.	Distribution of cooked food	...	60,000
5.	Cost of works sanctioned	...	75,000
		Total Rs...	3,74,405

About 3,75,000 Rupees; to this may be added batta given to the sepoys stationed in the district and to Government servants which will add, say Rs. 60,000, to the total.

The reluctance of the better classes to take relief in the shape of cooked food was sadly apparent in the famine, and there is not a doubt that a great many held out to their death.

It is impossible to say what would have been the improved state of affairs if the Government had promptly accepted the Collector's statements and given him assistance earlier, but the recorded deaths out of a population of 303,779 in the year between October 1863 and September 1865 are no less than 16,707. These figures apply to the principal Division only. In the Sub-Division there was not more than a severe scarcity.

In 1878, there was great fear of a famine. The high price of rice in consequence of the demand to supply the famine of Southern India, tempted the people in the middle of the year to part with their stocks. The rains failed to a considerable extent, and by October, though there was a fair ragi crop, there was very little prospect of a rice harvest. By December and January 1879 grain robberies commenced and similar other crimes, for which the excuse of hunger was given by the perpetrators. The poor people, beggars, &c., who infest the towns had to be fed by the Municipalites and slight relief to similar people in the villages was provided and a few small road repairs were commenced.

* The whole of this is not a cost to Government as until June, it was defrayed by public subscription. This figure does include the probable cost to Zemindars for their private charities.

The import of rice from Cuttack, however, did not fail, and the District Officers were able to feel sure that with the rains of the South-West monsoon their cause for anxiety would cease. They came later than usual however, and not until the fear of famine had taken possession of the people. At no time, however, was there any real absence of food; distress was caused entirely by high prices of grain. There was plenty in the district, and the difficulty of the poorer classes was to find employment and so earn money to buy their daily food, for the absence of rain put a stop to the ordinary work in the fields and fear of worse times rendered all classes loath to enter on any expenditure that could by any means be avoided.

An account of the schemes that have been proposed for the irrigation of the district and prevention of future famine may not be out of place.

In 1854, Captain Rundall reported as follows, on the capabilities of the rivers of the district for irrigation purposes :—

The means of Irrigation described.

" The means of Irrigation consists of channels taken from " the rivers, which traverse the " district, some of which are led " to reservoirs, which store the water brought by the freshes, " and some irrigate the fields at once.

" Of the two portions the Southern is the best furnished with " river channels, as it has the advantage of two large rivers " from whence to draw its supply. " From the Nangoolea* or Chi- " cacole river, one large channel " is taken off near the village " of Nimtoorladah, which runs " for a distance of 20 miles, and " waters land yielding a revenue " of Rs. 31,000. From the †Wum- " shadaura or Calingapatam " river there are 4 channels taken " off the right and 4 off the left bank. The former water land

	Rs.
Supplying Channel to Poorshotpore Tank.......... ..	9,918
Byree Dasey Buttay..........	15,448
The Garra and Omravilly...	8,262
The Calingapatam Channel.	990
	34,618
The Polaki Channel..........	32,000
The Looklam do.	5,000
The Jullmoor do.	16,488
The Nagaricutticum Channel	6,804
Total...	60,292

* Nagavali. † Vamsadhara.

" to the amount of Rs. 34,600, the latter to that of Rs. 60,000.

" On the left or Northern side of the Calingapatam river " whatever land is not irrigated by the above mentioned chan- " nels is supplied from tanks wholly dependant on the local " rains, with the exception of a small irrigation work lately " constructed across the hill stream called the Gareeboola- " gedda, from which a channel has been taken off supplying " the tanks lying between the village of Paltalagam and the " coast at Magaveram, affecting at present land assessed at " 4,500 Rs. and calculated to redeem a large quantity of waste " and jungle.

" The Itchapore talook, the next in order, to the north- " ward contains about Rs. 30,000 irrigated land, which is sup- " plied principally by 3 small channels taken off the Itchapore " river, and the rest by tanks fed from hill streams of which " that at the village of Montereddy is the largest.

" The Moherry talook has no river irrigation at all. " There are very few large tanks in it, the principal one " being close under the hills to the west of Berhampore at " the village of Lauty. Its wet lands however are assessed at " 60,500 Rs.

" The Poobacondah talook contains the principal irriga- " tion work in the northern part of the district. This is the " large channel taken off the Godahodo nullah, one of the " feeders of the Ganjam river. Under this channel which " runs nearly parallel to the southern bank of the river, there " are according to the talook accounts 9,292 acres of land " yielding a revenue of Rs. 26,372.

" On the northern bank there is a small channel taken " off the Ganjam river, at the Agraharum village of Anaman- " pilly for the supply of the Dollabilli tank at Poorshotpore " and intended to irrigate 9 villages besides, the total revenue " being Rs. 7,000. The rest of the lands in this talook are " watered by tanks dependant on the local rains.

" The Goomsur talook, the most extensive of all, has " no main supplying channel, but a number of small ones

" taken off from the different streams that traverse it, there " are no masonry annicuts or sluices, the method hitherto " pursued being to erect sand banks just after and before the " rains, so as to catch the earliest rising of the river, a most " precarious and unsatisfactory proceeding.

" The principal channels are in the Pilepadah and Vistnoo- " chakrum mootahs, each said to water about 10,000 Rs. " worth of land, but as I have no authentic statement of " the amount I cannot be sure. The rest of the channels affect " comparatively small areas of land.

The actual condition of the Works.

" Having thus briefly sketched the *means* of irrigation " possessed by each talook, I will " now proceed to state the actual " *condition* of the principal of these " works as far as I have been able to inspect them.

" The large channels in the Wadadah talook taken off " the *Nangoolea and †Wumshadara rivers, are all old native " works, they have been excavated with a great fall in their " beds, and having been unprovided with head sluices or any " masonry works to regulate the quantity of water entering " them, these channels have gradually become much enlarged " beyond their original dimensions, and consequently in high " freshes convey a much greater quantity of water than is " required, which is of course productive only of injury to the " crops. Such of the channels as I have had already surveyed " and levelled, have a fall of about 70 feet in a course of 20 " miles, and for want of attention have at their lower ends " become very crooked and winding.

" The tanks also in this (Chicacole) talook, both those " filled by the river channels, and those dependant only on the " rains are mostly unprovided with either calingulahs or " sluices, in consequence of which the bunds are liable to be " breached, while the ryots are obliged to cut holes in the bank

* Nagavali. † Vamsadharu.

" in order to obtain the water, and as these holes are seldom " strongly repaired, they are almost sure to become large " breaches during the ensuing monsoon. There are no anni- " cuts across these two rivers, so that the water in very low " freshes and in the summer season is lost to the country.

" Exactly the same may be said of the channel and " tanks in the northern talooks. The largest work there, viz., " the irrigating channel taken off the Godahodo nullah just " from a want of knowledge of the simplest principles of " Engineering is at times a source of great injury to the country " affected by it on account of the enormous body of water " which it conveys to the lower lands. The fall along this " channel is also 3 feet a mile, and in one place 6 feet. The " width at the head has enlarged to 60 yards, while at 2 miles " lower down it is 40 yards. This is altogether dispropor- " tionate to the quantity of land requiring to be watered, and " the bed has become so scoured out that sluices orginally " constructed in it have their floors 3 feet above the level of the " bed.

" The Heradaroo channel is the only one taken off the " Rooshkoolea river itself. It is intended to fill the Dollabilli " tank at Poorshotpore and to water 9 other villages ; but these " last complain that they are not properly supplied while the " people at Poorshotpore complain of having too much water.

" The principal channels in Goomsur, viz., the Dummarumma- " gedda and Mahanudee, are similar to the rest just described, " invaluable in moderate freshes, but productive of injury in " the high ones.

" The defects of this system of irrigation thus are apparent.

The defects of the present system.

" In the Wadadah talook a number " of channels have been excavated " independently one of another, each " having a separate head, and taken off from the level of the " bed of the river. By this arrangement owing to the con- " stant changes which take place in the bed of the river itself,

" while one channel is over abundantly supplied another " cannot get any water into it until the river has risen some 5 " or 6 feet, the velocity acquired by the great fall given to " these channels, has the effect of deepening their beds con- " tinually, which renders the necessity of cross banks being " raised every here and there to bring the surface of the water " to the level of the fields. These cross banks while they are " injurious to the channel by occasioning breaches are also the " cause of many disputes between the different villagers. " Another defect is that, in their present state they cannot take " advantage of the small freshes in the river, which in the event " of a late or a scanty monsoon is the cause of the whole culti- " vation being thrown back, which of course is prejudicial to " the proper growth of the crop if not sometimes endangering " its failure altogether. The result of this uncertainty must " necessarily be not only a considerable fluctuation in the " revenue, but a source of hardship to the ryot, who after " having engaged for the land is obliged to run the risk of the " season being unable to calculate on the production of his " crop.

The remedies and improvements proposed.

" Seeing then that such are the defects of the present system, " the remedies by which these are " to be overcome must be stated, and " in the improvements I am about to " suggest, I have been guided by the consideration of what is " required to secure the present extent of cultivation under " the existing channels as well as what will tend to bring a " larger quantity of land under the influence of river irriga- " tion.

To bring the several channels under the control of one head led off from a proposed annicut near Heeramundalum.

" I would therefore recommend first bringing all the pre- " sent channels as far as possible " under control by supplying them " from one main head. For this pur- " pose, I propose throwing an annicut " across the Calingapatam river just above the village of " Heeramundalum, where there is a favorable site for such a

" work, and lead a channel from thence, which shall follow the " highest level attainable with a fall of one foot per mile, which " will I think allow it to terminate in the backwater at Now- " padah. From this main head I would supply all the four other " channels on the northern bank, and by thus regulating the quan- " tity of water allow the land to have just as much water as was " needed; and at the same time not interfere with the proper " drainage of the country.

" The four channels on the south bank of the river may " likewise be supplied from the same source, but as lands " belonging to the Vizianagrum estate intervene, there may " be some objections to carrying out this project which do not " at present appear, and therefore I have not laid the line of " this channel down on the map.

" The Wadadah channel taken from the Nangoolea river " being the only one on that side, all that will be necessary at " present is to construct a head sluice to regulate the water " during the high freshes of the river, to repair the banks " where necessary, and to straighten the course of the channel ' by cutting away some of the most intricate windings. By " taking off a high level branch on a small fall, more land might " be brought under its influence, but as I have not yet the " exact levels for this taken yet, I could not mark out the " course it would follow.

" Between these two rivers there is a high ridge of country " extending from 2 to 4 miles in width, at present lying almost " wholly waste from want of means of irrigation. A great " deal of this however would be commanded by a high level " channel from the proposed annicut at Heeramundalum, and " by making new and restoring the old tanks I doubt not a " great portion of the tract, containing about 20 square miles, " will be redeemed.

" Besides supplying the existing channels in the northern " side, the proposed new main channel would convey water to a " number of tanks hitherto dependant on the local rains, con-

" vert a good quantity of dry land into wet, and allow of a large " extent of waste and jungle being redeemed, as it would com- " mand the whole country between it and the sea.

" The heads of the present channels I would not close up but " protect with head sluices, as in the event of more water being " required than the main channel could convey, or of some un- " foreseen accident happening at the head, these channels " would not then be deprived altogether of water, but draw " their supply, as now, direct from the river.

Combining navigation with irrigation from the proposed canal.

" But with this project, I have also held in view the feasi- " bility of establishing a water com- " munication for at least 6 months in " the year between the village of " Buttely in the confines of the Kimedy Zemindary, a great " emporium for trade, and the Salt pans at Nowpadah. The " whole rich valley of the Purlah Kimedy Zemindary would " thus be opened up, and an incalculable saving effected in the " transport of produce, which would tell with especial force on " the item of seeds, as the principal crop ripens in the month " of September, when there is the greatest quantity of water " in the river, and when carriage by land is most expensive. " The great demand for seeds has caused such a rise in the " prices, that any saving that can be effected in the cost of " carriage will tend to increase the export, and give additional " stimulus to the cultivation, as the present prices are very " remunerative. I have limited the time of navigation to 6 " months, but from what I have seen of the Calingapatam " river, I should say that there was enough water in it to " supply a navigable canal for 8 months in the year. The " supply for the remaining 4 months could without doubt be " obtained by having reservoirs in the Kimedy Hills, but this " is a point I have not yet attempted to investigate. With this " the subject of the desirability of establishing a salt depôt at " the foot of the Hills, bordering the Jeypore country naturally " suggests itself, and there can be but little doubt that the

" establishment of such a depôt would cause a very extensive " increase in the export of that article, as the diminished cost " of carriage would enable it to be supplied so much more " cheaply to the inhabitants in the interior, and become one " of the most effectual means of putting an end to the illicit " manufacture, which it is now almost impossible to prevent.

"I do not here enter into the details of this project, " and the enumeration of the several works required to carry " it into effect, but as far as I am able to calculate roughly, I " think the cost will be about 50,000 Rupees. As soon as the " country is more passable, I purpose having a careful survey " and levels taken, the particulars of which will be submitted " together with the estimate.

"Besides the above, the tanks must all be provided " with calingulahs and sluices, but as these are mere ordinary " works, they require no special notice.

"In the Itchapore talook there is so small a breadth " of land between the hills and the sea, that only a very " limited extent can be affected by channels from the river, " and therefore the improvements to be made must consist in " rendering the existing channels more secure, and prevent- " ing their being breached, as they now are, during the high " freshes of the river.

Project for supplying the Moherry taluk with an irrigating channel led off from the Rooshkoolea.

"The Moherry talook although having 60,000 Rupees " of wet land is, as stated above, " entirely dependant on the " local rains, and this talook has " therefore required careful con- " sideration. The chief means by which it can be benefited " with river irrigation, would appear to be by the construction " of an annicut across the Rooshkoolea near Aska, a mile " below the junction of the two rivers, from whence a channel " must be led on the right bank skirting the highest ground " up to the Godahodo Nullah which it must cross either by an " aqueduct or by the annicut hereafter proposed, and passing

" the village of Injelly be carried, as the levels allow, across " the highest country towards Munsurcottah, terminating in " the backwater at that place, and filling all the reservoirs " that lie below it.

Proposal to render the above navigable as well as irrigating canal.

" The benefit accruing from this work will necessarily be " very great, as it will convey " water to a hitherto wholly un- " irrigated tract of country, ren- " dering certain what has till now been very precarious, and " converting large extents of land into wet cultivation which " have hitherto yielded only dry crops or lain altogether fallow. " This channel would, like the one in Wadadah, be also avail- " able for navigation for 6 months of the year, but of the possi- " bility of extending it over a further period, I cannot speak " positively, as I know that the supply in the river after De- " cember is generally very small, and I do not know enough of " the country to say where extensive reservoirs might be con- " structed, though the general aspect of the country would " seem to indicate that many such localities exist among the " basins formed in the different ranges of hills that are scatter- " ed throughout it."

" The increase of revenue derivable from the increased " irrigation would, so the Tahsildar once stated to me, amount " to Rupees 50,000, and which I myself think might safely be " taken. The cost of the work on a rough calculation would " amount to a lac of Rupees.

" From this same point also, a channel can be taken which " shall provide for the irrigation of all the Poobacondah " talook lying to the north of the Ganjam river.

Canal from same annicut to supply northern portion of Poobaconda talook.

" For supplying the portion which lies to the south of " that river, it will be only neces- " sary to improve the existing " channel from the Godahodo " Nullah, by constructing an annicut across the latter, cutting a " new head to the channel, and protecting it with head and

" undersluices, correcting the fall in the bed with masonry " dams at the requisite spots, and thus enabling it to be of " more extensive use than it even now is.

Gumsur talook must be treated differently owing to the peculiar features of the country.

" The Gumsur talook will require a different system " altogether, the peculiar fea- " tures of the country will not " admit of the irrigation works " being brought under the control of one main feeder, con- " sisting as it does of a succession of narrow valleys separated " from each other by ranges of hills, the drainage from which " is discharged down the centre of each valley, as will be " perceived by a reference to the map,—a more minute and " detached system of works will be required, and which it " will require some little time and care to carry out so as to " allow of the country being properly supplied, while at the " same time the drainage is not intercepted. As yet I have " not had sufficient time to devote to the consideration of this " question, and am therefore unprepared to lay before the " Board any suggestion except that of improving the existing " channels, and of embanking the rivers. This last appears " to be a most necessary measure for the preservation of this " talook, and will require careful execution as the levels along " the banks of these several rivers vary considerably at inter- " vals. This project, as entered in my Budget for 1854-55 " lately submitted, I estimate would cost Rs. 75,000, and " I think that a competent officer should be appointed to " carry out the works. The loss from floods in this talook " are stated to be considerable, being, as a Tahsildar informed " me, from as much as 10 to 20,000 Rupees.

" For the Hautghur* talook, I am not able to suggest any- " thing at present from the reasons stated above; and the " talook of Sooradah† comprising comparatively so small an " extent, I have deferred visiting until I had more leisure.

* Atgadu. † Surada.

Facilities for carrying out the Coast Canal.

" I cannot close my remarks on the communications, without " pointing out, in reference to " the Report by the Committee " lately assembled for syste- " matizing the Public Works in the Presidency, the extremely " favorable nature of the country in the Ganjam district for " carrying out the Coast Canal. Perhaps in no district does " the line present so few difficulties, or could be opened sooner " than between Calingapatam and the Chilka Lake, and even " in this detached portion would prove of much value to the " commerce of the country, by enabling produce to be carried " to the most favorable shipping port. The Roadstead of " Munsoorcottah is very often for days inaccessible on account " of the high surf, while a few miles lower down, produce can " be shipped without risk at Sonapore, and the difference of " transit by water to the two places would be insignificant, " compared with the delay and anxiety caused by the deten- " tion of vessels in rough weather. There are a number of " hollows, called Tumparahs or tanks, extending for miles " parallel to the beach, and just at the back of the sand hills, " containing several feet of water in the centre. These only " require short cuts to be connected one with the other, and " these again with the Backwaters and long swamps, which last " would require but a very small amount of excavation to " render them navigable.

" In conclusion I would beg to sum up in one view the prin- " cipal works mentioned in the report, which are as follows :—

" An annicut across the Wumshadara river at " Heeramundalum, with channels on the northern " side to be rendered navigable, also as far as " circumstances will permit ... ...Rs.	55,000
" An annicut across the Rooshkoolea river below " Aska, with channels to water the Moherry and " Poobacondah talooks, also to be rendered navi- " gable as far as circumstances will admit .:.	1,00,000
" An annicut across the Godahodo Nullah head " and under-sluices, and a new head to the channel.	11,000

"The embanking of the Rooshkoolea, Lobara-
" kundee and Mahanaddee rivers ... ...Rs. 75,000

" Calingulahs and sluices to the different tanks. 1,00,000

" Improvements in Gumsur and Hautghur*
" talooks not yet ascertained, but from the revenue
" of each being a lac of Rupees, the probability is,
" the required expenditure will amount to one year's
" revenue, as there have been no extensive works
" ever yet undertaken in them 2,00,000

" Superintendence for the whole" 50,000

Total Rupees... 5,91,000

Of these, the anicut across the Godahodo alone has been constructed.

To what extent the bunding of the river that has been done, has been in accord with what is proposed I cannot say; but that to the Mahanadi on its left bank has recently been condemned.

On the proposed canals, Colonel Cotton gave his opinion that a canal from Naupada would be very useful and also one to Chicacole and one to Calingapatam and that they could be cut, locked, and kept up, for the money that the roads he was then making would cost. I think the Kistna and Godavery canals prove the fallacy of this. I doubt if there is a locked canal any where that can be kept in order for the same rate per mile as a road—and this scheme included reservoirs in the Hills adjacent from which the canal would be kept full in the hot weather.

In 1868 Captain Beckly was sent up to propose a remedy against future famine and his scheme is clearly shewn in the G. O. following :—

G. O., May 23rd, 1876, *No.* 1293, *P. W. D.*

The papers submitted in connection with the Rushikulya Project in Ganjam, and the review by the Chief Engineer for irrigation of the leading features of the scheme, appear to His Grace the Governor in Council to indicate that the water supply of the Mahanadi and Rushikulya rivers might be capable of being utilized so as probably to ensure with proper storage arrangement in other than unfavorable years the successful irrigation of about 120,000 acres of land.

2. The general conclusions arrived at by the Chief Engineer for Irrigation are that in two years out of four, with but slight aid from storage, the two rivers named would secure the irrigation of the full area abovementioned, and that in the other two years the area capable of being supplied would vary from 40,000 acres upwards, according to the extent and distribution of storage.

Note paragraph 4.

3. The Chief Engineer for Irrigation is not altogether certain that the project as submitted is the best that could be prepared, but as Major Beckly, who has throughout been employed upon the investigations, has after full consideration come to the conclusion that it is advisable to adopt this scheme rather than the alternative project of a reservoir of large capacity on the Rushikulya itself, as two Officers of experience have concurred to a greater or less extent in his views, and as there are some advantages of moment in drawing the irrigation supply of water from the Mahanadi as well as from the Rushikulya, no change of arrangements has been recommended.

4. The project as submitted for the consideration of Government provides for,

1st.—An anicut across the Mahanadi and a channel nearely 20 miles in length, to carry 90,000 cubic yards of water an hour, of which about 14,000 cubic yards would be utilized in the irrigation of 10,000 acres of land between the two rivers and the remaining 76,000 cubic yards an hour would be passed on to the Rushikulya to supplement the supply to the canal from that river. This section of the project is estimated to cost Rs. 4,30,000. The area drained by this river is 900 square miles.

2nd.—In order to ensure a constant supply of water between the freshes throughout the season of irrigation, a reservoir would be formed in the valley of the Andoni nullah near Bavankona. The site is a favorable one and as the nullah drains only 25 square miles, the principal supply would be obtained from the Gullery or Bodanoc river, an anicut across which and a supply channel therefrom have been provided for. This river has a catchment basin of 170 square miles. This reservoir is to hold 85 millions of cubic yards, and by accessions of water during the season the total storage is expected to be 110 millions of cubic yards. The estimate for this work is Rs. 5,79,300.

3rd.—An anicut across the Rushikulya just below the infall of the canal from the Mahanadi and a canal therefrom 63¼ miles in length, of which 44¼ miles are to be navigable. The discharge of the canal is to be 120,000 cubic yards an hour in the first 8 miles. The area, above the anicut, of the basin of the river is 820 square miles. This section is estimated to cost Rs. 14,12,500.

4th.—A reservoir on the Jorunadi, a tributary of the Rushikulya to be constructed near Surada and to be used for the same purposes as the similar reservoir at Bavankona. The capacity for storage of the Surada reservoir would be 80 millions of cubic yards and as the mean discharge of the Jorunadi annually is much in excess of this capacity, it has been assumed that 160 millions of cubic yards would be stored each season in this pond for use as and when required. This reservoir has been estimated to cost Rs. 4,10,000.

5. Out of a calculated total quantity of 558·72 millions of cubic yards of water required for a season's irrigation, about 270 millions would be stored, and it appears to be probable that this proportion of storage would suffice. Were additional storage requisite there are other sites at which water could be impounded.

6. The total estimated cost of the project is, exclusive of interest, Rs. 28,91,500, and inclusive of interest Rs. 33,09,100. The gross revenue is calculated by the Revenue Authorities at Rs. 2,03,000, and deductions on account of maintenance and revenue collections reduce the net revenue to Rs. 1,24,730,

giving a return of four per cent. on the outlay. This return is insufficient to make it advisable to recommend the sanction of the project as a Loan Fund Work, and the scheme is of such magnitude that it cannot be undertaken otherwise from the limited funds available for agricultural works generally. Moreover, even the small return of 4 per cent. would not be secured until after a long interval, and while it may be admitted that the great benefit which would be conferred on a portion of the District by such a project would secure indirect advantages to other and neighbouring parts of Ganjam, the proportion of the area which would be directly benefited to the whole District, is so small that it is more than doubtful whether the execution of the scheme would have any such appreciable effect in years of scarcity as would compensate for the postponement which its sanction would entail for many years throughout the Presidency of many needed improvements which can be effected at a moderate cost and with results much more easily determinable.

7. It is possible that in the future this project may assume a more certain aspect of profit, but after a very careful consideration of the reports of both the Revenue and Public Works Officers, His Grace in Council is clearly of opinion that the time has not come for undertaking it, and that no further expenditure in connection with it should be now incurred, except for the completion of the data on which any further consideration of the project should be based. These are :—

1st. The level of the sub-soil water at various points between the Ghâts and the sea in each month near the mouth of each river and also at convenient points near the foot of the Ghâts.

2ndly. The ascertainment of the actual cross section of each river, the height and the velocity during freshes in order that the discharge may be more accurately determined than has as yet been done, and their irrigating power may be more clearly understood.

The Chief Engineer for Irrigation will in communication with the District Engineer, prepare careful instructions for obtaining information on these points, and a report of the results should in due course be laid before Government.

There is a curious conflict of opinion between Captain Rundall and Captain Beckly; one of them hopes to convert great quantities of dry into wet land, the other remarks on the advantage that has accrued from the increase in the cultivation of ragi. I am with Captain Beckly and should like to see the ragi cultivation extended very much: it is a most useful crop and is more often spoilt by too much than too little rain.

Of course if there were money to spare and no other way of utilizing it, the carrying out of a scheme to render the full harvest of the district a certainty would be justifiable; but the very large profits anticipated by Mr. Rundall in 1854 were proved to have been due to a Tahsildar's inaccuracy by 1856; and the wet rates on which Captain Beckly founds his theory of profit have been recently raised by the Settlement Department.

It is certain that since the famine of 1865 the better class of ryots have been more provident in keeping stores of grain; but this would not help the very poor, or the coolies or weavers, &c., &c., for when the strain comes, the man with food grain will not sell any of his store till all danger is over. If the Famine Commissioner's proposition to store grain is to be acted upon, Ganjam can be rendered safe from famine at a very little cost, for the produce of rice is far in excess of the District wants, and I am by no means sure that such a scheme would not act as a preventive at least of panic or fear which first shows itself in the shape of high prices induced by the owners of food grain withholding it from the markets.

A perusal of Dr. Hunter's Orissa, page 131, vol. II, may prove instructive to those who anticipate large profits from Irrigation Works in Ganjam. His work shows clearly that the state of the Orissa ryot was infinitely worse than ever the Ganjam people were; yet after the Government works were in full working order, from 1866 to 1870-71, there was no Irrigation on a large scale because of the apathy of the ryot and the high rate, Rs. 10, demanded for the water, reductions were made subsequently but to no purpose. In 1870-71 the rate was further reduced from 2½ to 2 Rs. an acre (a very small reduction one would say) yet that and as I imagine chiefly the fear of a famine induced the ryots to apply for water with a result that 100,000 acres came under artificial irrigation at once. No doubt when the Government Irrigation was introduced into the Krishna District, there was similar hesitation about taking the water, but that was more from fear of the result to ancient dry lands than anything else. I doubt if it lasted so long and it certainly did not require famine pressure to dispel it. Here for four years the return for a very enormous outlay was next to nothing; and though there was a sudden very large accession of revenue at last, there is no certainty that the ryot is not paying more than he can afford and more than he need risk for the purpose of staving off a famine which may come any year in the next thirty.

A canal to connect the Chilka lake and Calingapatam is an old scheme approved by Colonel Cotton. It was taken up as a famine work in 1865, and is complete as far as the Ganjam river; but there is still something to be done at the river end for though open in the rains, in the hot season access to it is closed by a sand bank. It is a pity it cannot be finished at least as far as Gopalpur, but the difficulty is want of money. Ganjam has been entirely abandoned as a place of call for ships, and if the Orissa rice so plentifully used could be brought by the Chilka lake boats to Gopalpur it would be distributed in the interior as cheaply as possible by the bandies that having brought produce for export to Gopalpur now return empty or if they want paddy either go to Rumbha or beyond that to purchase it.

CHAPTER XIII.

NATURAL HISTORY.

MAMMALIA—DEER AND ANTELOPE—GAME BIRDS—SNAKES—FISHES—NETS FOR FISHING—FISHERMEN.

To commence with mammalia, tigers, man-eaters and otherwise are found throughout the district, but chiefly in the hilly parts of the Goomsur Taluq and along the line of the hills. In the hills and about the foot are found both species of the so-called cheetah, viz., the panther and the leopard. Bears and hyænas are found everywhere: wolves are not uncommon: and the two kinds of hill wild dogs have been noticed in Chapter IV.

Of smaller mammalia there are jungle cats, badgers, jackals, pigs, pengolin, hares, monkeys, mongoose, porcupine and squirrels. It is a curious fact that between Berhampore and Rambha, the common striped squirrel is hardly to be seen though quite common elsewhere. The Chilka Lake contains otters in considerable numbers. Of the deer kind there are the sambur, spotted deer, barking deer and mouse deer, nilgai on the slopes of the hills, and antelope along the coast and in the plains. Bison are in the hills and buffaloes from just over the border in Kalahandi are sometimes found straying into the district, while recently a herd of elephants (about 4) wandered down into the Chinna-Kimedi Máliahs.

The following is a list of animals with their names in English, Telugu and Uriya so far as they can be correctly ascertained.

English Names.	Telugu Names.	Uriya Names.
Madras Langur	...Gandangi or Kondamuchu Golonzo.	
Bengal Monkey ... } Madras do. ... }	Kôti	... Mankodo.
Slender Lemur	... Deväntri Pilli	... .
Large Fox Bat ... }	Chivukurayi	... } Chimmunia
Flying Fox ... }	Rushipakshi	... }
Long Armed Bat	... Pedda Gabbilum	... Bádará

English Names.		Telugu Names.		Uriya Names.
Coromandel Bat	...	Gabbi	...	Bádára
Common Musk Shrew / Musk Rat	...	Chooru Yelaka	...	Chalo Mussa
Indian Black Bear	...	Velugubanti	...	Bhallu
Indian Badger	...	Validikoti	...	......
Common Indian Otter		Neeti Kukka	...	Lodna
Tiger	...	Pedda Puli	...	Bágho
Panther / Leopard	...	Chinnapuli or Chirutapuli.		Koradapottria
Jungle Cat	...	Jinkapilli, Bavuripilli	...	Bhuva
Striped Hyæna	...	Dummalagondi, Kornogondu.		Goddua Bágho
Civet Cat	...	Ponnugupilli, Bootupilli.		Sáliyápotni
Madras Mongoose	...	Bayyanna or Mungi	...	Nevulo
Wolf	...	Tora or Tódélu	...	Dhenkya
Jackal	...	Nakka	..	Billuva
Wild Dog	...	Réchukukka	...	Boliyakukuro
Indian Fox	...	Poti Nara, Konki Nakka.		Konki Billuva
Red Squirrel	...	Bet-udata	...	......
Common Striped Squirrel		Udata	...	Nepporomussa
Indian Jerboa Rat	...	......		......
Indian Mole Rat	...	Golattukokku	...	......
Bandicoot Rat	...	Panthikokku	...	Bodo Mussa
Common Indian Mouse		Chuncheluka	...	Chuchundra
Porcupine	...	Yétupandi	...	Jhinko
Common Indian Hare	...	Kunthélu	...	Khuthuro
Elephant	...	Yenugu	...	Hatti
Wild Boar	...	Panthi	...	Barihá
Sambur Stag	...	Kaunzu	...	Somboro
Spotted Deer	...	Duppi	...	Jhyatho
Nilgai	...	Manpotu	...	Ghodango
Four-horned Antelope.		Konda Gorre	...	Kutra
Antelope	...	Nallapotu, Laidi	...	Horino
Wild Buffalo	...	Kárenumu	...	Goyilo
Scaly Ant-eater	...	Alawa	...	Gonda

The game birds to be had are the peacock, jungle fowl and spur fowl, partridges, quail, (rarely) plover snipé in fair profusion and wild fowl of all kinds; for those latter the Chilka Lake and the Tamparas already noticed, are a very favorite resort and flamingoes, pelican and acquatic birds of all sorts are to be found on and in them. The hill mina and the bhimraj famous for their talking and whistling powers and propensities are also to be found in the hills.

Appended is a list of game birds in the district with their Telugu and Uriya names as far as they can be ascertained.

English.	Telugu.	Uriya.
Lesser Florican	...Nela Nemali, Kamiladi pitta.	Kamolo Chodai
Painted Sand Grouse	...Sondu Polanka ...	Battel
Common do.	...Jam Polanka ...	
Pea Fowl	...Nemali pitta	...Moyuro
Red Jungle Fowl	...Adivi Kodi ...	Bono Kukkuda
Red Spur Fowl	...Yerra Jittu Kodi ...	
Black Partridge	...Konja pitta	...Titur
Painted do.	...Kakera kodi	...Kouzu Chodai
Quail	...Girza 1 t a ...	Gundru
Button Quail	.. Purudu pitta ...	
The Sarus Crane	... .	......
Demoiselle "Koolen"	...Wada Koraka	... .
Barred-headed Goose	...Pedda Báthu	...Bodo Homso
Comb Duck	...Guttu Chiluva Mukkudu báthu.	Sonno Homso
Common Teal ...	Chiluva bathu ...	Sile Chodai
Cotton Teal ...		
Whistling Teal	...Yerra Chiluva	... .
Brahminy Duck	...Bápana báthu	.. ..
Shoveller	... .	......
Grey Duck	...Komati báthu	... .
Pink-headed Duck	... .	......
Dun Bird or Pochard	... .	......
White-eyed Pochard	... .	......
Scoup	... .	......
Tufted Pochard	......	......
"Golden-eyed" duck of Sportsmen.	Nulla chiluva	... .
Snipe, Pin and Fan Tail, and Painted and Solitary.	Ullanki pitta	.. Chekku Chodai
Curlew	...Nullakankanam	...Budha Konko
Plover	... .	......
Bittern	.. ..	......
Flamingo ...	Rája hamsa, Samudrapu Chilluka.	Rájo Hamso

Poisonous snakes are unpleasantly numerous. The Ophiophagus Elaps is said to be found in the Hills, but the writer has not a personal acquaintance with this snake. The Cobra, Russell Viper, Bungarus of two kinds, Fasciatus and Coeruleus or the "Krait" are by no means uncommon, and a rock snake 17 feet long was killed in some low hills near Chatrapur two years ago.

The following is a list of names of snakes :—

Snakes.

English.	Telugu.	Uriya.
Cobra ...	...Nága Pamu	..Nago.
Rat Snake	...Jerripotu	...Dhamana.
Bungarus ...	Tutta Inapatutta. Tati tutta.	...Chitti or Roya.
Green Snake	...Pasirika pamu	...Kandonarajo.
Tree Snake	...Parugudu pamu	..Kandanarajo.
Russell Viper	...Ullu pamu or podda	...Pushokonia Buda.
Rock Snake	...Kondasalava	...Ohirajo.
Water Snake	...Neetipamu or Dhonda. Burada bukkadam.	
Krait	...Katla pamu.	
Two-headed Snake	...Rendutalala pamu. Nirugaddi.	Duinumdia Sapo Panibola.
A very thick short Snake said to be poisonous.	...	Puchakbudda.

The fisheries along the coast are not so good as those to be found further south and fishing villages are not so plentiful. The table fish that are caught are the Pomfret(*a*) white and black, the Seer(*b*), the Whiting(*c*), the Robal(*d*) and the Mullet(*e*), Turtles (*f*) are sometimes caught in the nets at Gopalpur.

(*a*) Telugu—*Chanduva.* Uriya—*Chandi*
(*b*) Telugu—*Vanjiram.* Uriya—*Manjiramo.*
(*c*) Telugu—*Sorangi.* Uriya—*Surungi.*
(*d*) Telugu—*Maga.* Uriya—*Mega.*
(*e*) Telugu—*Santa.* Uriya—*Koyyanga.*
(*f*) Telugu—*Tabelu.* Uriya—*Koyincho.*

The Chilka lake is full of fish but of a coarse uneatable kind.

There are some 16 different kinds of fresh-water fish in the District, but only three kinds, *Soulo, Báliyá and Rohi,* attain to any respectable size.

Indian fish have a practice of æstivating, if the expression may be permitted, that is of burying themselves in the mud, and thus lying concealed until the return of the rains permits them to regain once more their natural element.

When the floods come down in July and August, the fish deposit their eggs, and thousands of young fry make their appearance, but are destroyed in great numbers by the natives, who have no idea of sparing them on account of their small size.

Both breeding fish and small fry are indiscriminately caught by means of nets, baskets and other fixed engines.

The size of the mesh of nets employed in Ganjam is usually so small, that not even a minnow can get through, and the destruction of young fry is therefore proportionately great. Even the smallest sized fish are however eaten, but 12 species of fish out of the 16 kinds prevalent in the District would never appear to reach more than ½ a pound in weight.

For fishing in the Chilka lake and for sea fishing nets with small sized meshes might advantageously be prohibited, and it is eminently desirable that even the smallest sized mesh should be fixed at one inch from knot to knot, in order to prevent the wholesale destruction of small fry.

The number of fishermen in the District amounts to about 10,000, divided into 9 Odiyá castes, and 2 Telugu. The Odiyá castes are principally *Kento* and *Kondrá*, whilst the Telugu are called *Jalarivállu* and *Milavállu*.

Fishermen in Ganjam catch fish principally with nets, but some castes fish only with fixed engines, whilst others use both nets and fixed engines. On the Chilka and in the "Tamparas" along the coast, fish are speared by torch-light with a light pronged spear somewhat resembling an ell-spear. Baskets of different kinds and shapes are in common use as temporary fixtures. They resemble bird-cages, and are so constructed that when the fish get in, they cannot get out again. They are simply let down in the water sometimes baited but frequently without this addition.

The principal nets used are of three kinds:—*1st*, The casting-net, *2nd*, The drag-net, and *3rd*, The purse-net. The casting-net is commonly called *Pingadzálo* (from *pingibáro* to throw), and is thrown by hand from the right side, instead of from off the left shoulder as in Europe. On the Chilka lake the fishermen have a very neat and efficient way of throwing the casting-net by whirling it round the head like a lasso.

The drag-net (*Jikkadzálo*) is usually about 50 feet long with cross-sticks at regular intervals, so as to make the net bag out. It has no great depth, and is worked by two men, one at either end. The purse-net is sometimes called *Keramadzálo* and sometimes *Cussádzálo*. This net is fixed on a wooden triangle, and is chiefly used in narrow runs of water, and beneath small falls. Besides nets, other contrivances for catching fish are made resembling bamboo chicks. One of these called *benda* is stretched below falls of water, and when the fish drop upon it, they remain stranded, whilst the water passes through. Another instrument called *pottá* is held upright by the fishermen, and pushed before them, thus gradually drawing the fish into a corner with it, and so catching them. Fishing with rod and line is also occasionally practised.

In order to prevent the undue destruction of fish and fishing fry in Ganjam two steps might advantageously be taken.

1stly.—There should be a close season between the 15th June and the 15th August to protect spawning fish and every young fry in the fresh water fisheries.

2ndly.—For sea-fishing and fishing in the Chilka lake small sized meshes should be forbidden, and the distance from knot to knot should not be less than 1 inch, so as to avoid the capture of undersized fish.

The importance of fish as a food supply for the people should not be overlooked, and in Ganjam out of a population of 1½ millions, ⅞ths may be considered fish eaters.

CHAPTER XIV.

GEOLOGY.

MEMORANDUM ON THE GEOLOGY OF GANJAM, BY V. BALL, M.A., F.G.S.

The District of Ganjam has not yet been examined by the Geological Survey of India, and the following are the only available sources of information on the Geology :—

Firstly.—A brief account of the Circars on the coast of Orissa, by Dr. Heyne.(1)

Secondly.—Notes, chiefly Geological, of a journey through the Northern Circars in the year 1835, by Dr. Benza.(2)

Thirdly.—Notes by the present writer made during a brief visit to Mahendragiri in the year 1870.(3)

So far as is at present known the Geological formations represented in Ganjam are limited to the following :—

1. Metamorphic or Crystalline rocks.
2. Laterite.
3. Alluvium and Blown sand.
4. Kunkur or Gutin and Travertine.

Metamorphic or Crystalline Rocks.

Commencing with the oldest rocks there is not very much to be said about the possibility of their being subdivided into groups. The observations which have been made upon them are of a somewhat disconnected character even in the narrow outer margin along the foot of the Eastern Ghâts where they have as yet alone been examined. They refer moreover

(1) Tracts on India, London, 1814.
(2) Madras Journal of Lit. and Science, Vol. V, p. 48, 1857.
(3) Report on the Hill "Mahendragiri," Calcutta, 1878.

rather to the lithological characters of individual rocks than to their Geological or structural relations with one another. Taken as a whole, these rocks shew a prevalence of granitic varieties none of which however could be safely asserted to be of igneous or plutonic origin, indeed more or less distinct foliation and bedding structure with a north to south strike seems to prevail.

Near Berhampur there are some picturesque bosses of exfoliating gametiferous granitic gneiss. These are often much isolated, the intervening low ground being occupied by a considerable deposit of alluvium. Some portions of this granitic gneiss contain large crystals of orthoclase felspar and except for the great abundance of garnets, the rock has a general resemblance to a well known form which is found in the Western Highlands of Bengal.

All the hills to be seen from Berhampur, judging from their outlines, appear to be formed of metamorphic rocks. In some instances the natural angularity is modified by the existence of a capping of laterite.

A band of tough white quartzite which seems to be interbedded with the granitic gneisses is seen between the villages of Ramchunderpur and Pothara on the Gopalpur and Berhampur roads. It, or a similar band, was again observed considerably to the south near Kanchili.

The view of Mahendragiri, the culminating peak of the main North and South range below Berhampur, is from many points very fine, but perhaps especially so from the Huripur Dák Bungalow. As seen from thence there appear to be three distinct ranges with spurs which strike from them into the plains. Mahendra itself rises to an elevation of 4,923 feet. On the line of ascent to Mahendra from Sarvakota the principal rock seen is granitic gneiss of which there are several varieties. Dioritic gneiss is met with too, and, in some abundance, a felsite or petrosilex, which in places exhibits a pegmatitic character; very similar rocks to these were met with by the writer* on the western side of these Eastern Ghât ranges in the Kalahandi and adjoining States of the Central Provinces, and the supposition then put forward was that they represented original volcanic outbursts which had shared the effects of metamorphism with the sedimentary beds among which they had been originally intended.

The plateau of Mahendra, near the Bungalow, is formed chiefly of a porphyritic gneiss in which there are crystals of felspar quite two inches long, but the highest peaks are of granitic gneiss which is much cut up by joints into huge prismatic blocks. In some places this rock forms steep and imposing cliffs, in others it gives a craggy outline to the hills, while elsewhere it exposes considerable exfoliating surfaces. As far as the eye can reach from the summit of Mahendra the hills appear to be all formed of rocks having the same general characters. It is not certainly known, whether any crystalline limestone occurs among the metamorphic rocks of Ganjam or not.

To the north of Berhampur in the neighbourhood of the Chilka lake a decomposed gneiss is abundant. It is exactly similar to and no doubt continuous with a variety common in the eastern parts of Orissa. In its loose disintegrated condition it sometimes is mistaken for a sandstone. It generally contains numerous garnets.

Besides affording building stones, the durability of which may be estimated from the way in which certain ancient temples have withstood the ravages of time—these rocks contain iron ores in sufficient quantities at least to afford a supply for the native furnaces which were formerly,† if they are not still, to be found scattered over the country. Whether a really extensive deposit occurs anywhere is not known.

---

* Vide Records of Geological Survey of India, Vol. X, p. 184.

† Vide Heyne, l. c.

Laterite

Is found for the most part encrusting the gneiss along the eastern frontier of the rocks. It also occurs at considerable distances inland. In Kalahandi, on the western side of the Ghàts, there are many remarkable plateaus of considerable elevation which owe their flat tops to cappings of this rock, these are sometimes upwards of 100 feet thick. It is not improbable that similar plateaus may occur within the limits of Ganjam, regarding the Geology of the western parts of which, nothing appears to have been put on record.

Alluvium and Blown Sand.

Side by side the formation of alluvium and blown sand progress steadily together. The former is deposited at the mouths of rivers, estuaries and jheels which occur at intervals behind the sand ridges, all along the coast. In some cases there are deposits of considerable depth, but as a general rule it is probable that the gneiss rocks occur at no great distance from the surface. According to Dr. Benza, at several places down the coast, but more particularly at Waltair, pits were made in the alluvium for the purpose of extracting the shells of Mollusca which formerly lived in the brackish back-waters. These are said to occur in layers. They were, and I believe still are, burnt for lime.

The blown sand is confined to a belt of country of varying width, but which seldom exceeds a mile. The sand thrown up by the sea is carried forward by the prevailing winds and in some places gradually creeps on to the cultivated grounds. The *Pandanus* trees or screw pines which flourish in this sand, serve in a great measure to arrest its progress.

Kunkur or Gutin and Travertine.

As to the abundance of lime kunkur or gutin and its distribution, there is no information available to the writer; but it is believed to be used as a source of lime at Berhampur and elsewhere.

In the hills to the west there are reported to be some considerable deposits of calcareous tuff or travertine. This being a secondary product it is not improbable that rock limestone also occurs there, and indeed it is said, on native report, to be known to exist in parts of Kimedy.

Samples of this travertine have occasionally been forwarded to the Geological Survey Office under the belief that it consisted of fossil bones, its cellular structure having given rise to the idea which is expressed in the native name for it *Asurhar* or giant's bone.

CHAPTER XV.

SALT, ABKARRI, SEA CUSTOMS, STAMPS AND FORESTS.

Salt.—THE FOUR SALT FACTORIES IN THE DISTRICT—SPONTANEOUS SALT—SALT EARTH ALONG THE CHILKA COAST—THE GANJAM FACTORY—MODE OF PREPARING SALT AND THE TIME OCCUPIED—THE SURLA FACTORY—THE NAUPADA FACTORY—FISH-CURING DEPÔT—THE CALINGAPATAM FACTORY—THE SALT ESTABLISHMENT—SALT TRANSACTIONS FOR TEN YEARS—THE BRINJARIES—THEIR ROUTES TO GANJAM—FACILITIES PROPOSED FOR THE FURTHER DEVELOPMENT OF THE SALT TRADE. ABKARRI—PAST AND PRESENT REVENUE—FARMING AND EXCISE SYSTEMS—MESSRS. MINCHIN BROTHERS AND CO., LICENSED MANUFACTURERS AND SELLERS—THE HILL ABKARRI—PORTS OF CALL FOR STEAMERS—PRINCIPAL ARTICLES OF EXPORT AND IMPORT—STAMPS—EXTENT OF GOOMSUR FOREST TRACTS—THE SAL AND ITS SUPERIORITY—SURADA FORESTS—FUEL FOR ASKA FACTORY—SEIGNIORAGE RATES—MINOR PRODUCTS—POSSIBILITY OF ILLICIT FELLINGS.

Salt.

The following information in regard to the working of the Salt monopoly in the district is communicated by the Salt Assistant Commissioner in charge of the District Factories:

It will be seen that the cost to Government of making a garce of salt varies from Rs. 11 to Rs. 9-6-0, while the selling price is (Rs. 2-11-0 × 120 =) Rs. 322-8-0.

The manufacture of salt being by evaporation can only be undertaken in the hot weather, and the season commences about February, when the manufacturers prepare their pans, till such time as the amount reqnired is made or the rains put a stop to the work.

The orders are that there shall be in store a sufficient stock for the average sales of 18 months.

For the purposes of the Salt Department, the Ganjam District is divided into four circles,—Ganjam, Surla, Naupada and Calingapatam,—each of which contains a Salt Factory bearing the same name as the circle itself. Each circle is in charge of an officer designated an Inspector, who is aided by an Assistant Inspector in the general management of the circle, and by a two-fold subordinate establishment—a preventive force of petty officers and peons for employment along the Coast and in the interior of the district outside Factory limits; and a body of Sub-Inspectors, Clerks, Petty Officers and Peons for guarding the Salt Pans and Stores, and for the supervision of the manufacture and sale of salt, within the Salt Factory itself. The necessity for the preventive force arises from the fact that along the whole of the Ganjam coast, and also some little distance inland at various places, swamps and saliferous tracts of land are found, which are very injurious to the Salt revenue. In the swamps, spontaneous salt is found in the hot season and smuggled away by the people for their own consumption and for sale, and in the inland saliferous or salt earth tracts, the salt earth is scraped and carried away, stored in the people's houses, and when opportunity offers or a ready sale is practicable, converted into salt by boiling and either used for home consumption, or sold to neighbours at a large profit. These practices are carried on to a very considerable extent to the great detriment of the Government revenue. The mere possession of salt earth being declared by the High Court of Judicature, not illegal under the Laws hitherto in force, the Salt officials and police have been helpless in the matter, for no action could be taken unless the people were found in the actual possession of illicit salt, or unless the prosecution could prove that the intention of the possessors was to convert the salt earth into earth salt. This latter, of course, was almost impossible, the people generally declaring that they kept the stuff for the purposes of manure. It is notorious however, that in the Ganjam District salt earth is very rarely used for manure, and then only by the people living along the coast, for the cost of cooly hire for conveying the earth any distance would be too great. A change for the better is anticipated under an Act recently passed by the local Legislature, which makes the mere possession of salt earth an offence (without regard to the intent with which it is possessed) but which has not yet (February, 1882) come into force.

The Chilka Lake lying to the north of Ganjam, and partly in the Madras but chiefly in the Bengal Presidency, is another fruitful source of loss to the revenue. This lake is connected with the sea; its water is consequently always to a certain extent saline. During the months of April, May and June, and until the rains commence, it is quite as salt as the sea water. All along its shore, great quantities of salt earth are scraped and carried into the surrounding jungles and the interior and there converted into the illicit article and sold. Much is conveyed across the border into Bengal, and quantities are also taken across the hills into the countries west of Rambha.

The most northern factory in the Ganjam District is that at the town of Ganjam. There the pans are situated along the west bank of the canal connecting the Chilka Lake with the Rushikulia river. There are four platforms on which salt is stored after manufacture and receipt from the manufacturers. The first three platforms, or those called Nos. 1, 2 and 3, are situated in the neighbourhood of the town of Humma and in the Zemindary of that name, and some two miles north of the town of Ganjam; the fourth is the one called the Ganjam platform and is at Ganjam; there is a considerable tract of cultivated paddy land between this last and the other three platforms. The pans surround each platform and are in area about 370 acres; no rent is paid for the land. Transfer of the pans from one manufacturer to another is allowed with the sanction of the Chief Salt Officer of the district. The beds are on a stratum of black clay. The soil at Ganjam, however, is not so favourable as that at the Surla and Naupada factories for the making of salt; it, therefore, takes the manufacturers a much longer time to prepare their pans than it does at the other factories. The beds of the pans have first to be rendered perfectly smooth and level, after which they must be saturated with brine; after this has evaporated, the efflorescence that remains has to be well rammed or stamped into the beds, so that the floor may be as hard as possible. All this preparation takes about two months to complete. A set of pans consists of four reservoirs and as many producing pans as the manufacturer can afford to work, a set ranging from 1 to 4 acres. At the commencement of the season brine from the sea is baled into the 1st reservoir by hand labour; after remaining there a couple of days or so, it is allowed to run into No. 2 reservoir; after a few days this is allowed to run into the 3rd reservoir; finally after some days it is admitted into the 4th reservoir; there, when the density of the brine marks about 25 degrees on the Beaumé hydrometer, it is admitted into the small producing pans, where it evaporates and deposits salt which is scraped by the manufacturers as produced, *i. e.*, about every 3rd or 4th day and carried by them to the platforms. Care is taken that 30° Beaumé is not exceeded, as then the salt would contain an admixture of salts deleterious to health; after all the marketable or common salt is extracted from the brine, there remains in the pans what is called the *mother liquor* or *bitterns* which, if further evaporated to 34°, deposits chloride of sodium and sulphate of magnesium together, leaving a saturated solution of the chlorides of magnesium, calcium and potassium. After every fourth scraping, the mother liquor is removed from the pans and the beds are re-tamped. The supply of brine to the pans is obtained from the sea through a creek that meets the Chilka lake canal; feeding channels are dug all round the works so as to give each manufacturer easy access to the sea water; at the mouth of the main channel, where it connects itself with the creek and canal, a strong bund of earth is thrown across, having two sluices in it; as the tide comes in, it flows through these sluices into the feeding channels; immediately the tide begins to ebb, the sluices are shut, thus confining all the water received which is then bailed up by the manufacturers into their reservoirs; these tides, however, only serve during about 8 days in the month, *i. e.* for about 4 days each at full and change of the Moon; it is, therefore, of great importance to secure the brine at these times; a failure to do so would entail a loss on the manufacturers besides affecting the revenue through a short out-turn of salt for sale. The mode of manufacture, as detailed above, obtains in all the factories of the Ganjam District. The producing power of the pans is much the same, but Surla and Naupada being situated on better soil give larger crystals and produce salt quicker than the other two factories. The roads within the factory limits, leading from or communicating with the main roads are kept up by the Salt Department. The rate at which salt is sold at the Ganjam factory is the same as that of the other factories and is fixed by Government, *viz.*, Rs. 2-11-0 per Indian Maund of 82⅐ pounds. The kudivaram, or manufacturer's share, is Rs. 11-0-0 per garce or 120 maunds. The people of Cuttack in Bengal, of Sumbulpore, Goomsur, Atagada, Kalikota and Aska are the principal customers of this factory. The manufacturers belong principally to the Kayoto caste of Uriyas and to the Palli and Reddiki caste of Telugus.

Proceeding south the next factory is Surla, a small village about 4 miles east of Itchapore and 15 miles from Berhampore. The pans cover an area of about 672¾ acres. The principal customers of this factory are the people of the neighbouring taluks of Chinna and Purla Kimidi, and sometimes Cuttack traders and Brinjaries from Raygadda and Chotisgadda. The rate of kudivaram is Rs. 9-6-0 per garce. The manufacturers belong principally to the Reddika caste.

The next factory is that of Naupada, which is the largest in the district; this Factory is 65 miles south of Berhampore and is situated in the Chicacole Sub-Division; it is from 2½ to 3 miles from the sea. The pans cover an area of 990 acres, and are the quickest-producing pans in the district, also giving the largest crystals; the salt, however, is rather bitter to the taste, though perfectly wholesome; it is not so much sought after by the people of the immediate neighbourhood, who prefer that of Calingapatam. For transit, however, *i. e.* for carriage on pack bullocks or in bandies, it is preferred to any other salt in the district, the crystals being very hard and, comparatively speaking, large. The principal customers of this factory are the people of Kimidi, Palcondah, Jaipore, Parvatipore and Brinjáries from Raygadda and Chotisgadda. The rate of kudivaram is Rs. 9-6-0 per garce. The manufacturers here are Uriyas and Reddikis. At Bavanapad, a small fishing village about 4 miles from Naupada, there is a fish-curing establishment at which salt is sold to the fishermen at the reduced rate of six annas per maund for the purpose of curing fish. The establishment is experimental at present; the people do not frequent this depôt as much as they would, if the use of salt earth was strictly prohibited, nor do they seem to understand that, by using the Government salt, they would obtain a higher price for their commodity. Fish cured with salt-earth quickly deteriorates and becomes bad, whereas that cured with Government salt lasts for a long time and is much more wholesome and palatable.

4. The most southern factory is Calingapatam, situated on the sea, the pans not being more than ½ a mile in a direct line from the ocean. The salt produced here is highly approved of by all natives; people flock from all parts to purchase it, but unfortunately the producing power of the pans is exceedingly limited, joined to which, early rains nearly always put an end to the manufacture before the *dittam* or sanctioned quantity to be manufactured can be completed. The pans cover an area of 306 acres. The rate of kudivaram is Rs. 9-6-0 per garce. The principal customers are the people of Chicacole, Salur, Palcondah, Jaipur, Gunapur, Chipurapilly and places in the Vizagapatam District. Of late, Brinjáries are frequenting this factory in preference to going to Naupada. The manufacturers belong here all to the Reddiki caste; there are no Uriyas in the factory.

5. The sanctioned Salt Establishment of the district is at present as under :—

1 Assistant Commissioner in charge of the district under the orders of the Commissioner of Salt Revenue and Deputy Commissioner, Northern Division, with an Office composed of—

1 Head Clerk on Rs.	45 0 0	1 Attender on Rs.	8 0 0
1 2nd do. „	20 0 0	3 Peons, each „	7 0 0
1 3rd do. „	15 0 0	1 Sweeper „	6 0 0

Circles.	Permanent.							Temporary for 6 months on Rs. 6.	Pan guards during the manufacturing season only.			Remarks.
	Inspectors.	Assistant Inspectors.	Sub-Inspectors.	Clerks and Shroffs, on Rs. 10 to 20.	Jemadars, on Rs. 12 and 15.	Duffadars, on Rs. 9 and 10.	Peons, on Rs. 6 to 8.		Sirdar, on Rs. 20 to 30.	Jemadars, on Rs. 12 and 15.	Peons, on Rs. $6\frac{1}{4}$ and $7\frac{1}{2}$.	
Ganjam	1	1	4	4	3	7	44	20	1	6	46	
Surla	1	1	2	3	2	8	50	15	1	4	28	
Naupada	1	1	4	5	4	13	77	30	...	...	...	Strength of pan guards not yet settled.
Calingapatam ...	1	1	3	3	2	9	53	16	1	3	24	
Total...	4	4	13	15	11	37	224	81	3	13	98	

The Inspectors, Assistant Inspectors and Sub-Inspectors may be on any of the following rates of pay according to their grading in the general establishment of the Department :—

Inspectors . . ...Rs. 250, 300, 350, or 400.
Assistant Inspectors ...Rs. 150 or 175.
Sub-Inspectors ...Rs. 30, 40, 50, 60 or 70.

Arrangements however are in contemplation under which the Ganjam District will be incorporated with the Vizagapatam District into a single Salt Division under one Assistant Commissioner, the separate officer of that grade now allowed to the latter District being dispensed with.

The following Statement shews the Salt transactions for the last ten years in the district.

Official years.	Opening balance.	Manufactured.	Spontaneous salt.	Gain by weighment.	Miscellaneous.	Total received.	Consumption.		Total sales.	Total wastage.	Grand Total expended.	Grand Total Rupees realized.
							Home.	Inland.				
	Mds.	Mds.	Mds.	Mds.	Mds.	Mds.	Mds.	Mds.	Mds.	Mds.	Mds.	Rs.
1870-71	10,92,031	6,63,345	1,735	...	27	17,57,138	1,29,528	6,45,398	7,74,926	41,427	8,16,353	15,49,862
1871-72	9,40,785	7,68,781	61	208	67	17,09,902	1,42,173	6.89,849	8,32,022	41,504	8,73,526	16,64.191
1872-73	8,86,376	6,13,282	...	...	31	14,49,689	1,40,508	5,56,452	6,96,960	34,667	7,31,627	13,94,022
1873-74	7,18,062	9,73,817	...	...	3	16,91,882	1,63,170	6,64,762	8,27,932	47,984	8,75,916	16,55,934
1874-75	8,15,966	6,49,527	2	104	4	14,65,603	1,54,848	5,91,959	7,46,807	41,100	7,87,907	15,48,750
1875-76	6,77,696	9,43,120	1,408	113	...	16,22,337	1,60,013	7,97,873	9,57,886	55,832	10,13,718	19,99,993
1876-77	6,08,619	9,41,525	63	643	9	15,50,859	1,94,556	8,44,687	10,39,243	50,236	10,89,479	21,80,508
1877-78	4,61,380	6,04,862	4,902	517	96,913	11,68,574	1,67,972	8,53,378	10,21,350	37,638	10,58,988	21,88,970
1878-79	1,00,586	15,39,613	195	202	9	16,49,605	1,65,242	6,75,173	8,40,415	77,800	9,17,715	22,57,936
1879-80	7,31,890	8,21,292	250	113	22	15,53,567	1,96,897	6,18,256	8,14,653	40,700	8,55,353	21,88,640
1880-81	6,98,214	9,65,496	...	6	...	16,63,716	2,55,271	5,15,263	7,70,534	42,506	8,13,040	20,69,862

The market for the sale of Ganjam salt lies chiefly in the Central Provinces, and the great carriers of salt are the Brinjáries or rather Banjáras, who are somewhat similar in their manners and customs to the English gypsies. The Banjáras bring down to the coast comparatively little of the produce of the interior, but what they do bring consists chiefly of cotton, turmeric, iron and wheat. Many bullocks come down unladen. They take away salt and a little sugar. The salt is carried in sacks slung on either side of the bullocks' backs. There are two main roads followed by the Banjáras into Ganjam, firstly that viâ Sumbulpur through Bod and the Galleri Mutá of Gumsur leading by Berhampore to Ganjam, and secondly that through Bissumcuttack by Gunipuram and Kimidi to the salt pans of Náupada and Calingapatam.

The Banjáras themselves rarely proceed beyond Raipúr in the Central Provinces and travel but very short marches daily. On their arrival in Raipúr they deposit the salt in the stores in that city, and drive their bullocks to pasture in the jungles of Konkan, until the close of the rains again warns them to prepare for their annual journey. The Banjáras come down to the coast in December, January and February, and return to Raipúr in April, May and June. Under existing circumstances nearly the whole charge of transport falls upon the consumers of salt, who mostly live in the interior nearly 300 miles from the sea-coast. If the bullocks came down to the coast laden with wheat and other produce, the cost might be reduced one half, as the consumers of the inland produce would then bear their share of the burthen. Such is however not the case, and the transport of salt into the interior by means of pack oxen is therefore very costly. The roads lie chiefly through mountainous and jungly country. The oxen frequently fall sick and die. Sometimes when the grazing fails by the road-sides, whole droves of cattle perish, as the Banjáras never think of purchasing forage. Besides this the distance travelled daily does not as a rule exceed five miles, as the cattle must have time to supply themselves with food on the march. The hardships borne by the men are also great and much of their time is taken up with loading and unloading their oxen. The principal route traversed by the Banjáras between the Ganjam District and Raipúr is intersected by the river Vamshadhârâ and the obstructions that exist for its navigation as high up as Battili in the Parla-Kimidi estate might probably be removed at a comparatively small expense. A depôt for the sale of salt could then be established at Battili with every prospect of success. To reduce the cost of carriage and increase the sales of salt, the construction of good roads is the first consideration. The removal of all hindrances in the hill principalities of Kálahandi, Patna and Bastar, is the second. Canals would of course offer the greatest facilities of transport and as far as results go, the existence of the short canal between Ganjam and the Chilka Lake has been satisfactory. In the sub-division, the Vamshadhara river offers more especially very considerable facilities for the transport of salt into Jeypore and the interior generally and the material development of the Ganjam district is intimately connected with the extension of the trade in salt.

Abkarri is an old item of revenue. In 1810 it amounted to Rs. 43,648. Now the amount collected is Rs. 94,004. It is a tax on the manufacture and sale of intoxicating liquors which in this district are distilled from sugar-cane refuse (when it is properly rum), rice and ippa or mohwa flower. Cocoanut toddy is not known here, but the juice of the palmyra and of the date tree is collected. This revenue used to be collected by farming out the privilege of the manufacture and sale to the highest bidder. In 1869 the experimental excise system was introduced, and in 1875 the toddy and arrack farms were separated and the present system was introduced.

Messrs. Minchin Brothers and Co. are the arrack renters, and their lease commenced on the 1st July 1881 and will last three years. Their minimum guarantee is Rs. 60,000, and there is only one town, Berhampore, in which they pay a surcharge of Rs. 2,500. The liquor that they sell in the district known as "Pongoo" and "Kutcha," 30° and 60° under proof, is manufactured from the refuse of sugar-cane and jaggery, but they do manufacture small quantities of rice spirit and of mohwa or ippa flower spirit.

There are thirteen toddy renters whose leases also are for three years. At the end of 1880 there were 60 depôts and 807 shops for the storage and sale of arrack and 407 toddy shops.

In consequence of the report of the Special Assistant Agent, that the Goomsur Khonds in order that they might gratify their excessive taste for liquor, were mortgaging and parting with their lands to the liquor sellers or Sondies, and that such practice was likely to lead to trouble if it were allowed to extend, the Sondies were forbidden to manufacture or sell liquor in the Hills, and Messrs. Minchin Brothers and Co. were persuaded to try and introduce their rum into them, and at the same time the Khonds were given a special permission to manufacture such liquor as they require for their feasts, ceremonies and private consumption, but they were forbidden to sell it. The terms originally made with Messrs. Minchin Brothers and Co. were, that half the rate paid for liquor issued for consumption in the plains was to be paid for that sold in the Hills, and that the payment was to be on sales and not on issues. Since that in the present year, in consequence of Messrs. Minchin Brothers and Co.'s representation, that they were losing money, liquor of 60° under proof is now issued free. Messrs. Minchin Brothers and Co. have recently extended their operations to the other Máliahs, but it does not appear that they can afford to sell in those hills that are inhabited by the Savaras, and they have already asked to be allowed to withdraw.

The system so far has worked well enough, but the Abkarri Act III of 1864 (Madras), although it has or should have the force of law in the Hills, is a dead letter in regard to all its most important points.

The ports of the district are seven in number and are described in Chapter III, Gopalpur being the chief and Calingapatam the second.

The other ports with the exception of Ganjam are called minor ports. They contain a small establishment, and the trade at those ports often fluctuates. It is therefore difficult to say which of them has pre-eminence over the rest, but according to the experience of the past ten years, Bavanapad may be classed as the third port.

At Barwa the British India Steam Navigation Company's Steamers to and from Rangoon call regularly once in every fortnight; and some native vessels usually come there in the cold season from Madras to take rice, cashewnuts, cocoanuts and leaf platters. Messrs. Stephenson, Nixon and Co. exported a small quantity of rice to London from this port in 1880-81. Messrs. Wilson and Co. exported a good quantity of rice from Pundi and Sonnapur in the same year. The trade at Ganjam has decreased, and it now amounts to nothing.

Messrs. Simson Brothers.
" Stephenson, Nixon & Co.
" Wilson and Co.
" Minchin and Co.

The names of the European Firms carrying on business in this district are given in the margin. They chiefly export to England and France. Messrs. Minchin and Co. export large quantities of sugar to Colombo and Calcutta.

The principal articles of export from Gopalpur are rice, gingelly, turmeric, red powder, hides and skins, horns, rape and niger seeds, hemp, sugar, and myrabolans. Of these, rice, gingelly, and sugar-cane are grown in every taluq in the district, and Orissa and the Central Provinces send in large quantities of rice and gingelly. The other articles are chiefly obtained from the Goomsur Taluq and the Máliahs. Crystalized sugar is manufactured in the Aska factory by Messrs. Minchin and Co.

Cashewnuts, cocoanuts, coir ropes, coir yârn, and leaf platters are exported from Barwa and Pundi. Coir ropes and yarn to Rangoon, and the other articles to Madras.

Rice, gingelly, rape seeds and jaggery, are exported from Calingapatam. These articles are the produce of Chicacole and Parla-Kimedi Taluqs.

In 1879-80 and 1880-81 large quantities of salwood sleepers were exported from Gopalpur to Madras and Calcutta for the Harbour works and for the North Indian Railway respectively. The timber is obtained from the Government forests of Goomsur and Surada and the Zemindari Estates of Bodagoda, Ronabha and Korada.

The principal articles of import are cotton twist, piece goods, gunny bags, liquors, metals, kerosine oil, and ghee. The imports are chiefly made from Calcutta, Madras and Bombay.

In the Appendix will be found an abstract of the Sea-borne trade in the district.

There are 163 descriptions of Non-judicial stamped papers, Bills of Exchange and of Lading, and Adhesive Receipt stamps and 21 sorts of Court Fees' stamps. And if the number could only be diminished there would be joy in many a treasury. The District revenue from stamps was some 20,000 Rupees nearly 20 years ago, whereas it is now above one lakh.

The extent of the valuable forest tracts in Goomsur has been roughly estimated at 400 square miles as shewn below:—

	Sq. Miles.
Really good sal tracts	200
Indifferent sal tracts	100
Mixed forest	100
	400

The forests are traversed by the Loharakandi, Mahanadi, Baguva and the Rushikulya rivers, all except the Baguva being navigable for rafts.

The more valuable sal-yielding tracts are the Korcholi, Panchogodotolo, Jaganathprasad, Kukkuluba and Galleri Mutahs. Of these, the Kukkuluba Mutah is the best, but it is much spoilt by kumeri cultivation. The chief timber trees growing in this Mutah are Sal (Shorea robusta), Holondo (Nauclea cordifolia), Sahajo (Terminalia tomentosa), Bhandono (Dalbergia oajienensis) and Dohu (Conocarpus latifolia).

The sal wood of these forests is very superior, measuring 40 to 60 feet in length, and from 6 to 8 feet in girth, and it is stated that there are trees 12 feet in circumference. Its use was formerly confined to this district alone, but its utility is now widely known and there is a great demand for it for sleepers.

The sal in the other Mutahs is not so good, but there are other trees though less valuable. The burning of jungles to clear the land both for cultivation and for grazing purposes is a great hinderance to the growth of the saplings.

There are no reserved forests, and the reckless cuttings if permitted to continue will ere long denude the forests of all valuable trees. It is now in contemplation to form a few blocks into reserves. The Ranger reports that there are no virgin forests to be seen anywhere; though stumps of trees of superior dimensions are met with here and there.

The extent of the Surada forests is roughly estimated at 132 square miles, classed as follows:—

	Sq. Miles.
Good sal tracts	40
Indifferent sal tracts	20
Unreserved sorts of timber and firewood..	72
	132

The Rogoda, Peruju, Salingya and Pochangi Mutahs contain superior sal wood, and the very best is found to the west of Surada and in the Salingya Mutah where licensed fellers chiefly resort. In this Mutah there is plenty of young sal of from 20 to 30 years' growth.

Upwards of 10,000 tons of fuel are annually required for the Aska factory and are chiefly obtained from the hills and jungles around Surada, the Rushikulya, which runs close by, affording facilities for floating the fuel down to Aska at no great cost.

The rates of seigniorage just fixed by Government, and which will be hereafter levied, are shewn below compared with those at present collected:—

PRESENT.

Vernacular Names.	Botanical Names.	Rate per Bandy Load. Round logs. Rs.	Round logs. A.	Squared logs. Rs.	Squared logs. A.
Reserved Timber.					
1. Sal	Shorea robusta	1	8	1	14
2. Sissua	Dalbergia catifolia ...				
3. Khendu	Diospiros melanoxylon ...				
First Class Timber.					
1. Pia Sal	Pterocarpus marsupium ...	1	0	1	4
2. Bheyru	Chloroxylon Swietenia ...				
3. Pasi	Conocarpus aeuminatus ...				
4. Sohu	Soymida febrifnga ...				
5. Sahaju	Terminalia tomentosa ...				
6. Bandhono	Dalbergia oajeinensis ...				
Second Class Timber.					
1. Mohulo	Bassia latifolia	0	12	0	15
2. Kussum	Schleichera trijuga ...				
3. Dohu	Conocarpus latifolius ...				
4. Holondho	Nauclea cordifolia... ...				
5. Kadamba	Do. cadamba				
6. Munda Munde ...	Do. parvifolia ...				
7. Gombari	Gmelina arborea				
8. Kosi	Sriedelia retusa				
9. Mahanimo	Melia azedarach				
All jungle timbers (not classed)		0	8	0	10
Bandy load of firewood ... ... Annas 2 6					
Do. of charcoal ... ... „ 10 0					

PROPOSED.

Vernacular Names.	Rate per Bandy Load of Logs. Round. Rs.	Round. A.	Squared Rs.	Squared A.	Remarks.
First Class Timber.					
1. Sal	3	0	4	0	
2. Sissua					
3. Khendu					
4. Pia Sal					
5. Bheyru					
6. Holondho					
Second Class Timber.					
1. Pasi	2	0	3	0	
2. Sohu					
3. Sáhaju					
4. Bandhono					
5. Gombari					
6. Kussum					
Third Class Timber.					
1. Dohu ...	1	8	2	0	
2. Kadamba					
3. Munda Munde ...					
4. Mohulo					
5. Kosi					
6. Maha nimo					
7. Urjuno (Terminalia arjuna).					
All jungle timbers (not classed).	1	0	1	4	
Rs. A.					
Bandy load of firewood.. 0 4					
Do. of bamboos.. 0 5					
Do. of charcoal .. 1 5					
Cavady load of charcoal.. 0 1					

Messrs. Minchin Brothers and Co. pay however as a special case* a reduced rate of 4 annas the ton or 2 annas the cart load on fuel required by them for the factory.

*G. O., 24th Sept. 1879, No. 1923, R. D., para. 2.

Ebony, rosewood, satinwood, pia-sal (Pterocarpus marsupium) and Holondho (Nauclea cordifolia), besides sal, are chiefly used for furniture, while the Dohu (Conocarpus latifolius), though tough and durable, is not much used by natives for building purposes, merely from some prejudice against it that they have.

The minor forest products utilized in the district and exported to Calcutta, &c., are the Sundara gandi, the fruit of Rottlera Tinctoria, which is used in dyeing silk, the roots of the Achu (Morinda tinctoria) from the bark of which a pink color is extracted for dyeing cloths, (the wood of this is also suited for furniture), Gallnuts or Myrabolans and the bark of the Maddi (Terminalia tomentosa), which is used for tanning.

The free pass system is not introduced here owing, it is said, to the inadequacy of the present establishment to supervise free felling.

The Government forests are surrounded on all but the southern side by the Zemindari forests of Nyagur, Banpur, Atagada and Bodogoda. Those of Ronabha and Korada are enclosed by them and are always a source of annoyance. The timber cut in their jungles has to pass through Government forests and it is difficult to detect any illicit fellings in Government forests as the wood-cutters, though they may have cut it, in the latter, can always say it is Zemindary timber. Licenses to assist them are easily obtained for a trifle paid to the Zemindars' agents, or others who profess to be their agents.

The only forest depôt in the district is the one at Russellkonda.

CHAPTER XVI.

THE MUNICIPALITIES AND THE LOCAL FUND CIRCLES.

There are two Municipal Towns in the District,—Berhampore and Chicacole. The annual funds of these two institutions average Rs. 20,000 and Rs. 12,000 respectively. They are administered in accordance with the Act by Commissioners nominated by the Collector and approved by Government.

The duty of paying a percentage of the cost of the Police absorbs a very considerable part of the funds aforesaid, and there is but little left for the more legitimate purposes of the Act, namely, the improvement and sanitation of the towns. However, in both there has been a good deal done in the way of keeping the roads in better repair and cleaner. What is really wanted is an improvement in the domestic habits of the townspeople themselves; every attempt to purify and induce them to keep clean the insides of their houses and their compounds is resented, and neither body of Commissioners can fail to be unpopular and bring the Commission into disrepute if their attempts at sanitation lead them to interfere with private nuisances.

Neither Municipality has signalized itself by any great town improvement. In Berhampore a few stone drains have been put down, the main street has been improved and certain tanks in the centre of the town, which were a nuisance, have been partially filled up. In Chicacole, where a system of drainage is not necessary, the old market has been taken in hand and improved.

The Dispensaries in both towns are well officered, but they are not as popular (from the prejudices of the Northern people) as similar institutions are further south. For Berhampore it is proposed (when funds may be available) to remove the dispensary from its present situation on the outskirts of the town, and therefore a long way off from the bulk of the townspeople, to some more central spot.

There are eight Municipal schools, two of which are Girl schools, for which latter there is not any very great demand and a Government High School at Chicacole. At Berhampore there is the Government College; the schools are aided on the combined system by the Municipality.

The lighting of the towns is not as good as it might be, though sufficient for the wants of the native community.

For Local Fund purposes the District is divided into two circles,—the Chatrapur circle and the Chicacole circle.

In Chatrapur the roads are tolled, but the Chicacole circle has not been compelled to increase their funds in this way yet. Previous to 1877-78, the selling price of salt in Cuttack was higher than that in this Presidency generally and higher rates were fixed for the price of salt in the Ganjam Salt factories as they approached the boundary; to make up for the restriction in salt sales due to this cause, the Ganjam District used to receive a grant, which was spent on the roads, of Rs. 20,000. This grant was suddenly withheld in 1878-79, when the salt rates were equalised, and the only method of raising the money that was really necessary to keep up the existing roads that presented itself to the Commissioners was the imposition of tolls. They have not found themselves able to do without this addition to their income, for the grant already spoken of enabled officers in former days to construct more roads than they would have been able to keep up without it.

Road-making in this circle, or rather the keeping the roads in repair, is a very costly matter; for the traffic along them to and from the coast is very great indeed, and the material at hand very bad; also the time when the traffic is greatest is during the rains, when, of course the roads suffer infinitely greater damage than they would if dry.

The Schoolmasters in both circles are for the most part remunerated on the combined systems of salaries and results. There are nearly 200 schools.

In Chicacole, the great question now is to find funds for the repairs of the old bridge on the Langulia river, which will cost between 60,000 and 70,000 Rupees. The roads are in good order; there is less traffic upon them and consequently they are not so expensive to keep in repair.

In the two circles there are altogether seven out-lying Dispensaries. At present these are not popular, and, in fact, it depends entirely on the person in charge whether they become so or not.

There is a very good school at Kimedy, supported by the Court of Wards, which manages the affairs of the Zemindar; another at Chatrapur endowed by a late Collector Mr. Onslow, and a Normal School at Russelcondah. The Zemindar of Mandasa has a school in his chief town in which he takes an interest.

The improvement in the sanitation of villages is a matter of some difficulty. The cowshed and manure heap are generally in front of or in very close proximity to the dwelling house, and the street or roadway in front is generally undermined with grain pits. On the top of these the cattle assemble morning and evening, and the contents can hardly be sweetened by the percollation of their droppings.

The water-supply throughout the district is good. There is rain more or less for 5 months, and the sub-soil water is generally pretty close to the surface, so there is not any great call for expenditure of funds in this direction.

CHAPTER XVII.

MISSIONS.

The following is kindly communicated by Mr. Wood, the Missionary stationed in Berhampore.

"Berhampore was first visited by the General Baptist Missionaries from Orissa about the year 1827. Ten years later a Church of thirteen members was organized, and there was a school of eighteen destitute children. Schools and Orphanages in connection with the Mission have been continued ever since. Into these schools rescued Meriahs and famine orphans, with other poor children, both male and female, have been received to the number of several hundreds. The aim of the Missionaries has been all along to give the children a religious and an elementary secular training. The boys have been taught to earn their living as writers, domestic servants, mechanics, or farmers. A good number have settled in the neighbourhood, but some have migrated to different parts of the country.

A few of the boys have been trained in the Mission College at Cuttack, and have been settled as native preachers. Attention has been paid to the domestic training of the girls, to fit them to become suitable wives for the boys; and a great number of intermarriages have taken place between them. Some of the girls are also adepts in making crochet lace and knitting, and are able to earn something thereby.

The Mission has been and is an extensive evangelising agency in Ganjam, Goomsur, and wherever in the surrounding districts the Uriya language is spoken. A sub-station has been established at Russellconda, with a view to Mission agency among the Khonds; but has been somewhat neglected for some years for want of a European resident Missionary. There is also an agricultural village of about 150 inhabitants at Padre Palli, seven miles from Berhampore. At Berhampore there are two Christian villages. There are two Mission Chapels, one at Berhampore, and one at Padre Palli. The Mission possesses also a bungalow for the resident Missionary, with good school premises on the compound. The station is at present in charge of Rev. H. Wood.

The statistics, according to this year's report, are as follows :—

Adults baptized during the year............	19
Number of Communicants	162
Nominal Christians	177
Total Christian Community.....................	339"

The Roman Catholic Mission was originally at Berhampore, where a Convent was built; but its head-quarters are now at Surada, where there is an establishment for the education of children. The girls are under the care of a Sister, and there is also a Boys' school.

The inmates are children of native converts and famine children, *i. e.* those whose natural guardians died or deserted them in the famine. They are usefully brought up,—the female children to household work and the boys to agricultural labour.

The Roman Catholics, as well as the Baptists, have twice essayed to establish a Mission in the Khond Hills, and they too have failed; and the failure is always attributed to the malignancy of the Máliah fever.

APPENDICES.

No. I.—*Statement showing the number of Villages and Hamlets in the District of Ganjam, as they stood in Fasli* 1286.

Taluks.	Area in square miles.	GOVERNMENT.				ZEMINDARY.				INAM.				TOTAL.					
		Inhabited.		Uninhabited.		Inhabited.		Uninhabited.		Inhabited.		Uninhabited.		Inhabited.		Uninhabited.		Total.	
		No. of villages.	No. of hamlets.	No. of villages.	No. of hamlets.	No. of villages.	No. of hamlets.	No. of villages.	No. of hamlets.	No. of villages.	No. of hamlets.	No. of villages.	No. of hamlets.	No. of villages.	No. of hamlets.	No. of villages.	No. of hamlets.	No. of villages.	No. of hamlets.
1	2	3	4	5	6	7	8	9	10	11	12	13	14	15	16	17	18	19	20
Berhampore ...	983	332	214	15	5	998	290	114	15	66	1	...	22	1,396	505	129	42	1,525	547
Goomsur ...	373	699	175	65	14	302	55	57	5	100	1	2	...	1,101	231	124	19	1,225	250
Chicacole ...	876	142	252	4	...	1,267	567	102	32	94	75	4	...	1,503	894	110	32	1,613	926
Total...	2,232	1,173	641	84	19	2,567	912	273	52	260	77	6	22	4,000	1,630	363	93	4,363	1,723

No. II.—*Statement of Population arranged with reference to Caste according to the Census of* 1871.

Nationality.	Caste.	Population. Males.	Females.	Total.
Hindus ...	Brahmans	...	...	1,04,349
	Kshatriyas	...	...	3,170
	Chetties	Not	known.	18,516
	Vellar, (Agriculturalists) ...	...	...	3,11,518
	Idaiyars, (Shepherds and Pastural castes)	...	...	1,04,036
	Kammalan (Artizan)	...	...	44,217
	Kanakkan (Accountant caste) ...	...	...	32,260
	Kaikalar (Weavers)	...	...	48,196
	Vannaian (Labourers or slaves of Class IV)	...	...	30,398
	Kusavan (Potmakers) ...	...	...	11,969
	Satani (Mixed castes) ..	...	...	14,284
	Sembadavan (Fishermen) ...	...	...	49,741
	Shanar (Palm cultivating class)..	...	...	44,730
	Ambattan (Barbers)	...	...	21,518
	Vannan (Washermen) ...	...	...	34,579
	Others	...	...	4,76,107
	Pariahs (Out castes)	...	...	1,64,809
	Total...	...	...	15,14,397
Mahomedans...	Lubbays	...	...	4
	Mapillas	...	...	...
	Arabs	...	...	...
	Sheiks	...	...	1,968
	Syed	...	...	340
	Pathan	...	...	552
	Mogul	...	...	81
	Other Mahomedans	...	...	1,881
	Total...	...	...	4,826
Budhists ...	Budhists	...	...	45
Christians ...	Europeans	...	...	152
	Eurasians	...	...	205
	Others	...	...	...
	Total...	...	...	357
Other unspecified castes	....	...	...	508
	Grand Total...	...	...	15,20,088

NOTE.—The Vernacular names in column 2 are Tamil and are with difficulty applied to the people of this District. Also the heading "Caste" is most misleading as the words in brackets show.

No. II-A.—*Statement showing the Male population arranged with reference to occupation according to Census of* 1871.

Major Headings.	Minor Headings.	No. of Males employed.
Professional ...	Government Service (Civil)	3,535
	Military	2,182
	Learned professions	4,058
	Minor do.	8,355
Domestic ...	Personal Service	50,197
Commercial ...	Traders	33,770
	Conveyors	2,441
Agricultural ...	Cultivators	2,34,586
Industrial ...	Dress	16,023
	Food	18,867
	Metal	7,763
	Construction	8,560
	Books	23
	Household goods	3,536
	Combustibles	570
Indefinite and non-productive	Laborers	90,363
	Property	2,911
	Unproductive	4,980
	Others	1,937
	Total...	4,89,657

No. II-B.—*Statement showing the number of Houses, Population and Cattle in each Taluq of the Ganjam District.*

Items.	Number of Houses.					Population.			Agricultural Stock.						
	Terraced.	Tiled.	Thatched.	Unspecified.	Total.	Males.	Females.	Total.	Tilling Cattle.	Cows.	She Buffaloe.	Sheep.	Ploughs.	Horses.	Ponies.
Berhampore Taluq ...	192	1,858	38,155	4,347	44,552	1,19,857	1,24,088	2,43,945	47,820	33,901	8,560	6,873	20,388	34	60
Goomsur Taluq ...	145	1,403	28,823	3,285	33,656	79,300	78,761	1,58,061	33,353	21,440	4,348	404	14,135	13	...
Chicacole Taluq ...	155	1,508	30,964	3,529	36,156	84,425	84,669	1,69,094	21,718	4,900	2,238	3,775	10,232	8	10

No. II-C.—*List of Castes.*

Brahmins. బ్రాహ్మణకులం.

1. Telugu Brahmins ...తెనుగుబ్రాహ్మణులు. ఆంధ్రబ్రాహ్మణులు.
2. Oriya Brahmins ...ఓఢ్రబ్రాహ్మణులు. ఉత్కళబ్రాహ్మణులు.
3. Hindustani Brahmins ...హిందుస్థానిబ్రాహ్మణులు.
4. Bengali Brahmins ...బంగాళిబ్రాహ్మణులు.
5. Guzrati Brahmins ...ఘూర్జరబ్రాహ్మణులు.
6. Maharatta Brahmins ... మహారాష్ట్రబ్రాహ్మణులు.
7. Carnatic Brahmins ...కర్ణాటకబ్రాహ్మణులు.
8. Dravida Brahmins ...ద్రావిడబ్రాహ్మణులు.

Kshatryas. క్షత్రియకులం.

1. Kshatriyulu ...క్షత్రియులు.
2. Khonduvalo ...ఖొండువాళో.
3. Katrautu ...కత్రౌతు.
4. Bhayipuo *alias* Santo (illegitimate) ...బాయిపో - అంతరులు.
5. Rowtara ...రౌతురా.
6. Maghee ...మాఘు.
7. Rajputs ...రజపుత్తులు.

Vysias. వైశ్యకులం.

1. Gavara Komatlu ...గౌరకోమట్లు.
2. Kalinga Komatlu ...కళింగకోమట్లు.
3. Kanchura Komatlu ...కంచరకోమట్లు.
4. Guzarati Komablu ...గుజరాతికోమట్లు.

Sudras. శూద్రకులం.

1. Telaga ...తెలగాలు.
2. Adivelama ...ఆదివెలములు.
3. Baligi ...బలిజలు.
4. Bodiredlavallu ...బొదిరెడ్లవాళ్లు.

5. Ayyaralu ...అయ్యరాకులు.
6. Perike ...పెరికలు.
7. Akulavallu ...ఆకులవాళ్ల.
8. Ralla Balji ...రాళ్ల బలిజీలు.
9. Gajula Balji ...గాజులబలిజీలు.
10. Linga Balji ...లింగబలిజీలు.
11. Modalari ...మొదలారులు.
12. Pillalu ...పిల్లలు.

Kapulu. కాపులు.

1. Velama ...వెలమలు.
2. Beléma ...బెలిమా.
3. Yanadi Velama ...యానాదివెలమలు.
4. Kamma ...కమ్మలు.
5. Bosontia ...బొసాంటియాలు.
6. Kalinji ...కాళింజీలు.
7. Kalingulu ...కాళింగులు.
8. Nunia ...నుణియా.
9. Kolata ...కోలాటవాళ్లు.
10. Reddika ...రెడ్డికలు.
11. Vupparialu ...ఉప్పరియాలు.
12. Kapavallu ...కాపవాళ్లు.
13. Gajula Kapulu ...గాజులకాపులు.
14. Tudu Kapulu ...తుడుకాపులు.
15. Kampo ...కంపో.
16. Doluva ...డొలువా.
17. Potia ...పొట్యా.
18. Oodiya ...ఒడియా.
19. Banayita ...బెణాయితా.
20. Molosupodia ...మొలాసాపొడ్యా.
21. Bolasi ...బొలాసీలు.
22. Alia ...అలియాలు.
23. Aruva ...అరువాలు.
24. Kudumo ...కుడుమో.

Golla.	గొల్లలు.
1. Golla	...గొల్లలు.
2. Yerragolla	...ఎర్రగొల్లలు.
3. Mekalagolla	...మేకలగొల్లలు.
4. Kakustagolla	...కాకుస్టగొల్లలు.
5. Gowdu	...గవుడువాళ్లు.
6. Apola Gowdu	...అపొలాగొళ్లు.
7. Battuva Gowdu	...బత్తువాగొళ్లు.
8. Sollokhondia Gowdu	...సొల్లొఖొండియా గొళ్లు.
9. Gowdu Halisi	...గొడుహాలిసి.

Panchananam.	పంచాననులు.
1. Kamsali	...కంసాలి.
2. Asari	...ఆసరి.
3. Rampakari	...రంపకారి.
4. Kammari	...కమ్మరి.
5. Kanchari	...కంచరి.
6. Ashttalohi	...అష్టలోహి.
7. Sunnari	...సున్నారి.
8. Badayi	...బడాయి.
9. Korti	...కొర్తి.
10. Muli	...ములి.
11. Pothiria	...పొథిరియా.
12. Khodra	...ఖోద్రా.
13. Tambra	...తాంబ్రా.
14. Kundara	...కుందరా.
15. Ostali	...ఒస్టాలి.
16. Sonkari	...సొరకారి.
17. Kavusia	...కావుంశ్యా.
18. Jaura	...జౌరా.
19. Lohura	...లొహురా.
20. Bonia	...బొణియా.
21. Komsari	...కొంసారి.

Dendra.	డేంద్రకులం.
1. Devangulu	...దేవాంగులు.
2. Dendra	...దేంద్రవాళ్లు.
3. Pattusali	...పట్టుసాలీలు.
4. Sali	...సాలీలు.
5. Kaikalu	...కైకాలువాళ్లు.
6. Ranguni	...రంగుణీలు.
7. Tonti	...తొంటీలు.
8. Koli	...కోలీ.
9. Dera	...డేరా.
Karanalu.	కరణాలు.
1. Sistu Karanam	...శిష్టుకరణాలు.
2. Bomma Karanam	...బొమ్మాళికరణాలు.
3. Boyicia Karanam	...బొయిశ్యాకరణాలు.
4. Madjula Karnam	...మజ్జులకరణాలు.
5. Balaga Karnam	...బలిగకరణాలు.
6. Odiya Karnam	...ఓడ్రకరణాలు.
7. Mahanty	...మహాంతులు.
Pujaries.	పూజారులు.
1. Dammulavallu	...దమ్ములవాళ్లు.
2. Jakkulavallu	...జక్కులవాళ్లు.
3. Ravulo	...రావులో.
4. Mali	...మాలీ.
5. Muni	...మునీ.
6. Jani	...జానీ.
7. Sipiti	...సిపిటి.
Kummari.	కుమ్మలు.
1. Kummari	...కుమ్మరి.
2. Kumbharo	...కుంభారో.
Vupparlu.	ఉప్పలు.
1. Vuppara	...ఉప్పరలు.
2. Vaddari	...వడ్డారి.
3. Mattia	...మాట్యా.

Mangallu.	మంగళ్లు.
1. Mangali	...మంగలి.
2. Bhondari	...భోండారి.
Chakallu.	చాకళ్లు.
1. Chakali	...చాకలి.
2. Sukladhari	...శుక్లాదారి.
3. Dhoba	...ధోభా.
Meela.	మీలలు.
1. Pallevallu	...పల్లివాళ్లు.
2. Vadavallu	...వాడవాళ్లు.
3. Yedivadavallu	...ఏడి వాడవాళ్లు.
4. Meela	...మీలవాళ్లు.
5. Jalari	...జాలారివాళ్లు.
6. Khandra	...ఖంద్రవాళ్లు.
7. Kevutu	...కెవుటవాళ్లు.
8. Tiyaro	...తియారోవాళ్లు.
9. Nolia	...నొలియా.
10. Khotuya	...ఖోటుయా.
Sondi.	సొండీలు.
1. Gamallu	...గమళ్లు.
2. Segedi	...సెగెడిలు.
3. Yatavallu	...యాతవాళ్లు.
4. Sondi	...సొండి.
5. Siolo	...స్యాలో.
Telukulavallu.	తెలుకులువాళ్లు.
1. Deva Telukulavallu	...దేవతెలుకులువాళ్లు.
2. Telukulavallu	...తెలుకులువాళ్లు.
3. Telli	...తెలి.
Others.	యితర్లు.
1. Bondili	...బొందిలీలు.
2. Gudia	...గుడియా.
3. Darji	...దర్జీ.

4. Rangirizu ...రంగిరిజాలు.
5. Pitabalji ...పిట్ట బలిజలు.
6. Nagarapuvallu ...నగరపువాళ్లు.
7. Battraju ...భట్రాజులు.
8. Mutharachavallu ...ముతరాజవాళ్లు.
9. Summialu ...సుమ్యాలు.
10. Vatra ...వట్రాలు.
11. Chamdayitya ...చండాయిత్యా.
12. Neyyalavallu ...నైయ్యలవాళ్లు.
13. Kurakulavallu ...కూరాకులవాళ్లు.
14. Gavaravallu ...గవరవాళ్లు.
15. Pondra ...పొందరా.
16. Pachilia ...పచ్చిలియా.
17. Togarlu ...తొగర్లు.
18. Tohoro ...తొహురో.
19. Satani ...సాతానులు.
20. Dasari ...దాసరులు.
21. Jogulavallu ...జోగులవాళ్లు.
22. Jangum ...జంగము.
23. Viramushtivallu ...వీరముష్టివాళ్లు.
24. Senkudasari ...శంకుదాసరి.
25. Bukkavallu ...బుక్కావాళ్లు.
26. Singamvallu ...సింగంవాళ్లు.
27. Vipruavinodulu ...విప్రువినోదులు.
28. Ranjavallu ...రంజవాళ్లు.
29. Kalukuntlavallu ...కాలుకుట్లవాళ్లు.
30. Pichakuntlavallu ...పిచ్చకుట్లవాళ్లు.
31. Bommatalavallu ...బొమ్మలాటవాళ్లు.
32. Kumbhakalisavuddillu ...కుంభకలిశవడ్డీలు.
33. Pondito ...పుండితవాళ్లు.
34. Katikarivallu ...కాటుకారివాళ్లు.
35. Nagaswaramvallu ...నాగస్వరంవాళ్లు.
36. Pamulavallu ...పాములవాళ్లు.
37. Bandangivallu ...బండంగివాళ్లు.

38. Yeetivallu ...ఈటివాళ్లు.
39. Dommaravallu ...దొమ్మరవాళ్లు.
40. Neravidiavallu ...నేరవిధ్యవాళ్లు.
41. Garidivallu ...గారిడివాళ్లు.
42. Katikapulavallu ...కాటి కాపులవాళ్లు.
43. Ponnadilu ...పొన్నాడీలు.
44. Dasi ...దాసీలు.
45. Gudesetti ...గుడిశెట్లి.
46. Nagavamsamvallu ...నాగవంశంవాళ్లు.
47. Sanulu ...సానులు.
48. Bogunapuevallu ...బోగపువాళ్లు.
49. Kurmapuvallu ...కూర్మపువాళ్లు.
50. Drare ...ద్రారి.
51. Godugulavallu ...గొడుగులవాళ్లు.
52. Medarivallu ...మేదరవాళ్లు.
53. Tollari ...తొల్లారి.
54. Magura ...మాగురా.
55. Muchi ...ముచ్చి.
56. Chitrakari ...చిత్రకారి.
57. Potrasunia ...పొత్రసునియా.
58. Jalagadugulavallu ...జలగడగులువాళ్లు.
59. Dudekulavallu ...దూదేకులవాళ్లు.
60. Tulabhena ...తులాభేనా.
61. Bolidia ...బొలిదియా.
62. Bolidhiatelli ...బొలిధియాత్రెల్లి.
63. Bouddhia ...బౌద్ధియా.
64. Hayegudia ...హాయిగుడియా.

Hill people. కొండజాళ్లు, కొండమనుష్యులు.

1. Pittalavallu ...పిట్టలవాళ్లు.
2. Gytalu ...గయితలు.
3. Yanativallu ...యానాటివాళ్లు.
4. Jatapuvallu ...జాతపువాళ్లు.
5. Khandilu ...ఖండీలు.

6. Gullavallu ...గుల్లవాళ్లు.
7. Agarlu ...అగర్లు.
8. Boyulu ...బోయీలు.
9. Gadabalu ...గదబలు.
10. Sabaravallu ...శబరవాళ్లు.
11. Savara ...సవరలు.
12. Jara Savra ...జరాసవరలు.
13. Kapa Savra ...కాపుసవరలు.
14. Avisa Savra ...అవిశాసవరలు.
15. Sudda Savra ...శుద్ధసవరలు.
16. Jennalu ...జన్నాలు.
17. Tekkali Savra ...టెక్కలిసవరలు.
18. Yerakalavallu ...యెరుకలివాళ్లు.
19. Pano ...పాణో.
20. Kondo ...కోదులు.
21. Sonno Kondo ...సొన్నుకోదులు.
22. Bado Kondo ...బోడుకోదులు.
23. Buda Kondo ...బుడాకోదులు.
24. Sankara ...సంకరా.
25. Lodderajulu ...లొడ్డె రాజులు.

Pariahs. చండాలులు.

1. Relli ...రెల్లి.
2. Mala ...మాల.
3. Madiga ...మాదిగ.
4. Arisa Mala ...అరిశమాల.
5. Gosangy ...గోసంగి.
6. Maladasari ...మాలదాసరి.
7. Paidi ...పైడి.
8. Arisa Paidi ...అరిశపైడి.
9. Godari ...గొడారి.
10. Boya ...బోయా.
11. Chadara Boya ...చదరబోయా.
12. Suddakulustulu ...శుద్ధకులస్థులు.
13. Sunnapuvallu ...సున్నపువాళ్లు.

14. Dombo ...డోంబో.
15. Pano Dombo ...పాణోడోంబో.
16. Sani ...సాణి.
17. Ghasi ...ఘాషి.
18. Bavuri ...బావురి.
19. Jaggili ...జగ్గిలి.
20. Chachadi ...చచ్చడి.
21. Dandasi ...దండాసి.
22. Arisa Dandasi ...అరిశదండాసి.
23. Chitra Ghasi ...చిత్రఘ్రాసి.
24. Samantya ...సామత్యా.
25. Haddee ...హడ్డి.
26. Muchi ...ముచ్చి.

No. II-D.—*Statement of population in Ganjam District as per Census of* 1881, *roughly tabulated up to 17th June* 1881.

Taluqs.	Houses.		Population according to the Census of 1881.			Resident Population.		Floating Population.		Difference between Columns 8 and 11.
	Occupied.	Unoccupied.	Males.	Females.	Total.	Males.	Females.	Males.	Females.	
Berhampore*	52,913	2,177	1,45,541	1,55,027	3,00,568	1,42,433	1,54,399	3,108	628	
Chicacole*	40,120	947	99,023	1,01,730	2,00,753	96,377	1,01,240	2,646	490	
Goomsur ... { Plain Villages ...	...	...	85,640	88,536	1,74,176	83,710	88,271	1,930	265	
Goomsur ... { Hill Tracts... ...	34,423	783	28,652	26,461	55,113	...	...	...	...	
Surada	4,244	158	9,348	9,052	18,400	9,058	8,967	290	65	
Aska	20,578	1,180	57,321	58,699	1,16,020	56,142	58,595	1,179	104	
Purshottapore	4,659	456	13,044	13,619	26,663	12,583	13,555	461	64	
Ganjam	14,099	435	37,958	38,033	75,991	35,947	37,676	2,011	357	
Itchapore	14,641	374	37,345	39,044	76,389	36,231	38,665	1,114	379	
Sompet ... { Plain Villages ...	...	...	25,938	28,258	54,196	25,635	28,159	303	99	
Sompet ... { Mandasa Hill Tracts	12,189	256	2,250	2,116	4,366	...	...	...	...	
Sompet ... { Budarasingi do. ...	...	...	414	366	780	...	...	...	...	
Tekkali	20,114	256	51,348	53,639	1,04,937	49,668	53,204	1,680	435	
Narsannapett	2,830	11	7,627	7,632	15,259	7,320	7,571	307	61	
Parlakemidi....	49,174	1,374	1,20,083	1,20,429	2,40,512	1,17,328	1,19,834	2,755	595	
Pratapagiri or Chinnakimedi ...	6,798	341	18,415	18,915	37,330	18,080	18,848	335	67	
Jalantra ... { Plain Villages ...	...	...	11,074	11,066	22,140	10,769	10,998	305	68	
Jalantra ... { Hill Tracts ...	4,194	138	865	863	1,728	...	...	...	...	
Sirgada	3,191	65	5,843	5,873	11,716	5,592	5,869	251	4	
Urlam	2,446	60	5,728	5,780	11,508	5,571	5,752	157	28	

* The figures for these Taluqs include the population of the Municipalities, but are exclusive of the 6,212 houses in the Municipality.

No. II-D.—*Statement of population in Ganjam District as per Census of* 1881, *roughly tabulated up to* 17*th June* 1881.—Concluded.

Taluqs.	Houses.		Population according to the Census of 1881.			Resident Population.		Floating Population.		Difference between Columns 8 and 11.
	Occupied.	Unoccupied.	Males.	Females.	Total.	Males.	Females.	Males.	Females.	
Hill Tracts.										
Specl. Asst. Agent's Establishment.	...	...	31	...	31	31	...	...	...	
Sub-Magistrate's Establishments at Ramagiri	...	...	16	2	18	16	2	...	...	
Baliguda	...	...	12	...	12	12	...	...	...	
Udayaghiri	...	...	24	16	40	24	16	...	...	
Total... { Plain Villages ...	...	...	7,81,276	7,55,332	14,86,608	7,12,444	7,51,623	18,832	3,709	
Total... { Hill Tracts ...	...	...	32,181	29,806	61,987	...	...	...	...	
	...	...	83	18	101	83	18	...	...	
Grand Total...	2,85,608	9,011	7,63,540	7,85,156	15,48,696	...	...	...	...	†28,608
Municipalities Berhampore* ...	...	...	11,520	11,967	23,487	11,026	11,913	494	54	
Chicacole	3,279	193	7,497	8,852	16,349	7,296	8,794	201	58	

* Vide Remark against the Taluq.

† The number of houses occupied and unoccupied has been taken from the sanctioned Supervisor's list prepared at the preliminary enumeration.

No. III.—*Statement of Rent Roll of the Ganjam District for Fasli* 1286.

Items.	Single Puttahs.		Joint Puttahs.		Total Puttahs.	
	Number.	Assessment.	Number.	Assessment.	Number.	Assessment.
		RS.		RS.		RS.
Below 10 Rupees ...	19,171	70,403	2,027	7,659	21,198	78,062
Above 10 Rs. but below 30 Rs...	10,584	1,79,908	1,531	31,804	12,115	2,11,712
30 „ 50 „ ...	2,978	1,09,328	668	26,617	3,646	1,35,945
„ 50 „ 100 „ ...	1,555	1,00,578	444	30,978	1,999	1,31,556
„ 100 „ 250 „ ...	361	49,121	137	19,921	498	69,042
„ 250 „ 500 „ ...	28	9,300	47	15,583	75	24,883
„ 500 „ 1,000 „ ...	1	589	9	6,243	10	6,832
„ 1,000 ...	...	...	2	2,792	2	2,792

No. IV.—*Statement showing the different sources of Irrigation belonging to Government.*

Taluqs.	Tanks.			Channels.			Anicuts.			Wells.		
	No of Tanks.	Average extent of Cultivation within the last 5 years.	Assessment including all charges for water, &c.	Number of Channels.	Average extent of Cultivation within the last 5 years.	Assessment including all charges for water, &c.	No. of Anicuts.	Average extent of Cultivation within the last 5 years.	Assessment including all charges for water, &c.	Number of Wells.	Average extent of Cultivation within the last 5 years.	Assessment including all charges for water, &c.
		Acres.	RS.		Acres.	RS.		Acres.	RS.		Acres.	RS.
Collector's Division—												
Goomsur Taluq ..	405	12,313	37,185	322	16,676	54,764	...	...	...	19	76	19
Principal Assistant Collector's Division—												
Chicacole	701	28,836	76,953	13	30,727	1,09,503	...	...	...	42	80	252
Senior Assistant Collector's Division—												
Berhampore	1,452	61,402	1,64,694	148	24,219	82,699	1	526	2,085	...	...	...

No. V.—*Statement showing the average Rainfall for a series of 10 years in the District of Ganjam, in Inches and tenths of Inches.*

Faslies.	Official year.	July.		August.		September.		October.		November.		December.		January.		February.		March.		April.		May.		June.		Total.	
		I.	T.	I.	T.	I.	T.	I.	T.	I.	T.	I.	T.	I.	T.	I.	T.	I.	T.	I.	T.	I.	T.	I.	T.	I.	T
1280	1870-71	5	...	6	2	10	1	14	4	2	2	...	...	...	...	1	5	1	6	3	4	2	2	6	...	52	6
1281	1871-72	5	9	4	8	6	5	...	5	...	...	...	...	...	..	...	2	...	1	...	3	1	7	15	7	35	7
1282	1872-73	10	1	7	...	8	2	12	5	2	2	1	...	...	...	...	...	...	6	...	6	1	7	1	7	45	6
1283	1873-74	4	1	9	5	7	1	12	1	1	1	1	7	...	6	...	1	...	3	...	3	2	4	6	8	46	1
1284	1874-75	7	5	4	9	4	3	14	1	1	7	...	1	...	5	...	...	...	...	..	9	2	3	3	5	39	8
1285	1875-76	5	2	4	9	14	6	7	6	...	...	...	...	...	...	...	...	1	3	...	6	1	9	3	4	39	5
1286	1876-77	4	5	7	...	9	8	9	...	...	...	...	...	...	9	2	3	1	8	2	6	7	9	3	3	49	1
1287	1877-78	3	6	4	8	6	4	2	...	...	1	...	...	...	...	...	1	...	6	...	3	2	6	1	4	21	9
1288	1878-79	6	7	12	8	6	9	12	9	5	6	13	...	...	...	...	...	...	9	...	...	5	3	2	5	66	6
1289	1879-80	6	7	8	6	6	8	4	6	3	3	1	...	...	2	1	1	...	1	...	1	2	8	9	7	45	...

No. VI.—*Statement showing the prices of grain for a series of 10 years in the District of Ganjam.*

Faslis.	Official years.	Rice, 1st sort, per garce.	Rice, 2nd sort.	Paddy, 1st sort.	Paddy, 2nd sort.	Cholum.	Cumboo.	Ragi.	Varagu.	Horse gram.	Ulandu.	Wheat.	Salt RS.	Salt A.
1280	1870-71	269	250	107	100	149	119	120	111	166	...	...	240	0
1281	1871-72	314	287	129	117	166	155	153	...	160	...	...	240	0
1282	1872-73	246	222	98	87	146	128	133	...	182	...	...	240	0
1283	1873-74	250	219	98	87	134	130	122	...	134	...	...	257	8
1284	1874-75	266	239	106	94	160	146	123	...	123	...	...	257	8
1285	1875-76	286	258	114	108	177	182	123	...	183	...	...	257	8
1286	1876-77	348	314	133	123	229	160	178	...	229	...	...	257	8
1287	1877-78	666	551	267	229	320	320	320	...	320	...	...	257	8
1288	1878-79	492	471	186	174	277	269	278	...	289	...	592	257	8
1289	1879-80	360	320	117	110	156	181	162	...	131	...	320	257	8

CHICACOLE.

No. VI-A.—*Prices per Madras garce in every tenth year from* 1803 *to* 1880.

Dates.	Rice. 1st sort.			Rice. Last sort.			Ragi or Natchney.			Horse Gram.			Kandulu.			Pesalu.			Minumalu.			Wheat.			
	Rs.	A.	P.	Rs.	A.	P.	Rs.	A.	P.	Rs.	A.	P.	Rs.	A.	P.	Rs.	A.	P.	Rs.	A.	P.	Rs.	A.	P.	
1803...	168	11	0	...	...	...	87	4	0	87	4	5	157	1	6	168	11	8	107	10	2	142	8	0	
1813...	199	8	0	...	...	...	119	0	0	196	0	0	161	0	0	210	0	0	175	0	0	247	8	0	
1823...	128	14	0	94	1	10	72	0	8	81	5	4	144	13	10	134	10	2	120	2	7	201	14	5	
1833...	160	8	3	155	12	0	94	1	11	88	14	3	100	0	0	133	5	4	192	0	0	320	0	0	
1843...	91	7	4	63	5	4	44	4	2	38	12	5	66	0	10	75	12	3	74	11	11	110	10	3	"The low prices of the different description of grains are owing to the abundant outturn of the harvest and to the large stock of grain still remaining in the country."
1853...	140	15	6	110	13	4	9	8	11	78	14	7	121	1	9	144	7	1	125	9	6	131	1	9	
1863...	234	0	0	216	0	0	123	0	0	117	0	0	...	...	...	...	...	...	238	0	0	208	0	0	
1873...	228	9	1	208	3	4	136	14	0	142	1	5	...	...	...	...	...	...	223	5	4	320	0	0	
1880...	...	...	...	251	12	1	144	0	0	100	0	0	...	...	...	...	...	...	240	0	0	342	13	8	

No. VII.—*Statement showing the particulars of Cultivation, &c., for a series of 10 years.*

Faslis.	Cultivable extent.	AREA OCCUPIED.						Deduct Remissions.	Remainder.
		Dry.		Wet.		Charge for Water, &c.	Total Assessment.		
		Extent.	Assessment.	Extent.	Assessment.				
1	2	3	4	5	6	7	8	9	10
	Acres.	Acres.	RS.	Acres.	RS.	RS.	RS.	RS.	RS.
1280	...	1,10,454	1,40,954	1,82,271	5,24,845	...	6,65,799	22,262	6,43,537
1281	3,39,373	1,10,888	1,41,251	1,82,175	5,25,458	...	6,66,709	99,619	5,67,090
1282	Do.	1,11,006	1,41,646	1,82,777	5,27,761	89	6,69,496	1,270	6,68,226
1283	Do.	1,10,862	1,41,794	1,82,758	5,27,969	70	6,69,833	16,123	6,53,710
1284	Do.	1,10,236	1,41,255	1,82,397	5,27,605	93	6,68,953	8,467	6,60,486
1285	Do.	1,10,815	1,41,915	1,81,898	5,26,841	26	6,68,782	697	6,68,085
1286	Do.	1,16,092	1,41,721	1,87,771	5,27,818	156	6,69,695	8,871	6,60,824
1287	Do.	1,16,967	1,42,621	1,88,100	5,28,736	48	6,71,405	81,439	5,89,966
1288	Do.	1,74,495	1,43,097	1,88,082	5,48,954	...	6,92,051	2,716	6,89,335
1289	...	1,41,213	1,73,873	1,80,924	5,50,371	1,218	7,24,962	20,538	7,04,424

No. VII.—*Statement showing the particulars of Cultivation, &c., for a series of 10 years*—concluded.

Faslis.	All Miscellaneous Items.	Total Rayotwari Demand.	Revenue from Permanently settled Estates.	Jadi or Shrotriem Villages.	Total Land Revenue Demand.	Arrears, previous years.	Total demand for the year.	Gross Collections.	Balance at the end of Fasli.
	11	12	13	14	15	16	17	18	19
	RS.	RS.	RS.	RS.	RS.	RS.	RS.	RS.	RS.
1280	70,742	7,14,279	4,31,005	24,858	11,70,142	41,515	12,11,657	11,18,403	93,254
1281	70,354	6,37,444	4,31,005	24,858	10,93,307	93,254	11,86,561	8,74,728	3,11,833
1282	70,681	7,38,907	4,31,005	24,858	11,94,770	3,11,833	15,06,603	12,56,877	2,49,726
1283	73,087	7,26,797	4,31,081	24,858	11,82,736	2,49,726	14,32,462	11,69,514	2,62,948
1284	78,497	7,38,983	4,31,555	24,802	11,95,340	2,62,948	14,58,288	13,18,652	1,39,636
1285	69,633	7,37,718	4,37,773	24,766	12,00,257	1,39,636	13,39,893	11,74,791	1,64,922
1286	65,365	7,26,189	4,37,703	24,766	11,88,658	1,64,922	13,53,589	12,05,880	1,47,700
1287	79,365	6,69,331	4,37,703	24,766	11,31,800	1,47,700	12,79,500	10,83,027	1,96,473
1288	73,903	7,63,238	4,38,588	24,766	12,27,303	1,96,473	14,23,776	12,87,985	1,35,691
1289	77,710	7,82,134	4,38,662	24,613	12,45,409	1,35,791	13,81,200	12,92,123	89,077

No. VII-A.—*Statement showing the area under*

Taluqs.	Rice.	Ragi.	Cholum.	Wheat.	Varagu.	Cumbu.	Dholl.	Black gram.	Chamalu.	Jenugulu or
	Acres.	Acres.	Acres.	Acres.	Acres.	Acres.	Acres.	Acres.	Acres.	Acres.
Berhampore. ...	1,23,392	39,897	81	...	...	3,154	2,764	3,057	195	...
Goomsur ...	79,669	15,334	...	..	...	...	1,257	267	1,670	...
Chicacole ...	75,934	21,148	772	...	...	5,909	283	359	177	...
Total ..	2,78,993	76,379	853	...	...	9,063	4,304	3,683	2,042	..

the principal crops cultivated in Fasli 1289.

Green gram.	Sugar-cane.	Cotton.	Indigo.	Oil seeds and nuts of various sorts.	Horse gram.	Cocoanut topes.	Betel-leaf garden.	Aricanut topes.	Cheyroots, Dyeng roots.	Plantain garden.	Mango topes.	Tobacco.	Other products.
Acres.	Acres.	Acres.	Acres.	Acres.	Acres.	Acres.	Acres.	Acres.	Acres.	Acres.	Acres.	Acres.	Acres.
4,285	637	272	...	11,220	2,568	1,402	40	31	...	825	3,644	55	4,721
6,639	904	2,445	...	14,838	707	66	...	...	...	3	2,322	349	2,068
161	103	655	...	1,641	2,326	530	...	106	...	75	1,088	284	1,149
1,1085	1,644	3,372	...	27,699	5,601	1,998	40	137	..	903	7,054	688	7,938

No. VIII.—*Statement showing the particulars of the several Tenures other than Ryotwari.*

Names of the Zemindaries and Inam Villages.	The entire beriz of the Estate.	Peishcush or Quit-rent.
Zemindaries.		
	RS.	RS.
1 Palur	7,658	533
2 Humma	8,491	1,163
3 Biridi	22,440	4,457
4 Kallikot	3,64,510	18,976
5 Bodagada	27,536	4,230
6 Dharakot	80,451	25,039
7 Sergada	36,165	5,823
8 Pratapagiri	1,22,060	20,827
9 Vizianagaram	1,00,968	23,324
10 Chikati	1,22,138	33,915
11 Surangi	21,596	3,545
12 Jarada	17,609	2,025
13 Jalantra	40,135	7,384
14 Budárasingi	3,443	525
15 Mandasa	69,175	14,035
16 Kattingia	...	50
17 Parla Kimedi	4,53,184	87,825
18 Tarla	36,898	4,000
Malukdaries.		
1 Atagada	...	59,929
2 Aska	8,896	4,849
3 Kurla	10,045	5,428
4 Devábhumi	10,327	5,188
5 Baruva	9,339	3,900
6 Peta	11,291	3,900
7 Raghunadhpur	43,422	9,818
8 Nandigam	26,867	9,128
9 Do. Penta	881	549
10 Do. Chinna Gokarnapally	237	111
11 Jalagam	17,821	9,735
12 Do. Bharanigam	198	82
13 Temburu	10,533	4,910
14 Do. Naugam	5,415	2,257
15 Khallada of Naugam	4,273	2,257
16 Pothuluru Naugam	159	68
17 Do. Bejjipalli	590	328
18 Pata Tekkali	...	9,316
19 Gopalpur	9,525	3,699
20 Pedda Jungam	961	424
21 Tallavalasa	965	424
22 Chinna Jungam	956	425
23 Chakipalli	1,621	869

No. VIII.—*Statement showing the particulars of the several Tenures other than Ryotwari.*—(Continued.)

Names of the Zemindaries and Inam Villages.	The entire beriz of the Estate.	Peishcush or Quit-rent.
Malukdaries.—(Continued.)	RS.	RS.
24 Konusula Kotturu	1,460	393
25 Tarlipeta	852	256
26 Boddam	581	89
27 Belamara Palavalasa	2,248	1,043
28 Chittivalasa	9,272	2,074
29 Jayangi Gangaram	5,841	1,002
30 Yelamanchili		654
31 Rajapuram	76	76
32 Susaram	1,041	833
33 Seddibehara Kotturu		102
34 Malagam	1,095	571
35 Jonnapadu	246	92
36 Akkayyavalasa	1,457	278
37 Soudam	2,794	686
38 Danta	6,179	2,309
39 Jilaru	9,374	3,654
40 Jalasamudram	6,420	2,383
41 Santalakshmipuram	2,558	1,192
42 Urlam	52,561	12,467
43 Devady	...	1,113
44 Karakavalasa	84,743	4,048
45 Mulagavalasa		3,978
46 Gottipalli	7,674	2,034
47 Do. Yembaram	7,089	2,015
Berhampore Taluk Agraharams.		
1 Donnay Berhampore	695	236
2 Baluta	150	32
3 Santarapuram	280	64
4 Bhikkaripally	808	132
5 Brahmapalli	255	67
6 Misripalli...	848	96
7 Vidianadhapore	80	76
8 Sukunda	527	131
9 Rangipuram	803	360
10 Dubbapalli	308	158
11 Manohara	400	138
12 Krupasindupuram	700	114
13 Lanja	493	144
14 Darasarakhandi	894	195
15 Venkatarayapalli	100	52
16 Jagannadhapore	154	23
17 Sitaramapuram	170	30

No. VIII.—*Statement showing the particulars of the several Tenures other than Ryotwari.*—(Continued).

Names of the Zemindaries and Inam Villages.	The entire beriz of the Estate.	Peishcush or Quit-rent.
Berhampore Taluk Agraharams.—(Continued.)		
	RS.	RS.
18 Ranajhalli	370	90
19 Burutoli	434	142
20 Hundetho	617	164
21 Santoshapuram	567	143
22 Dayanedhipuram	200	64
23 Udayi Buragam	585	236
24 Sriramachandrapuram	900	200
25 Sriramapuram	670	171
26 Pattupuram	176	44
27 Balakristnapur	300	59
28 Raghunadhapur	225	50
29 Kirtipuram	832	191
Amanyas.		
30 Madanamohanapuram	196	100
31 Rathnapuram	100	25
32 Kumarapuram	396	9
33 Langapalli	1,150	474
34 Jagayyapalli	533	8
35 Haradakhandi	2,003	6 annas
36 Rayapuram	825	283
37 Angu	1,579	304
38 Hattapuram	754	129
39 Govindapuram	360	40
40 Jaganadhapalli	185	45
41 Sompuram	300	60
42 Palasi	442	80
43 Pottapuram	730	300
Mokhasas.		
44 Padmapuram	1,017	125
45 Koithapalli	240	30
46 Rajanallupally	500	102
47 Rampalli	306	69
48 Pratapuram Khujipalli	577	137
49 Saradapuram	731	109
50 Punarakhandy	480	130
51 Mohanapalli	500	150
52 Sappuvapalli	1,600	370
53 Daribhadra	560	168
54 Do Madhurasnikalapalli	40	12
55 Dobhadi	833	204

No. VIII.—*Statement showing the particulars of the several Tenures other than Ryotwari.*—(Continued.)

Names of the Zemindaries and Inam Villages.	The entire beriz of the Estate.	Peishcush or Quit-rent.
Mokhasas.—(Continued).	RS.	RS.
56 Khusalapalli	330	50
57 Munshipeta	50	25
58 Aminsahebpeta	200	56
59 Mandiyapalli	120	...
60 Sathukuttuni	180	...
61 Singabadi	170	...
62 Sinderapuram	3,500	...
63 Purnalakam	151	...
64 Pholophola	200	...
Goomsur Taluk Agraharams.		
1 Pratapadhanumjayapuram	348	41
2 Sadasivapuram	169	18
3 Narainpuram including Vagrakota hamlet ...	250	31
4 Kshatriavarupuram	536	57
5 Pratapalakshmipuram	282	30
6 Vasudevapuram	809	90
7 Viralakshmipuram	89	10
8 Sirikoy	161	66
9 Gopinadhapuram	1,548	168
10 Neladevipuram	601	53
11 Sadarakrushnasaranapuram	791	89
12 Harisaranapuram	345	37
13 Krushnasaranapuram	97	11
14 Viradhanunjayapuram	152	18
15 Konchipada	160	36
16 Lakshminarasupuram	451	48
17 Vijayadhanunjayapuram	353	40
18 Narayanapuram	661	78
19 Vijayakrushnasaranapuram	150	50
20 Masgarajapuram	688	70
21 Jagannadhapuram	230	25
22 Dhanunjayapuram	800	81
23 Gangadharapuram *alias* Chancharapalli ...	192	23
24 Gopalpuram	265	31
25 Vistnarakuttibadi	41	5
26 Koitagada *alias* Kunjabeharipuram... ...	250	30
27 Muliapalli	67	9
28 Gadapungudi *alias* Vijayagopalpuram ...	119	69
29 Arabhipalli	130	64
30 Kukkulunda	598	72
31 Irinavapalli *alias* Kojjara	100	50
32 Mandopoukolo	10	.6
33 Bhathuvapalli	22	11

No. VIII.—*Statement showing the particulars of the several Tenures other than Ryotwari.*—(Continued.)

Names of the Zemindaries and Inam Villages.	The entire beris of the Estate.	Peishcush or Quit-rent.
Mokhasas.		
	Rs.	Rs.
34 Danachendanapedi	471	55
35 Sunniapalli	281	37
36 Sitapada *alias* Sothaboro	96	12
37 Akulapada	213	26
38 Mattikanni	198	25
39 Pathulisayi	201	25
40 Moholya	399	50
41 Kontaduro	264	33
42 Bolladi	410	50
43 Chaddabhumi	265	50
44 Gochabadi	551	177
Chicacole Taluk Agraharams.		
1 Dipavali	610	207
2 Sativada	1,273	422
3 Fakirutekia (a hamlet of Do.)	859	49
4 Antlavaram	99	188
5 Raghavapuram	295	46
6 Jafarabada	296	152
7 Vatchavalasa	623	246
8 Jalluvalasa	1,006	166
9 Nizambada	394	356
10 Akkavaram	477	86
11 Goodem	1,409	123
12 Laukam	798	108
13 Vunjungipeta	147	45
14 Ragulupeta	392	54
15 Lingalavalasa —	202	75
16 Chenulavalasa	748	372
17 Ponnampeta...	390	131
18 Jagannadhapuram	618	125
19 Kasimvalasa	238	22
20 Bhyravasastrulapeta	357	106
21 Jaggusastrulapeta	146	79
22 Mallusastrulapeta	200	78
23 Jallavalasa	200	29
24 Pandrangi Srinivasa Charyulapeta	288	97
25 Chintalapeta...	...	259
26 Akkulapeta	...	298
27 Bobbilipeta	...	408

No. VIII.—*Statement showing the particulars of the several Tenures other than Ryotwari.*—(Continued.)

Names of the Zemindaries and Inam Villages.	The entire beriz of the Estate.	Peishcush or Quit-rent.
Chicacole Taluk Agraharams.—(Continued.)	RS.	RS.
28 Vungaradapeta *alias* Vandanapeta	1,318	51
29 Shermahamadpuram		27
30 Anandapuram	1,171	69
31 Hanumantapuram		134
32 Parvatisvarunipeta	449	205
33 Venkayyapeta	641	229
34 Chinnajonnalavalasa	308	172
35 Kudiram	916	235
36 Do. Sivaramakondapeta *alias* Atchannapeta...	111	14
37 Kattiyacharulapeta	834	269
38 Krushnasastrulapeta	213	47
39 Chintada	2,394	386
40 Jurakapeta	417	96
41 Sitarampuram	613	65
42 Krushnapuram	423	175
43 Jimmapuram	656	327
44 Jandamvalasa	979	223
45 Peddajonnalavalasa	290	222
46 Palavalasa	479	336
47 Ravipadu	172	81
48 Channayavalasa	923	120
49 Satyavaram	6,963	1,192
50 Sundarapuram	955	293
51 Amitikotturu	108	19
52 Harischandrapuram *alias* Subramanyapuram ...	284	40
53 Jillalavalasa	224	54
54 Mahamadpuram	435	101
55 Gotivada	2,096	918
56 Kondapolavalasa	391	185
57 Karavanga	1,154	222
58 Narayanavalasa	1,496	264
59 Rellapadu		30
60 Mavidivalasa	528	171
61 Alladapeta	356	55
62 Jannangi	1,758	266
63 Vandrada	785	336
64 Venkatapuram	1,496	249
65 Lingalavalasa	2,532	393
66 Srimannarayanapuram	435	66
67 Atchutapuram	1,186	201
68 Suramapuram	522	83
69 Harischendrapuram	4,132	626

No. VIII.—*Statement showing the particulars of the several Tenures other than Ryotwari.*—(Concluded.)

Names of the Zemindaries and Inam Villages.	The entire beriz of the Estate.	Peishcush or Quit-rent.
Chicacole Taluk Agraharams.—(Concluded.)	RS.	RS.
70 Sariabaddasadu	360	69
71 Chinnabommidi	375	84
72 Priya	968	231
73 Ramaiyavalasa	940	161
74 Pirvada	282	63
75 Gokiyavalasa	232	100
76 Kusumpolavalasa	798	393
77 Kollivalasa	908	113
78 Karazada	1,274	159
79 Varahanarasimhapatam...	1,666	399
80 Ravikuntipeta *alias* Ramachendrapuram ...	870	109
81 Venkatapuram	892	111
82 Budittupeta *alias* Godiyakara	63	80
83 Thallannvalasa	590	...
84 Chidivalasa	618	...

No. IX.—*Statement showing the Collections under the several heads of Revenue in the District of Ganjam for a series of* 10 *years.*

Faslies.	Official Years.	Land Revenue.	Abkarri.	Assessed Taxes.	Sea Customs.	Land Customs	Salt.	Stamps.	Total.
		RS.	RS.	RS.	RS.	RS.	RS.	RS.	RS.
1280	1870-71.	11,15,364	83,521	46,115	31,236	...	14,95,968	81,764	28,53,968
1281	1871-72.	8,72,807	73,894	13,114	48,863	...	14,31,118	78,259	25,18,055
1282	1872-73.	12,56,877	75,427	12,042	87,463	...	15,46,113	80,557	30,58,479
1283	1873-74.	11,68,841	77,718	27	1,56,799	...	15,47,652	85,832	30,36,869
1284	1874-75.	13,17,685	84,553	...	1,13,733	...	16,90,497	94,986	33,01,454
1285	1875-76.	11,73,482	88,975	50	67,206	...	19,63,960	93,385	33,87,058
1286	1876-77.	11,99,086	89,037	1,042	6,812	13	23,67,515	1,08,122	37,71,627
1287	1877-78.	10,77,996	94,643	...	2,979	...	20,46,731	1,26,998	33,50,347
1288	1878-79.	12,82,749	74,153	36,809	9,780	...	...	1,27,663	15,31,154
1289	1879-80.	12,87,108	91,620	25,602	61,728	...	...	1,21,231	15,87,289

No.IX-A.—*Statement showing the gross receipts and charges under the following heads during the official years ending* 1880-81.

RECEIPTS.

Official Year.	Land Revenue.	Forest.	Excise.	Assessed Tax.	Customs.	Stamps.
		RS.	RS.	RS.	RS.	RS.
1871-72	9,58,693	3,884	74,713	13,491	48,913	80,998
1872-73	11,42,316	3,439	76,245	12,345	51,072	74,176
1873-74	12,61,860	2,363	72,388	45	1,41,519	90,118
1874-75	12,72,721	4,785	93,031	14	1,46,907	94,072
1875-76	12,68,882	4,322	85,271	51	77,917	93,728
1876-77	11,30,219	4,089	82,926	1,042	25,281	1,00,816
1877-78	11,20,323	3,945	99,629	...	2,937	1,25,446
1878-79	13,19,439	3,476	72,140	36,581	6,767	1,29,980
1879-80	12,99,939	4,107	94,530	25,493	27,400	1,19,684
1880-81	12,64,361	25,541	1,07,481	12,133	1,53,479	1,23,098

DISBURSEMENTS.

Official Year.	Land Revenue.	Forest.	Excise.	Assessed Tax.	Customs.	Stamps.
		RS.	RS.	RS.	RS.	RS.
1871-72	1,55,003	2,641	...	2,172	6,647	2,992
1872-73	1,56,680	2,770	65	737	7,568	3,916
1873-74	1,63,345	3,037	41	65	7,564	2,374
1874-75	1,31,281	3,330	702	...	7,962	2,378
1875-76	1,34,789	4,036	766	...	8,166	2,543
1876-77	1,58,835	3,134	299	...	9,586	2,608
1877-78	1,41,510	3,299	83	...	9,670	3,289
1878-79	1,19,457	2,673	97	385	7,754	2,517
1879-80	1,60,037	2,846	174	1,203	9,510	2,955
1880-81	1,54,668	2,933	128	99	10,101	3,080

No. X.—*Statement showing the total values of Trade in the District of Ganjam for a series of seven years.*

Official Years.	Value of Imports.			Value of Exports.			Value of Re-exports.	Gross duty.
	Merchandise.	Treasure.	Total.	Merchandise.	Treasure.	Total.		
	RS.	RS.	RS.	RS.	RS.	RS.	RS.	RS.
1874-75	12,42,113	4,90,948	17,33,061	42,99,227	5,50,000	48,49,227	...	1,46,132
1875-76	8,15,759	1,50,567	9,66,326	27,42,834	15,13,000	42,55,834	...	76,990
1876-77	11,50,560	16,66,658	28,17,218	49,71,874	7,00,500	56,72,374	...	24,393
1877-78	15,11,355	9,17,657	24,29,012	54,86,221	8,12,300	62,98,521	...	1,610
1878-79	10,84,892	82,030	11,66,922	26,31,311	16,65,138	42,96,449	...	5,217
1879-80	13,37,818	80,000	14,17,818	32,41,786	16,75,964	49,17,750	...	*26,354
1880-81	12,38,945	2,76,855	15,15,800	46,21,757	16,50,000	62,71,757	...	*1,52,420

* In 1879-80 there was a refund of Rupees 11 and in 1880-81 Rupees 28.

SEA CUSTOMS.

No. XI.—*Statement showing the value of Export Trade, with particulars of articles, in the District of Ganjam, from the year* 1874-75 *to* 1880-81 (*both inclusive.*)

Articles.	1874-75.	1875-76.	1876-77.	1877-78.	1878-79.	1879-80.	1880-81.
	RS.	RS.	RS.	RS.	RS.	RS.	RS.
Bones	...	1,691	60	1,346	317	266	499
Cotton Goods	4,092	23,915	17,993	9,387	3,908	2,485	5,068
Drugs	151	750	206	65	319	300	155
Indigo	3,672	50,771	35,560	11,433	7,216	13,050	18,518
Dyes of sorts	1,22,726	2,29,974	1,65,259	4,70,009	3,03,014	74,828	99,470
Feathers	...	1,120	...	...	30	120	309
Fish-maws	300	245	230	...	300	300	787
Fruits and Nuts	2,687	3,118	8,502	19,566	19,561	23,428	15,675
Paddy	4,334	8,292	1,45,552	2,11,711	6,362	623	20
Rice	26,30,208	7,55,404	25,74,827	19 60,036	4,08,480	7,09,655	19,19,910
Wheat	1,487	7,943	5,338	2,211	3,440	4,877	8,537
Grain of sorts	64,748	36,123	4,86,011	7,30,628	90,656	76,293	78,117
Hides	2,54,750	1,99,137	1,41,775	2,52,891	2,69,627	2,64,354	2,80,551
Horns	7,483	42,825	20,144	38,747	57,198	23,919	66,079
Ivory and Ivoryware	...	350	...	...	...	...	...
Mats	1,567	3,366	738	3,213	5,668	3,617	4,461
Molasses	4	318	118	40	28,521	1,13,191	38,705
Coir and Coir rope	22,991	18,144	15,775	28,592	22,486	17,814	19,133
Hemp	23,978	24,532	23,837	40,020	54,779	3,952	51,489
Oils	711	198	8	75	88	...	...
Perfumery	...	...	500	...	...	32	...
Seeds	7,67,540	9,57,985	6,95,845	10,84,035	7,60,148	13,40,420	13,93,452

SEA CUSTOMS.—(*Concluded.*)

No. XI.—*Statement showing the value of Export Trade, with particulars of articles, in the District of Ganjam, from the year* 1874-75 *to* 1880-81 (*both inclusive.*)

Articles.	1874-75.	1875-76.	1876-77.	1877-78.	1878-79.	1879-80.	1880-81.
	RS.	RS.	RS.	RS.	RS.	RS.	RS.
Shawls, Cashmere	...	...	...	300	...	...	...
Silk, Piece Goods	1,600	1,721	1,240	4,019	4,408	2,160	5,516
Spices	58	940	3,824	339	678	15	..
Spirits	1,28,873	1,02,557	91,212	2,33,246	2,43,509	1,43,518	1,22,401
Sugar	2,17,786	2,18,422	4,25,478	2,16,832	2,00,174	3,42,645	3,24,842
Timber and Wood	758	3,038	1,085	233	657	10,648	1,14,520
Tobacco	32	126	164	655	82	81	20
Wax and Wax candles ...	4,874	8,110	14,611	8,405	5,355	4,917	3,696
Sundries	30,408	40,773	37,247	54,687	38,080	36,446	39,850
Total...	42,97,318	27,42,088	49,13,134	53,82,721	25,35,091	32,13,954	46,11,780

SEA CUSTOMS.

No. XII.—*Statement showing the value of Imports at the several ports in Ganjam District, from the official year* 1874-75 *to* 1880-81 *(both inclusive.)*

Names of Articles.	1874-75.	1875-76.	1876-77.	1877-78.	1878-79.	1879-80.	1880-81.
	RS.	RS.	RS.	RS.	RS.	RS.	RS.
Millinery and Wearing Apparel	18,310	35,771	18,461	33,488	25,304	26,587	19,711
Gold and Silver Lace and Thread	...	...	...	...	...	520	..
Books and Stationery ...	6,045	4,961	5,659	9,860	6,101	4,294	4,043
Twist and Yarn	1,55,313	2,34,337	3,58,684	3,72,526	3,88,394	6,34,829	6,39,227
Piece Goods, dyed ...	33,702	23,060	12.294	39,125	26,172	21,320	14,617
Piece Goods, plain ...	68,394	61,176	53,442	46,364	38,852	47,899	53,840
Drugs	4,191	3,404	1,094	3,003	4,179	6,455	4,106
Dyes	574	7,656	4,766	1,686	1,389	4,620	3,378
Betel-nut, raw ...	3,699	3,020	3,110	2,396	13,394	15,465	9,365
Glassware	29,277	19,206	20,736	16,382	22,801	19,060	22,285
Paddy	...	...	5,625	9,012	3,045	960	...
Rice	1,778	...	3	19,026	6,334	16,364	5
Grain of sorts	2,744	1,116	1,031	116	3,570	796	79
Gunnies and Gunny Bags ...	2,44,154	56,110	1,75,913	1,06,410	22,060	65,500	1,12,271
Jewellery	200	300	...	8,000	...	787	...
Machinery	1,857	2,550	647	2,411	10,197	2,706	7,792
Malt Liquors	7,775	5,511	10,758	7,582	6,701	5,011	3,106
Metals	3,50,247	1,68,598	1,87,696	3,82,899	2,34,228	1,57,419	1,21,728
Porcelain and Earthenware ...	2,048	563	1,139	2,013	1,451	1,460	820
Provisions	13,220	9,237	19,317	8,125	10,958	37,357	27,861

SEA CUSTOMS.—*(Concluded.)*

No. XII.—*Statement showing the value of Imports at the several ports in Ganjam District, from the official year* 1874-75 *to* 1880-81 *(both inclusive.)*

Names of Articles.	1874-75.	1875-76.	1876-77.	1877-78.	1978-79.	1879-80.	1880-81.
	RS.	RS.	RS.	RS.	RS.	RS.	RS.
Seeds	7,466	8,413	63,304	7,989	41,074	29,117	7,578
Silk raw	4,000	8,470	7,026	3,464	18,070	540	480
Silk, Piece Goods... ...	920	2,830	615	5,312	7,689	6,086	1,090
Spices	14,145	17,379	9,492	14,212	6,516	10,348	6,827
Spirits	13,092	4,679	8,162	8,152	6,899	6,413	5,279
Tea	1,121	319	1,564	1,558	1,195	911	525
Timber and Planks ...	...	...	296	60	8,123	...	2,846
Wines	20,406	6,252	11,196	10,941	9,176	7,449	8,953
Woollens	2,425	4,959	10,123	9,153	8,471	10,308	2,744
Sundries	67,445	50,128	63,805	82,684	75,757	1,29,290	91,964
Total...	10,74,548	7,40,008	10,55,958	12,08,944	10,08,100	12,69,371	11,72,502

No. XII-A.—*Statement showing the Receipts and Charges of Port Funds in the District of Ganjam for a series of 6 years.*

Names of Ports.	Chief Items.	1875-76.	1876-77.	1877-78.	1878-79.	1879-80.	1880-81.
		RECEIPTS DURING THE OFFICIAL YEAR.					
		Rs.	Rs.	Rs.	Rs.	Rs.	Rs.
Ganjam* ...	Port Dues ...	2,248	557	111	67	9	574
	Other Receipts...	21	14	62	72	5	11
Gopalpur ...	Port Dues ...	19,789	14,686	14,717	8,955	9,655	11,183
	Other Receipts...	184	176	295	105	347	262
Calingapatam.	Port Dues ...	3,377	1,526	3,683	2,061	2,555	5,151
	Other Receipts...	43	97	53	870	413	130
	Total...	25,662	17,056	18,921	12,130	12,984	17,311
		EXPENDITURE DURING THE OFFICIAL YEAR.					
Ganjam* ...	Port Estabt. ...	454	456	538	566	576	576
	Other charges ...	2,248	54	239	148	248	140
Gopalpur ...	Port Estabt. ...	1,231	2,262	2,099	2,382	2,376	2,376
	Light do. ...	312	312	333	333	312	312
	Other charges ...	2,621	464	756	731	706	1,275
Calingapatam.	Port Estabt. ...	456	476	519	588	547	605
	Light do. ...	...	151	477	493	472	472
	Other charges ...	2,785	768	1,298	2,553	979	815
	Total...	10,107	4,943	6,259	7,794	6,216	6,571

* There is no Light House at Ganjam.

No. XIII.—*Statement showing the Number and Tonnage of Vessels which arrived at and departed from the District of Ganjam.*

Official Years.	Arrivals.							
	Square Rigged.				Native Craft.		Total.	
	Steamers.		Sailing Vessels.					
	Number.	Tonnage.	Number.	Tonnage.	Number.	Tonnage.	Number.	Tonnage.
1874-75 ...	221	222,454 } Vessels.		......	74	14,980	295	237,434
1875-76 ...	247	286,116 } Vessels.		......	59	9,358	306	295,474
1876-77 ...	198	229,399	105	57,155	109	16,906	412	303,460
1877-78 ...	207	221,764	119	61,227	54	8,069	380	291,060
1878-79 ...	249	267,609	24	16,188	82	8,329	355	292,126
1879-80 ...	219	263,947	46	27,292	49	5,271	314	296,510
1880-81 ...	255	328,194	51	42,165	43	6,949	349	377,308

Note.—The steamers and the sailing vessels were grouped together in the returns for the years 1874-75 and 1875-76. They cannot now be separated.

Departures.

Official Years.	Steamers Number.	Steamers Tonnage.	Sailing Vessels Number.	Sailing Vessels Tonnage.	Native Craft Number.	Native Craft Tonnage.	Total Number.	Total Tonnage.
1874-75 ...	221	222,454 } Vessels.		......	74	14,980	295	237,434
1875-76 ...	247	286,116 } Vessels.		......	59	9,358	306	295,474
1876-77 ...	197	228,149	106	58,984	109	16,906	412	304,039
1877-78 ...	208	221,842	122	62,901	54	8,069	384	292,812
1878-79 ...	243	267,456	30	18,331	82	8,329	360	294,116
1879-80 ...	218	262,737	39	22,604	49	5,271	306	290,612
1880-81 ...	256	328,761	50	40,265	43	6,949	349	375,975

Note.—The number of vessels that arrived in this District has been shown as the number departed. This remark applies to the case of Native Craft.

No. XIV.—*Statement showing the Number and Value of Suits disposed of in the Civil Revenue Courts for a series of 10 years.*

	Number of Suits disposed of in different Courts.													
	Ordinary Suits.								Small Causes.					
	Village Munsiffs.	Revenue Courts.	District Munsiffs.	Principal Amins.	Judges of Small Causes and Principal Sadar Amins.	Civil Judges and Judicial Commissioners.	Total number of Suits.	Total value in Rupees.	District Munsiffs and Assistant Agents and Assistant Commissioners.	Principal Sadar Amins.	Judges of Small Causes Courts.	Civil Judges and Judicial Commissioners.	Total number of Small Causes.	Total value in Rupees.
1	2	3	4	5	6	7	8	9	10	11	12	13	14	15
								RS.						RS.
1871... ...	493	...	1,500	...	...	17	2,010	11,34,689	2,304	...	...	...	2,304	58,170
1872... ...	517	...	1,637	...	...	29	2,183	3,42,886	2,179	...	...	...	2,179	53.530
1873... ...	580	...	1,799	...	...	14	2,393	3,32,700	2,134	...	...	...	2,134	58,277
1874... ...	484	103	1,761	...	...	3	2,351	3,33,774	2,066	...	...	...	2,066	51,797
1875... ...	511	116	1,774	...	...	13	2,414	3,64,886	2,019	...	...	...	2,019	53,070
1876... ...	367	178	1,705	...	...	27	2,277	4,18,043	1,838	...	...	...	1,838	43.303
1877... ...	816	178	2,252	...	...	29	3,275	4,55,642	2,174	...	...	...	2,174	40,945
1878	612	1	1,752	10	...	12	2,387	5,14,605	1,810	...	...	...	1,810	59,910
1879... ...	536	141	2,162	...	...	12	2,851	4,24,588	2,401	...	...	...	2,401	59.118
1880... ...	467	182	2,485	...	...	24	3,158	5,77,242	2,330	...	...	...	2,331	59,371

No. XV.—*Statement of persons tried, convicted and acquitted, and of property lost and recovered.*

Nature of Offences.	Number of persons tried during the year.	Acquitted or discharged.	Convicted.	Remaining under trial.	Property.	
					Stolen.	Recovered.
1	2	3	4	5	6	7
1870.						
1. Murder	7	6	1	...	3	3
2. Culpable homicide	8	2	6	2	...	...
3. Rape...	5	2	3	...	...	...
4. Hurts and assaults ...	1,794	1,178	616	70	...	...
5. Other offences against the person	77	37	40	3	883	28
6. Dacoity	16	16	...	...	3,008	2,000
7. Robbery	22	9	13	...	910	713
8. House-breaking	270	65	205	...	5,991	1,815
9. Theft	870	332	538	13	13,923	3,295
10. Other offences against property.	571	390	181	8	7,477	2,386
11. Other offences against the Penal Code	2,177	1,033	1,144	14	837	2
Total...	5,817	3,070	2,747	110	33,032	10,242
12. Special and Local Laws ...	2,173	518	1,655	26	361	250
Total...	7,990	3,588	4,402	136	33,393	10,492
1871.						
1. Murder...	14	8	6	...	19	...
2. Culpable homicide ...	9	4	5	...	...	...
3. Rape	2	1	1	...	...	...
4. Hurts and assaults... ...	2,066	1,369	697	21	60	...
5. Other offences against the person	81	49	32	...	547	465
6. Dacoity	...	...	...	...	...	...
7. Robbery	29	13	16	...	322	143
8. House-breaking	306	103	193	9	8,462	2,700
9. Theft	1,074	462	612	3	14,857	4,922
10. Other offences against property	551	350	201	25	...	...
11. Other offences against the Penal Code	1,926	955	971	92	3,967	700
Total...	6,058	3,324	2,734	150	28,224	8,930
12. Special and Local Laws ...	2,374	592	1,782	...	133	55
Total...	8,432	3,916	4,516	150	28,357	8,985

No. XV.—*Statement of persons tried, convicted and acquitted, and of property lost and recovered.*—Continued.

Nature of Offences.	Number of persons tried during the year.	Acquitted or Discharged.	Convicted.	Remaining under trial.	Property.	
					Stolen.	Recovered.
1	2	3	4	5	6	7
1872.						
1. Murder...	15	2	13	1	156	146
2. Culpable homicide	5	2	3	2	...	...
3. Rape	...	...	...	...	...	...
4. Hurts and assaults... ...	1,512	932	580	112	...	...
5. Other offences against the person	85	56	29	22	..	...
6. Dacoity	36	13	23	7	458	165
7. Robbery	1	1	...	...	10	1
8. House-breaking	341	109	232	24	13,538	1,861
9. Theft	1,034	387	647	44	21,938	4,926
10. Other offences against property.	1,160	754	406	58	14,749	4,108
11. Other offences against the Penal Code	1,147	321	826	49	373	257
Total...	5,336	2,577	2,759	319	51,217	11,464
12. Special and Local Laws ...	2,478	574	1,904	31	1,494	1,354
Total...	7,814	3,151	4,663	350	52,711	12,818
1873.						
1. Murder...	19	14	5	13	2,175	977
2. Culpable homicide ...	8	6	2	...	...	...
3. Rape	...	...	...	3	...	...
4. Hurts and assaults... ...	1,010	548	462	...	...	...
5. Other offences against the person	84	37	47	1	...	...
6. Dacoity	17	7	10	...	6	...
7. Robbery	15	9	6	...	484	11
8. House-breaking	234	70	164	5	14,038	2,139
9. Theft	814	333	481	83	12,694	4,266
10. Other offences against property.	1,089	618	471	11	12,770	632
11. Other offences against the Penal Code	952	266	686	42	82	8
Total...	4,242	1,908	2,334	158	42,244	8,033
12. Special and Local Laws ...	1,833	288	1,545	6	39	36
Total...	6,075	2,196	3,878	164	42,283	8,069

No. XV.—*Statement of persons tried, convicted and acquitted, and of property lost and recovered.*—Continued.

Nature of Offences.	Number of persons tried during the year.	Acquitted or discharged.	Convicted.	Remaining under trial.	Property. Stolen.	Property. Recovered.
1	2	3	4	5	6	7
1874.						
1. Murder	15	15	...	6	...	...
2. Culpable homicide	6	3	3	...	...	...
3. Rape	...	...	...	...	...	...
4. Hurts and assaults... ...	1,173	455	718	50	10	4
5. Other offences against the person	81	14	67	1	18	...
6. Dacoity	11	11	...	...	104	...
7. Robbery	12	7	5	3	188	162
8. House-breaking	244	46	198	21	12,829	2,352
9. Theft	907	297	610	101	10,607	3,220
10. Other offences against property.	766	451	315	53	1,447	472
11. Other offences against the Penal Code	2,260	417	1,843	33	369	162
Total...	5,475	1,716	3,759	268	25,572	6,372
12. Special and Local Laws ...	2,663	360	2,303	43	217	110
Total...	8,138	2,076	6,062	311	25,789	6,482
1875.						
1. Murder	31	17	14	20	69	65
2. Culpable homicide... ...	7	5	2	...	...	...
3. Rape	...	...	...	1	...	...
4. Hurts and assaults ...	1,156	574	582	78	...	...
5. Other offences against the person	64	13	51	6	24	24
6. Dacoity	...	...	...	7	20	2
7. Robbery	1	1	...	...	154	2
8. House-breaking	361	44	317	23	23,744	9,203
9. Theft	1,103	288	815	99	17,717	3,660
10. Other offences against property	809	412	397	25	3,479	1,114
11. Other offences against the Penal Code	1,952	342	1,610	82	...	...
Total...	5,484	1,696	3,788	341	45,207	14,070
12. Special and Local Laws ...	1,938	288	1,650	49	312	101
Total...	7,422	1,984	5,438	390	45,519	14,171

No. XV.—*Statement of persons tried, convicted and acquitted, and of property lost and recovered.*—Continued.

Nature of Offences.	Number of persons tried during the year.	Acquitted or discharged.	Convicted	Remaining under trial.	Property. Stolen.	Property. Recovered.
1	2	3	4	5	6	7
1876.						
1. Murder	36	23	13	...	460	50
2. Culpable homicide... ...	24	15	9	...	...	...
3. Rape	...	..	...	...	...	...
4. Hurts and assaults... ...	1,511	661	850	18	...	...
5. Other offences against the person	39	11	28	4	...	..
6. Dacoity	...	...	...	...	...	...
7. Robbery	4	...	4	...	51	3
8. House-breaking	430	95	335	22	18,633	9,115
9. Theft	1,111	344	767	46	15,576	4,036
10. Other offences against property.	982	558	424	21	3,279	2,194
11. Other offences against the Penal Code	1,950	510	1,440	59	153	...
Total...	6,087	2,217	3,870	170	38,122	15,398
12. Special and Local Laws ..	2,485	353	2,132	25	203	54
Total...	8,572	2,570	6,002	195	38,325	15,452
1877.						
1. Murder	13	19	14	1	117	76
2. Culpable homicide ...	21	6	15	3	...	...
3. Rape	2	1	1	1	...	...
4. Hurts and assaults ...	1,345	590	755	14	1	1
5. Other offences against the person	72	8	64	3	94	1
6. Dacoity	...	...	...	...	...	...
7. Robbery	7	5	2	2	62	13
8. House-breaking	449	55	394	12	25,000	12,539
9. Theft	1,489	336	1,153	34	17,494	6,014
10. Other offences against property.	923	466	457	30	6,913	1,003
11. Other offences against the Penal Code	2,076	311	1,765	22	152	16
Total...	6,417	1,797	4,620	122	49,833	19,663
12. Special and Local Laws ...	2,230	287	1,943	2	287	81
Total...	8,647	2,084	6,563	124	50,120	19,744

No. XV.—*Statement of persons tried, convicted and acquitted, and of property lost and recovered.*—Concluded.

Nature of Offences.	Number of persons tried during the year.	Acquitted or discharged.	Convicted.	Remaining under trial.	Property.	
					Stolen.	Recovered.
1	2	3	4	5	6	7
1878.						
1. Murder...	18	9	9	1	90	66
2. Culpable homicide... ...	16	12	4	...	...	...
3. Rape	...	...	...	...	...	...
4. Hurts and assaults... ...	1,270	544	726	20	...	..
5. Other offences against the person	32	4	28	...	2	...
6. Dacoity	14	13	1	...	629	111
7. Robbery	11	3	8	6	453	179
8. House-breaking	982	157	825	12	34,445	7,123
9. Theft	2,300	323	1,972	84	32,998	9,540
10. Other offences against property.	1,118	471	647	33	4,070	2,138
11. Other offences against the Penal Code	1,834	240	1,594	12	...	...
Total...	7,595	1,781	5,814	168	72,687	19,157
12. Special and Local Laws ...	2,333	198	2,135	20	357	151
Total...	9,928	1,979	7,949	188	73,044	19,308
1879.						
1. Murder...	30	19	11	...	2,274	261
2. Culpable homicide	7	3	4	1	4	...
3. Rape	...	...	...	...	...	...
4. Hurts and assaults... ...	1,154	421	733	5	21	20
5. Other offences against the person	66	20	46	1	...	...
6. Dacoity	4	2	2	8	243	62
7. Robbery	5	...	5	...	39	...
8. House-breaking	362	23	339	11	31,810	6,922
9. Theft	1,381	250	1,131	60	29,185	6,375
10. Other offences against property.	728	318	410	38	5,172	1,388
11. Other offences against the Penal Code	2,227	477	1,750	26	251	108
Total...	5,964	1,533	4,431	150	68,999	15,131
12. Special and Local Laws ...	2,223	293	1,930	3	418	293
Grand Total...	8,187	1,826	6,361	153	69,417	15,424

Note.—Column 2 includes Columns 3 and 4, but not Column 5.

No. XVI.—*Statement showing the expenditure on Public Works from Imperial, Provincial, and Special Funds, for the years* 1875-76, 1876-77, 1877-78, 1878-79, 1879-80.

Years.	Imperial.						Provincial				Special.			
	Miscellaneous Public Improvements.	Communications.	Civil Buildings.	Military	Agricultural.	Total.	Civil Buildings.	Communications.	Miscellaneous Public Improvements.	Total.	Civil Buildings.	Communications.	Miscellaneous Public Improvements.	Total.
New Works.	Rs.	Rs.	Rs.	Rs.	Rs.	Rs.	Rs.	Rs.	Rs.	Rs.	Rs.	Rs.	Rs.	Rs.
1875-76 ...	...	...	316	958	2,412	3,686	8,330	15,554	205	24,089	...	...	...	...
1876-77 ...	...	...	1,654	969	2,777	5,400	8,352	17,224	...	25,576	1,975	...	1,441	3,416
1877-78 ...	...	...	651	1,092	6,322	8,065	9,931	7,987	...	17,918	4,145	...	335	4,480
1878-79 ...	...	...	133	6	1,123	1,262	6,425	3,995	...	10,420	562	...	271	833
1879-80 ...	...	...	1,019	...	2,405	3,424	4,368	930	...	5,298	1,228	...	...	1,228
Total...	...	...	3,778	3,025	15,039	21,837	37,406	45,690	205	83,301	7,910	...	2,047	9,957
Repairs.														
1875-76 ...	119	...	66	757	33,535	34,477	4,863	...	...	4,863	...	...	...	...
1876-77 ...	...	...	372	1,654	48,707	50,733	7,626	...	...	7,626	74	...	155	229
1877-78 ...	480	...	263	2,334	61,632	64,709	6,391	1,800	...	8,191	261	...	449	710
1878-79 ...	...	...	1,007	459	24,421	25,887	3,359	1,800	...	5,159	52	...	605	657
1879-80 ...	15	...	210	349	25,379	25,953	3,710	593	...	4,303	175	...	...	175
Total...	614	...	1,918	5,553	1,93,674	2,01,759	25,949	4,193	...	30,142	562	...	1,209	1,771

No. XVII.—*Statement showing the Receipts of Local Funds under Act IV of* 1871, *for the last* 5 *official years.*

Receipts.	1875-76.			1876-77.			1877-78.			1878-79.			1879-80.		
	RS.	A.	P.	RS.	A.	P.	RS.	A.	P.	RS.	A.	P.	RS.	A.	P.
1. Balance	115,611	10	8	112,092	8	2	83,321	7	9	18,251	0	8	47,540	15	7
2. Provincial grants for Roads	60,773	0	0	20,000	0	0	20,000	0	0	......			......		
3. Provincial grants for Schools	......			......			......			......			......		
4. Provincial grants for General purposes ...	5,000	0	0	5,000	0	0	5,000	0	0	5,000	0	0	......		
5. Surplus Pound Fund	1,507	0	0	2,543	0	0	600	0	0	1,100	0	0	580	0	0
6. Avenue	21	5	0	17	8	0	17	13	0	10	15	0	45	5	6
7. Fishery Rents	6,154	0	7	6,148	7	5	5,864	4	2	7,448	4	11	8,931	5	0
8. Ferry Rents	1,627	2	0	1,726	1	4	2,947	6	8	3,140	7	2	83	0	0
9. Miscellaneous	685	0	9	285	12	10	40	0	2	5	11	0	......		
10. Road Cess under Act III of 1866 ...	115	4	9	36	9	7	18	0	10	96	0	2	22	2	7
11. Land Cess under Act IV of 1871 ...	170,225	11	10	176,322	2	6	149,370	5	5	191,624	12	8	191,535	11	7
12. Tolls under Act IV of 1871	......			......			......			6,288	3	10	13,694	0	6
13. House Tax	......			......			......			......			......		
14. Fees in Schools and Training Institution ...	......			......			......			......			......		
15. Contributions	590	0	0	460	0	0	6,188	2	9	1,419	13	1	180	0	0
16. Educational Receipts	5	12	0	......			......			11	0	0	......		
17. Sale proceeds of Elementary books ...	256	6	2	375	14	8	598	1	0	353	15	11	439	4	3
18. Fees from Travellers' Bungalows ...	260	15	1	265	9	3	177	12	0	262	13	9	319	6	0
19. Balance of Bungalow Fund	......			......			......			......			......		
20. Fines, Penalties and Refunds	......			15	4	5	54	4	0	455	6	0	81	8	0
21. Sale of other property	......			......			......			13	10	0	......		
22. Public Works Receipts	106	5	10	3	8	0	3	11	0	......			......		
23. Do. Refund of Expenditure... ...	2,606	0	11	......			20,657	12	10	88,698	13	2	1,322	4	9
24. Miscellaneous	314	12	0	306	5	9	334	9	10	887	6	9	100	5	1

No. XVII.—*Statement showing the Receipts of Local Funds under Act IV of* 1871, *for the last* 5 *official years*.—Continued.

Receipts.	1875-76.	1876-77.	1877-78.	1878-79.	1879-80.
	RS. A. P.	RS. A. P.	RS. A. P.	RS. A. P.	RS. A. P.
25. Donations for Hospitals, &c.	1,000 0 0	1,000 0 0	1,015 0 0	1,568 8 6	1,121 6 0
Miscellaneous No. of do.	......	20 11 9	......	2 14 0	52 14 0
Miscellaneous sale of Medicines ...	......	14 12 11	34 5 0	6 3 4	......
26. Contributions for works unconnected with schools or endowed foundations ...	1,581 9 3	195 6 0	......	......	......
27. Miscellaneous Debt Account	4,296 10 1	7,675 11 0	......	1,400 15 11	362 0 0
28. Contribution from Parlakimedi for Sanitary purposes	360 0 0	360 0 0	360 0 0	360 0 0	360 0 0
29. Interest on Arrears of Land Revenue ...	......	......	......	......	170 15 8
Total Rupees...	373,098 10 11	334,865 0 7	296,103 0 5	323,395 15 5	266,942 8 6

No. XVII.—*Statement showing the Expenditure of Local Funds under Act IV of* 1871, *for the last* 5 *official years*.

Expenditure. *New Works.*		RS. A. P.	RS A. P.	RS. A. P.	RS. A. P.	RS. A. P.
1. Communications..	By P. W. Department...	47,513 3 11	48,315 3 8	55,432 6 11	35,544 12 10	9,599 2 8
	„ other Agency ...	......	......	1,019 14 3	......	54 10 6
2. Tolls and Ferries.	„ P. W. Department...	......	......	......	......	......
3. Civil Buildings ...	„ P. W. Department...	......	......	943 1 1	1,141 7 10	976 0 3
	„ other Agency ...	100 0 0	......	446 13 0	56 0 0	......
4. Sanitary and Miscellaneous.	„ P. W. Department...	6,462 12 5	7,399 3 2	5,854 4 7	3,772 0 7	2,058 4 7
	„ other Agency ...	1,248 0 0	632 0 0	......	......	......

No. XVII.—*Statement showing the Expenditure of Local Funds under Act IV of* 1871, *for the last* 5 *official years.*—Continued.

Expenditure.	1875-76.	1876-77.	1877-78.	1878-79.	1879-80.
Repairs.	RS. A. P.	RS. A. P.	RS. A. P.	RS. A. P.	RS. A. P.
5. Communications.. { By P. W. Department...	93,448 6 0	97,100 12 8	93,110 15 10	1,19,974 11 0	59,866 8 11
" other Agency ...	......	688 4 0	2,414 15 4	1,533 11 11	1,695 1 10
6. Tolls and Ferries. " P. W. Department...	49 5 8	......	......	......	......
7. Civil Buildings ... { " P. W. Department...	......	......	2,617 12 0	451 2 6	754 10 6
" other Agency ...	......	......	......	32 0 0	......
8. Sanitary and Miscellaneous. { " P. W. Department...	2,527 10 4	1,169 9 11	3,734 6 10	2,067 12 10	1,090 11 4
" other Agency ...	......	......	......	......	......
9. Public Works Department Supervision ...	33,941 12 10	35,043 5 3	40,423 4 1	40,737 15 11	18,586 5 9
10. Petty Establishment	......	15 0 3	......	......	......
11. Tolls and Ferries	......	......	......	1,400 15 11	3,865 1 1
12. Tools and Plant	1,452 15 7	2,510 1 6	11,783 10 10	4,463 2 5	1,858 10 2
13. Refund of Receipts	......	0 2 0	2 8 0	......	12,026 13 10
14. Contributions	150 0 0	705 8 0	525 0 0	525 0 0	525 0 0
Total Grant I...	1,86,894 2 9	1,93,609 2 5	2,18,339 0 9	2,11,700 13 9	1,12,957 1 5
15. Payment for Inspection	2,005 7 7	2,088 1 7	3,103 7 11	3,499 7 5	3,835 0 5
16 Local Fund Schools	628 14 5	454 1 7	13,287 8 8	18,259 13 5	10,478 15 3
17. Purchase of books	363 6 5	785 9 6	608 3 10	1,310 1 1	432 0 6
18. Commission on sale of books	27 15 10	54 8 1	73 0 8	36 5 0	19 0 5
19. Salary Grants	......	......	30 0 0	......	8,794 11 6
20. Results Grants	5,759 0 0	9,800 0 0	4,970 8 0	3,006 3 0	2,069 9 0
Total Grant II...	8,784 12 3	13,132 4 9	22,072 13 1	26,111 13 11	25,629 5 1

No. XVII.—*Statement showing the Expenditure of Local Funds under Act IV of 1871, for the last 5 official years.*—Concluded.

Expenditure.	1875-76.			1876-77.			1877-78.			1878-79.			1879-80.		
Repairs.	RS.	A.	P.	RS.	A.	P.	RS.	A.	P.	RS.	A.	P.	RS.	A.	P.
21. Hospitals and Dispensaries	4,935	1	4	12,081	3	6	11,026	14	11	13,652	3	11	8,818	11	4
22. Vaccine Establishment	4,129	9	3	5,278	14	5	5,731	9	9	6,241	1	7	6,464	8	4
23. Sanitary Establishment and cleansing of tanks and wells	36,188	6	1	11,063	9	8	9,274	15	8	11,053	7	5	9,314	14	11
24. Travellers' Bungalow Establishment ...	1,670	1	0	500	7	7	677	12	10	909	7	0	867	8	4
25. Contributions and Medical College Contribution	2,600	0	0	1,700	0	0	1,700	0	0	2,000	0	0	4,068	0	0
Total Grant III...	49,523	1	8	30,624	3	2	28,411	5	2	33,856	3	11	29,553	10	7
26. Establishment at the Presidency in the Collector's and Local Fund Board Establishments and Contingencies	2,230	5	5	2,539	12	3	2,951	11	2	2,112	2	1	2,770	8	2
27. Refund of Cesses	4,282	0	10	......			......			......			......		
Total Grant IV...	6,512	6	3	2,539	12	3	2,951	11	2	2,112	2	1	2,770	8	2
28. Miscellaneous Debt Accounts	9,292	0	10	11,638	2	3	6,077	2	0	1,400	15	11	27	13	3
29. Total Expenditure	2,61,006	7	9	2,51,543	8	10	2,77,852	0	2	2,75,182	1	7	1,70,938	6	
30. Balance...	1,12,092	3	2	83,321	7	9	18,251	0	3	48,213	13	10	1,13,347	1	
Grand Total...	3,73,098	10	11	3,34,865	0	7	2,96,103	0	5	3,23,395	15	5	2,84,285	7	10

No. XVIII.—*Statement showing the Receipts and Expenditure of Special Funds, for a series of 5 years.*

FUNDS.	1875-76.														
	Balance at the beginning of the year.			Receipts during the year.			Total.			Expenditure during the year.			Balance at the end of the year.		
1	2			3			4			5			6		
	RS.	A.	P.	RS.	A.	P.	RS.	A.	P.	RS.	A.	P.	RS.	A.	P.
1. Jungle Conservancy Fund	658	11	3	68	0	9	726	12	0	183	11	4	543	0	8
2. Cattle Pound do	871	5	4	2,992	0	5	3,863	5	9	2,734	10	5	1,128	11	4
3. Surplus Pound do	...	...	...	1,000	0	0	1,000	0	0	1,000	0	0	...	...	...
4. Village Service do	423	3	5	447	10	10	870	14	3	180	0	0	690	14	3
5. Nanal Grass do	...	...	...	...	...	...	...	...	...	...	...	...	...	...	...
6. Public Bungalow do	...	...	...	...	...	...	...	...	...	...	...	...	...	...	...
7. Endowment do	...	...	...	...	...	...	...	...	...	...	...	...	...	...	...
8. Canal and Ferry do	...	...	...	...	...	...	...	...	...	...	...	...	...	...	...
9. Irrigation Cess do	...	...	...	...	...	...	...	...	...	...	...	...	...	...	...
Total...	1,953	4	0	4,507	12	0	6,461	0	0	4,098	5	9	2,362	10	3

No. XVIII.—*Statement showing the Receipts and Expenditure of Special Funds, for a series of 5 years.*—Continued.

FUNDS.	1876-77. Receipts during the year including balance.	1876-77. Expenditure during the year.	1876-77. Balance at the end of the year.	1877-78. Receipts during the year including balance.	1877-78. Expenditure during the year.	1877-78. Balance at the end of the year.
	7	8	9	10	11	12
	RS. A. P.	RS. A. P.	RS. A. P.	RS. A. P.	RS. A. P.	RS. A. P.
1. Jungle Conservancy Fund	682 11 10	190 7 6	492 4 4	707 4 10	219 3 0	488 1 10
2. Cattle Pound do	3,878 14 9	2,653 0 7	1,225 14 2	4,403 10 8	3,117 13 9	1,285 12 6
3. Surplus Pound do	1,000 0 0	1,000 0 0	... ...	1,200 0 0	1,200 0 0	... ...
4. Village Service do	1,095 1 10	179 0 0	916 1 10	1,632 3 9	180 0 0	1,452 3 9
5. Nanal Grass do	... ...	... ...	... ...	... ...	... ...	... ...
6. Public Bungalow do	... ...	... ...	... ...	... ...	... ...	... ...
7. Endowment do	... ...	... ...	... ...	... ...	... ...	... ...
8. Canal and Ferry do	... ...	... ...	... ...	... ...	... ...	... ...
9. Irrigation Cess do	... ...	... ...	... ...	... ...	... ...	... ...
Total...	6,656 12 5	4,022 8 1	2,634 4 4	7,943 2 10	4,717 0 9	3,226 2 1

No. XVIII.—*Statement showing the Receipts and Expenditure of Special Funds, for a series of 5 years.*—Concluded.

FUNDS.	1878-79.			1879-80.		
	Receipts during the year including balance.	Expenditure during the year.	Balance at the end of the year.	Receipts during the year including balance.	Expenditure during the year.	Balance at the end of the year.
	13	14	15	16	17	18
	RS. A. P.	RS. A. P.	RS. A. P.	RS. A. P.	RS. A. P.	RS. A. P.
1. Jungle Conservancy Fund	640 8 7	222 11 10	417 12 9	602 5 6	269 0 8	333 4 10
2. Cattle Pound do	4,351 11 7	3,915 4 5	436 7 2	2,785 0 8	2,555 15 7	229 1 1
3. Surplus Pound do	.. ..	... ...	... ...	... ...	... ...	... ...
4. Village Service do	1,916 0 3	179 0 0	1,737 0 3	2,101 12 7	168 0 0	1,933 12 7
5. Nanal Grass do	... ...	... ...	... ...	... ...	... ...	... ...
6. Public Bungalow do	... ...	... ...	... ...	... ...	... ...	... ...
7. Endowment do	... ...	... ...	... ...	... ...	... ...	... ...
8. Canal and Ferry do	... ...	... ...	... ...	342 8 8	... ...	342 8 8
9. Irrigation do	... ...	... ...	... ...	... ...	... ...	... ...
Total...	6,908 4 5	4,317 0 3	2,591 4 2	5,831 11 5	2,993 0 3	2,838 11 2

No. XIX.—*Statement showing the progress of Education in the Ganjam District for a series of 10 years.*

Description of Schools.		1870-71.			1871-72.			1872-73.			1873-74.			1874-75.		
		No. of Schools.	No. of pupils.		No. of Schools.	No. of pupils.		No. of Schools.	No. of pupils.		No. of Schools.	No. of pupils.		No. of Schools.	No. of pupils.	
			Boys.	Girls.		Boys.	Girls.		Boys.	Girls.		Boys.	Girls.		Boys.	Girls.
A. Government Schools—	College...	...	...	...	...	...	..	...	...	...	...	...	...	...	..	...
1. Maintained from Imperial or Provincial Funds.	Higher...	1	150	...	1	159	...	1	157	...	1	198	...	1	211	...
	Middle...	5	279	...	5	188	...	5	190	...	5	193	...	5	238	...
	Lower ...	...	...	...	...	...	...	...	...	...	16	777	...	16	812	...
2. Maintained from Local or Municipal Funds.	Higher...	...	...	...	...	...	...	...	...	...	...	...	...	...	...	...
	Middle...	...	...	...	...	...	...	...	...	...	1	58	...	1	108	...
	Lower ...	...	...	...	...	...	...	...	...	...	...	...	...	...	...	...
B. Schools Aided— 1. Salary Grant ...	Higher...	...	...	...	...	...	...	...	...	...	...	...	...	...	...	...
	Middle...	5	244	...	5	214	...	5	198	..	5	220	...	6	226	...
	Lower...	...	..	...	...	...	...	...	...	...	3	54	...	3	61	...
2. By Results Grants ...	Higher...	...	...	...	...	...	...	...	...	...	...	...	...	...	...	...
	Middle...	...	...	...	...	...	...	...	...	..	7	155	...	7	293	3
	Lower ...	...	...	...	...	...	...	...	...	...	167	4,359	39	193	4,918	50
3. Combined, Salary and Results Grant.	Higher...	...	...	...	...	...	...	...	...	...	...	...	...	...	..	...
	Middle...	...	..	...	...	...	...	...	...	...	...	...	...	...	...	...
	Lower...	...	...	...	...	...	...	...	...	...	...	...	...	...	...	..
C. Schools under inspection for Grants, but not examined.	Higher...	...	...	...	...	...	...	...	...	...	...	...	...	...	...	...
	Middle...	...	...	...	...	...	...	..	...	...	73*	*	*	106*	*	*
	Lower ...	...	...	...	...	...	...	...	...	...	...	...	...	...	...	...
D. Schools solely maintained by Zemindars or Proprietors, but under Government Inspection.	Higher...	...	...	...	...	...	...	...	...	...	...	...	...	...	...	...
	Middle...	1	18	...	1	25	...	1	17	...	1	27	...	1	28	...
	Lower ...	...	...	...	...	...	...	...	...	...	...	...	...	1	33	...
Candidates passed the Matriculation	...	1	...	...	1	...	...	1	3	...	1	1	...	1	7	...
Do. do. F. A. Examination	...	...	...	...	...	...	...	...	...	...	...	...	...	...	..	...
Total ..		13	691	...	13	586	...	13	565	...	280	6,042	39	341	6,935	53

* The pupils of these Schools are included in the number of pupils of Aided Lower Class Result Schools.

No. XIX.—*Statement shewing the progress of Education in the Ganjam District for a series of 10 years.*

Description of Schools.		1875-76.			1876-77.			1877-78.			1878-79.			1879-80.		
		No. of Schools.	No. of pupils.		No. of Schools.	No. of pupils.		No. of Schools.	No. of pupils.		No. of Schools.	No. of pupils.		No. of Schools.	No. of pupils.	
			Boys.	Girls.		Boys.	Girls.		Boys.	Girls.		Boys.	Girls.		Boys.	Girls.
A. Government Schools—	College...	...	...	...	...	...	...	...	...	...	1	208	...	1	211	...
1. Maintained from Imperial or Provincial Funds.	Higher...	1	203	...	1	180	...	2	338	...	1	165	...	1	171	...
	Middle...	5	329	...	5	283	...	4	148	...	3	141	...	3	167	...
	Lower....	16	849	...	16	709	...	16	703	...	16	656	...	16	810	...
2. Maintained from Local or Municipal Funds.	Higher...	...	...	...	...	...	...	...	...	...	...	...	...	...	...	...
	Middle...	1	126	...	1	100	...	1	124	...	1	131	...	1	144	...
	Lower ...	3	20	81	3	20	74	3	10	76	3	39	66	3	39	63
B. Schools Aided— 1. Salary Grant ...	Higher...	...	...	...	...	...	...	1	100	...	1	98	...	...	...	...
	Middle...	4	216	...	3	127	9	2	126	...	2	112	...	3	209	...
	Lower....	1	24	...	...	...	...	...	...	...	...	...	...	...	...	...
2. By Results Grants ...	Higher...	...	...	...	...	...	...	...	...	...	...	...	...	...	...	...
	Middle...	...	...	...	...	...	...	...	...	...	...	...	...	...	...	...
	Lower....	251	4,572	32	247	3,848	29	209	3,705	67	172	2,588	77	145	2,413	99
3. Combined, Salary and Results Grant.	Higher...	...	...	...	...	...	...	...	...	...	...	...	...	...	...	...
	Middle...	...	...	...	...	...	...	...	...	...	...	...	...	...	...	...
	Lower....	...	...	...	38	1,129	24	184	4,602	144	191	4,324	135	196	4,733	135
C. Schools under inspection for Grants, but not examined.	Higher...	...	...	...	...	...	...	...	...	...	...	...	...	...	...	...
	Middle...	...	...	...	...	...	...	...	...	...	...	...	...	...	...	...
	Lower....	292	3,950	...	390	5,069	151	178	2,447	60	184	2,309	123	182	2,422	60
D. Schools solely maintained by Zemindars or Proprietors but under Government Inspection.	Higher...	...	...	...	...	...	...	...	...	...	...	...	...	...	...	...
	Middle...	2	67	...	2	56	...	1	38	...	1	32	...	...	...	...
	Lower....	1	44	...	1	46	...	3	98	...	3	78	...	4	108	...
Candidates passed the Matriculation ...		1	8	...	1	13	...	1	8	...	1	1	...	2	7	...
Do. do. F. A. Examination...		...	...	...	...	...	...	...	...	...	...	...	...	1	3	...
Total ...		578	10408	113	708	11,580	287	605	12,447	347	580	10,912	401	558	11,497	357

No. XIX-A.—*Statement showing the number of Successful Candidates in the Uncovenanted Civil Service Examinations for a series of five years, from* 1876-77 *to* 1880-81.

Years.	General Test.	Special Tests.														Remarks.
		I A. Civil Higher Grade.	I B. Civil Lower Grade.	II A. Criminal Higher Grade.	II B. Criminal Lower Grade.	III A. Revenue Higher Grade.	III B. Revenue Lower Grade.	IV. Salt Test.	V. Sea Customs.	VI. Account Test.	VII A. Translation Higher Gde.	VII B. Translation Lower Gde.	VIII A. Precis Higher Grade.	VIII B. Precis Lower Grade.	IX. Pleaders' Test.	
1876-77 ...	11	...	...	8	1	2	7	...	1	...	...	22	7	...	3	
1877-78 ...	25	1	1	8	4	3	3	4	...	1	1	8	10	1	1	
1878-79 ...	58	4	...	2	3	4	3	1	...	...	2	16	13	1	...	
1879-80 ...	39	1	...	3	1	4	1	1	...	...	1	17	11	1	...	
1880-81 ...	121*	...	...	4	4	4	2	3	...	...	2	17	18	...	8	* These passed in the Middle School Examination, of whom 8 were placed in the 1st Class. General Test was abolished.

No. XX.—*Statement showing Receipts and Expenditure of the two Municipalities for a series of 5 years.*

Years.	Municipal Towns.	Receipts.												Expenditure.							Balance.
		Rate on House & Lands.	Trade Tax.	Tolls.	Tax on Carriages and Animals.	Registration of Carts.	Licenses.	Fines.	State Contribution.	Arrears including balance.	Miscellaneous.	Other receipts and advances recovered.	Total.	New Works.	Repairs.	Conservancy.	Police.	Establishment.	Miscellaneous.	Total.	
1875-76	Berhampore	4,704	106	6,900	917	517	514	136	30	2,591	1,636	1,668	19,719	2,047	2,310	4,539	...	2,242	6,064	17,202	2,517
1876-77	Do.	3,847	64	6,650	934	528	30	498	47	2,517	1,200	2,083	18,388	1,929	2,721	4,190	...	2,071	6,806	17,717	671
1877-78	Do.	3,842	17	7,100	1,308	597	60	975	46	671	1,119	1,902	17,637	192	1,791	4,606	...	1,985	6,694	15,268	2,369
1878-79	Do.	4,017	...	6,750	1,186	578	28	927	...	2,369	1,734	4,471	22,060	746	3,053	4,666	...	1,970	11,046	21,421	639
1879-80	Do.	5,776	...	6,950	1,121	546	44	771	...	639	1,306	4,805	21,958	342	2,787	4,066	...	1,975	11,265	20,435	1,523
1875-76	Chicacole.	1,684	...	5,240	451	263	...	8	16	2,371	1,278	2,645	13,957	1,617	1,735	2,585	...	1,200	5,112	12,249	1,708
1876-77	Do.	1,706	...	5,061	477	255	5	32	2	1,708	1,882	1,959	13,087	211	1,553	2,466	...	1,208	4,321	9,759	3,328
1877-78	Do.	1,366	...	3,055	509	278	...	123	...	3,328	1,783	1,953	12,405	237	2,883	2,538	...	1,115	4,657	12,400	5
1878-79	Do.	1,926	...	2,688	403	208	...	65	...	5	1,746	2,928	9,969	457	1,062	2,348	...	1,114	4,889	9,870	99
1879-80	Do.	1,747	1,979	1,960	324	166	...	124	...	99	1,763	2,987	11,149	81	1,014	2,383	...	1,890	5,594	10,962	187

No. XXI.—*List of Civilians in the Ganjam District who were Chief Officers or Collectors, from the time it became a British possession.*

No.	Names and Rank.	Date of assuming charge of the District.	Date of relinquishing charge of the District.	Period of the management. Y.	M.	D.	Remarks.
1	Edward Cotsford, Esq., Resident ...	A. D. 1768	1774	7	0	0	
2	Charles Smith, Esq., Chief ...	„ 1775	1778	4	0	0	
3	Morgan Williams, Esq., Chief ...	„ 1779	1780	2	0	0	
4	John Turing, Esq., Resident ..	„ 1781	1782	2	0	0	
5	John Maxwell Stone, Esq., Chief ...	„ 1783	1785	3	0	0	
6	Hugh Maxwell, Esq., Ag. Chief ...	„ 1786	1786	1	0	0	
7	Morgan Williams, Esq., Chief ...	„ 1787	1788	2	0	0	
8	Henry Crawford, Esq., Resident ..	„ 1789	1790	2	0	0	
9	Thos. Snodgrass, Esq., Resident ...	„ 1791	1792	2	0	0	
10	William Gordon, Esq., Ag. Resident ..	„ 1793	1793	1	0	0	
1	Walter Balfour, Esq., Collector ...	1 Apr. 1794	28 Feb. 1797	2	11	0	
2	Thos. Snodgrass, Esq., Collector ...	1 Mar. 1797	31 Aug. 1880	3	6	0	
3	William Brown, Esq., Collector ...	1 Sept. 1880	8 Aug. 1802	1	11	8	
4	Peter Cherry, Esq., Collector ..	9 Aug. 1802	4 Dec. 1804	2	3	6	
5	Augustus Robson, Esq., Collector ..	5 Dec. 1804	16 Sept. 1806	1	9	11	
6	Robert Alexander, Esq., Collector ..	17 Sept. 1806	28 Dec. 1808	2	3	12	
7	G. F. Travers, Esq., Collector ...	29 Dec. 1808	8 June. 1809	0	5	11	
8	H. Spottiswoode, Esq., Collector ...	9 June 1809	23 July 1817	8	1	14	
9	Peter Reado Cazalet, Esq., Ag. Collector.	24 July 1817	18 Feb. 1819	1	6	25	Asst. Ag. Collr.
		19 Feb. 1819	29 Jan. 1827	7	11	9	Asst. Collector.
10	Robert Bayard, Esq., Collector ...	30 Jan. 1827	11 Jan. 1830	2	11	13	
11	Samuel Smith, Esq., Sub-Collector ...	12 Jan. 1830	2 Feb. 1830	0	0	22	Sub-Collector, in charge.

No. XXI.—*List of Civilians in the Ganjam District who were Chief Officers or Collectors, from the time it became a British possession.*—Contd.

No.	Names and Rank.	Date of assuming charge of the District.	Date of relinquishing charge of the District.	Period of the management. Y.	M.	D.	Remarks.
12	Henry Lacon, Esq., Collector ...	3 Feb. 1830	27 May 1830	0	3	25	
13	James Fraser, Esq., Sub-Collector ...	28 May. 1830	26 Oct. 1830	0	4	29	Sub-Collector, in charge.
14	Robert Eden, Esq., Ag. Collector.	27 Oct. 1831	15 Jan. 1831	0	2	19	Ag. Collector.
		16 Jan. 1831	16 Feb. 1832	1	1	1	Collector.
15	George Maertney Ogilvie, Esq. ...	17 Feb. 1832	16 Mar. 1835	3	1	0	
16	James Arthur Robert Stevenson, Esq. ...	17 Mar. 1835	19 June 1837	2	2	3	
17	Robert Alexander Bannerman, Esq. ...	2 Feb. 1838	25 Nov. 1843	5	10	24	
18	Thomas Andrew Anstruther, Esq., Ag. Collector ...	9 Dec. 1843	Leave to Cape 19 Nov. 1844	0	11	10	
19	Pat. Boileau Smollett, Esq., Ag. Collector...	20 Nov. 1844	24 Nov. 1845	1	0	5	
20	R. A. Bannerman, Collr.	25 Nov. 1845	12 May 1849	3	5	7	
21	Charles John Shubrick.	13 May 1849	26 July 1849	0	2	7	Pl. Asst. Collr., in charge.
22	Arthur Pooley Onslow, Esq., Collector ...	29 July 1849	24 Jan. 1854	4	5	28	
23	William Knox, Esq., Ag. Collector ...	25 Jan. 1854	4 July 1854	0	5	10	
24	Thomas Prendergast, Collector ...	4 July 1854	7 Oct. 1854	0	3	4	
25	William Knox, Acting Collector ...	7 Oct. 1854	1 Apr. 1858	3	5	24	
26	Thomas David Lushington, Collector ...	1 Apr. 1858	29 Apr. 1858	0	0	29	
27	George Thornhill, Esq.	29 Apr. 1858	26 May. 1858	0	0	28	
28	Thos. John Knox, Esq., Acting Collector ...	26 May 1858	19 Aug. 1858	0	2	26	
29	Gordon Sullivan Forbes, Esq., Collr.	19 Aug. 1858	31 Jan. 1860	1	5	0	
30	Robert Davidson, Esq., Acting Collector ...	1 Feb. 1860	10 Apr. 1860	0	2	10	
31	G. S. Forbes, Esq., Collector ...	10 Apr. 1860	20 Oct. 1863	3	6	10	
32	C. T. Longley, Esq., Acting Collector ..	20 Oct. 1863	20 Nov. 1863	0	1	1	

No. XXI.—*List of Civilians in the Ganjam District who were Chief Officers or Collectors, from the time it became a British possession.*—Concld.

No.	Names and Rank.	Date of assuming charge of the District.	Date of relinquishing charge of the District.	Period of the management. Y. M. D.	Remarks.
33	G. S. Forbes, Esq., Collector ...	21 Nov. 1863	16 Mar. 1864	1 3 26	
34	Captain H. L. Grove, Offg. Collector ..	16 Mar. 1864	12 Apr. 1864	0 0 27	
35	G. S. Forbes, Esq., Collector ...	13 Apr. 1864	1 Oct. 1864	0 5 14	
36	E. B. Foord, Esq., Ag. Collector ...	1 Oct. 1864	2 Sep. 1865	0 11 1	
37	G. D. Leman, Esq., S. Asst. Collector ..	2 Sep. 1865	4 Sep. 1865	0 0 3	Pl. Asst. Collr.
38	G. Thornhill, Esq., Ag. Collector ...	4 Sep. 1865	24 Jan. 1866	0 4 20	
39	G. S. Forbes, Esq., Collector ...	24 Jan. 1866	14 May 1867	1 3 21	
40	D. F. Carmichael, Esq...	14 May 1867	7 Apr. 1869	1 10 21	
41	H. G. Ellis, Esq., Ag. Collector ...	7 Apr. 1869	31 Dec. 1870	1 8 24	
42	James Hope, Esq., Pl. Asst. Collector ...	1 Jan. 1871	4 Mar. 1871	0 2 4	
43	F. C. Carr, Esq., Ag. Collector ...	4 Mar. 1871	10 July 1871	0 5 6	
44	C. G. Master, Esq., Ag. Collector ...	10 July 1871	14 Feb. 1874	2 8 4	
45	W. F. Grahame, Esq., Ag. Pl. Asst. Collr.	14 Feb. 1874	2 Mar. 1874	0 0 15	
46	R. Davidson, Esq., Ag. Collector ...	2 Mar. 1874	7 June 1876	2 3 5	
47	C. G. Master, Esq., Collector ...	7 June 1876	5 May 1877	0 10 27	
48	W. F. Grahame, Esq., in charge ...	5 May 1877	20 June 1877	0 1 0	
49	Jeremiah Garnet Horsefall, Esq., Offg. Collr.	20 June 1877	26 Nov. 1877	0 5 5	
50	G. D. Leman, Esq., Collector ...	26 Nov. 1877	15 Apr. 1879	1 4 19	
51	William Alexander Happell, Esq., Pl. Asst Collector, in charge..	10 Apr. 1879	25 Apr. 1879	0 0 10	
52	W. D. Horsley, Esq.	26 Apr. 1879	11 Sep. 1880	1 4 16	
53	A. E. C. Stuart, Esq.	12 Sep. 1880	20 Sep. 1880	0 0 11	
54	G. D. Leman Esq. ...	21 Sep. 1880	21 Sep. 1881	1 1 0	
55	H. St. H. Goodrich, Esq., Ag. ...	21 Sep. 1880	......		

No. XXII.—*Statement showing the names of Imperial and District Post lines the names of Head and Sub-Post Offices the*

Mail Lines.						Post Office, with their Mail
Imperial.			District.			
From	To	Miles.	From	To	Miles.	Offices.
Chicacole.	Rambha ...	130	Heramandalam.	Battili ...	28	*Chicacole Rambha.*
			Do. ...	Nagarikatakam..	4	
Do. ...	Calingapatam	17	Sompet ...	Mandasa ...	14	Chicacole to Narasannapet
* Do. ...	Kimedi Viâ Heramandalam.	43	Ichapur ...	Sonnapur ...	5	Narasannapet to Naupada.
			Chatrapur ...	Ganjam ...	5	Naupada to Kasibugga ...
			Aska ...	Surada ...	22	Kasibugga to Sompet ...
Naupada.	Tekkalli ...	5	Do. ...	Digupudi ...	19	Sompet to Ichapur ...
Kasibugga	Kimedi ...	24				Ichapur to Berhampore...
Do. ...	Pundi ...	7				Berhampore to Chatrapur.
Do. ...	Tarlakota ...	4				Chatrapur to Ganjam ...
Sompet ...	Baruva ...	5				Ganjam to Rambha ...
Gopalpur.	Russellkonda..	59				*Gopalpur Russellkonda.*
Do. ...	Chatrapur ...	9				
Aska ...	Purushottapur.	16				Gopalpur to Berhampore.
						Berhampore to Aska ...
						Aska to Russellkonda ...
						Aska Purushottapur.
						Aska to Boyirani ...
						Boyirani to Purushottapur.
						Chicacole Kimedi.
						Chicacole to Heramandalam
						Heramandalam to Kimedi.
						Parla-Kimedi Pundi.
						Parla-Kimedi to Kasibugga
						Kasibugga to Pundi ...

* Portion of the line is of Imperial and the

with the distance in miles from one Post Office to the other on the lines: also detached letter box stations in the Ganjam District.

distance from each other on the Lines.			Post Offices in the District	Detached Letter Box Stations attached to the Imperial Post Office.		Remarks.
District.	Head Office.	Sub-Office.	Branch Office.	Sheet Iron Letter Box Stations.	Attached to the Imperial Post Office.	
			Old Berhampore.	Sergada	Aska.	
				Mondimorayi	do.	
14	Disbursing and	Calingapatam		Ballibhadra	do.	
20	Sortiug	Heramandalam		Pulasara	Boyirani.	
17	Berhampore.	Battili		Varanasi	Battili.	
21	*Sorting Office.*	Nagarikatakam		Ampuva	Berhampore.	
15	Chicacole.	Parla-Kimedi		Konchoor	do.	
15		Naupada		Golantra	do.	
13		Tekkalli		Padmapuram	do.	
5		Kasibugga		Gujaratipett	Chicacole.	
10		Pundi		Srikurmam	do.	
		Tarlakota		Mulagavalsa	do.	
		Sompet		Akkupalli	Kasibugga.	
		Mandasa		Bramhuatarla	do.	
9		Baruva		Kowti	do.	
25		Ichapur		Tekkalipatnam	do.	
25		Sonnapur		Naupada	Digupudi.	
		Gopalpur		Pattupuram	do.	
		Chatrapur		Humma	Ganjam.	
		Ganjam		Lakshminarusupett.	Heramandalam.	
		Rambha		Kottur	do.	
6		Aska		Chikati	Ichapur.	
10		Russellkonda		Kowti	do.	
		Surada		Patrapur	do.	
		Digupudi		Gurandi	Parla-Kimedi.	
		Boyirani		Haripur	Mandasa.	
28		Purushottapur.		Mottur	do.	
15		Narasannapet.		Pitali	do.	
				Urlam	Narasannapet.	
				Jalmur	do.	
				Atagada	Naupada.	
24				Kotabommali	do.	
7				Pratapur	Purushottapur.	
				Amalapadu	Pundi.	
				Kallikot	Rambha.	
				Bellugunta	Russellkonda.	
				Kullada	do.	
				Surla	Sonnapur.	
				Kotumu	Sompet.	
				Ampuram	do.	
				Jalantra	do.	
				Bodogoda	Surada.	

rest District Post Establishment.

MADRAS POLICE, GANJAM DISTRICT.

No. XXIII.—*Allocation List.*

Division.	Population.	No. of Villages.	No. of Beats.	Stations.	Sanctioend Strength. Inspectors.	Sub-Inspectors.	Head Constables. 1st Grade.	2nd Grade.	3rd Grade.	4th Grade.	Constables.	Total.	Remarks.
				Principal Division.									
A.				Chatrapur Reserve ...	1	...	1	1	1	3	35	42	
				„ Treasury ...	...	...	...	..	...	1	6	7	
				„ Jail ...	...	...	...	...	...	...	3	3	
				Circuit Writer ...	...	...	..	1	...	...	...	1	
				District Magt.'s Orderlies	...	...	...	1	...	...	4	5	
				Rampa Mausabdar's Guard	...	..	...	...	...	...	4	4	
				Press ...	...	...	...	...	1	...	...	1	
				School ...	1	..	...	...	1	1	...	3	
				Head Quarter Office ...	2	...	1	3	1	1	2	10	
				Stores ...	...	...	...	1	1	...	...	2	
				Total...	4	...	2	7	5	6	54	78	
E.	5446	177	6	Iohapur ...	1	1	.	...	...	1	15	18	a. b. 1 Process Server included.
	833	66	4	Golantra ...	...	...	...	...	...	1	4	5	
	88	97	4	Chikati Nuagam ...	...	...	...	...	...	1	4	5	
	3014	52	3	Surangi ...	...	...	...	..	1	...	4	5	
	...	392	17	Total...	1	1	...	...	1	3	27	33	
† E.	4309	57	5	Sompet ...	1	...	...	1	...	...	11	13	a. b. 1 Do.
	6739	28	3	Baruva ...	..	...	...	...	...	1	4	5	
	846	110	4	Harripur ..	...	...	...	...	1	...	4	5	
	206	71	4	Kanchili ...	...	...	..	...	...	...	5	5	
	...	266	16	Total...	1	...	...	1	1	1	24	28	
* F.	21634	......	...	Berhampore Town........	...	...	1	1	1	...	27	31	b. d.
				Total...	...	...	1	1	1	...	27	31	

a. 3 Constables for Subsidiary Jail included.

b. 1 Orderly to Sub-Magistrate included.

d. 1 European Head Constable included.

MADRAS POLICE, GANJAM DISTRICT.—*Contd.*

No. XXIII.—*Allocation List.*

Division.	Population	No. of Villages.	No. of Beats.	Stations.	Sanctioned Strength. Inspectors.	Sub-Inspectors.	Head Constables. 1st Grade.	2nd Grade.	3rd Grade.	4th Grade.	Constables.	Total.	Remarks.
				PRINCIPAL DIVN.,—*Contd.*									
F.		65	6	Berhampore Taluq ...	1	1	...	...	...	1	20	23	*a. b. c.* 3 Process Servers included.
				" Treasury ...	...	..	...	...	..	1	6	7	
				S. A. Magt.s' Orderlies...	...	...	...	...	...	...	2	2	
	2416	33	3	Gopalpur ...	...	...	...	1	...	...	6	7	
	397	40	4	Jagganadapore ...	...	...	...	...	...	1	5	6	
	553	84	4	Roygam ...	...	...	...	...	...	1	4	5	
	1093	30	4	Konchur ...	...	...	...	...	1	...	5	6	
	...	252	21	Total...	1	1	...	1	1	4	48	56	
½ F.	2900	105	6	Purushottapur ...	1	...	1	...	...	...	13	15	*a. b.* 1 do.
	3052	70	5	Boyirani ..	...	...	...	...	...	1	5	6	
	2392	76	5	Pulsara ...	...	...	...	1	...	...	5	6	
	715	84	5	Benganaupada ...	...	...	...	...	...	1	4	5	
	...	335	21	Total...	1	...	1	1	...	2	27	32	
G.	2625	89	6	Russellkonda ...	1	...	1	...	...	...	14	16	*a. b.* 1 do.
				" Treasury ...	...	...	...	...	...	1	6	7	
	439	56	3	Moojagada ...	...	...	..	..	...	1	5	6	
	857	160	5	Baroda ...	...	...	...	1	...	...	7	8	
	330	36	4	Kucholy ...	...	...	...	...	...	1	4	5	
	520	67	4	Juggunadaprasad ...	...	...	...	...	...	1	5	6	
	1689	57	4	Bellugunta ...	..	...	...	1	...	...	5	6	
	...	465	26	Total...	1	...	1	2	...	4	46	54	
½ G.	3116	65	5	Surada ...	1	...	1	...	...	..	15	17	*a. b.* 1 do.
	2015	65	4	Bodagada ..	...	...	...	...	1	...	7	8	
	427	77	4	Gungapur ...	...	...	...	...	1	...	6	7	
	1099	50	4	Bugada ...	...	...	...	...	...	1	4	5	
	997	68	4	Ballipadra ...	...	...	...	...	1	...	5	6	
	...	325	21	Total...	1	...	1	...	3	1	37	43	

a. 3 Constables for Subsidiary Jail included.
b. 1 Orderly to Sub-Magistrate included.
Constables for Court House guard included.

MADRAS POLICE, GANJAM DISTRICT.—*Contd.*

No. XXIII.—*Allocation List.*

Division.	Population.	No. of Villages.	No. of Beats.	Stations.	SANCTIONED STRENGTH.								Remarks.
					Inspectors.	Sub-Inspectors.	Head Constables. 1st Grade.	2nd Grade.	3rd Grade.	4th Grade.	Constables.	Total.	
				PRINCIPAL DIVN.—*Concld.*									
H.	4163	47	5	Ganjam ...	1	...	1	..	...	...	13	15	*a.b.*1 Process Server included.
	2018	58	4	Chatrapur ...	...	...	...	1	...	...	8	9	
	2543	71	4	Rambha ...	...	...	...	1	...	..	6	7	
	37	61	3	Punditigam ...	...	...	...	...	...	1	4	5	
	...	237	16	Total...	1	...	1	2	...	1	31	36	
I.	4255	110	6	Aska ...	1	...	1	...	...	...	15	17	*a. b.* 1 do.
	1816	87	5	Sergada ..	..	...	...	...	1	...	6	7	
	1877	72	5	Poramari ...	...	...	...	1	..	...	7	8	
	589	81	5	Jahada ...	...	...	...	...	1	..	5	6	
	1867	31	4	Injilly ...	...	...	...	1	...	...	5	6	
	1363	127	6	Pudmanabapur ...	...	...	...	1	...	...	6	7	
	...	508	31	Total...	1	...	1	3	2	...	44	51	
				KIMEDI SUB-DIVISION.									
* **B.**	15360	...	...	Chicacole Town ...	...	1	...	...	1	1	25	28	
				Total...	...	1	...	...	1	1	25	28	
B.		116	6	Chicacole Taluq ...	1	...	...	1	...	1	20	23	*a. b.* 3 do.
				Treasury ...	...	...	...	...	...	1	6	7	
				P. A. Magistrate's Orderlies ...	...	...	...	...	...	...	2	2	
	6721	75	5	Narasannapet ...	...	..	...	1	...	...	14	15	*a. b.* 1 do.
	8192	59	5	Julmur ...	...	...	...	...	1	...	5	6	
	480	109	4	Mulagavulsa ...	...	...	..	1	...	...	5	6	
	4675	51	4	Calingapatam ...	...	...	...	1	...	...	5	6	
	...	410	24	Total...	1	...	...	4	1	2	57	65	

a. 3 Constables for Subsidiary Jail included.

b. 1 Orderly to Sub-Magistrate included.

MADRAS POLICE, GANJAM DISTRICT.—*Contd.*

No. XXIII—*Allocation List.*

Division.	Population.	No. of Villages.	No. of Beats.	Stations.	Sanctioned Strength. Inspectors.	Sub-Inspectors.	Head Constables. 1st Grade.	2nd Grade.	3rd Grade.	4th Grade.	Constables.	Total.	Remarks.
				KIMEDI SUB-DIVN.—*contd*									
C.	5206	53	3	Raganádapur ...	1	...	1	...	...	...	17	19	*a.b.*1 Process Server included.
	1992	149	7	Bomally ...	...	...	...	...	1	...	6	7	
	1926	127	6	Pundi ...	...	...	...	...	...	1	3	4	
	700	77	4	Tekkali Patnam ...	..	...	...	...	1	..	5	6	
	1715	69	4	Kasibugga ...	...	...	...	1	...	...	9	10	
	...	475	24	Total...	1	...	1	1	2	1	40	46	
D.	...	...	...	Kimedi Reserve ...	1	...	...	2	2	2	44	51	
D.	4525	136	10	Kimedi ...	1	1	...	...	...	1	28	31	*a. b.* 1 do.
	2287	100	5	Gurandi ...	...	...	...	...	1	...	6	7	
	978	61	4	Tembur ...	...	...	...	...	...	1	5	6	
	1475	62	4	Sarvakota ...	.	...	...	1	...	...	6	7	
	3201	76	5	Heramundalum ...	...	...	...	1	...	...	5	6	
	629	40	4	Nowtalah ..	...	...	...	...	...	1	4	5	
	..	...	...	Asst. Superintendent's Office ...	...	...	1	...	...	1	1	3	
	...	475	32	Total...	2	1	1	4	3	6	99	116	
½ D.	4056	32	5	Varanasy ...	1	...	...	1	...	...	9	11	
	431	41	4	Hadduobangy ...	...	...	...	...	1	...	6	7	
	433	30	4	Guradi ...	...	...	...	..	...	1	8	9	
	708	34	4	Peddadimili ...	...	...	...	...	...	1	6	7	
	...	137	17	Total...	1	...	...	1	1	2	29	34	
K	275	85	4	Kolakota ...	1	...	...	1	...	...	7	9	
	789	126	4	Sarungo ...	...	..	...	...	...	1	6	7	
	241	51	3	Nuwagada ...	...	...	...	...	1	...	6	7	
	929	109	4	Udayagiri ...	...	...	...	...	1	...	16	17	*a. b.*
	1008	118	5	Ramgiri ...	...	...	...	...	...	1	6	7	
	5	57	3	Budvabadi* ...	...	...	...	...	...	1	8	9	
	...	546	23	Total...	1	...	...	1	2	3	49	56	

a. 3 Constables for Subsidiary Jail included.
b. 1 Orderly to Sub-Magistrate included.
* This station will be abolished and the men removed to Udayagiri.

MADRAS POLICE, GANJAM DISTRICT.—*Contd.*

No. XXIII.—*Allocation List.*

Division.	Population.	No. of Villages.	No. of Beats.	Stations.	Sanctioned Strength. Inspectors.	Sub-Inspectors.	Head Constables. 1st Grade.	2nd Grade.	3rd Grade.	4th Grade.	Constables.	Total.	Remarks.
				Balliguda Sub-Division.									
M	......	......	...	Balliguda Reserve ...	1	1	...	1	2	5	91	101	*a.*
	......	......	...	Stores ...	...	...	...	...	1	...	...	1	
	......	......	...	School ...	...	...	...	1	...	1	...	2	
	......	......	...	Special Assistant Agent's Orderlies ...	...	...	...	...	...	...	2	2	
	......	......	...	Do. Office Guard...	...	...	...	...	...	...	2	2	
	......	......	...	Assistant Supt.'s Office...	...	...	1	...	...	1	1	3	
	......	......	...	Total...	1	1	1	2	3	7	96	111	
1st M	......	150	4	Tumiribund ...	1	...	1	...	1	...	20	23	
	......	40	2	Lunkaghur ...	...	...	...	1	...	1	19	21	
	......	82	4	Belghur ...	...	...	1	...	1	1	27	30	
	......	277	4	Balliguda ...	...	...	...	...	1	...	5	6	
	......	549	14	Total...	1	...	2	1	3	2	71	80	
2d M	......	131	5	Daringabadi ...	1	...	...	1	..	1	13	16	
	......	117	4	Shubernagiri Nuagam ...	...	...	..	1	...	1	13	15	
	......	75	4	Budaguda ...	...	...	...	...	1	1	12	14	
	......	323	13	Total...	1	...	...	2	1	3	38	45	
3d M	......	225	5	Baminigam ...	1	...	1	..	1	...	20	23	
	......	152	4	Mohana ...	...	...	...	1	...	1	12	14	
	......	91	4	Nalaghat ..	...	...	...	1	1	...	13	15	
	......	60	4	Lohagudi ...	...	...	...	...	1	1	10	12	
	......	528	17	Total...	1	...	1	2	3	2	55	64	
N	......	117	5	Udiaghiri ...	1	...	...	1	1	...	13	16	*a. b.*
	......	204	5	Possara ...	...	...	...	...	1	1	13	15	
	......	216	5	Raikia ...	...	...	...	1	...	1	28	30	
	......	171	4	Koosadundi ...	...	...	...	...	1	1	13	15	
	......	708	19	Total...	1	...	...	2	3	3	67	76	

a. 3 Constables for Subsidiary Jail included.
b. 1 Orderly to Sub-Magistrate included.

ABSTRACT.

Divisions.	Stations.	Sanctioned Strength. Inspectors.	Sub-Inspectors.	Head Constables. 1st Grade.	2nd Grade.	3rd Grade.	4th Grade.	Total.	Constables. 1st Class.	2nd Class.	Total.	Grand Total.	Remarks.
	Principal Division.												
A.	Chatrapur Head Qrs. ...	4	...	2	7	5	6	20	17	37	54	78	
E.	Ichapur ...	1	1	...	...	1	3	4	9	18	27	33	
½E.	Sompet ...	1	..	...	1	1	1	3	8	16	24	28	
*F.	Berhampore Town ...	...	...	1	1	1	...	3	9	18	27	31	
F.	Berhampore Taluq ...	1	1	...	1	1	4	6	16	32	48	56	
½F.	Purushottapur ..	1	...	1	1	...	2	4	9	18	27	32	
G.	Russellconda ...	1	...	1	2	...	4	7	15	31	46	54	
½G.	Surada ...	1	...	1	..	3	1	5	12	25	37	43	
H.	Ganjam ...	1	...	1	2	...	1	4	10	21	31	36	
I.	Aska ...	1	..	1	3	2	...	6	15	29	44	51	
	Total ..	12	2	8	18	14	22	62	120	245	365	442	
	Kimedi Sub-Divn.												
*B.	Chicacole Town ...	...	1	...	..	1	1	2	8	17	25	28	
B.	Chicacole Taluq ...	1	...	...	4	1	2	7	20	37	57	65	
C.	Raganádapur ..	1	...	1	1	2	1	5	13	27	40	46	
D.	Kimedi Reserve ...	1	...	...	2	2	2	6	16	28	44	51	
D.	Kimedi Taluq ...	1	1	1	2	1	4	8	18	37	55	65	
½D.	Varanasi ...	1	...	...	1	1	2	4	10	19	29	34	
K.	Kolakota .	1	...	...	1	2	3	6	16	33	49	56	
	Total...	6	2	2	11	10	15	38	101	198	299	345	
	Balliguda Sub-Division.												
M.	Balliguda Head Qrs. ...	1	1	1	2	3	7	13	32	64	96	111	
1 M.	Tumirbund ...	1	...	2	1	3	2	8	24	47	71	80	
2 M.	Budaguda ...	1	...	...	2	1	3	6	12	26	38	45	
3 M.	Baminigam ...	1	...	1	2	3	2	8	18	37	55	64	
N.	Udiaghiri ...	1	...	...	2	3	3	8	22	45	67	76	
	Total...	5	1	4	9	13	17	43	108	219	327	376	
	Police Force General ... Including 16 Process servers.	23	5	14	38	37	54	143	329	662	991	1,163	

* 1 European Head Constable included.

SALT GUARDS.

Factories.	Sub-Inspectors.	Permanent.								Grand Total.	Temporary.								Grand Total.	Remarks.
		Head Constables.					Constables.				Head Constables.					Constables.				
		1st Grade.	2nd Grade.	3rd Grade.	4th Grade.	Total.	1st Class.	2nd Class.	Total.		1st Grade.	2nd Grade.	3rd Grade.	4th Grade.	Total.	1st Class.	2nd Class.	Total.		
Ganjam ...	1	1	...	2	2	5	8	16	24	30	1	1	2	3	7	17	35	52	59	
Ichapur ...	1	...	1	1	1	3	8	16	24	28	...	1	1	2	4	8	16	24	28	
Naupada ...	1	1	...	1	2	4	10	20	30	35	1	1	2	3	7	21	41	62	69	
Umaravilli ...	1	...	1	1	1	3	8	16	24	28	...	1	1	3	5	10	19	29	34	
Total...	4	2	2	5	6	15	34	68	102	121	2	4	6	11	23	56	111	167	190	

For fish-curing at Naupada 1 4th Grade Head Constable and 4 2nd Class Constables are sanctioned.

PRIVATE GUARDS.

	4th Grade Head Constables.	1st Class Constables.	2nd Class Constables.	Total.
Berhampore Bank Guard ...	...	1	2	3
Aska Factory Guard ...	1	3	6	10
Kimedi Palace Guard ...	1	1	2	4
Kimedi Treasury Guard ...	1	2	3	6
Total...	3	7	13	23

The Jail guards should be calculated at the rate of 1 to 7 prisoners for Berhampore District Jail and 1 to 5 for Russelconda Hill as follows :—

A party of Police consists of 15 men of all ranks, viz., 2 Heads and 13 Constables.

In two parties or 30 men of all ranks.

1st Party.	*2nd Party.*
1 Head, 2nd Grade	1 Head, 1st Grade.
1 Head, 4th Grade	1 Head, 3rd Grade.
4 Constables, 1st Class	4 Constables, 1st Class.
9 Constables, 2nd Class	9 Constables, 2nd Class.

With 33 men or 2½ Parties for Jail the allowance of Heads & Constables is—

1 Head, 1st Grade; 1 Head, 2nd Grade; 1 Head, 3rd Grade; 2 Heads, 4th Grade; 11 Constables, 1st Class; and 22 Constables, 2nd Class.

No. XXIV.—*Statement showing the results of the measures adopted in the District of Ganjam, with the view of exterminating wild animals and venemous snakes, for a series of 5 years.*

1	2									3									4																	
	No. of persons killed by									No. of cattle killed by									No. of animals and snakes destroyed and amount of rewards paid for their destruction.																	
Years.	Elephants.	Tigers.	Leopards and Panthers.	Bears.	Wolves.	Hyænas.	Other animals.	Snakes.	Total No. of persons killed.	Elephants.	Tigers.	Leopards and Panthers.	Bears.	Wolves.	Hyænas.	Other animals.	Snakes.	Total No. of cattle killed.	Elephants.	Amount of reward.	Tigers.	Amount of reward.	Leopards and Panthers.	Amount of reward.	Bears.	Amount of reward.	Wolves.	Amount of reward.	Hyænas.	Amount of reward.	Other animals.	Amount of reward.	Snakes.	Amount of reward.	Total number destroyed.	Total amount of rewards paid.
																						Rs.		Rs. a.		Rs. a.				Rs. a.						Rs. a.
1876	...	10	17	6	...	...	...	27	60	..	140	166	...	...	11	...	...	317	...	..	21	881	169	2,746-0	54	237-0	...	...	29	78-0	3	1	...	...	276	3,943-0
1877	...	14	5	4	...	...	3	56	82	...	163	121	1	...	6	1	...	292	...	...	25	843	182	2,925-8	57	277-8	...	...	27	66-8	...	...	...	...	291	4,112-8
1878	1	21	...	5	...	...	16	19	61	...	51	155	6	...	6	...	...	218	...	...	16	419	128	1,611-8	57	274-8	...	...	39	74-0	...	...	...	..	240	2,379-0
1879	1	14	36	3	...	...	1	14	69	...	34	145	10	...	14	2	...	205	...	...	22	636	173	2,333-0	61	358-0	1	4	41	116-8	...	...	...	..	298	3,447-8
1880	...	18	22	2	...	..	...	19	61	...	43	112	5	...	9	2	...	171	..	...	13	485	155	2,311-0	69	414-0	5	25	43	161-0	...	...	...	...	285	3,396-0

No. XXV.—*List showing the Distribution and Locality of Government Offices and Institutions in the Ganjam District.*

Taluk or Zemindari Division, (to be written lengthways.)	Name of Town or Village.	Head Quarters of Collector.	Do. of Principal Assistant Collector.	Do. of Senior Assistant Collector.	Do. of Deputy Collector.	Do. of Tahsildars.	Do. of Dy. Tahsildars and Sub-Magts.	Post Office.	Police Station.	Central Jail	District Jail.	Sub-Jail.	Sub-Registrar.	District Court.	Sub-Court.	Munsif.	Public Bungalow or Rest House.	Municipality.	Dispensary.	School.	Chaplain.	Telegraph Station.	Railway Station.	Salt Factory.	Sea Port.	Light-House.	Head Qrs. of Police Officers (Gazetted).	Do. of D. P. W. ditto.	Do. of Telegraph ditto.	Do. of Forest ditto.	Do. of Inspecting Post Masters.	Do. of Inspector of Schools.	Do. of Assistant Collector.	Do. of Special Assistant Collector.	
1	2	3	4	5	6	7	8	9	10	11	12	13	14	15	16	17	18	19	20	21	22	23	24	25	26	27	28	29	30	31	32	33	34	35	36
Berhampur Taluk.	Ganjam						1	1	1			1	1				1		1	1				1	1										
	Chatrapur	1			1			1	1			1							1	1							1						1		
	Purushottapur						1	1	1			1	1							1															
	Injilly							1	1								1			1															
	Jaganádapur								1																										
	Gopalpur							1	1								1		1	1					1										
	Sonnapur							1	1								1								1										
	Konchur							1	1																										
	Berhampore			1		1	1	1	1		1	1	1	1				1	1	1	1	1						1							
	Golantra							1	1																										
	Ichapur						1	1	1			1	1				1			1															
	Roigam							1	1																										

Chicacole Taluk.	Chicacole	...	1	...	...	1	...	1	1	...	...	1	1	...	...	1	...	1	1	1	...	1	...	...	...	...	...	...	...	...	...	...	...	...	
	Narsannapet	...	...	...	...	...	1	1	1	...	...	1	...	...	...	...	...	1	...	1	...	...	...	...	...	...	...	...	...	...	...	...	...	...	
	Jalmur	...	...	...	...	...	...	1	1	...	...	...	...	...	...	...	...	...	...	...	...	...	...	...	...	...	...	...	...	...	...	...	...	...	
	Calingapatam	...	...	...	...	...	...	1	1	...	...	...	...	...	...	...	...	...	1	1	...	...	...	...	1	1	...	...	...	...	...	...	...	...	
	Bomalli	...	...	...	...	...	...	...	1	...	...	...	...	...	...	...	...	...	...	1	...	...	...	...	...	...	...	...	...	...	...	...	...	...	
	Nagaricuttacam	...	...	...	...	...	...	1	1	...	...	...	...	...	...	...	...	...	...	1	...	...	...	...	...	...	...	...	...	...	...	...	...	...	
Goomsur Taluk.	Gangupuram	...	...	...	...	...	...	...	1	...	...	...	...	...	...	...	...	...	...	1	...	...	...	...	...	...	...	...	...	...	...	...	...	...	
	Russellconda	...	...	...	...	...	1	1	1	...	1	1	1	...	...	...	1	...	1	1	...	...	...	...	...	...	1	...	...	...	...	...	...	...	
	Mojagada	...	...	...	...	...	...	...	1	...	...	...	...	...	...	...	...	...	...	1	...	...	...	...	...	...	...	...	...	...	...	...	...	...	
	Kurcholy	...	...	...	...	...	...	...	1	...	...	...	...	...	...	...	...	...	...	...	...	...	...	...	...	...	...	...	...	...	...	...	...	...	
	Juggernatprasad	...	...	...	...	...	...	...	1	...	...	...	...	...	...	...	...	...	...	1	...	...	...	...	...	...	...	...	...	...	...	...	...	...	
	Bellagunta	...	...	...	...	...	...	1	1	...	...	...	...	...	...	...	...	...	...	1	...	...	...	...	...	...	...	...	...	...	...	...	...	...	
	Suradah	...	...	...	...	...	1	1	1	...	...	1	...	...	...	...	...	...	...	1	...	...	...	...	...	...	...	...	...	...	...	...	...	...	
	Buguda	...	...	...	...	...	...	...	1	...	...	...	...	...	...	...	...	...	...	1	...	...	...	...	...	...	...	...	...	...	...	...	...	...	
	Ballipudra	...	...	...	...	...	...	1	1	...	...	...	...	...	...	...	...	...	...	...	...	...	...	...	...	...	...	...	...	...	...	...	...	...	
Beridi Zemindary	Rambha	...	...	...	...	...	...	1	1	...	...	...	...	...	...	...	...	...	...	1	...	...	...	...	...	...	...	...	...	...	...	...	...	...	
Kallikot & Atagada Zemindary	Panditogam	...	...	...	...	...	...	...	1	...	...	...	...	...	...	...	...	...	...	...	...	...	...	...	...	...	...	...	...	...	...	...	...	...	
	Bengunaupada	...	...	...	...	...	...	...	1	...	...	...	...	...	...	...	...	...	...	...	...	...	...	...	...	...	...	...	...	...	...	...	...	...	
	Boiranee	...	...	...	...	...	...	1	1	...	...	...	...	...	...	...	...	...	...	...	...	...	...	...	...	...	...	...	...	...	...	...	...	...	
	Pulasara	...	...	...	...	...	...	1	...	...	...	...	...	...	...	...	...	...	...	1	...	...	...	...	...	...	...	...	...	...	...	...	...	...	
PeddaKimedi Zemindary	Digupudy	...	...	...	...	...	...	1	1	...	...	...	...	...	...	...	...	...	...	1	...	...	...	...	...	...	...	...	...	...	...	...	...	...	
	Padmapuram	...	...	...	...	...	...	1	1	...	...	...	...	...	...	...	...	...	...	1	...	...	...	...	...	...	...	...	...	...	...	...	...	...	
Bodogoda Zemindary	Bodogoda	...	...	...	...	...	...	1	1	...	...	...	...	...	...	...	...	...	...	1	...	...	...	...	...	...	...	...	...	...	...	...	...	...	
Sergada Zemindary	Sergada	...	...	...	...	...	...	1	1	...	...	...	...	...	...	...	...	...	...	1	...	...	...	...	...	...	...	...	...	...	...	...	...	...	
Chinna-Kimedi Zemindary	Poramari (Pudamari)	...	...	...	...	...	...	...	1	...	...	...	...	...	...	...	...	...	...	1	...	...	...	...	...	...	...	...	...	...	...	...	...	...	
Dharakot Zemindary	Jahada	...	...	...	...	...	...	...	1	...	...	...	...	...	...	...	...	...	...	1	...	...	...	...	...	...	...	...	...	...	...	...	...	...	
Chekah Zemindary.	Chekatinowgam	...	...	...	...	...	...	1	1	...	...	...	...	...	...	...	...	...	...	1	...	...	...	...	...	...	...	...	...	...	...	...	...	...	

No. XXV.—*List showing the Distribution and Locality of Government Offices and Institutions in the Ganjam District*—continued.

Taluk or Zemindary Division.	Name of Town or Village.	Head Quarters of Collector.	Do. of Principal Assistant Collector.	Do. of Senior Assistant Collector.	Do. of Deputy Collector.	Do. of Tahsildars.	Do. of Dy. Tahsildars and Sub-Magts.	Post Office.	Police Station.	Central Jail.	District Jail.	Sub-Jail.	Sub-Registrar.	District Court.	Sub-Court.	Munsif.	Public Bungalow or Rest House.	Municipality.	Dispensary.	School.	Chaplain.	Telegraph Station.	Railway Station.	Salt Factory.	Sea Port.	Light-House.	Head Qrs. of Police Officers (Gazetted).	Do. of D. P. W. ditto.	Do. of Telegraph ditto.	Do. of Forest ditto.	Do. of Inspecting Post Master.	Do. of Inspector of Schools.	Do. of Assistant Collector.	Do. of Special Assistant Collector.	
1	2	3	4	5	6	7	8	9	10	11	12	13	14	15	16	17	18	19	20	21	22	23	24	25	26	27	28	29	30	31	32	33	34	35	36
Surangi Zemindary.	Surangi ...	...	...	...	...	...	...	...	1	...	...	...	...	...	...	...	...	...	...	1	...	...	...	...	...	...	...	...	...	...	...	...	...	...	
Jalantra Zemindary.	Kanchili ...	...	...	...	...	...	...	...	1	...	...	...	...	...	...	...	1	...	...	1	...	...	...	...	...	...	...	...	...	...	...	...	...	...	
Chekati and Jalantra Zemindaries	Sompet ...	...	...	...	...	...	1	1	1	...	...	...	...	...	...	...	...	...	1	1	...	...	...	...	...	...	...	...	...	...	...	...	...	...	
Mandasa Zemindary.	Haripur ...	...	...	...	...	...	...	1	1	...	...	...	...	...	...	...	1	...	...	1	...	...	...	...	...	...	...	...	...	...	...	...	...	...	
	Mandasa ...	...	...	...	...	...	...	1	1	...	...	...	...	...	...	...	...	...	...	1	...	...	...	...	...	...	...	...	...	...	...	...	...	...	
Tarla Zemindary.	Kasibugga ...	...	...	...	...	...	...	1	1	...	...	...	...	...	...	...	1	...	...	...	...	...	...	...	...	...	...	...	...	...	...	...	...	...	
	Tarla ...	...	...	...	...	...	...	1	1	...	...	...	...	...	...	...	...	...	...	...	...	...	...	...	...	...	...	...	...	...	...	...	...	...	

Parla-Kimedi Zemindary.	Parla-Kimedi	...	...	...	...	...	...	1	1	1	...	...	1	1	...	...	1	...	...	1	1	...	...	...	...	...	...	1	...	...	...	...	...	...	...
	Temboor	...	...	...	...	...	...	...	...	1	...	...	...	...	...	...	...	...	...	...	...	...	...	...	...	...	...	...	...	...	...	...	...	...	...
	Kottur	...	...	...	...	...	...	...	...	1	...	...	...	...	...	...	...	...	...	...	...	...	...	...	...	...	...	...	...	...	...	...	...	...	...
	Nowtala	...	...	...	...	...	...	...	...	1	...	...	...	...	...	...	...	...	...	...	1	...	...	...	...	...	...	...	...	...	...	...	...	...	...
	Varanasy	...	...	...	...	...	...	...	1	1	...	...	...	...	...	...	...	...	...	...	1	...	...	...	...	...	...	...	...	...	...	...	...	...	...
	Haddubangy	...	...	...	...	...	...	...	...	1	...	...	...	...	...	...	...	...	...	...	...	...	...	...	...	...	...	...	...	...	...	...	...	...	...
	Guradi	...	...	...	...	...	...	...	...	1	...	...	...	...	...	...	...	...	...	...	1	...	...	...	...	...	...	...	...	...	...	...	...	...	...
	Peddadimeli	...	...	...	...	...	...	...	...	1	...	...	...	...	...	...	...	...	...	...	...	...	...	...	...	...	...	...	...	...	...	...	...	...	...
	Battili	...	...	...	...	...	...	...	1	1	...	...	...	...	...	...	...	...	...	...	...	...	...	...	...	...	...	...	...	...	...	...	...	...	...
Vizianagrum Zemindary.	Hiramandalam	...	...	...	...	...	...	...	1	1	...	...	...	...	...	...	...	...	...	...	1	1	...	...	...	...	...	...	...	...	...	...	...	...	...
Proprietory...	Aska	...	...	...	...	...	...	1	1	1	...	...	1	1	...	...	1	...	...	1	1	...	...	...	...	...	...	...	...	...	...	...	...	...	...
	Baruva	...	...	...	...	...	...	1	1	1	...	...	...	...	...	...	...	1	...	...	...	...	...	1	...	...	...	...	...	...	...	...	...	...	...
	Mulagavalsa	...	...	...	...	...	...	...	1	1	...	...	...	...	...	...	...	...	...	...	...	...	...	...	...	...	...	...	...	...	...	...	...	...	...
	Raghunadhapuram	...	...	...	...	...	...	...	...	1	...	...	...	...	...	...	...	...	...	...	...	...	...	...	...	...	...	...	...	...	...	...	...	...	...
	Pundi	...	...	...	...	...	...	...	1	1	...	...	...	...	...	...	...	...	...	...	...	...	...	...	...	1	...	...	...	...	...	...	...	...	...
	Tekkalipatnam	...	...	...	...	...	...	1	1	1	...	...	1	...	...	...	1	1	...	...	1	...	...	...	...	...	...	...	...	...	...	...	...	...	...
	Naupada	...	...	...	...	...	...	...	1	1	...	...	...	...	...	...	...	...	...	...	1	...	...	...	1	...	...	...	...	...	...	...	...	...	...
	Pata Tekkali	...	...	...	...	...	...	...	...	1	...	...	...	...	...	...	...	1	...	...	...	...	...	...	...	...	...	...	...	...	...	...	...	...	...
	Gopalapuram	...	...	...	...	...	...	...	...	1	...	...	...	...	...	...	...	1	...	...	...	...	...	...	...	...	...	...	...	...	...	...	...	...	...
	Bavanapad	...	...	...	...	...	...	...	...	1	...	...	...	...	...	...	...	...	...	...	...	...	...	...	...	1	...	...	...	...	...	...	...	...	...
Goomsur Máliahs.—*Ctd.*	Linepada	...	...	...	...	...	...	...	...	...	...	...	...	...	...	...	...	...	...	...	1	...	...	...	...	...	...	...	...	...	...	...	...	...	...
	Udayagiri	...	...	...	...	...	...	1	...	1	...	...	1	...	...	...	...	...	...	...	1	...	...	...	...	...	...	...	...	...	...	...	...	...	...
	Possara	...	...	...	...	...	...	...	...	1	...	...	...	...	...	...	...	...	...	...	1	...	...	...	...	...	...	...	...	...	...	...	...	...	...
	Raikia	...	...	...	...	...	...	...	...	1	...	...	...	...	...	...	...	...	...	...	1	...	...	...	...	...	...	...	...	...	...	...	...	...	...
	Kusadandi	...	...	...	...	...	...	...	...	1	...	...	...	...	...	...	...	...	...	...	...	...	...	...	...	...	...	...	...	...	...	...	...	...	...
	Teangia	...	...	...	...	...	...	...	...	1	...	...	...	...	...	...	...	...	...	...	...	...	...	...	...	...	...	...	...	...	...	...	...	...	...
Pedda-Kimedi Máliahs.	Udayagiri	...	...	...	...	...	...	1	...	1	...	...	1	...	...	...	...	...	...	...	1	...	...	...	...	...	...	...	...	...	...	...	...	...	...
	Nuagada	...	...	...	...	...	...	...	...	1	...	...	...	...	...	...	...	...	...	...	1	...	...	...	...	...	...	...	...	...	...	...	...	...	...
Chinna-Kimedi Máliahs	Balliguda	...	...	...	...	...	...	1	...	1	...	...	1	...	...	...	...	...	...	...	1	...	...	...	...	...	...	...	...	...	...	...	...	...	...
	Tummiriband	...	...	...	...	...	...	...	...	1	...	...	...	...	...	...	...	...	...	...	1	...	...	...	...	...	...	...	...	...	...	...	...	...	...
	Lankaghar	...	...	...	...	...	...	...	...	1	...	...	...	...	...	...	...	...	...	...	...	...	...	...	...	...	...	...	...	...	...	...	...	...	...
	Belghar	...	...	...	...	...	...	...	...	1	...	...	...	...	...	...	...	...	...	...	...	...	...	...	...	...	...	...	...	...	...	...	...	...	...
	Naagam	...	...	...	...	...	...	...	...	1	...	...	...	...	...	...	...	...	...	...	...	...	...	...	...	...	...	...	...	...	...	...	...	...	...

No. XXV.—*List showing the Distribution and Locality of Government Offices and Institutions in the Ganjam District.*—Concluded.

Taluk or Zemindari Division, (to be written lengthways.)	Name of Town or Village.	Head Quarters of Collector.	Do. of Principal Assistant Collector.	Do. of Senior Assistant Collector.	Do. of Deputy Collector	Do. of Tahsildars.	Do. of Dy. Tahsildars and Sub-Magts.	Post Office.	Police Station.	Central Jail.	District Jail.	Sub-Jail.	Sub-Registrar.	District Court.	Sub-Court.	Munsif.	Public Bungalow or Rest House.	Municipality.	Dispensary.	School.	Chaplain.	Telegraph Station.	Railway Station.	Salt Factory.	Sea Port.	Light-House.	Head Qrs. of Police Officers (Gazetted).	Do. of D. P. W. ditto.	Do. of Telegraph ditto.	Do. of Forest ditto.	Do. of Inspecting Post Masters.	Do. of Inspector of Schools.	Do. of Assistant Collector.	Do of Special Assistant Collector.	
1	2	3	4	5	6	7	8	9	10	11	12	13	14	15	16	17	18	19	20	21	22	23	24	25	26	27	28	29	30	31	32	33	34	35	36
Chinna-Kimedi Máliahs.	Serangada ...	...	...	...	...	...	...	...	1	...	...	...	...	...	...	...	...	...	...	1	...	...	...	...	...	...	...	...	...	...	...	...	...	...	
	Daringabadi	...	...	...	...	...	...	...	1	...	...	...	...	...	...	...	...	...	...	1	...	...	...	...	...	...	...	...	...	...	...	...	...	...	
	Budaguda ...	...	...	...	...	...	...	...	1	...	...	...	...	...	...	...	...	...	...	...	...	...	...	...	...	...	...	...	...	...	...	...	...	...	
	Baminigam...	...	...	...	...	...	...	...	1	...	...	...	...	...	...	...	...	...	...	...	...	...	...	...	...	...	...	...	...	...	...	...	...	...	
	Nolagat ...	...	...	...	...	...	...	...	1	...	...	...	...	...	...	...	...	...	...	...	...	...	...	...	...	...	...	...	...	...	...	...	...	...	
	Mahasingi ...	...	...	...	...	...	...	...	...	...	...	...	...	...	...	...	...	...	...	1	...	...	...	...	...	...	...	...	...	...	...	...	...	...	
Parla-Kimedi Máliahs.	Gumma ...	...	...	...	...	...	...	...	...	...	...	...	...	...	...	...	...	...	...	1	...	...	...	...	...	...	...	...	...	...	...	...	...	...	
	Kolakota ...	...	...	...	...	...	...	...	1	...	...	...	...	...	...	...	...	...	...	...	...	...	...	...	...	...	...	...	...	...	...	...	...	...	
	Serango ...	...	...	...	...	...	...	...	1	...	...	...	...	...	...	...	...	...	...	...	...	...	...	...	...	...	...	...	...	...	...	...	...	...	
Bodogoda Máliahs.	Mohana ...	...	...	...	...	...	...	...	1	...	...	...	...	...	...	...	...	...	...	1	...	...	...	...	...	...	...	...	...	...	...	...	...	...	
	Lohagudi ..	...	...	...	...	...	...	...	1	...	...	...	...	...	...	...	...	...	...	...	...	...	...	...	...	...	...	...	...	...	...	...	...	...	

No. XXVI.—*Statement showing the Revenue and Magisterial charges of the Divisional Officers in the District of Ganjam.*

Designation of office and Head Quarters.	Names of Divisional Officers.	Revenue.		Magisterial.		Remarks.
		Taluqs and portions of Taluqs comprised in each Division.	Population.	Taluqs and portions of Taluqs comprised in each Division.	Population.	
Collector and District Magistrate, Chatrapur.	Goomsur Tahsildar.	Whole of the Goomsur Taluq.	1,57,960	Goomsur Taluq, exclusive of the following Mutahs :— 1. Nuagoda, 2. Gondibada, 3. Malo, 4. Rogada, 5. Salingia, 6 Pochangi, 7. Priya, 8. Bondagocha, 9. Kudika, 10. Bhutapilli, 11. Payalapada, 12. Vishnuchakram, 13. Ballipadra.	92,409	
	Surada Deputy Tahsildar and Sub Magistrate.	The 13 Mutahs of Goomsur of which he has Magtl. charge.	...	The above enumerated Mutahs of Goomsur. The following Estates are under Surada :—1. Bodogoda, 2. Korada, 3. Ronaba, and 4. Pandakhallo Mutah.	...	
	Purushottapur Deputy Tahsildar and Sub Magistrate.	The 3 Mutahs of Berhampore of which he has Magtl. charge.	...	Narasingapuram, Sikkiri and Konchura Mutahs of the Berhampore Taluq.	56,840	
				The Kollada Mutah of the Atagada Estate.	...	
	Ganjam Deputy Tahsildar and Sub Magistrate.	The 2 Mutahs of Berhampore of which he has Magtl. charge.	...	Sitarampuram and Manusurkota Mutah of the Berhampore Taluq,	38,987	
				And the Estates of		
				Palur	4,173	
				Humma	2,754	
				Biridi	10,960	
				Kallikot	42,589	

No. XXVI.—*Statement showing the Revenue and Magisterial charges of the Divisional Officers in the District of Ganjam.*—Continued.

Designation of office and Head Quarters.	Names of Divisional Officers.	Revenue.		Magisterial.		Remarks.
		Taluqs and portions of Taluqs comprised in each Division.	Population.	Taluqs and portions of Taluqs comprised in each Division.	Population.	
Senior Assistant Collector and Magistrate, Berhampore.	Berhampore Tahsildar.	Whole of the Berhampore Taluq.	2,43,685	The Berhampore Taluq. The Dura, Golantra and Kukkudakhandi Mutahs and the	66,098	
				Pedda-Kimedi Zemindari except Naupada Mutah.	34,560	
	Aska Deputy Tahsildar and Sub Magistrate.	Bavanipuram Mutah of the Goomsur Taluq.	...	Bhavanapuram Mutah of the Goomsur Taluq,	4,664	
				And the Estates of Dharakot ...	31,262	
				Sergada	9,595	
				Chinna-Kimedi ...	28,849	
				Aska	7,712	
				Devabhumi ...	3,539	
				Kurla	5,457	
	Berhampore Town Sub Magistrate.	None ...	...	The town of Berhampore	21,417	
	Ichapur Deputy Tahsildar and Sub Magistrate.	The Mutahs of Berhampore of which he has Magtl. charge.	...	Ichapur, Kairti and Mantreddi Mutahs of the Berhampore Taluq,	59,454	
				And the Zemindari of Chikati except Talatampara Mutah.	33,717	
				Sursangi	12,919	
				Jarada	5,813	
				Naupada Mutah of the Pedda-Kimedi Zemindari	6,350	

No. XXVI.—*Statement showing the Revenue and Magisterial charges of the Divisional Officers in the District of Ganjam.*—Continued.

Designation of office and Head Quarters.	Names of Divisional Officers.	REVENUE.		MAGISTERIAL.		Remarks.
		Taluqs and portions of Taluqs comprised in each Division.	Population.	Taluqs and portions of Taluqs comprised in each Division.	Population.	
Senior Assistant Collector and Magistrate, Berhampore.	Sompet Deputy Tahsildar and Sub Magistrate.	None ...	...	Talatampara Mutah of the Chikati Zemindari.	7,702	
				Jalantra	18,450	
				Baruva	8,454	
				Mandasa	34,508	
				Budarasinga	3,244	
	Ramagiri (Máliah Portion.) Sub Magistrate and District Munsiff.	None ...	...	Pedda-Kimedi, Surangi, Budarasingi, Jarada and Mándasa Maliahs.	26,937	
Principal Assistant Collector and Magistrate, Chicacole	Chicacole Tahsildar and Sub Magistrate.	Whole of the Chicacole Taluq.	2,00,655	Chicacole Taluq exclusive of the following Divisions :—	91,298	
				Uttara Khandam, 3 Mokhasa villages of the Southern Division, one Agraharam of the Western Division, Polaki and Palatalagam Divisions.		
	Tekkali Sub Magistrate.	None ...	...	Tekkali Estates	58,054	
				Tarla	24,639	
				Chakipalli	1,018	
				Konusulakothur	574	
				Tarlipeta	388	
				Chinnatungam	395	

No. XXVI.—*Statement showing the Revenue and Magisterial charges of the Divisional Officers in the District of Ganjam.*—Continued.

Designation of office and Head Quarters.	Names of Divisional Officers.	Revenue.		Magisterial.		Remarks.
		Taluqs and portions of Taluqs comprised in each Division.	Population.	Taluqs and portions of Taluqs comprised in each Division.	Population.	
Principal Assistant Collector and Magistrate Chicacole.	Tekkali.—*continued.*			Peddatungam	564	
				Tallavalasa	347	
				Jerjangi	2,336	
				Yelamanchili	643	
				Boddam	217	
				Belamarapalavalasa	855	
				Gopalapurum	5,165	
				Chittivalasa	5,698	
	Parla-Kimedi Sub Magistrate.	None ...	...	Parla-Kimedi	2,52,391	
	Narasannapet. Deputy Tahsildar and Sub Magistrate.	The Divisions of Chicacole Taluq of which he has Magtl. charge.	...	The following Divisions and Villages of Chicacole Taluq :—	60,107	
				Polaki, Uttara Khandam, 3 Mokhasa villages of the Southern Division and one of the Western Division.		
				Urlam	11,061	
				Danta	3,220	
				Tilaru	6,180	
				Sowdam	1,030	
				Akkayyavalasa	788	
				Santalakshmipuram	485	
				Talasamudram	923	

No. XXVI.—*Statement showing the Revenue and Magisterial charges of the Divisional Officers in the District of Ganjam.*—Concluded.

Designation of office and Head Quarters.	Names of Divisional Officers.	Revenue.		Magisterial.		Remarks.
		Taluqs and portions of Taluqs comprised in each Division.	Population.	Taluqs and portions of Taluqs comprised in each Division.	Population.	
Principal Assistant Collector and Magistrate, Chicacole.	Narasannapet.—*contd.*			Susaram	320	
				Rajapuram	266	
				Siddibehara Kotturu	109	
				Jounapadu	138	
				Mulagam	916	
Special Assistant Agent, Balliguda.	Udayagiri. Deputy Tahsildar, Sub Magistrate and District Munsiff.	None ...	...	Goomsur Máliahs, Chokkapad, Chali, Posara, and Gutigada Mutahs of the Goomsur Taluq.	35,566	
	Balliguda. Sub Magistrate and District Munsiff.	None ...	...	Surada and Kattingia Máliahs and portions of the Chinna-Kimedi and Bodogoda Máliahs.	73,551	
	Ramagiri. Sub Magistrate and Deputy Tahsildar.	None ...	...	The remaining portions of the Chinna-Kimedi and Bodogoda Máliahs.	...	

APPENDIX No. XXVII.

Extract from the Report of the Committee of Circuit as written under Mr. Russell's letter, No. 16, dated 10th September 1787, to the address of Mr. H. Crawford, Manager of the Havéli lands, Chicacole Circar.

3. In delivering our observations on the heads of Inquiry specified by our Hon'ble Masters, We shall adhere to the same arrangement as they have observed and as the Havaily Lands of Chicacole and Cassim Cotah are under the immediate direction of Government, we shall commence our Report with that subject.

Produce of the Havaily.

4. The Havaily produces chiefly Paddy the small grains not being in the proportion of more than ⅓rd. Its manufactures were formerly very considerable, consisting of fine and coarse Muslins, Sarces, Mooras, &c., and Long Cloth of 12 and 14 Punjum, the fine cloth and Muslins were sent to Hydrabad and Money returned, a trade now totally lost from the more skilful Weavers having left the Havaily to settle in the Zemindaries so that its present manufactures are of the coarser sorts only.

Population of the Havaily.

5. The population is by no means proportioned to the extent of country and at least one quarter of the land is entirely neglected, evils which must be attributed to the exactions and injustice of Renters in resuming the Enams and instituting oppressive collections and to the influence and artifice of the Vizianagarum Cutcherry in compelling and decoying away all the ablest artificers and numbers of other Inhabitants.

The Revenue.

6. The Revenue of this Havaily in the time of Anverdeen Cawn whose administration is still spoken of as an example is said to have amounted to 4 Lacks of Rupees. We find it at present producing Rupees 3,78,190-13-9 per annum.

Source of Revenue in the Havaily.

7. Government's share of the Crops, Duties on Jancans and Bazaars, Taxes on Gardens, Tradesmen, and Artificers and the Sea Customs are the sources of Revenue. The latter were very considerable

formerly at the Ports of Calingapatam and Mauphees Bunder on exports of Grain, Ghee and Oil for Madras, salt, fine cloth and Muslin and Wax, for Bengal and Bimlipatam, and on the Import of Raw silk, Taffaties, Copper, Iron, Spices, Betle-nut, and some Elephants, but are now fallen extremely low, from the scarcity of manufactures and poverty of the People.

Mode of collection in the Havaily.

8. In the collections it has been customary to receive Government share of the Produce in specie but the proportions have always been ascertained by a yearly valuation of the crops $\frac{1}{3}$rd being allowed the fixed Inhabitants $\frac{2}{5}$th to strangers and $\frac{1}{2}$ to Tellingees and those who cultivated Dry Grain; previous however to dividing the shares 1 Rupee per Garce on the whole was collected by the Circar. The repair of Tanks and Water Courses fell to the share of Government and the people supplied themselves with seed, Bullocks and Labourers: those who undertook to cultivate Waste Ground were allowed $\frac{2}{3}$rd for two years, for Fields that had only been neglected, $\frac{4}{5}$th for the first season paying afterwards at the rate of other Inhabitants; on clearing Hilly or Woodlands, they had one year's profit complete, on the second, the Circar took $\frac{2}{5}$th, on the Third $\frac{1}{2}$, on the Fourth $\frac{3}{5}$th, and in the fifth they were assessed like others, but in some places they were allowed the whole produce for 5 years and afterwards paid to Government according to usual custom, all which Regulations though observed in form are no longer essential, the Renter collecting from the under Renters at whatever rate he thinks fit to impose as was evinced in the last year's Jammabundy when the price of Paddy being at 40 Rupees, he took Government share of this article in part of their rent at a valuation of 17 Rupees which occasioned a loss of 23 Rupees per Garce to those under Renters who were therefore under the necessity of reducing the Cultivator's share in order to satisfy the demand of the Renter, whereby the People had nothing but their Dry Grain to subsist on and that being expended were obliged by necessity to purchase their daily food from the Renter's store at the exorbitant Price of 43 Rupees per Garce Annapinda Vissanah the under Renter of Cassim Cotah and also several other under Renters inform us that the heavy Rents exacted from them by Sitteram Rauze had obliged them to deprive the Inhabitants of

their proper proportions. The allowances to new settlers do not occur of late years, owing to the discouraging conduct of the Renter. The Taxes upon Tradesmen and manufactures have been raised within these two years from ½ and 2 Rupees to 3 and 7 Rs. per man, the Duties of the arrack sellers have been doubled and the cloth which used to pay from 3 to 7½ Rupees per cent., is raised in some instances to 9 and 17 as may be seen in No. which for this and various other oppressive taxes that are a grievous burthen upon the people, the cause of much complaint and considerable Desertions.

9. Although the offices of the Mussleman Cutchery have been long since disused the Renter continues for his own profit but to the discouragement of Trade, the Fees and Perquisites formerly attached to those employments and notwithstanding the Bazaar Duties of Chicacole were originally appropriated to charitable purposes, the produce is applied entirely to his advantage.

10. The great decrease in sales of salt at Nowpadah where they were accustomed to make about 1,500 Garce annually is attributed not only to the embargo on the Importation at Bengal but also to the enormous duties (stated as amounting to 167 Rupees on every 100 Bullocks load of salt) that are exacted at different Chokies from the Brinjarics and Merchants, and have occasioned ultimately a great loss to the company in that article of the Revenues.

11. The people have no Property in the Ground, neither is there any security for their Effects and Persons as We have known in many instances. No Courts of Justice are existing in the Havailly the Renters' decision being the only resource of the Injured, so that those who have money generally escape by a well applied Present while the poor who are perhaps the really aggrieved frequently undergo a corporal punishment; This authority leaves him frequently judge or Party in his own cause, therefore an equitable distribution of justice is not to be expected. During the Mahomedan Government an Adaulut was established at Chicacole in which the Amuldar nominated by the Nabob was supposed to preside but he appears to have disposed of the authority and profit which were established at 25 per cent. on the amount of Property. The Head Inhabitants of Villages have been long accustomed to settle trifling causes.

12. The periods of payment were formerly six beginning in September and ending in February but for these three last years the kists have been reduced to four, the 1st Kist taken in July is three months before even the small Grain Harvest, The 2nd in September brings the payments on the great crop also in advance, the third is taken in November and the last in January, a mode that exposes the people to great distress and the payment of Heavy Interest.

Times of Payment.

13. It appears that the Renter has not only resumed most of the Enam Lands granted to many Individuals, by the Mahomedans, and during the French administration, but hath also taken away the whole of the Free Gift Lands to Bramins and others excepting those village servants who now pay a nazar of 5 Rupees per Garce and when the Bramins have at times applied to him in distress he has granted them a few Garce of Grain as a Charity. Many of the Agraharam also are joined to Government collections, and the Shotreeum on those remaining is increased considerably.

14. The fortified places in the Havelly were Chicacole, Jelmore and Cassim Cotah, all of which are in Ruins. Chicacole the antient seat of Government had a good stone Fort built under the Mahomedan Nabobs by a joint contribution of the dependant Zemindars but of which only one *Bastion* remains. The Town once very extensive flourishing and a great mart for all sorts of commodities has partaken of the general decay and is now composed of mean Houses and thatched Cottages inhabited by few else than the Families of the Sepoy Battalions.

Fortified Places.

15. According to former Regulations the Tanks should be repaired by Government or the Renter, but the present one does not appear to have disbursed by any means a sufficient sum for this necessary purpose and as the inhabitants by reason of their sufferings can have little incitement or ability to make advances of which another will reap the benefit, the Tanks are only patched up from time to time; but no where repaired in a substantial and durable manner so that frequently during an heavy rain the imperfect bank yielding to the pressure within a whole year's store of Water is lost to the village and the people often reduced to the most extreme want.

State of the Tanks.

16. We do not meet with any balances upon the villages as the Renter after ascertaining the Price of Grain and the amount of Government share, should any individual be deficient, completes his own proportion, by increasing the payments of others. The same practice applies to Purganah at large the more fertile being compelled to make up the wants of others less *prolific.*

Enam Lands.

17. By the account of alienated Lands your Lordship, &c, will perceive the amount of Enam is computed at ——— Rupees most of which lands having seized by the Havaily Renter many of the Mahomedans who subsisted on them in idleness have been obliged to pursue some other way of life, which, with the encouragement those of Cicacole have received, at the Durbar of Phazel Beg and their own bias to the lazy life always found in moorish cutcheries have together decreased their numbers considerably in the Havaily and prevented our making a thorough and personal investigation of the validity of their several pretensions. We have however examined the Sanads that were produced and observing that very few bear the Seal of Hydrabad Durbar which we consider as absolutely requisite to authenticate such Deeds, and that most appear to have been granted to Moollahs, Servants and Dependants of Nabobs, who however absolute upon the spot from their Military command and the distance of their Court being in fact nothing more than Renters, could not be legally empowered to make any alienations of the Circar lands, We therefore cannot but consider the expectations of these claimants to be very illfounded, neither can such Sanads as were liable to the exception and rejection of a succeeding Nabob be any wise binding upon the Hon'ble Company. Though it is by no means our wish to deprive any Individual of what he may have been accustomed to regard as his Property yet the fraudulent practices of Renters and other abuses under the head of Enams, make it absolutely necessary. We should point out the insufficiency of the claim before us. But as it is probable considering the benign and generous intentions of our Hon'ble Masters towards their subjects in general and as many of these Enamdars, are real objects of Benevolence, whom age or misfortunes have deprived of their resource, that your Lordship, &c., may be disposed to relax the Circar Rights in favour of these sufferers, We take leave to suggest with deference that as the

Renter has already by seizure of these lands affixed to himself the Odium that would have attended Governments resumption of them however well founded. We preceive no necessity for depriving the Revenue again of their very valuable addition now enjoyed by the Renter without payment of any equivalent and as a considerable part of the Havaily though capable of cultivation remains in a very wild state from the reasons already assigned perhaps it might be advisable as we understand it would be acceptable to the Parties to bestow allotments thereof in proportion to their present claims upon these necessitous objects which on the decease of them and their wives, may revert back to the Circar, imposing upon them a light annual payment, to determine their dependance on Government and enable the cutchery to ascertain the time of their reversion as We cannot but regard the absence of those Mahomedan Enamdars whom necessity or choice has drawn from the Company's possessions a fortunate event and considering also the very exceptionable tenure by which they claim the Enams. We do not take upon us to recommend them to attention, being rid of such troublesome dependants, We would avoid every unnecessary measure likely to entice them back again, nor needlessly embarass the peace of Government, and quiet of the natives by associating with them so licentious factious and indolent a Race.

18. With respect to any future mode of managing the Havaily Lands We can by no means approve the system of Renting, However restrained and regulated, for after attentively considering it in every point of view, it still recurs in every modification as ultimately ruinous and under the fairest arrangements as accelarating the dissolution of countries that had otherwise been flourishing and populous. Decrease in Cultivation, &c., has been attributed to the shortness of Renters leases not allowing them to *risque* money in extensive improvements. The experiment of a long lease has been tried in the Instance of the present Renter and the consequences are found to be still more destructive than of any former system. But as it is our Wish to bring the Regulations deemed necessary for the Prosperity of this whole Circar into one point of view, We shall decline entering further upon the subject at present.

A true extract.

(Signed) F. H. DRAKE, *Secretary.*